# AMERICAN FOLK MUSIC AND MUSICIANS SERIES

SERIES EDITOR: RALPH LEE SMITH

1. *Wasn't That a Time! Firsthand Accounts of the Folk Music Revival*, edited by Ronald D. Cohen. 1995, paperback edition, 2002.
2. *Appalachian Dulcimer Traditions*, by Ralph Lee Smith. 1997, paperback edition, 2001.

SERIES EDITORS: RALPH LEE SMITH AND RONALD D. COHEN

3. *Ballad of an American: The Autobiography of Earl Robinson*, by Earl Robinson with Eric A. Gordon. 1998.
4. *American Folk Music and Left-Wing Politics, 1927–1957*, by Richard A. Reuss with JoAnne C. Reuss. 2000.
5. *The Hammered Dulcimer: A History*, by Paul M. Gifford. 2001.

SERIES EDITORS: RONALD D. COHEN AND ED KAHN

6. *The Unbroken Circle: Tradition and Innovation in the Music of Ry Cooder and Taj Majal*, by Fred Metting. 2001.
7. *The Formative Dylan: Transmission and Stylistic Influences, 1961–1963*, by Todd Harvey. 2001.

SERIES EDITOR: RONALD D. COHEN

8. *Exploring Roots Music: Twenty Years of the JEMF Quarterly*, edited by Nolan Porterfield. 2004.
9. *Revolutionizing Children's Records: The Young People's Records and Children's Record Guild Series, 1946–1977*, by David Bonner. 2007.
10. *Paul Clayton and the Folksong Revival*, by Bob Coltman. 2008.
11. *A History of Folk Music Festivals in the United States: Feasts of Musical Celebration*, by Ronald D. Cohen. 2008.
12. *Ramblin' Jack Elliott: The Never-Ending Highway*, by Hank Reineke. 2010.
13. *Appalachian Dulcimer Traditions: Second Edition*, by Ralph Lee Smith. 2010.
14. *A Pete Seeger Discography: Seventy Years of Recordings*, by David King Dunaway. 2011.
15. *The Ballad Collectors of North America: How Gathering Folksongs Transformed Academic Thought and American Identity*, edited by Scott B. Spencer. 2012.
16. *Arlo Guthrie: The Warner/Reprise Years*, by Hank Reineke. 2012.

# Arlo Guthrie

## The Warner/Reprise Years

*Hank Reineke*

American Folk Music and Musicians, No. 16

THE SCARECROW PRESS, INC.
*Lanham • Toronto • Plymouth, UK*
2012

Published by Scarecrow Press, Inc.
A wholly owned subsidiary of The Rowman & Littlefield Publishing Group, Inc.
4501 Forbes Boulevard, Suite 200, Lanham, Maryland 20706
www.rowman.com

10 Thornbury Road, Plymouth PL6 7PP, United Kingdom

British Library Cataloguing in Publication Information Available

**Library of Congress Cataloging-in-Publication Data**

Reineke, Hank, 1961–
  Arlo Guthrie : the Warner/Reprise years / Hank Reineke.
      p. cm. — (American folk music and musicians ; No. 16)
  Includes bibliographical references and index.
  ISBN 978-0-8108-8331-4 (cloth : alk. paper) — ISBN 978-0-8108-8332-1 (ebook)
  1. Guthrie, Arlo. 2. Folk singers—United States—Biography. I. Title.
  ML420.G978R45 2012
  782.42164092—dc23
  [B]                                                              2011053499

Printed in the United States of America

To my wife, Christa, who makes everything possible.

# Contents

# Series Editor's Foreword

This is Hank Reineke's second contribution to the American Folk Music and Musicians Series, following on his biography *Ramblin' Jack Elliott: The Never-Ending Highway*. It joins other biographical studies, such as Bob Coltman's *Paul Clayton and the Folksong Revival*, Todd Harvey's *The Formative Dylan*, and Fred Metting's joint biography of Ry Cooder and Taj Mahal, *The Unbroken Circle*. Reineke explores the public side of Arlo Guthrie's life, focusing on his musical and political contributions without delving too deeply into his personal life.

As Reineke argues, Arlo was not just following in the footsteps of his famous father, Woody, but carving out his own claim to fame through his musical compositions and unique performance style, beginning in the turbulent 1960s. He quickly attracted a large fan base that has continued into the twenty-first century. In this intriguing study Reineke has drawn upon a wealth of sources to delve deeply into Arlo's recording career while exploring his prolific output through the vehicle of this lucid and detailed discography.

Ronald D. Cohen

# Preface

Arlo Guthrie sits atop a stool on the apron of the Carnegie Hall stage, knees bent, with both feet resting on the spindle nearest the floor. He is surrounded by a bank of acoustic guitars, a small table where he rests his harmonicas, and Carnegie's formidable black grand piano. The folk singer is seven songs into his program, which is comprised, characteristically, of original songs ("Chilling of the Evening"), songs written or amended by his father, Woody Guthrie ("I Ain't Got No Home," "Buffalo Skinners"), songs of Bob Dylan ("When the Ship Comes In"), and such deep album tracks as the vaudeville-era "Ukulele Lady" and David Mallet's "Garden Song." Things are going well, as they always seem to in New York City, this being the artist's old hometown. Directly following his "Old Shep" pastiche, "Me and My Goose," Guthrie moves from the piano and returns to his Martin M-38 guitar. His right thumb begins to alternate between the instrument's bass strings, and he moves into a windy tale of how, a lifetime earlier, he had been trying desperately to stay in college. It was then autumn 1965, and, as Guthrie explained, "You were either going to school or visiting Asian nations all expenses paid." But since his strategy hadn't worked out as planned, Guthrie chose to embark on a career in music while an intrigued U.S. Army simultaneously pondered what to do with this budding flower child. Arlo admitted that his earliest attempts at songwriting were less than transcendent, and to illustrate the point he treats Carnegie to one example of his earliest efforts at song craft. Leaning into the microphone he begins to sing in his usual flat and nasal tone, "I don't want a pickle." There is an explosion of cheers and applause, and the song's equally ridiculous second line is lost in the reverberating echoes of the hall. This retooled version of the song, half-spoken, half-sung, serves as something of a career biography, Guthrie recounting how the popularity of his nonsense song had been such an embarrassment that "I started talking in the middle of this song, hoping that I could talk my way out of singing that stupid chorus again. As time went by this song got longer and longer until pretty soon I could start this song on one coast and finish it three weeks later on the other coast." He recalled that writing "The Motorcycle Song" had almost permanently damaged his self-merit as a songwriter, until he "discovered about three years ago that they were studying the lyrics to this song in colleges and universities around the country. No wonder we're in trouble." The audience laughs at the absurdity of "The Motorcycle Song" as a subject of disciplinary study, but evidence suggests that reality and myth intersect with surprising regularity in Guthrie's shaggy-dog tales.[1]

Though I cannot corroborate sightings of "The Motorcycle Song" in any of my college texts, I can confirm that it was featured in the lesson plan of my secondary school education. One book on the reading list of my English class was *Richard Goldstein's The Poetry of Rock*. Though the slim paperback was a little overreaching in its premise, it was still a welcome diversion from the *de rigueur* studies of the scribbles of Chaucer and Shakespeare. Great writers, yes, but my sixteen-year-old-mind was simply not able to comprehend, much less marvel at, their masterful turns of old English phrase. I could better relate to the rock 'n' roll texts offered in *The Poetry of Rock*, as these verses were far more accessible and affirmed the value of the LPs I played endlessly on my turntable at home. There, on page 52 of the volume (which included such famous word sketches as Bob Dylan's "Subterranean Homesick Blues," the infamous stanza concerning government wiretaps protectively "deleted at the request of the publisher"), was Arlo's "The Motorcycle Song." Though already a huge Guthrie fan, I was surprised to find this particular song in the Goldstein collection. As the owner of all of Arlo's albums released to date, I knew that the folk singer had written songs with far better poetic flourish than "I don't want a pickle / Just want to ride on my motor-sickle." But Goldstein set the record straight, explaining that "The Motorcycle Song" wasn't about the fun of motorcycling at all but rather "about having a 'free head.'" "Rock writers have learned that equality is not quite the same as liberty," he opined. "So when they speak about being free, they generally mean free from hang-ups, from authority, and most of all from obligation." I don't recall putting much stock in that interpretation even then. But Goldstein was a well-regarded critic who sounded like he knew what he was talking about, so that was enough for me to consider that a song—even "The Motorcycle Song"— might have multilayered meaning.[2]

In autumn 1967 twenty-year-old Arlo Guthrie had played his freshly penned "The Motorcycle Song" at the *déclassé* Bitter End on MacDougal Street in Greenwich Village, a mile or so downtown from Carnegie's plush seats. Though the folk singer would later grouse that he didn't care for "interpretation of any kind," he was apparently more amenable to such analysis in his early years. Contemplating the "Significance of the Pickle" at Paul Colby's famed nightclub, Guthrie allowed, "I thought I'd leave that to musical historians, you know? People like, uh . . . Alan Lomax, and all those people. They can have fun figuring it out." I'm not confident that Lomax, the distinguished ethnomusicologist, song collector, and architect of cantometrics, had ever considered putting "The Motorcycle Song" under his microscope, but it certainly would have been fun to read what he came up with.[3]

In keeping with Guthrie's expressed wish of a half-century ago, I too will forego interpretations of the songwriter's occasionally opaque lyrics in this volume. I've no talent for the discipline, and wisdom and age have taught me that songs mean different things to different people at various times of their lives, and sometimes even to the original composer. What I will attempt to provide here is a reasonably comprehensive, fact-based, and cross-referenced accounting of Guthrie's career as a stage and recording artist for the Reprise and Warner Bros. labels. It's surprising that while Guthrie's storied career has now passed the half-century mark, there has been only one book published thus far to document the pilgrim's progress. Laura Lee's *Arlo, Alice and Anglicans* (Lee, MA: Berkshire House Publishers, 2000) is a wonderful read and one that more completely recounts Guthrie's relationship with Alice and Ray Brock and the events comprising the "Alice's Restaurant Massacree." But Lee's welcome study was, by design, less of a Guthrie biography than a history of "The Lives of a New England Church," the book's emphatic subtitle. *Arlo Guthrie: The Warner/Reprise Years*, on the other hand, is the first volume solely dedicated to studying the milestones of the celebrated folk singer's career in music.

As Arlo Guthrie has spent the better part of his life on a concert stage and in the public eye, the basic biographical sketch of his life is familiar to most of his fans and admirers. But this simple biography is too often fraught with factual and timeline errors, and the fan pages and Wikipedia entries are rarely filtered through corroborative processes. Guthrie's storytelling abilities are legendary and have no doubt added to the myths and confusions, but his tales have also opened small windows through which we can catch glimpses of personal history. Regardless, there remains enough evidence to suggest that the singer has managed to retain his privacy and remain a mostly taciturn figure off stage. Janet Maslin, a Guthrie fan and music critic whose reviews have appeared in the *New York Times*, the *Village Voice*, and *Rolling Stone*, once astutely observed that Arlo "has a rare capacity for establishing intimacy without ever revealing anything specific about himself." In a *Rolling Stone* feature the writer Joe Klein, a biographer of Woody Guthrie, noted that Arlo tended to lapse "into a splutter of demonstrative pronouns . . . when the subject of himself comes up in conversation." Though wariness of journalistic intrusion into his private matters is understandable, it must be said that Guthrie has also been very generous and forthcoming in recounting some aspects of his storied life and extremely candid about his interest in matters of spirituality. Perhaps it wasn't too surprising to learn that the most comprehensive and satisfying published accounts of Arlo's life came early on when the singer was in the midst of building his career. The best of these early features were Sara Davidson's "Arlo Guthrie" from the *Boston Globe Sunday Magazine*, June 9, 1968; Susan Braudy's "As Arlo Guthrie Sees It . . . Kids Are Groovy, Adults Aren't" from the *Sunday New York Times Magazine*, April 27, 1969; Paul D. Zimmerman's "Alice's Restaurant's Children" from *Newsweek*, September 29, 1969; and Joe Klein's award-winning profile of the artist in *Rolling Stone*, March 10, 1977. The best midcareer assessment came via Jeff Tamarkin's wonderful interview with Guthrie in the pages of the record-collecting magazine *discoveries* (August 1997) on the occasion of the artist's fiftieth birthday. Though interviews with Guthrie continue to appear in magazines and, more regularly, in local newspapers where he is scheduled to perform, the majority of these contemporary conversations tend toward retellings of stories honed to perfection on stage or rehashes of the origins of the "Alice's Restaurant" legend. It also should be noted that an interview is merely one more type of performance, and not everything related therein should be taken as gospel but should be gauged in context.[4]

There are limitations to a biography as well, and I would imagine that any child of a famous parent would be aware of the form's shortcomings. Arlo once described his father, Woody Guthrie, as "a folk-song singer, writer of books and ballads, traveler, and victim of movies about him." Though Arlo would carve his own niche in American popular music history, fate would see to it that he would also be remembered, in part, as an integral part of his father's legacy. Being the son of Woody Guthrie was mostly a blessing but also an occasional burden. If Arlo has lived his entire life, in the assessment of one *Washington Post* writer, at the "center of the fringe," one can understand his wariness about revealing too much of himself or of his friends and colleagues to curious strangers. When Guthrie was asked forthrightly by Aiyana Elliott, the documentary filmmaker and daughter of his friend Ramblin' Jack Elliott, his thoughts on why her busking father had chosen to follow his unorthodox path, the singer flatly answered, "Maybe you're not supposed to know. . . . Maybe [there are] parts of him that you're never going to know." This was OK since Arlo was convinced that in the final tally myths were more lasting than statistics and likely more important. Most children of school age in America could tell you that John Henry was the steel-drivin' man, but who remembers the name of Simon Ingersoll, inventor of the steam drill? Once, when addressing a gathering of academics, Woody Guthrie fans, and folk-music scholars at Case Western Reserve University in Cleveland, Arlo admitted freely that whatever people came up with that week was fine as "I have never been an opponent to myths."[5]

In the final analysis it's the career and musical milestones of the artist, and not the artist himself, that I concern myself with here. Though I had hoped to obtain the cooperation of Guthrie's Rising Son Records for this project, my enquiry received no response so this book will remain, alas, an unauthorized accounting of Arlo's career. Having Guthrie's cooperation on the book would have been helpful, as not having official blessing made the research more of a challenge. But I've tried to diligently reconstruct the trajectory of the first half of Guthrie's career by combing through hundreds of concert and record reviews, reading every published interview (circa 1965–1982) that I could source, and listening through countless oxidizing cassettes that have preserved a score of dimly remembered or long-forgotten radio shows, television programs, and privately circulated concert recordings. The results of this research are offered here in this book, though with the caveat that opinions expressed at age eighteen may not necessarily reflect the beliefs of the same traveler decades on.

One of Guthrie's primary exhortations is his belief that life is best fulfilled when the decision is made to consciously choose to live "in the moment." It was Arlo's belief that was how his father had existed, "being right there and not worrying about what the future was going to be . . . or what the past had been. But just grasping it, and munching it fully and completely, as if it was the only moment that was ever going to be. He did that. I try to do that in my own way." In the following pages I hope you will find a worthwhile gathering of moments in the life of Arlo Guthrie.[6]

## NOTES

1. Arlo Guthrie, Carnegie Hall, New York City, November 30, 1991.

2. Richard Goldstein, *Richard Goldstein's The Poetry of Rock* (New York: Bantam Books, 1969), 52.

3. Arlo Guthrie, Bitter End Café, New York City, October 1, 1967.

4. Janet Maslin, "Arlo Guthrie Lives Up to His Name," *Village Voice* 21, no. 46 (November 15, 1976), 97; Joe Klein, "Notes on a Native Son," *Rolling Stone*, no. 234 (March 10, 1977), 50–57.

5. Arlo Guthrie, "House of the Rising Son," *Esquire*, September 1984, 80; Paul Richard, "Arlo Guthrie at 30," *Washington Post*, July 29, 1977, B1; Aiyana Elliott, Paul Mezey, Dan Partland, and Dick Dahl (producers), *The Ballad of Ramblin' Jack*

(motion picture), Lot 47 Films/Winstar Video, 2000; Arlo Guthrie, "Going Back to Coney Island," in *Hard Travelin': The Life and Legacy of Woody Guthrie*, edited by Robert Santelli and Emily Davidson (Hanover, NH, and London: Wesleyan University Press, 1999), 41.

    6. Arlo Guthrie, "Going Back to Coney Island," 41.

# Acknowledgments

Writing is an often lonely, but more often than not cooperative, exercise. I'm therefore totally indebted to many who have helped me along the way. First and foremost, I need thank my immediate family: my wife Christa and daughters Emily and Sara, who time and again have waited patiently for me to finish typing late into the night. It's the closest family members who most often suffer through the author's alternating intervals of uncertainty and unbridled enthusiasm. But it's also been my family that continues to inspire me. A special thank-you is owed to my mother, Janet Reineke, for giving her then seven-year-old son his first records: a collection of 78s featuring Hank Williams and Tex Ritter. These fragile acoustic- and steel guitar–driven records have left an obvious and lasting impression, and the music I most treasure has alternately enriched and ruined my life. Thanks, Mom. Thanks too to the assorted members of the Phillips, Thiel, and Ustupski families for their encouragement, their support, and their sharing of computer skills with this self-confessed Luddite.

I would also like to offer special thanks to series editor Ronald D. Cohen, who has not always graciously encouraged my writing but whose skillful editing and vast knowledge of the history and players of American folk music has improved this manuscript at every turn. Ron's enthusiasm is infectious and has often made this recalcitrant author continue to push forward and keep spilling words on paper. Thanks too to Bennett Graff at Scarecrow for his encouragement and intermittent prods to keep me on task when I would just as soon have coasted for a while.

I also need to offer my sincerest gratitude to retired journalist William "Bill" Blando, formerly of the Albany-based *Knickerbocker News*. Bill was no doubt surprised when I telephoned thirty-three years later to inquire if he was the newsman of the same name who had interviewed twenty-year-old

Arlo Guthrie at the Caffé Lena in late autumn 1967. Through sheer serendipity (and a successful Google search), he was. And though Bill informed me that the *Knickerbocker News* had long ceased publishing (having merged with a rival newspaper in 1988), he kept me on the trail of his interview by graciously putting me in contact with news editor Fred LeBrun and news research director Sarah Hinman Ryan of the *Albany Times Union*. Sarah selflessly—some might say "amazingly"—excavated two vintage *Knickerbocker News* clippings from the absorbed file morgue on only the merest sliver of bibliographic info I could provide. Thanks to all of you for your kindness and work on behalf of a stranger!

Thanks to Jeff Place at Smithsonian/Folkways for his friendly e-mails and for sharing the details of the 1965 Woody Guthrie tribute concert at New York's Town Hall. Thanks to Professor Maurice Isserman of Hamilton College for directing me to the Labor Archives and Research Center of San Francisco State University in search of some rare materials I was seeking. Thanks too to Catherine at the Labor Archives for going beyond the call of duty and searching through back numbers of *People's World* in search of materials. Thanks to Walt Saunders of *Bluegrass Unlimited* magazine for his assistance in identifying the source of an old WNYC broadcast recording I had of the 1974 West Virginia Bluegrass Folk Festival.

Thanks to Joe Kivak, David Cox, Kevin Avery, Jeffrey Johnson, Bill Thaute, Larry Hansen, and Peter Tesoro for their selfless sharing of information and materials over many years. Thanks to Mitch Blank for his interest in and support for this project and for generously opening up his amazing archives to share recordings of Guthrie's earliest appearances on Pacifica radio station WBAI in New York City. Thanks to Ron Mandelbaum at Photofest for shepherding me through hundreds of photographs and generously offering advice and suggestions on the sourcing of images. Thanks, too, to Marc Allen for his "divine" suggestion and his friendship, to Kurt Asan for the helpful loan of his Doobie Brothers album, and to Jim Phillips for the great photos.

Though they don't know me from Adam, as the saying goes, the members of the Guthrie family have been integral figures in my own life and, most assuredly, the lives of countless others. The music and prose of Woody Guthrie has inspired me in countless ways as a writer, guitar player, and student of American history. Arlo's music has provided the soundtrack to my life. A wary but friendly Joady Guthrie was among the first musicians I interviewed (incongruously on the second floor of a fluorescent-lit McDonalds restaurant on West 3rd Street in Greenwich Village) when I first started writing in 1983. And there's not a single contemporary admirer of Woody Guthrie who doesn't owe enormous gratitude to two members of the Guthrie family: to Marjorie Guthrie for seemingly saving every scrap of her husband's output and to their daughter Nora Guthrie for her skillful stewardship in preserving, and extending, the cultural legacy of her father's lifework. So, along with all the good people listed in this book's dedication, those who *actually* walked along with me "a little part of the way" (to paraphrase a poignant lyric of Weaver Fred Hellerman), I offer here a note of sincere gratitude to the entire Guthrie clan for brightening the lives of countless strangers.

*Chapter One*

# Standing at the Threshold

On the Sunday afternoon of June 1, 1947, the folk singer Woody Guthrie was scheduled to sing at a "People's Picnic" in San Francisco, California. It was the sort of comradely booking that Guthrie liked best, but it was a commitment that he would not, with regret, be able to honor. Guthrie's wife, Marjorie Mazia Guthrie, had telephoned Woody from their home in Brooklyn, telling her famously itinerant husband that it was time he planned his return home. The doctor had told Marjorie that the child she and Woody were expecting could "be born any minute now" and upon receipt of that news Woody was determined to get back to Coney Island for the blessed event. Through a charming column published in *People's World*, the San Francisco–based communist newspaper (to which Guthrie had been a contributor since May 1939), Woody apologized to his comrades in San Francisco for skipping out on their scheduled event. "Wife having baby over which I have no control," Guthrie explained to his readers. "Awful glad and awful sorry at the same time."[1]

Guthrie, who had been residing in New York City, more or less, since 1940, was not on the West Coast by accident. Several months earlier, on the morning of February 10, 1947, four-year-old Cathy Ann Guthrie, the first child of Woody and Marjorie, tragically passed away at Coney Island Hospital from burns sustained in a fire at the small home they shared at 3520 Mermaid Avenue. The loss, a painful tragedy from which Woody would never truly recover, brought a somber pall to the usually creative and hopeful hamlet that was the Guthrie household. In the months prior to Cathy's passing, Woody had been invited to travel to Spokane, Washington, to sing some of his Columbia River ballads at a gathering of the National Association of Rural Electric Cooperatives. Though Guthrie had been originally hesitant to accept that booking, the situation at home had since changed. The opportunity

*This familiar Reprise Records publicity image was used in the company's 1968 promotional campaign of the artist. Photofest.*

to escape the recent grim events at home now seemed a tempting notion. Out on the Pacific coast, Guthrie reasoned he could revisit old friends and family and accept some of the bookings he would receive from time to time from comrades out west. But the sad passing of Cathy Ann had shaken him badly. One year earlier Guthrie expressed a wish that Cathy be an integral collaborator in this family of artisans. Watching Cathy sing and twirl in the family living room, Woody wrote, "AND IT FLEW ACROSS MY MIND when I watched the seat of your britches dance into the front room that I would do right well for myself and for the whole human race if I could put down on paper, film, clay, canvas, wax, metal, or on some windier material, the song you sang for me, and the way you sang it." Woody's dream of nurturing a singing and dancing Guthrie clan had dimmed with Cathy's passing, but now, with the imminent arrival of their second child, that vision blossomed again. "Can't take no more jobs to sing along Westerly seaboard," Woody would write proudly from Los Angeles, "but will take all bookings for The New Improved Modern Cannon Ball Guthrie Family anywhere east from Coney Island." The idea of a singing family troupe wasn't *that* fanciful a concept, and one had to assume that Guthrie meant every word of it. Woody's long-standing musical heroes were the Carters, the "First Family" of country music, and Guthrie was clearly intrigued by the notion of establishing a musical brood of similar design. It was Woody's dream that his as-yet unborn second child with Marjorie might, right from the beginning, contribute to the music making. He wrote in *People's World*: "If I can get back in time to catch him right early, maybe I can talk him (or her) into taking up the bones, tambourines, silver spoons, or to travel with us and knock off my rhythms on my oatmeal box." "You might think I'm running out on you West Coast folks when I make this run," Guthrie wrote, "but when I think of hitting the trail with a singing new baby and a dancing wife, well, it's got its good points. . . . You get a better deal anyhow when you hire the whole Guthrie family. It will only cost you three bucks more and my wife don't drink, she don't smoke, dip, chew, cuss, fight nor gamble. She dances and teaches and I learnt her how to shift our '47 Cadillac Buick Studie just about a month ago."[2]

One afternoon in the autumn of 1946, with Marjorie already "fragrant" (Woody's term for pregnant), the Guthries were walking along the deserted beachside of Coney Island. Woody, walking a few steps forward of his wife, was pulling daughter Cathy in a small cart behind him. From Marjorie's view, the snapshot of Woody dragging the wagon was "uncanny." The image closely resembled "a picture I'd drawn of a little boy named Arlo when I was in school," Marjorie recalled. As a young girl the former Marjorie Mazia Greenblatt had enjoyed the children's book *Arlo* (Newton Upper Falls, MA: Arlo Publishing Company, first impression 1915) by Bertha Browning Cobb and Ernest Cobb. The hardcover book featured a plate illustration of an original Charles Copeland drawing of the book's young hero, Arlo, his pants rolled up at the cuffs, alongside his faithful dog, Krit, pulling a small wagon filled with laborer's tools. This memory flash caused Marjorie to shout to her husband, "Woody, I drew you!" Guthrie stopped in his tracks and turned toward Marjorie, who proceeded to tell him the story of *Arlo*.

She explained that the storybook recounted the adventures of a nine-year-old child named Arlo who was, unbeknownst to him, the son of an exiled count beloved by the simple people of the mountain. The child had been told that his natural parents were dead, and he was left in the care of a local mountain woman. This was for the child's own safety as the mountain was currently under the control of a wicked duke. The duke had violently driven Arlo's parents from their castle a few years earlier as the exiled count "was a kind man, and did not make his people pay all their money to the Duke, who ruled the District." Following a switching by a beleaguered caretaker who had lost all hope that the count and duchess might someday reclaim their son, Arlo and Krit set off on their own for the mountains. It was there that they met Comrade, a beloved fiddler who roamed the mountains playing music for the locals, secretly passing notes among the rebels opposed to the reign of the unloved duke. "Most of all Comrade loved the simple tunes which the village folk played and sang at their work," the book explained. "It is the music that comes from the heart that fills the world with joy," Comrade told Arlo shortly after agreeing to teach the boy to fiddle in the old-time mountain style. Comrade explained to the young runaway, "The simple tunes that simple people sing fill the world with happiness." In the end, the revolution that Comrade longed for finally came, and the wicked duke was disposed, replaced by the exiled count. It was the duchess who first realized that the nine-year-old boy playing the violin at a formal concert they were attending was their long-lost son when the boy began to play a sweet lullaby on the fiddle, the very same lullaby she had often sung to the child before the wicked duke had forced the family to separate.

Woody listened as Marjorie related the story and mulled it over a bit; he decided that it *had* to be a sign of some kind. "If the baby is a boy we'll name him Arlo," Woody suggested. "It's a good name for a professional," Guthrie sniffed, unlikely as that suggestion would seem. Surprisingly, it was Marjorie who was first to beg off the notion. This was Brooklyn, after all, and wasn't the name Arlo, at the very least, a too teaseable appellation for a young city-born boy? "What if he just wants to be an ordinary kid?" Marjorie pondered. Popular legend has long suggested that should the second-born child of Woody and Marjorie Guthrie be a son, they'd give him the middle name of "Davy." This choice of name was offered as homage to the title character of "Gypsy Davy," an old, traditional ballad of British origin that Guthrie had reworked and recorded for Moses Asch in April of 1944. But Marjorie later dismissed this as outright fiction, stating that the name Davy had its provenance, from the beginning, in American popular culture: "When Arlo was born, there was a big rage for Davy Crockett. . . . We named him Arlo Davy, so he could use Davy if he didn't like Arlo."[3]

Arlo Davy Guthrie was born at 9:47 a.m. on the Thursday morning of July 10, 1947, at Brooklyn's Jewish Hospital, a breech baby. The event sparked a series of birth announcements, each handcrafted and individually addressed to the recipients. Guthrie wrote to friend-in-folklore Alan Lomax that little Arlo "had to dive feet first because the Brooklyn Jewish Hospital was so little and so noisey [*sic*] and so packed." Woody wrote to Natanya Neuman, a nineteen-year-old neighbor whom the Guthries had used as a babysitter for Cathy Ann, that the birthing experience had been so near painless for Marjorie that the family was already planning their next addition to the brood. That night, with Marjorie and child resting at the hospital, Woody returned alone to their small home on Mermaid Avenue and wrote to another friend, the record engineer Moses Asch, care of Asch's Disc Company of America. Woody had recently been enjoying Asch's recent 78 rpm folio *Piano Compositions by Alan Hovhaness and John Cage, Played by Maro Ajemian and Alan Hovhaness* (Disc 875) and was intrigued and fascinated by the atonal music and off-kilter piano playing of the two avant-garde musicians. Woody, changing some of the birth details regarding his son's arrival, wrote:

> I need something like this oddstriking Hovaness [*sic*] and Cage music to match the things I feel in my soul tonight. . . . Marjorie gave birth this morning at 10:10, July the Tenth, to a big seven pound baby boy over in the third ward of the Brooklyn Jewish Hospital where Classon crosses Prospect Avenue.[4]

Woody Guthrie wasn't writing to Asch as a fan. He too had been recording sides for the Disc label. In the winter that preceded the arrival of Arlo Davy Guthrie, February or March of 1947 as best as Moses Asch could recollect, Woody Guthrie had recorded a cycle of children's songs for Disc. The songs had been written for, and sometimes with the contributions of, his beloved daughter Cathy Ann, whom Woody had playfully nicknamed "Stackabones." The Sunday of the house fire at the Guthries', Woody had stopped by Asch's office and brought home several copies of the booklet that was to accompany his children's album *Songs to Grow On*. It was a cruel twist that Cathy Ann would never get to hear the album that she had been so instrumental in helping to create. Guthrie's folk-singing friend and collaborator, Pete Seeger, offered as consolation that the songs that Cathy Ann had inspired Woody to write would garner little "Stackabones" a measure of immortality. It was true that, in time, the children's songs of Woody Guthrie would be regarded as classics among families from progressive backgrounds and occasionally beyond. Six of the best songs from the sessions were collected by Asch and issued as a 78 rpm folio, on his Disc label, titled *Songs to Grow On: Nursery Days* (Disc 605). One of the songs from the *Songs to Grow On* folio, "Don't You Push Me," was prominently featured in the July/August 1947 issue of

*People's Songs*, a newsletter and song sheet that collected and published the best topical songs documenting the labor struggles of postwar America. On occasion, *People's Songs* featured a page titled "Singing People," the left-wing monthly's version of a tabloid gossip column. It was there that editors Pete Seeger and Irwin Silber dutifully recorded the birth of the child they heralded as "WOODY GUTHRIE THE SECOND": "CONGRATULATIONS to Woody and Marjorie Guthrie. The new addition is a boy, named Arlo. Rumors are that Arlo is already refusing to be Pushed Around (see 'Songs to Grow On,' page 3)."[5]

The arrival of Arlo Davy Guthrie would rekindle memories of Cathy Ann and of painful memories unresolved. With his recent sojourn on the West Coast abruptly ended by the arrival of Arlo Davy, Woody found himself once again tied down in a domestic situation, never his strong suit. In a "dimestore [*sic*] stenographer's pad" titled *Coney Island Short Hauls*, Guthrie, a habitual diarist, would write down fragments of the thoughts, troubled and otherwise, going through his mind. On August 2, 1947, less than a month following Arlo's birth, the balladeer would moodily scribble that attending to the needs his newborn son left him unable to read and write as often he wished. In this case, he comforted himself that it was all OK as "I just can't hear the same kind of singing in my written or printed page here that I felt through Arlo's wool shawl giving him his nippling bottle this morning before sun. . . . My sagey brush here in my baby's nurse room dances homier and happier than a dozeful Sandburg." His short musings in the month following Arlo's birth tended to similar sentiments, ricocheting wildly between descriptions of wistful moments with his son (on August 7, Woody composed a little suckling poem for his child, "Hi Little Arlo"), to rants against fascism, revelations of sexual longings for women other than his wife, and barbed criticisms of such literati as Carl Sandburg, Walt Whitman, Robert Burns, and Pushkin, who, in Woody's opinion, all celebrated the working class but couldn't write in their tongue. Other times Guthrie's writing seemed to brighten, as on August 29, 1947, when everything seemed right with the world, with "Arlo Guthrie, 8 wks old . . . sucking your bottle here on my lap good and warm." Guthrie's mood had, presumably, lifted as he wrote of recently going down to the bank to cash a check for $1,155.56, his royalty payment for cousin Jack Guthrie's best-selling recording of his "Oklahoma Hills."[6]

On February 12, 1948, Woody Guthrie sat down at his typewriter and knocked off a six-paragraph letter to the editors ("All and everybody") of *People's Songs*. He rued that he would not be able to join his friend, the songwriter Earl Robinson, in Chicago for that day's Abraham Lincoln birthday concert to benefit the Civil Rights Committee. In consolation, Woody wrote that he was reading approvingly through the newly published *The People's*

*Song Book*, a collection of American topical songs, old and new, which had been thoughtfully assembled over the course of the previous year by the editors of *People's Songs*. Guthrie wrote, "Our 7 month old son, Arlo Davy, says tell you that you sure did pick out a good flavor of glue and starch to use on that stiff back binding. Arlo and the book went to press at just about the same time. They're both able to sit up on their own powers al-one [*sic*]. And the book and the baby are just about as loud, as plain, as clear, and as honest as each other." On Christmas night of 1948, the Guthries welcomed a second son, Joady Ben Guthrie, into the fold. Joady's unusual name was chosen as homage to the character of Tom Joad from John Steinbeck's classic Dust Bowl novel *The Grapes of Wrath*.[7]

From the beginning, it was clear that the Guthrie children were to be brought up in a rarefied atmosphere. In 1949, when Arlo was all of three years old, Marjorie and Woody brought the child to the Greenwich Village apartment of Huddie "Lead Belly" Ledbetter, the great Louisiana bluesman and songster. Shortly after Lead Belly and Woody started in playing their guitars, Arlo suddenly jumped up from the floor where he was playing, grabbed the harmonica that he had brought along, and started to blow on the harp and dance to the music. "He twirled and twirled and then did a two-step to the music," his mother recalled. Lead Belly thought it was wonderful, blessing the child with a kiss. His mother remembered that from his earliest days Arlo would walk around the family home with a borrowed guitar and racked harmonica draped around his neck. "Yeah," Arlo acknowledged years later. "Everybody thinks Dylan started that."[8]

On January 2, 1950, Arlo and Joady were blessed with a sister, Nora Lee Guthrie, named after Woody's own mother, Nora Belle Tanner, who succumbed, undiagnosed, to the rare illness of Huntington's disease in an asylum for the insane in Norman, Oklahoma, in September 1930. The Guthrie household was now filled with three children, all born within a three-year span. Marjorie recalled these days as endlessly busy. It was almost "like having triplets. . . . Twenty-four bottles and thirty-six diapers a day, with Woody and I washing and rinsing together at a big double sink." Woody Guthrie wasn't a model parent; his drinking and indiscreet philandering and his tendency to wander off for days on end understandably caused a great deal of stress in the marriage. Marjorie, who preferred not to dwell on negative emotions, would only acknowledge bravely that Woody "was a family man to the best of his ability."[9]

Many friends thought Marjorie tended to view her marriage to Woody through the prism of rose-colored glasses and that sharing life with the moody balladeer was more difficult than she allowed. Marjorie once remarked ruefully to the folk singer Ramblin' Jack Elliott, then Woody's nineteen-year-old protégé and an on-again-off-again houseguest, "Sometimes I don't think it's possible to be a great artist and also be a great human being in the same body." Elliott, who lived off and on with the Guthrie family in the years 1951 and 1952, recollected that Woody was a great father to his children, at least during the intervals "when he wasn't being a drunk or a meanie." Elliott told *Folk Roots* magazine that Woody's parenting style was somewhat unorthodox. He remembered six-year-old Arlo having "free rein" of Woody's valuable collection of 78 rpm records, and "every once in awhile one would drop off the back of the piano and break. Woody didn't seem to mind at all. It was his way of raising kids. Let them touch and feel and have everything, especially the things that were valuable." When Woody's spirits were high and his personal demons were at bay, he was a wonderful parent. Marjorie told the *New York Times* that a favorite early-morning family game was "huggin, buggin' time." Either she or Woody would yell "huggin', buggin' time," and the three kids would excitedly race from their rooms and climb into their parents' convertible sofa bed in the family's living room. Woody, a talented but self-taught artist, constantly sketched the children as they played, and he would often compose and play his nonsense songs for them on the guitar. One occasional morning ritual was when Woody would load the three children in a carriage and push them through the snow for a visit to Nathan's hot dog stand on Surf Avenue. While Marjorie tended to straightening up their home without the children, or Woody, underfoot, everyone else would feast on "hot patooties," Woody's name for Nathan's golden French-fried potatoes. In the late spring and summer when the weather was more pleasant, the family would build sand castles on the beach and stroll on the boardwalk at Coney Island where they would marvel at the spinning carousel, though they could rarely afford a ride on it. Most of Arlo's earliest memories of his father before his various hospitalizations were in such vivid snapshots. "One thing you've got to remember," Guthrie told *Melody Maker* in 1965, "is that Woody has been in hospital since I was six. I can remember a few things about him—walking on Coney Island, the sound of his typewriter, odd fragments like that." Of all the children, Arlo was the only one of the three that could even treasure such fragmented recollections: Woody went into the hospital for the first time in 1952, when his son was barely age five. Arlo offered that Joady and Nora probably enjoyed "less of a recollection of my dad as being their father [at home] . . . the rest of the time was visiting him in the hospital on weekends, or bringing him home for weekends. And that went on for 15 years." One of the watershed moments came when Woody bought Arlo his first good guitar. In fact, it was a *very* good guitar—a Gibson LG-2 three-quarter-sized six-string, an instrument that retailed for nearly eighty dollars in 1955. Marjorie was aghast that Woody would go off and, without her consent, purchase such an expensive instrument for a child—for *two* children, actually, as a neighborhood kid had gone along for the ride to the music store and had gotten one as well. The Guthries and their neighbors weren't people of means; the family lived almost exclusively off Marjorie's modest income from her dance school in Brooklyn. Arlo could still recall Woody's passionate defense of his purchase, that if you started a child off on a good guitar rather than a cheap knockoff instrument the only limit would be "the kid himself." Guthrie still owns that instrument to this day.[10]

Though Woody and Marjorie would, after a long estrangement, formally divorce in October 1953, the former Mrs. Guthrie maintained that she never separated from her husband "in my heart and in my actions." The fact of the matter was that Marjorie was, for the most part, the sole provider of the Guthrie household, and though she had been an assistant to the dance legend Martha Graham and taught six days a week at the Marjorie Mazia School of Dance in Sheepshead Bay, there was very little money. Her divorce from Woody was based solely on the realities she faced as a single parent of three children. "People forget that we were poor," Marjorie would tell the *New York Times*. "They ask, 'What was it like to be married to a famous man?' But we were poor all during his lifetime."[11]

Marjorie threw her considerable energies into rearing the three children she shared with Woody. Though his mother confirmed that her son's first instrument, taken up at age three, was the harmonica, the first instrument that Arlo Guthrie was to achieve any proficiency at was the recorder. This was entirely his mother's doing. Marjorie recollected to a writer from the *Boston Globe* that Arlo's first instrument was "the recorder because I believe the recorder is the pre-instrument instrument." Joady and Nora were also introduced to music training through the study of the recorder, and from the beginning the Guthrie children were taught to play three-part Bach pieces rather than old folk tunes. Marjorie was also determined that her eldest son would learn to play the piano, though this desire was met with resistance. "I forced him to play the piano for two years," she recalled, "until he had the basic facility, and then I said, 'Now you beg me for lessons.'" Guthrie remembered this scenario differently, offering forthrightly, "That never happened. . . . After two years I absolutely refused to go near the piano. I would get these little motherly beatings."[12]

Beginning in the autumn of 1956, Marjorie and a new husband, Al Addeo, would load the Guthrie children into the family car for occasional weekend visits with Woody, now a patient at Greystone Park Psychiatric Hospital in Morris Plains, New Jersey. It was important to Marjorie that her children get a sense not only of who their father was but also of the illness that he was struggling with. In September 1952 Guthrie was diagnosed as suffering from

Huntington's disease (sometimes referred to as Huntington's chorea), a de-
generative nerve disease for which there is no cure. Though the father and son
were unable, due to the obstructions of age and illness, to discuss important
family matters, Marjorie told *Newsweek* magazine that from the outset, "Arlo
and Woody had a spiritual link. They listened to music even when Woody
couldn't talk anymore. There was that common bond." There were, in fact,
a lot of records lying about the house that could be listened to. Long-playing
records featuring a Woody Guthrie song or two were constantly arriving in
the mail at the Guthries' new home in Howard Beach, Queens, so the children
were exposed to a lot of different artists and musical styles. Though, as a
young man coming of age in the late 1950s, Arlo much preferred the smooth-
sounding harmonies of the Everly Brothers to the high-singing of Lead Belly,
Marjorie recalled that Arlo forever remained his father's son. Arlo was able
to absorb the essence of Woody through the impressions of such old friends
as Pete Seeger, Cisco Houston, and Ramblin' Jack Elliott, singers whose
allegiance to the elder Guthrie was lifelong. "It was a way of keeping my
family alive," Marjorie reasoned. But with the exception of Jack Elliott, who
boarded on and off with the Guthries in 1951 and 1952, these artists weren't
regularly passing through the Guthries' homes in Coney Island or Howard
Beach. Once established as a performing artist in his own right, Arlo's press
kit featured his "Oughtabiography," which invariably began:

> He was born in Coney Island, New York on July 10, 1947. Music has always
> been a part of his daily life. His father, Woody, legendary troubadour from
> Oklahoma, has been one of the most influential and creative songwriters of
> our time. Arlo grew up around folk music. Their household was frequented by
> Leadbelly [*sic*], Josh White, Pete Seeger, the Weavers and many other folksing-
> ers during Arlo's early years. It seems natural then, that Arlo would continue
> this musical tradition.

This was all true, to a degree, but as Guthrie told filmmaker Jim Brown during filming of his award-winning documentary *The Weavers: Wasn't That a
Time!* he mostly knew these revered folk-music legends not as artists but as
members of his extended family. "We'd go someplace to hear them sing, or
we'd go to their house to visit, but it was always my mom or someone who
was doing the talking, and us kids just went out and played on the swings."
But his mother believed it was her responsibility to take her son from Queens
into Manhattan whenever any of Woody's old friends were scheduled to play
at some *déclassé* Greenwich Village nightclub. Arlo remembered the smooth-
singing Cisco Houston, Woody's best friend, musical partner, and fellow
Merchant Marine seaman, as "gentle and nice," always enjoying time spent
in his company. Though Jack Elliott, the youngest of the old guard, had been

off rambling through Western Europe for most of 1955 through 1960, upon his return he taught the young Guthrie a wagon's load of old cowboy songs, a "Beat" persona, and more than a few bad habits. From the Pete Seeger concerts he would attend, Arlo learned the rudiments of banjo playing and song leading and was introduced to a repertoire of hundreds of folk songs. Guthrie would often find himself in the company of Woody's blues-singing friends Brownie McGhee and Sonny Terry. Though the two bluesmen were barely on speaking terms, they still had the business acumen to keep their successful act together. Arlo gleaned many of Sonny's wailing, railroad blues harmonica secrets firsthand and always thought of Brownie and Sonny as his "uncles." He remembered the two bluesmen as "always fighting, but not in front of me."[13]

Not all lessons learned would come secondhand. Until December of 1956 when the severity of his illness would end all written correspondence, Woody would send letters to Marjorie and his children from his hospital bed on "Ward forty. Graystone [*sic*] Park, N.J." In a letter addressed to "Deary Arlo Davy" from September of 1956, Woody tried his best to comfort his nine-year-old son. Arlo had been born with a weak eye, necessitating his wearing of thick-lens prescription glasses. Woody counseled his son regarding the "weakedly blinded eye" that all of humankind suffered on one level or another, and that's just the way it was: "Don't whine to God Don't even complain one little bitsy word back to god Be silent Be quiet Be thankyful Be faithyful Be grateful Be gaylyful Be Joydyful Be thankyful to god for giving you your very very life on gods earthy here." Sometimes it was difficult to be "joydyful." As the Guthrie children were all very young when Woody went into the hospital, Arlo remembered that on the occasions that Marjorie would sign Woody out of the hospital for a day, it was a little embarrassing to seen on the street with their staggering-ill father. Guthrie would recall that, as youngsters, neither he nor his siblings really had any real insight into what was going on with Woody. "I felt uneasy sometimes," Arlo would later admit, "because being in public with somebody who looks like he is drunk, wobbling around, can be embarrassing for a kid." But the children were made to understand that what was happening to Woody was not of his own doing; Woody was suffering from a disease over which he had no control. It wasn't the responsibility of the family to correct the misperceptions of people on the street who stared, or giggled, or made judgments.[14]

Guthrie has long maintained that he didn't know that his father was—in the left-wing, artsy circles of New York City at least—relatively famous. Though he had never been much of a student, he was having so many problems in the public elementary school that he was attending that Marjorie was forced to intercede. She enrolled him at the Brooklyn Community-Woodward School, a "progressive" school located at 321 Clinton Avenue, near the corner of First and Prospect Park West. Founded in 1928 by Miss E. Frances Woodward, the school was among the first in the United States to offer alternative teaching methods for small children, including the use of "outdoor classes and other educational innovations." Many of the students attending Woodward were the offspring of well-off parents with left-wing sensibilities—one schoolmate was the chess prodigy Bobby Fischer—and Guthrie remembered that on his first day there, while attending a school assembly, the school's chorus stood on their risers and sang "Pastures of Plenty" and "This Land Is Your Land." To say that he was surprised to hear his father's songs sung at his new school would be an understatement. As a young child he simply had no idea that Woody's songs were performed anywhere outside of the Guthrie home or among Guthrie's friends. Journalist Joe Klein suggested that Woodward was "an integral part of the New York left-intellectual culture, and one of the few places where people *would* know Woody's songs in the Fifties." Prior to his enrollment at Woodward, Arlo recalled to filmmaker Jim Brown a time when, at age nine, "our school took a trip to go to see a Pete Seeger concert somewhere in Brooklyn." That would have been in April of 1956 when the Woodward school made plans to host a Seeger concert at the Brooklyn Academy of Music. The proposed Seeger concert attracted the attention of some local, and some very angry, veterans' groups who contacted the equally outraged Brooklyn Borough president John Cashmore to plead that the concert should not be held at the academy as the venue was a "tax-supported institution." Cashmore defiantly told the press that he shared the veterans' anger and that "I am sure nearly everyone agrees with me when I say there is no room—on the stage or even in the wings—for left-wingers, be they speakers, lecturers, ballad singers or other types of entertainers." The evening of the concert, Guthrie recalled that he and his schoolmates got off the bus and "out in front of the theater are all these guys walking around with signs saying 'Don't go, he's a Commie.'"

"Is he *really* a Commie?" Guthrie asked one demonstrator. "Oh, yeah, he's a Commie" was the response.

Guthrie recalled to Brown that he and his friends offered to take all of the anti-Seeger pamphlets off the protestor's hands: "So we got all the pamphlets and then we walked inside and they didn't have any more pamphlets. That was our first political action that was sort of based on a 'Pete' event." It wouldn't be the last. In his program notes to one of his yearly Carnegie Hall concerts, Guthrie "remembered the times when I was a kid and as I grew up, that I marched along with Pete Seeger and others—Ban The Bomb—Civil Rights—End the War in Vietnam—No Nukes—Clean Air & Water and so on. We sang and shouted, chanted and laughed, and took note of who we were and where we thought we were headed. We were determined that if the world was going to hell, it wasn't going quietly."[15]

Though the Woodward School was, environmentally and temperamentally, a better fit for him, Arlo didn't necessarily "buckle down" or improve as a student. But the teaching staff at Woodward, many of whom had suffered the McCarthy-era blacklist and had long been disenfranchised with traditional teaching methodologies, were more empathetic to Arlo's idiosyncratic musings. Able to see beyond the youngster's brooding, Guthrie's social studies teacher, Ann D. Greenstein, would note in his eighth-grade report card that his "understanding of social problems indicates his ability to empathize with people and analyze situations with intelligent judgment." But that same report card was still littered with such unwelcome citations as "careless work habits," "employs research skills in a superficial manner," and "only occasionally completes an assigned task." He also remained something of a loner. His art teacher at Woodward observed that while Arlo had recently shown an interest in painting watercolors, he "works best by himself." Arlo's music teacher at Woodward was none other than Margot Mayo, who in the 1940s occasionally employed a young Pete Seeger (and friends) as string-band instrumentalists for the square dances she would organize on 13th Street in Greenwich Village. Of her student she wrote:

> Arlo is talented musically, but needs a great deal of help and guidance in self-discipline. He is a "natural" musician, but tends to fool around, hit wrong notes, and to just get by with what comes easily. In this year, though, he has shown amazing growth in poise, and in technique in guitar-playing. He still hasn't enough self-discipline to play in an orchestra. He is definitely a solo player, so far at least.[16]

Though he wasn't raised in any particular faith, it was decided that Arlo should celebrate his transition to manhood with a traditional bar mitzvah. Though Woody was a Protestant, Marjorie was Jewish, and she and the children often shared suppers and instruction with her Russian-born parents, the Yiddish poet Aliza Greenblatt and husband Isidore, both dedicated Zionists with socialist political sympathies. The Greenblatts had earlier all but disowned their daughter when they learned that Marjorie was planning to marry the gentile Woody Guthrie. It was only after the tragedy of Cathy's passing that the Greenblatts softened, readily embracing and tending to the needs of their remaining grandchildren. It was likely through the intervention of the deeply religious Greenblatts that the Guthrie children were expected to study Hebrew. At his Carnegie Hall concert of November 24, 1990, Guthrie recalled, "When I was kid living not far from here in Howard Beach, [we] used to have a Rabbi come by and teach us Hebrew. . . . He wasn't very good at it, and I don't know that he actually tried that hard. . . . He was a weird guy. He seemed very nice and sort of peaceful when he came, but after trying to teach us for a while—me and my brother and sister—something happened [to him]. It was *Kahane*." "Kahane" was the controversial Rabbi Meir Kahane, the Zionist and founder of the militant Jewish Defense League, who three weeks prior to Guthrie's Carnegie concert had been assassinated by the Egyptian-born gunman El Sayyid Nosair.

Guthrie's bar mitzvah was held at a loft on 2nd Avenue on Manhattan's Lower East Side, at a dance studio operated by a colleague of Marjorie's. Harold Leventhal famously described the event as "the first (and probably only) Hootenanny Bar Mitzvah in history." It's true that the celebration brought most of Woody Guthrie's old friends out of the woodwork. Attending were Pete Seeger, the Weavers, Cisco Houston, and William "Bill" Doerflinger, the editor at the E. P. Dutton publishing house who arranged for Woody's first novel, *Bound for Glory*, to be published in March 1943.[17]

Though his new stepfather wasn't the least bit interested in music, Marjorie continued to see to it that Arlo understood the tradition of which he was, genealogically at least, very much a part. As early as age fifteen, his mother began bringing him on weekends to such nightclubs as Gerdes Folk City in Greenwich Village to see whoever might be appearing that night: Cisco Houston, Judy Collins, Odetta, Ramblin' Jack Elliott. Though he was technically forbidden by law to attend these barroom events due to the state's strict alcohol beverage control laws, he was nonetheless embraced with welcome arms. He was, after all, Woody's kid, and most of the managers of the nightclubs knew that his mom was with him in the rare event that someone should complain. The funny thing is that Marjorie really didn't like going out to the nightclubs; she was clearly uncomfortable with the revelry, the boisterous crowds, the late nights, the drinking, and the cigarette smoking. "That whole scene was totally alien to my mother's way of life," Arlo recalled to *Melody Maker*. "Naturally I loved it," he added, "being at the age where you love everything your parents don't. [Wherever] Cisco or Jack was going, I'd say 'Take me, take me, I wanna go.'" It's impossible to overestimate Marjorie's selfless devotion to Woody and her three children. She was, in her own way, helping her eldest understand not only who his absentee father was but what Woody represented to many people. In a sense, by trying to get Arlo to understand who Woody was she was helping her son come to terms with who *he* was. It was a tough balancing act. Marjorie was well aware that such lessons, no matter how well intentioned, could well have an opposite effect on a rebellious teenager. She told writer Susan Braudy that she had to walk a fine line: "I didn't want to force Woody on him. Arlo had to be exposed to many things so he could be himself . . . most children reject what their parents are like. I didn't want Arlo to reject Woody."[18]

Ramblin' Jack Elliott once noted that even when healthy and working and banging away on his typewriter and guitar, Woody Guthrie wasn't all that well known among the general populace. He was only familiar to a cadre of intellectuals and "politically aware" people from New York City, Chicago, and Los Angeles. But this would change when folk music began its improbable transformation from a coterie art of interest only to academics and leftists and was absorbed into the pop-music mainstream. One afternoon in either late January or early February of 1961, the Guthrie children were at home in Howard Beach with a babysitter caring for them until Marjorie returned from teaching class at her dance school. There was a knock at the front door, and Arlo went to see who it was. The door opened to reveal a rag-a-muffin sort of character, nineteen years old, with wild, crazy hair sticking out from under a corduroy cap. He introduced himself as Bob Dylan, telling the family that he had just rambled in from the West and had come looking for Woody. The babysitter, according to Arlo's recollection, was "really frightened" of the uninvited guest. There *was* something about him that was a little odd, from the mumbling way he talked to the way his narrow eyes moved about the room. The babysitter, Joady, and Nora were all uncomfortable; they wanted the stranger to leave, but Arlo, enamored of Dylan's "high, lace-up engineer boots," invited the teenager into the house. They chatted a little about Woody and the hospital and music, and before long Dylan was demonstrating how to play the harmonica in the bluesy "cross-harp" style, bending notes by sucking air into the instrument rather than blowing out. After an uncomfortable hour-long visit, the babysitter finally convinced Dylan to leave, telling him that it would be best if he planned his next visit when Mrs. Guthrie would be home. Nora and Joady were relieved to see the stranger go, but Arlo wasn't. The guy was pretty interesting.[19]

It wasn't too long before their paths would cross again. One Saturday night, February 16, 1961, Marjorie brought thirteen-year-old Arlo into mid-Manhattan to see Ramblin' Jack Elliott's New York City concert debut at Carnegie Chapter Hall on West 57th Street. Bob Dylan was there too, fresh from Minnesota, where, as a budding Woody Guthrie acolyte, he had studied the recordings that Elliott had made in England years earlier. Elliott, Woody's most gifted musical mimic and protégé, had more or less been out of the United States for most of 1955 through 1960, almost single-handedly creating a cult of Woody Guthrie fandom throughout England and parts of Western Europe. Elliott's concert at Carnegie Chapter Hall was an emotional one, a musical homecoming that ended in several curtain calls and moved Marjorie (and many of Woody's old friends who had feared that Guthrie's voice had been permanently stilled) to grateful, happy tears. Woody's genius would not be forgotten as long as Ramblin' Jack was traveling the back roads of America. Afterwards, Jack encouraged everyone at Carnegie to head downtown to catch Cisco Houston's late set at Gerdes Folk City. Though only his friends and associates were aware of it, Cisco had been diagnosed with an inoperable form of cancer and told his time wasn't long. Before planning to spend his last days with his sister's family out west, Cisco chose to say farewell to friends and fans in New York City with a week-long engagement at Gerdes. The engagement was a tough struggle for the weakened Cisco, and he needed friends to play a song or two so he could rest and get through the long nights. It was likely the night of the Jack Elliott concert that young Arlo Guthrie was asked by Cisco to climb onto the stage and sing a few songs. It was a moment that Guthrie would painfully remember for all time. He recalled the stale smell of beer and sawdust on the floor, the peeling paint, the sight of the pipes that twisted in and out of the ceiling and connected the rooms. Houston had been sharing the bill with the Grandison Singers, so by the time Cisco's set winded down, it was late into the night. Just before finishing up, Cisco spied Marjorie Guthrie and son sitting at a small table in the club. He introduced Marjorie from the stage to warm applause. Then he introduced Arlo and asked him to sing a few songs. Those gathered applauded with polite encouragement, hoping to coax Woody's reluctant son to the stage. Guthrie recalled he "froze in time." "It was the usual painful agony of birth," Arlo would later write. "I couldn't walk, talk [or] think. I was just there." He climbed on stage and sat on the stool, his legs dangling and knees nervously beating out a rhythm of their own. He sang three or four songs, including a talking blues and his father's "Pastures of Plenty." "If I hadn't been so pathetic, it would have at least been fun for everyone," Arlo would recall, but he got through the ordeal more or less unscathed, and the audience clapped warmly. But when he stepped off stage, he vowed, "I'll never do *that* again." He also remembered that evening as bittersweet. It was the final night of Cisco's stand, and everyone knew it. In Guthrie's own words, "My being born had been his farewell."[20]

Though the Guthrie children were reared in the shadow of the Manhattan skyline, Arlo longed for the presumed solitude and easygoing charm of country life. The Guthrie children got a taste of this life each summer when Marjorie would bring the children along to a summer camp in New York's Adirondack Mountains, trading her talents and expertise as a dance instructor for her children's room and board. In the summer of 1959, with her children outgrowing the youth-oriented activities and atmosphere of the Adirondack camp, Marjorie proactively paid a visit to the prestigious Indian Hill School in Stockbridge, Massachusetts, seeking a similar arrangement.

Indian Hill, founded in 1952, was the brainchild of the Julliard-trained baritone Mordecai Bauman and his wife Irma. Mordecai Bauman was an interesting gentleman. He had been introduced to the German communist composer Hanns Eisler in 1935 by fellow Julliard student Elie Siegmeister. Eisler alarmed Bauman with tales of anti-Semitism and fascism stirring in his homeland—and throughout all of Western Europe—and the outraged baritone responded by aligning with the artists and causes of the Left sworn to combat it. Following the end of World War II, Bauman continued to work for progressive causes and supported the ill-fated campaign of Progressive Party candidate Henry Wallace in 1948. Though folk music was not his métier, Mordecai befriended such comrades as composer Earl Robinson (*Ballad for Americans*) and Pete Seeger. He also heartily supported *People's Songs* in its effort to get progressive songs out to politically sympathetic artists, lending his impressive baritone to rallies on sound trucks when called to do so.

The Baumans founded Indian Hill as a communal school where teachers and students boarded and shared dinners together. The educational emphasis at Indian Hill was not on folk music but on the fine arts, classical music, and dance. The Baumans had been friends with Marjorie for some time. Mordecai had worked alongside her at an arts program for a New Jersey YMCA, and she eventually worked out a similar tuition-for-services trade arrangement with Indian Hill. Beginning in 1960, Marjorie would close her school of dance in Brooklyn each summer to teach classes at Indian Hill. The pay wasn't great, but she could bring her children along for a two-month retreat from Queens that would allow them to breathe the fresh air of the Berkshire Mountains in western Massachusetts.

Arlo attended Indian Hill in the summers of 1960 through 1962, but though he loved the mountain setting and the calm stillness of the nights, he wasn't particularly interested in the school's fine arts program. He recalled Indian Hill, with some derision, as an institution, "where all the young prodigies went for violin and viola and cello and piano, and for theater and for dance." Folk music was welcome—Pete Seeger would often visit and play his banjo for the wide-eyed students, all fans familiar with him and what he represented—but the Baumans were devotees of "high art." They appreciated folk music and were interested in its effectiveness as agit-prop, but musically folk songs were dismissed as a source of simple, rough melodies in desperate need of polishing by the masters. Guthrie remembered the attitude of the staff at Indian Hill with little fondness. "You want to play that folk stuff, take your guitar and go off in the woods," he remembered them telling him. "But don't you play it around everybody else." It was only after his first concert at Carnegie Hall that Guthrie would be belatedly celebrated by the staff at Indian Hill as "an alumnus."[21]

In the autumn of 1962, Arlo enrolled as a high school freshman at the Stockbridge School, a similar progressive institution founded in the years following World War II by the German socialist Hans Maeder. As the student body at Stockbridge rarely exceeded some 200 students, there were many opportunities to grow as both a student and as an internationalist. It's interesting that Arlo Guthrie's name would first make the sacrosanct pages of the *New York Times* not as a musician—or as the offspring of a musician—but as, of all things, a *student*. In March 1964, thirty-six students of the Stockbridge School (tuition $2,700 as per the *Times*) visited with Puerto Rican–born students of Manhattan's poor and struggling Benjamin Franklin High School. Most of the Stockbridge School's junior class were to set off on a visit to Puerto Rico on March 23 and were hoping to learn a little about the island's customs from those that would know them best. "'It's a culture shock,' said Arlo Guthrie, 16, a Stockbridge student," reported the *Times*. "'We hope to find out more about people and more about ourselves.'" Marjorie Guthrie had already accepted that her eldest son was not going to distinguish himself as a scholar. She would tell the *Boston Globe* that at "the Stockbridge School, at least he played music the whole four years. The kids there were playing music night and day, and I thought it was great."[22]

There was a lot of music. It was during his sophomore year at the Stockbridge School that Guthrie teamed up with three classmates to form his first band. These friends, Jeff Boverman, Steve Elliott, and Geoff Outlaw, were kindred spirits; all three were from New York City, and all shared Arlo's interest in music. The band was formed on a whim. The school had been planning a class-exchange trip to Canada, and Guthrie figured that he and his friends would "give the Canadians some entertainment." So they formed a folk-singing group that was, interestingly, less Woody and Cisco and more Weavers–Kingston Trio–Travelers 3–Brothers Four. The band had a pop-folk sound, a sound in commercial vogue at the time, and they had worked out simple vocal harmonies, synched with satisfaction to their robust guitar, bass, and banjo playing. Following the class trip to Canada, the group chose to stay together to perform informally at school assemblies and for friends. In the early winter of 1963, five months after first forming, the Almanacs Four were invited on a local radio station in neighboring Pittsfield, Massachusetts, in the heart of the Berkshires. They opened the program with a robust folk-pop reading of the moonshiner's song "Darling Corey," and as the song closed the program's host picked up the string: "That's the sound of folk music. . . . WBEC has in the studio today a group from the Stockbridge School, four young men who made it their hobby to sing this most popular type of music. They call themselves the Almanacs Four and their spokesman is Mr. Arlo Guthrie." A somewhat hesitant spokesman, Arlo talked haltingly about the formation of the group before leading his band mates in "This Land Is Your Land," notably including the rarely sung and vaguely radical "shadow of the steeple" verse. Following the song, the band members were asked if any of them had the benefit of professional training. Guthrie replied, "Well, not really taught by a teacher. . . . We mostly taught ourselves." In his own case, he mentioned that his "father played [the guitar] and most people think he taught it to me, but it was my mother really. She started me off on a few chords and I became interested and I just kept going and learned the rest." Jeff Boverman's training was even less formal. He admitted to being taught to play bass in "five minutes" by Arlo. When asked if the outfit had any thoughts of going professional as a "vocal group," Guthrie said, "Well, it's kind of hard to say. If we get any better, I think we will. For a while anyway. . . . It's strictly amateur for now." The band closed the show with the old spiritual "Sinner Man," their vocal arrangement showing a clear debt to the Erik Darling–era Weavers. When asked how these folk songs differed from conventional popular music, Arlo explained: "Well, I would say, in our country, when the people came over they brought along a whole lot of things and one of them was music. It was put into *American* terms, in which words were changed. You still find a lot of songs that can be traced back to all parts of Europe and some in Africa. Especially blues. It's been formed into American culture." The group would stay together through graduation, eventually developing their musical and singing talents and shedding their pop folk for a more bluegrass-oriented sound.[23]

Though he would later rail that the institution was merely another "survival school—that's all any school is," the Stockbridge School was a good fit for Arlo. If nothing else, "you learn how to get along when you're not learning anything," he would grouse. But it was at the school that Guthrie would meet two people who, in their own easygoing ways, would change the course of his life. Alice Brock was born Alice Pelkey in a middle-class neighborhood in Brooklyn, though her father's family had roots in Pittsfield, Massachusetts, neighboring Stockbridge. She wasn't necessarily a wild child, but she had a mind of her own. She was of early age when sent to reform school, reportedly for two years, by parents tired of dealing with her orneriness. She briefly attended Sarah Lawrence College in Bronxville, New York, but according to one newspaper feature her campus "political activities . . . did not exactly endear her to the administration." So she dropped out of school, created art, explored her interest in cooking, and drifted until 1962, when she met Ray Brock while waitressing in New York City. Brock was a "struggling architect" and sculptor from Tidewater, West Virginia, when they first met, but Ray too was a blithe spirit, recently divorced and anxious to free himself from the straitjacket of the buttoned-down American Dream.

In 1962 the couple moved to Stockbridge, not too far from the home of Alice's parents in Lenox, Massachusetts, where Ray and Alice accepted positions at the Stockbridge School, he as a carpentry and sculpting instructor, she as the school's librarian. The Brocks had a great rapport with the kids attending. Ray was not only a gifted craftsman but also a first-class raconteur who spun long, winding tales that more or less mirrored his philosophical views. The Brocks were caring, interesting, colorful figures, and the friendships they made with the students during their single semester at the school were long lasting. These friendships would extend far beyond graduation. Always restless, the Brocks traveled to Martha's Vineyard, off Cape Cod, where they briefly opened a hostel in the summer of 1963 for "traveling teens and some 15 members of their own following." As Alice recalled, "[we] took half the student body [of the Stockbridge School] with us." It was during the summer of 1963 that Arlo and Joady became close friends with Alice and Ray, the brothers preferring the scene on the Vineyard, with the attendant sun and beaches, to another dreary summer of fine arts studies at Indian Hill. But the idyll on Martha's Vineyard was short lived as, at the end of summer, the Brocks decided to return to New York City to remake themselves once again. The couple might have stayed on in Manhattan indefinitely, living inexpensively as artsy bohemians on the Lower East Side, had it not been for Alice's mother, Mary Pelkey. Pelkey was a realtor in the area, and it was she who decided to buy the old Trinity Church for the nominal sum of $2,000. The church, a soon-to-be-deconsecrated Episcopal house of worship in the hamlet of Van Deusenville, was situated in the area of Great Barrington, Massachusetts. The building was first erected in 1764 and remained a house of worship for nearly 200 years. In 1962 the challenges of a diminishing congregation, age, and structural neglect would force the church to shutter its doors. Though Pelkey had no real interest in the church herself, there was method to her madness. Remembering that her daughters had always loved passing by the picturesque New England church during the family's many car trips through the area, she was betting that Alice and Ray might be persuaded to abandon the hassles of Manhattan for a return to the peaceful idyll of the Berkshires. They were, and in June of 1963 the Brocks took ownership of the Trinity. It wasn't long before the talented Ray Brock found work in an architectural firm in nearby Pittsfield. With the money earned there he donned a tool belt and, with the assistance of his many young friends from the Stockbridge School, began to transform the old Trinity Church into a something resembling a home. Trying his best to leave the infrastructure of the sanctuary intact, Ray designed and built several small rooms, a bathroom, and a series of stairways on the perimeter of the assembly. In the soaring bell tower of the church, he installed a small but serviceable kitchen for Alice, whose cooking skills, everyone agreed, had really blossomed.[24]

Many of the young people who had helped the Brocks remodel the old church moved in. There had been no grand design to form a commune, and

Guthrie recalled everything happened more or less organically. He remembered, "It happened to be an unconscious [development] at first. No one said, 'Let's have a community.' No one said, 'You do this and you do this, you sleep here and you sleep here.' People just started gathering. It just happened that way." Aside from owners Alice and Ray, there were usually anywhere from eleven to fourteen young people residing at the Trinity at any given time, with most content to pass through, returning from time to time to recharge their spiritual batteries. Some of the earliest tenants were Guthrie, Geoff Outlaw, Rick Robbins, Steve Elliott, Liza Condon, and Michael Lerner. Though they hadn't chosen to take on the role—and would have preferred *not* to—Alice and Ray, both ten years older than their friends, found that they had assumed the roles of surrogate parents. In many ways it was a family in the best sense of the word. Alice herself never thought of her home as a commune, though she acknowledged, "I suppose it grew out of the same roots—the need to belong to something and for some feeling of family. These were kids who felt they didn't belong in the outside world, and who, because of this, didn't get along too well with their families." In the wake of the media attention that would later surround the filming of the *Alice's Restaurant* movie, journalist Saul Braun, freelancing for *Playboy*, visited Great Barrington and came to a similar conclusion. Braun found that most of the young people gathered at the Trinity were held together by a single common thread. It was Braun's finding that for "an unusually large number" of young people living at the Trinity, the church was not a second home but, in some ways, their *first* home since many had been children of "broken or well-bent marriages."[25]

Though the good times were plentiful, they wouldn't last long. Alice was, by her own admission, becoming increasingly unhappy with the scene at the church, desperately looking for her own place in the universe. "I was twenty-five, married, and crazy," Alice would later write in her book *My Life as a Restaurant*. "I was captive in a situation I had very little control over other than the role of cook and nag—being a hippy housewife was not satisfying." It was around this time, April 1966 as best as Alice could recollect, that her mother the realtor, sensing her daughter's ennui, told Alice of a vacant luncheonette in town that was up for sale. The small luncheonette was situated down a short alley, sandwiched between Nejaime's Grocery and Kempton's Insurance, just off of Stockbridge's Main Street. The opening of a restaurant had never been a dream of Alice's. "I had a world of fantasies; none included a restaurant," Alice conceded, but she was immediately taken by the idea, and a down payment was made. The modest luncheonette was in fact never named "Alice's Restaurant," but was listed in the local directory as simply The Back Room. The young people at the church were happy for Alice—it was great to have a friend with a restaurant—but The Back Room was too formal a name, so they simply called the eatery "Alice's Restaurant." As Guthrie remembered, "We were sitting around one night and Alice said she was thinking of opening a restaurant. So I wrote her an advertisement, which became the chorus, 'You can get anything you want at Alice's Restaurant.'" Though it is often reported that the "Alice's Restaurant" chorus began its fabled life as a radio advertising jingle written by Arlo for his friend, Alice laughed at that notion. "I never had a commercial on the radio. I couldn't afford that."[26]

In the spring of 1965, with graduation from the Stockbridge School in plain sight, nearly all of the young people associated with the Trinity were confronted with the realities of establishing lives separate from friends. Arlo's musical skills had developed to the point that folk-music impresario Harold Leventhal invited the youngster to perform at a concert he was producing in midtown Manhattan. On April 17, 1965, *Sing Out!* magazine and Leventhal cosponsored a Town Hall concert to feature "Songs of, by, for and to Woody Guthrie." Old friends such as Pete Seeger, Brownie McGhee, Sonny Terry, Jack Elliott, Marianne "Jolly" Robinson, and Logan English were the principal singers that evening, with two youngsters, twenty-five-year-old Patrick Sky and eighteen-year-old "Arlow [*sic*] Guthrie" (as per the *New York Times*), on hand to represent the continuum. Arlo performed early in the program, singing a duet with Jack Elliott on "Oklahoma Hills" and taking a solo turn on Woody's World War II patriotic song "My Daddy (Flies a Ship in the Sky)." Sadly, Arlo's father *wasn't* flying terribly high in 1965. Woody was continuing to deteriorate incrementally, slowly wasting away in his bed at Brooklyn State Hospital and able to communicate only through the softest of hand presses or with the gentlest blink of an eye. The fact that Woody had been institutionalized and off the scene for so long caused *New York Times* critic Robert Shelton to note that at the concert, "some of the performers had trouble keeping their comments about Mr. Guthrie in the present tense."[27]

Upon graduation from the Stockbridge School in June 1965, and with little discernible ambition, Arlo chose to accept brief summer employment as an office boy for Harold Leventhal Management, Inc. Leventhal had been a longtime friend of the Guthrie family. Breaking into the music business as a "song-plugger" for Irving Berlin, Harold, a lifelong leftist, would eventually establish himself as a successful concert and theater producer and manager of Pete Seeger, the Weavers, Cisco Houston, Judy Collins, and a slate of other progressive-minded folk singers and artists. Leventhal was also one of the principal architects of the Guthrie Children's Trust Fund, launching the enterprise in 1956 so that the small stream of songwriting and publishing royalties that Woody was, at long last, generating might benefit Woody's children with Marjorie. Leventhal remembered Arlo, with some affection, as a "Come-When-He-Wants-To, In-Residence; Part-Time (and Sometimes Part Part-Time) Guitar-Pickin' Office Boy." As he would later reminiscence on in his notes to Arlo's first LP:

> Of course, whenever there were things to be done such as opening or sealing the mail, pasting clippings, answering the phone, going down for coffee, and the myriad spectrum of responsible office-boy duties, Arlo was not available. He was busy. Practicing the guitar. Writing songs. Singing duets with Pete Seeger whenever Pete walked in the office. Swapping stories with ex-Weaver Lee Hays, an old crony of Woody's. He was generally kept too busy with these important matters to be bothered with minor office details.[28]

Though they differed in age by some thirty-odd years, Guthrie and Lee Hays were cut from the same cloth. Doris Willens, the biographer of Hays, recounted a time when a group of youngsters, including Arlo, were sent out to help redecorate Lee's West End apartment. While everyone rolled up their sleeves for an afternoon of work, the notoriously glacial Hays watched in amusement as Arlo situated himself atop a stepladder and played his guitar, spinning out impromptu verses about whatever was happening around him. "As a master of sitting there while others did the work," Willens wrote, "Lee doffed his cap to Arlo's . . . method of doing the same thing." Guthrie learned a lot from Lee Hays, the rotund bass singer of the Weavers, whose curmudgeonly demeanor and dry but masterful comic storytelling skills were without peer. As a child, Arlo had been brought along to a number of Weavers' concerts, and he carefully watched and listened as Hays spun extended folksy tales mixing progressive politics with common-sense values. Guthrie recalled to Jim Brown, the talented filmmaker who documented the Weavers' 1980 reunion concert at Carnegie Hall, that the things he remembered best about the Weavers' concerts was the group's "humor onstage, Lee's stories especially. Punctuating lines, timing, those kind of things. . . . [They] have become a part of me; I learned them as a kid, watching the group on stage." Hays was also taken with Woody and Marjorie's eldest, writing to Harold Leventhal that he found Arlo a "very sociable, humorous, talented boy," though the bass singer thought perhaps the more introspective and self-contained brother, Joady, ultimately "may make the larger contribution in later years, being the troubled one." Of the three siblings, Joady, who also wrote songs and expertly played guitar, seemed to be the one most burdened with his inheritance of the Woody Guthrie legacy.[29]

In a rare interview Joady offered a grim picture of his childhood in Howard Beach, telling the *San Francisco Chronicle*, "My father was literally never there. . . . My mother was there, but she wasn't around. My brother was miserable. My sister was miserable. I was miserable." Shortly after releasing his late-to-debut album, *Spys on Wall Street*, in 1985, Joady, age thirty-seven, told a writer from *Broadside* that he was put off by the mythologizing of his father, arguing, "Woody wasn't the great prophet that he was made out to be. . . . He didn't have all of the answers and he didn't know how to take care of himself while he was writing all of those songs." If Arlo and Nora shared Joady's sentiments they seemed to keep such memories to themselves.[30]

Arlo's summer employment with Leventhal soon turned into a season of half-employment. He announced he was planning to travel, alone, to England and Scandinavia for the duration of July and August 1965. As he didn't have any money, Arlo's cross-Atlantic adventure would be underwritten by the Guthrie Children's Trust Fund. Guthrie's sudden decision to travel abroad was hastened by a more pressing announcement. Flush with the gentle prompts of well-meaning friends and with the knowledge that school would provide a safe haven from military conscription, Arlo surprised everyone in the extended Guthrie family by proclaiming that he had given the matter a lot of thought and was now planning on attending college. Marjorie Guthrie was aghast at the thought. Arlo had never been much of a student, and though she was not one to underestimate the value of college and continuing education, her son's uncharacteristic decision seemed foolish. "I didn't want Arlo to go," she remembered. "Who was going to take him? Only a school with no standards."[31]

Guthrie's airplane landed at London airport in early July 1965. Handing off his passport to an official in the terminal, the young officer read aloud his name. "Arlo Guthrie," he read and then, looking up at the pale, skinny, long-haired, teenager in horn-rimmed glasses, asked, "Are you any relation of Woody's?" "Well, I'm his son," Arlo shyly replied. It wasn't a surprise. By 1965 the name of Woody Guthrie was no longer known only to a handful of scholars and left-wing types. This was due in part to the meteoric rise of Bob Dylan. The young singer had long since cast off his image as a wandering misfit knocking on the door of the Guthrie home and was now in the midst of turning the popular-music world on its head. Dylan had only recently completed a wildly successful tour of England—and it was through Dylan's fame and worshipful praise of Woody that the fame of the Dust Bowl balladeer had grown exponentially. Not having any particular destination in mind, Arlo, toting his guitar and a rucksack, climbed into a taxi, telling the driver to simply "drop me off where the people are." He was driven to Piccadilly Circus. This, coincidentally, was the very same neon-splashed plaza that his buddy Ramblin' Jack Elliott had visited on his first night in London almost a decade earlier. The night of Elliott's arrival in September of 1955, he and his wife had mindfully stayed at a bed-and-breakfast on the outskirts of London; Arlo, hoping to conserve the limited cash he had on hand, was intending to rest that first evening as inexpensively as possible—in a seat of a seedy all-night cinema. But he soon abandoned that accommodation when he was near-groped by a male patron, who may or may not have mistaken the long-haired Guthrie for a girl. He walked the streets cautiously the rest of the night, more mindful of his surroundings. The next day he traveled up to Manchester Square, where the Beatles maintained an office at EMI. Though there were, disappointingly, no Beatles to be found, he did chat a bit with a sympathetic staffer and was given the telephone number of the writer Karl Dallas.[32]

Dallas was a well-known figure in London's folk-music circles. He was the publisher of the small-press magazine *Folk Music* and well known as a supporter of radical causes. Dallas was, more importantly in this instance, a great fan of Woody Guthrie and more than happy to welcome to England the son of the legendary Dust Bowl troubadour. Dallas brought Arlo to a meeting of the Singer's Club in London, a left-wing song-swapping session formed as an offshoot of Ewan MacColl and A. L. Lloyd's Ballad and Blues Organisation. Dallas, who would occasionally contribute articles to the *Daily Worker*, Great Britain's communist newspaper, would gleefully report that the Singer's Club was in the midst of hosting, as it so often would, an "evening of political songs, many of them anti-American." Dallas informed Peggy Seeger, the wife of balladeer Ewan MacColl and Pete's expatriate half-sister, that Woody's son had come along with him. Upon Peggy's passing that news on to those attending there was, to no one's surprise, an explosion of comradely applause, and Arlo was asked to sing a song or two. Though Arlo had been greeted warmly, Dallas sensed that the shy teenager was uncomfortable with the attention. It wasn't that the politics of the event were off-putting to him. He told Dallas afterward that he mostly "agreed with what those songs had to say about what our government is doing in the world." But he suspected that he was welcomed warmly not on the basis of his own talent but because of his lineage. "I'd hate to think people were listening to me and comparing me with Woody," he told Dallas. "He's a legend . . . and I can't beat it." Dallas would recall some two years after that first meeting that while he understood why Arlo was determined not to ride on his father's coattails, he nonetheless "counseled him to remember that his audiences would expect him to sing at least some of his father's songs." Dallas would go on to describe the Arlo Guthrie he met in 1965 as merely one more "guitar-picking kid with a pleasant but not sensational singing style," albeit one with valuable, if possibly damaged, genetics and "some interesting songs of his own which showed great promise."[33]

Dallas was a contributing writer to England's premier pop-music weekly, *Melody Maker*, and Arlo consented to sit for a brief interview. He admitted to Dallas that memories of his father were generally confined to "odd fragments" since his father had been ill a long time. He went on to explain how it was his mother who taught him his first guitar chords, but as Woody was in the hospital for most of his childhood, "I don't know if you'd call us a singing family. There was always a lot of music, and we've got more broken-down instruments around that we've worn out than you can imagine." He told Dallas that his future plans were sketchy beyond an immediate interest in attending college. Though he loved music he wasn't too certain that "I'll become a professional singer. I've still got to go through college [first]," he cautioned, expressing a vague desire in mastering "some instrument like a piano." During his relatively short time in England, Guthrie accepted Dallas's welcome offer of a pallet on the floor of his apartment, where, in his recollection, Arlo "eked out his money, visited the Keele Folk Festival, hopped over to Scandinavia and back, played a lot of guitar and drank a lot of Scotch whisky."[34]

Guthrie returned to the United States. It was September 1965, and, with the new school year set to begin, Marjorie Guthrie was readying to send her eldest child off to college. "I packed him up and said to myself, 'How long is he going to last?'" She grumbled to one journalist that Arlo's going off to college "was a big joke." In truth it hadn't been easy searching for a college that, given the sorry state of his transcripts, was willing to accept him into its program. They finally received word that Guthrie would be welcomed at the liberal arts school of Rocky Mountain College in Billings, Montana. In later years, Arlo would joke that the college was the closest to New York City willing to accept him into its program. But in an interview from 1969, he claimed to have purposefully chosen rural Montana simply because he liked "the country there." Three years following his single semester at Rocky Mountain, he would tell writer Arthur Whitman, somewhat hazily, "I had a reason for going [to college], but I don't remember what it was. Maybe I wanted to get away from the east coast and east coast things." If that was his intention, he succeeded. The Billings, Montana, of 1965 wasn't a terribly progressive community, and his experiences there hardly mirrored life in either New York City or Stockbridge. His fellow students, most of the college faculty, and all of the cowboy-hat-wearing locals were little enamored of a guitar-strumming flower child who wore his hair to his shoulders. The townspeople, according to Arlo, "didn't know what to think of me. They'd follow me down the street in single file, making remarks. I guess they thought I was a freaked-out kid they could study." Though there was a school chaplain sympathetic to his situation, he made few friends in Billings, and his tenure at Rocky Mountain lasted all of three to six weeks, depending on the interview. If Arlo was a little vague on his reasons for attending college, there was no confusion about why he chose to leave. When he first enrolled in the physical education program, the course was centered more or less on such innocuous activities as bowling and similar recreations. But things began to go awry almost immediately when the class morphed from pleasant games into something resembling "basic training . . . you had to wear packs and drill, like soldiers. . . . I said 'Training for what? I can get this tin-soldier stuff in the east, so I came back home.'" Though she secretly wished to be proven wrong, Marjorie had been right all along; her son was totally unsuited for college. He defended his decision to abandon the school, sourly telling the *Washington Post* that college life simply wasn't able to offer "what I was looking for. Education today is not relevant in anyone's life. Going to college is like visiting the supermarket. You pick out this and that, but what do you come away with?"[35]

That's not to say that his time in Billings wasn't life changing. One night Arlo was listening to the radio when Bob Dylan's new single "Positively Fourth Street" (released September 7, 1965) came on. It was as if he had been struck by lightning. He was already something of a Dylan fan, of course, but there was something almost absurd about the fact that the local DJs were spinning "Positively Fourth Street" out in the desolation of Montana. He later recalled to Folk City co-owner Robbie Woliver that his first thought on hearing the single was, "Oh, God. That's incredible that they're playing this song on the radio." He admitted that hearing the Dylan song that night was the principal factor in his abandoning his college fantasy; Dylan's angry anthem made him come to terms with the fact that he was on the wrong course. In the years that followed Arlo would offer, with no sense of familial guilt, that his songwriting had always been "more influenced by Dylan's songs than by my father's. They made an impact on me the same way my father's songs made an impact on Ramblin' Jack Elliott." Arlo recalled that, in these earliest days of his musical consciousness, it was Dylan's music, not Woody's, that "made me feel things I was thinking were important. I knew I had to do what I wanted to do." That was, of course, to make his own music. He decided that he would need to return home if he was to take advantage of his celebrated surname. He called his mother at their home in Queens, explaining his decision to try to make it as a folk singer: "I sing at football games and I sing at church, so I might as well be home and sing." Guthrie recalled that while his mother was resigned to welcoming him home, she did so with mixed feelings. Without college, her eldest son would be of interest to the military in less than a year's time. And although Arlo had never been much of a student, Marjorie valued education and self-discipline and faithfully hoped that her wayward son might still blossom in a college environment. Mostly she expressed disappointment that her son was giving up so soon. It was becoming an unwelcome trend. Guthrie recalled that Marjorie's response was the typical "Jewish mother thing—if you don't go to college, you can't be a doctor or a lawyer."[36]

It was an odd time to begin a career in folk singing; the brief but vibrant period of topical songwriting à la Dylan-Ochs-Paxton was already passé, with even the most earnest folkies moving into experimentations with rock 'n' roll. Rock 'n' roll was transforming. The form was beginning to shed its teenybopper reputation and embrace more thoughtful and provocative lyrics. Though Los Angeles had supplanted New York as the home of the "happening" music industry, Guthrie chose to return to the East, staying for a time with his mother and a new stepfather, Louis Cooper, in Howard Beach, Queens. He scraped together enough money to purchase a 1957 red MGA from Pete Seeger's son, Dan. The sports car, which Arlo remembered as "just like the one Elvis always drove in his movies," would, presumably, get him to the gigs he was wishing on. He made plans to visit Stockbridge in late November, as a call had gone out that Ray and Alice Brock were hosting a Thanksgiving Day feast at the Trinity. When Guthrie pulled into Stockbridge on Thanksgiving morning, he found the Brocks in the process of readying for their guests by cleaning debris from the main assembly of the church. The trash included the remnants of building supplies, plaster board, bottles, garbage, boxes of papers, and even a good-sized but well-worn divan. Guthrie had arrived at the church with his friend, Richard J. "Rick" Robbins, and the two volunteered to transport the garbage to the dump in Great Barrington. The problem was that the dump was closed on Thanksgiving Day, so they would, as Guthrie would fatefully note, need to find "another place to put the garbage." The two young men suddenly remembered that there was a collection of rubbish at the base of a hill off Prospect Street, a residential area just across the road from Arlo's alma mater, the Indian Hill School. It was there that the two disposed of the trash by throwing the contents of the red VW microbus down the slope. The problem was that this alternate site was on the estate of one Nelson Foote Sr., who didn't care much for hippies or the leftie kids at Indian Hill and wasn't pleased to see his backyard used as a dumping ground. As a student at Indian Hill, Arlo had been cautioned by Indian Hill staff for three consecutive summers "to stay away" from Foote's property. But the students found Mr. Foote's antagonism amusing, the Baumans recollecting that Guthrie and his friends would often sit on a wall dividing the properties to listen to Mr. Foote's "passing tirades." Guthrie and Robbins probably would have gotten away with the disposal had an eyewitness not telephoned the Stockbridge Police Department to report the crime.[37]

The chief of police of Stockbridge was William J. Obanhein, a no-nonsense sort not enamored of hippies or alternative lifestyles. The locals referred to the hippie kids in the area as the "church people," and Chief Obanhein didn't care much for them. The chief was a true-blue American, a "John Wayne type," who had earlier been a model of the beloved artist-illustrator and Stockbridge resident Norman Rockwell. It was "Officer Obie," as Obanhein was referred to by the young people of the area, who spent "a disagreeable two hours" on Thanksgiving Day poking through the trash before finding a slip of paper with Ray Brock's name on it. Following the paper trail, the chief drove to the Trinity and, after finding Guthrie and Robbins and the telltale red VW microbus on the premises—Alice was not at the church at the time—escorted the two men to the Stockbridge jailhouse. The arrest, which in two years' time would elevate Chief Obanhein to iconic comic-villain status, was far less dramatic then Guthrie's resulting talking-blues song might suggest. Following the success, and notoriety, of *Alice's Restaurant*, it was important to the chief that he set the record straight. "I didn't put any handcuffs on them," Obie told a feature writer from *Playboy* magazine. Though it was true that he carted the two litterbugs off to the Stockbridge Jail—this was a matter of the law, after all—the chief didn't, as Guthrie muses in the song, "take off the toilet seats, so we couldn't hit ourselves in the head and drown." "I didn't take the toilet seats off, 'cause we don't have any seats," Obie shrugged. "I told the architect who designed the cells you can't have things like that, 'cause when people come in here, they're like to rip them off." What *was* true was that following their arrest Guthrie and Robbins called Alice, expecting that she would come down to the station and bail them out. Before long a seething Alice arrived at the station, outraged at the sight of her friends behind bars. She called the chief, among other mostly unprintable things, a "fascist." The language was harsh but, as she would later tell *Newsweek*, the no-nonsense Obie was infamous for being hostile to the young people in the community, that he "would handcuff anybody" for the smallest of infractions. He was, in a sense, being true to that image when, in a heavy-handed attempt to cool Alice's tantrum, Obie told her that if she didn't stop carrying on, he'd arrest her as well.[38]

The wheels of justice turned quickly in Washington County, and the following day, Friday, November 27, Guthrie and Robbins were scheduled to appear before Special Justice James E. Hannon at the district court in neighboring Lee, Massachusetts. The justice, to Obie's dismay, was not able to page through the numerous photographs that he had taken of the crime scene; Hannon suffered from blindness in both eyes and would not be examining any visual evidence. But he accepted the guilty pleas of Guthrie and Robbins, handed down fines of twenty-five dollars each, and made them spend the better part of a rainy Saturday afternoon removing the debris from the bottom of the hill near Prospect Street. Obie monitored the cleanup from the dry comfort of his blue Ford Galaxie 500 police car, telling the *Berkshire Eagle*, with satisfaction, that he was of the mind that Guthrie and Robbins "found dragging the junk up the hillside much harder than throwing it down." He also added that "he hoped their case would be an example to others who are careless about disposal of rubbish."[39]

It should have ended there. But the surreal incident was the topic of conversation back at the church for weeks, and as Guthrie and his friends told and retold the tale of the absurd event, a story—part true and part fanciful—began to emerge from the entertaining banter. Alice remembered that elements of what would later transmute into the "Alice's Restaurant Massacree" had their genesis almost immediately following the arrest. "We were sitting around after [Thanksgiving] dinner and wrote half the song," she remembered, "and the other half, the draft part, Arlo wrote."[40]

The draft was on everyone's mind. In July of 1966 Arlo would turn nineteen, the age of which he would be eligible for the draft. He had earlier registered for conscientious-objector status, but that request was still pending by the army. His biggest problem was that he was no longer attending college and therefore was ineligible to get a deferment to allow him to wait out the war in an institution of higher learning. His mother and Harold Leventhal were already trying to work out a strategy that would keep the boy stateside, but Guthrie had already decided that, no matter what, he simply wasn't going to Vietnam—that as a strong opponent of the war he would refuse to take the induction oath. With the draft situation still unsettled, Arlo began to fashion himself a folk-singing career in 1966. He was mostly playing "basket houses" at first, sharing what monies were collected with his fellow up-and-coming folk singers in and around Philadelphia and Manhattan.[41]

Through the wranglings of an early agent, Charles Bowbeer, Arlo was to perform at the Caffé Lena in Saratoga Springs, New York, before he was to travel to Chicago in the early winter of 1966. Guthrie had been offered a five-night residency at Poor Richards, a saloon at 1363 North Sedgwick Street in Chicago's Old Town section. The string of shows, lasting from February 2 through 6, would constitute Arlo's premiere engagement in the Windy City. Other than being advised that he was booking "the son of the one-and-only" Woody Guthrie, the owner-manager of Poor Richards, Richard Harding, wasn't sure what to expect from his blind hire. But it was soon apparent that Woody's kid was no *prima donna*; Harding was impressed that Guthrie didn't seem at all interested in sailing through life on his father's reputation. Harding told the Chicago-area correspondent for *Billboard* that Bowbeer's only request of management was a modest one: "They wondered if we could find space for their sleeping bags."[42]

That's not to say that Arlo wasn't going to benefit from his notoriety as the son of Woody Guthrie. He was going to attract attention; there was no doubt about it. In attendance at one of Arlo's shows at Poor Richards was a writer from the entertainment industry trade sheet *Variety*. It's interesting to note that the template of what would become Arlo's traditional stage show was in place from the beginning. *Variety* offered that the young Guthrie was "relaxed on stage, and [had] an easy time of communicating with his audience." He traded between his guitar, a racked mouth harp, and an autoharp throughout the evening, telling stories, singing Dylan songs, encouraging audience participation, and treating those gathered to a resplendent finger-picked guitar version of John Philip Sousa's "The Stars and Stripes Forever." "Blues, hymns, and the like are dispatched casually with his effective folksy voice," the review trailed off. The *Variety* writer confidently concluded that though as-yet unrecorded, "Guthrie should be considered for wax exposure."[43]

He returned to Manhattan where, on Friday evening, February 11, Guthrie appeared with Lionel Kilberg, Lynn Rosner, and others on a folk-music program at Town Hall in midtown Manhattan. Then, on Friday night, February 25, the same weekend of his write-up in *Variety*, Guthrie made his West Coast professional debut at the Ash Grove, Ed Pearl's famed Los Angeles nightspot on Melrose Avenue. The Ash Grove residency, which was to run through March 6, was shared with Mississippi bluesman Skip James. Midway through Guthrie's Ash Grove shows, Jean Heller, a reporter from the Associated Press, separately filed a story originally published in the *San Francisco Examiner* as "He's Sung His Last." The article reminded readers that although Woody Guthrie "tramped" out of the Oklahoma Dust Bowl of the 1930s to find a better life, "he never really did find it, and now his time is running out." The pensive feature was soon disseminated to newspapers throughout the country under a variety of titles. It was easy to forget that the institutionalized Woody Guthrie was still alive and breathing.[44]

In March 1966 Arlo received notice that he was expected to appear at the army building at 39 Whitehall Street in lower Manhattan. Even though he had officially registered for conscientious-objector status, Uncle Sam still expected him to report for his draft examination. He grudgingly reported on the assigned morning for his physical and mental examinations, and the surreal experience would, unexpectedly, inspire a second chapter to his still-evolving, long-winded "Alice's Restaurant" saga. "Yeah, it sure was a drag," Guthrie later recalled to Sara Davidson of the *Boston Globe*. "It may be funny on the record, but it was a drag in there." Guthrie had prepared a four-paragraph-long statement that he planned on reading to the draft examiners. Guthrie's "A Letter Read to the Draft Board," dated March 8, 1966, partly read: "I do not believe that war is a means to attain good, nor that it creates love or respect for something good. I do not believe that today, anyone can win a war. Everyone involved can only lose." He continued that going to war would be a repudiation of his spiritual ideals, as "God is the love that people have for one another and this love is what I have devoted my life to." In the end, Guthrie was classified by the Army as 4F, which designates a candidate as "unqualified for military service," usually due to a physical or mental defect. Sitting around the kitchen table with his mother and stepfather in 1968, Guthrie was free to laugh off the episode, telling the *Boston Globe* that he believed "it says mental illness" in his official dossier. But saying something like that—even in jest—in the presence of a journalist was too much for Marjorie Guthrie, who quickly interrupted to correct her son's self-deprecating joke. "It says unsuitable for the Army at this time," she allowed. Director Arthur Penn, who would later adapt the story of *Alice's Restaurant* to the big screen, agreed with the findings of the draft examiner: "If I were the army," Penn told one reporter, "*I* wouldn't take him."[45]

It is ironic that as one branch of the U.S. government was red-penciling the son another was planning to celebrate the father. On April 6, the Guthrie family and Folkways Records founder Moses Asch were in Washington, DC, received as welcome but unlikely guests of the federal government. Some 2,000 government employees and invited guests had gathered for a U.S. Department of the Interior ceremony where Woody Guthrie, in absentia, was to receive the department's "Conservation Service Award." "You have summarized the struggles and the deeply held convictions of all those who love our land and fight to protect it," wrote department secretary Stewart L. Udall to Woody in a letter addressed to Brooklyn State Hospital. The cycle of Columbia River songs that Woody had written while on the government's payroll for a planned film designed to promote the construction of the Bonneville Dam were celebrated, with Udall promising that the Bonneville Power Administration had plans to name a substation for him, "in recognition of the fine work you have done to make our people aware of their heritage and their land." Marjorie, Arlo, Joady, and Nora were on hand to accept the award on Woody's behalf. Arlo, in suit and tie, had brought his guitar to the ceremony and sang several of Woody's ballads at the fête, most accompanied by Mr. and Mrs. Charles Perdue, the former a government geologist and president of the Folklore Society of Greater Washington. Nearly every photograph of the event shows the Guthrie family justifiably beaming in pride, their father rightly recognized at long last as a patriot rather than a subversive. Upon learning that Woody was going to honored, Marjorie visited her ex-husband at Brooklyn State Hospital so that she could tell him the news. He was totally bedridden by this time but could, if only barely, communicate by blinking his eyelids or moving his hand ever so gently. Marjorie told the press, "When we told him about the award, his eyes opened wide and glowed." Moses Asch's eyes glowed too at the official ceremony that afternoon. He sang along with Arlo from the sidelines, telling a reporter afterwards that the award was nothing less than a "great occasion," a long-awaited "official recognition of an authentic culture that this country has long denied." Not everyone saw it that way, of course. Irwin Silber, the far-left editor of *Sing Out!* thought the award a travesty. "For Woody, the great American process of canonization set in just about the same time he stopped singing and writing. We prefer our heroes sedentary and committed to their image. That way they cannot embarrass us."[46]

The Guthrie award was reported nationally, with most mentioning briefly that Woody's young son Arlo was himself a fledgling folk singer. Shortly following the Washington, DC, event, Arlo accepted a second engagement at Poor Richards, the series of shows concluding on the second weekend of April. It was sometime during that weekend at the nightclub that Guthrie was approached for an interview by Richard Steele, a correspondent for *Newsweek* magazine. Steele's interest in Guthrie was somewhat unclear; after all, Arlo was still unknown, unsigned, and unrecorded, extremely green as a stage artist. It's probable that Steele's curiosity was brought about by Jean Heller's recent AP feature and the recent reports of Arlo's participation at the award event in Washington, DC. In any event, Steele was easily charmed by Guthrie's music, humor, and easy demeanor and afterwards set off for his typewriter. Nonplussed by the surprising interest of *Newsweek* in his career, Arlo returned east to Pennsylvania, where he was booked to perform a four-day residency, April 14 through 17, at the Main Point in Bryn Mawr, the Gilgarra Trio opening.[47]

On May 23, 1966, a month following his second engagement at Poor Richards, eighteen-year-old Arlo Guthrie received his first national press coverage when *Newsweek* published Steele's article ("Woody's Boy") in the pages of the widely circulated magazine. It was a very encouraging feature, the writer managing to introduce Arlo to the readers of *Newsweek* with a poetic flourish or two of his own:

He cannot help stirring up a past that he himself never knew. Skinny frame encased in blue jeans, face half hidden behind dark prescription glasses, his familiar, thirsty, twangy voice hauntingly evokes the parched earth and the barren highways of the Depression. "Once in awhile," Arlo Guthrie says, "when I'm singing 'Talkin' Dust Bowl Blues,' I hear Woody's voice, not mine. It's like having a ghost with you."

It sounded promising, but the truth of the matter was that the ghost on stage singing and playing the guitar, racked harmonica, and autoharp had not yet fully materialized. This fact wasn't lost on Steele. He made note that while Arlo possessed the "natural ease of a born entertainer," his singing was occasionally off-pitch. He fumbled with his guitar capo, clumsily switching between keys midway through a song. This latter stagecraft might have been intentional, an endearing time-wasting trait often employed by Guthrie's mentor Ramblin' Jack Elliott. *Newsweek* also offered that the young Guthrie hadn't yet blossomed as a songwriter. "Sometimes I get mad and have to say something—like about Watts," young Arlo told Steele, referencing the race-fueled police riot of August 1965. "But you don't accomplish very much singing protest songs to people who agree with you. Everybody just has a good time thinking they're right." *Newsweek* noted that although Arlo rarely chose to sing his own songs, "Woody's spirit informs everything Arlo sings."

*Marjorie Cooper (the former Mrs. Woody Guthrie) and Arlo admire the Conservation Service Award presented to her former husband, in absentia, by the U.S. Department of the Interior on April 6, 1966. The photograph was taken at the office of Arlo's manager, Harold Leventhal, on April 23, 1966. Author's collection.*

What Arlo did choose to sing, the article went on, were "traditional songs, impudent satires, Bob Dylan songs and songs that protest human inequities and the war in Vietnam."[48]

On April 23, Jean Heller of the Associated Press was at the 57th Street office of Harold Leventhal Management, Inc. The AP photographer accompanying Heller that afternoon captured an image of Marjorie and Arlo (his face hidden behind dark sunglasses) admiring the Conservation Award, now neatly framed and hanging on the wall along with assorted other treasured mementos of Woody Guthrie memorabilia. The resulting publicity surrounding Heller's AP feature that March, as well as the recent award, reminded the public-at-large that Guthrie, who had been warehoused out of sight at Brooklyn State Hospital, was still alive, though his condition continued to rapidly deteriorate. The press release that accompanied the photograph read, "Several hundred letters . . . have arrived since an Associated Press story carried the singer's plight around the world." Marjorie, the AP feature noted, was now remarried to the seaman Lou Cooper, an old friend. "Lou is grand," Marjorie told Heller. "He understands how Woody and I are still so close. When you love someone, you love him all your life." Marjorie's enduring love for Woody, as well as her championing of her ex-husband's legacy, was extraordinary. But there really wasn't much to do when visiting Woody aside from seeing to it that he was comfortable and reading to him. Lately there was plenty to read. Since the publication of Heller's original AP feature, over 300 letters addressed to Woody had arrived at the hospital, and Marjorie, seeing the mail as nothing short of a blessing, read each and every one to her former husband. "Mostly he loves the letters," Marjorie told Heller. "And they have been beautiful." The news item also made a short note that Woody's son was in the wings, ready to carry on the Guthrie legacy. In a somewhat premature though well-intentioned assessment, Heller wrote that eighteen-year-old Arlo was already "a *successful* folk singer." Showing the writer a photograph of himself as a baby cradling his father's guitar, Arlo told the reporter, "I played a guitar for the first time when I was six months old. . . . It seemed sort of natural for me to keep it up."[49]

Harold Leventhal thought so too. One week following the *Newsweek* feature, *Billboard* reported that "Arlo Guthrie, 18-year-old son of Woody Guthrie, signed with the Harold Leventhal office for personal management." In his notes to Guthrie's debut album *Alice's Restaurant*, Leventhal recalled that it was some three months following his departure for college that Arlo was back at the high-rise office on 57th Street in Manhattan. In Leventhal's recollection, "I called in my secretary, dictated a few letters to some coffee-houses, made a long distance call to Club 47 in Cambridge, Mass., [and] got Arlo his first job." Guthrie was scheduled to perform for the first time at the cozy

Club 47, at 47 Palmer Street, on June 9 and 10. Though Charles Bowbeer had been acting as Guthrie's agent and plugging on the folk singer's behalf in the early winter of 1966, it wasn't until Arlo became a client of Leventhal that his professional opportunities multiplied. Though it was important to Arlo that he "make it" in the music business on his own terms, this was, of course, one occasion where he certainly benefited from peerless connections. He was, after all, the son of Woody Guthrie. In 1966, with such Guthrie acolytes as Dylan and Donovan topping the charts, this was enough for Arlo to enjoy a certain *carte blanche* in the folk-music world. It wasn't that he lacked talent, but he was still very green on stage and as a songwriter. He wasn't necessarily all that special of a performer yet. His earliest shows were more than a little rickety and, according to one Leventhal staffer, those sets consisted mostly of "watered-down Dylan and Woody Guthrie." "He was going through the imitative learning process we all go through. He was good," the staffer continued. "But we'd have taken him on even if he wasn't. You don't throw your own kid out." In truth, there wasn't any question that Arlo would eventually be taken on as a client of Harold's. "As far as I'm concerned," Leventhal frankly told writer Susan Braudy, "my relationship to Woody and the fund necessitated my managing Arlo. Arlo is an extension of Woody, and I have an emotional stake in that."[50]

"Arlo Guthrie: Woody's Son Comes to Gerdes" read the *Village Voice* advertisement. Guthrie was slated to make his professional debut at Gerdes Folk City on Tuesday evening, July 5, at 9:30. He was booked as the support act for Bucky and Walter, a duo billing themselves, immodestly, as "The Voices of Bluegrass." The cobill was to last through Sunday evening, July 10, Arlo's nineteenth birthday. Marjorie Guthrie was there to support her son at his Gerdes debut, but in truth very few others were. The news that Woody's kid was performing at Gerdes caused no stir in the Village, especially as Odetta and Chad Mitchell were sharing a bill at Art D'Lugoff's Village Gate the very same week. His mother recalled there were at most seven people in attendance that first night. On one evening during the course of the six-night engagement, Arlo had to contend with a completely drunk and noisy patron. Guthrie was in the middle of one of his rambling monologues when the drunk catcalled, "Don't talk. Play music."

"Everything's music," Arlo answered, without missing a beat.[51]

A cassette tape, sourced from the Gerdes sound system, circulates of at least one of that week's shows at the nightclub, and the surviving audio document provides a fascinating snapshot of the singer at the beginning of his career. He opened his set with "Alice's Restaurant," but, aside from the title and memorable chorus, the storytelling song meandered and had absolutely nothing in common with the version he would famously wax a summer later.

There was no talk of littering or of his recent tribulations at the draft board. Guthrie recalled that "when I first did ["Alice's Restaurant"] at Gerdes Folk City in New York, it wasn't anything like the last version. It developed on stage. I added things as they happened and took away."[52]

Following "Alice's Restaurant," Guthrie moved into "Buffalo Skinners." It was a traditional song, but one rewritten and recorded by Woody for Moses Asch in March 1945. The song was well known amongst folkies as it had been one of Jack Elliott's premier showpieces since the mid-1950s, but though Arlo would play the song straight, the preface was his alone. Guthrie's long-winded introduction to "Buffalo Skinners" was likely the result of his getting a copy of the notorious privately published street pamphlet "Fuck the System." Though the pamphlet had been actually written by Abbie Hoffman, the future founder of the Youth International Party, the writer-activist had published the short treatise under the pseudonym of "George Metesky," the name of a famously disgruntled ex-employee of the United Electric Light and Power Company dubbed the "Mad Bomber" by the New York tabloids. "Fuck the System" was chock-full of information, with revelations on where street people in the East Village could find free or low-cost items to help them survive on little or no cash. One of the more interesting factoids presented was that the Department of the Interior was willing to give American citizens "a real live buffalo if you can guarantee shipping expenses and adequate grazing area." Though the government's only interest in doing this was "to keep the herds at a controllable level," this bizarre offer of a free buffalo was perfect fodder for this early Guthrie stage soliloquy:

> Here's a song about buffalos. You don't see buffalos in cowboy movies anymore 'cause they ain't got enough of them to rent. But you can buy 'em. Buy 'em for a quarter a piece. . . . If you rent buffalos they cost a lot, but if you buy 'em they're real cheap. But if you buy 'em you got to feed 'em. . . . That's why, like, on movie sets in Hollywood they don't have any buffalos. 'Cause if they buy them they got to feed them, and they [cost] a lot to keep them there. But, friends, you can be the first on your block to own a herd. Send in a dollar and you get four of them, man. Just bring them into your basement and you can say 'C'mon down and see my herd.' And you can get rubber tipped dart guns and shoot them down. Have a lot of fun. You can walk them in the middle of your street. Put up signs saying, "Watch Out. Buffalo Trail." Or "Please Curb Your Buffalo." [Unintelligible] . . . all the kids on the block would have a good time, I'm sure. Parents might not dig it much, seeing all their kids out there getting trampled by a herd of buffalo.[53]

Following "Buffalo Skinners," Guthrie moved into a straight cover of Ernest Tubb's "Take Me Back and Try Me One More Time." This was another song that Guthrie had likely gleaned from Jack Elliott, who had recorded the song on his influential *Country Style* LP for Prestige-International (1962). But if the guitar arrangement was Elliott's, the introduction was, again, 100 percent Arlo Guthrie:

> Here's a song from Texas. It's about. . . . Well, it's not really about anything it used to be about. It's actually an old cowboy song, but you'll find that if you listen to the words very carefully it would make an excellent next campaign speech for Lyndon Johnson. Now this song, of course, is from Texas and so is Lyndon. And I'm sure he knows the song. And if he doesn't, he'll learn it, because . . . folk music was "in" [here in] the city here about two years ago, so any week now it should be hitting the White House. They're always a little bit behind guessing what's happening. So, here's a song that he'll be singing when the next election comes. The words haven't been changed or anything like that. Of course "folk-rock" may be in the White House by that time . . . but I kind of doubt it. So when you see our president standing up with a guitar, singing this song, just say, "I told you so."

Throughout this performance, and eventually throughout his career, Guthrie would seamlessly thread humorous commentaries on topical matters with guitar-based songs in traditional settings. Guthrie's fourth song that night was an original of sorts. "Right now I'm going to sing a song that, uh, was written because I heard a song on the TV I didn't like. And the song on TV was about how my dog was bigger and shinier than your dog, 'cause he eats Ken-L-Ration. OK. That used to be a good song by Tom Paxton and when a song like that gets destroyed by TV it's like the death of the song. So I killed a song you for." The song that Arlo was referring too was Tom Paxton's "My Dog's Bigger Than Your Dog." It had appeared on Tom's first LP, *I'm the Man Who Built the Bridges*, recorded in concert at the Gaslight Café in 1962. The Paxton song caught the ear of one advertising agency, which licensed the song, with some small lyric changes, to be used as a television commercial jingle to help sell Ken-L-Ration Dog Food. It wasn't that much of a big deal (Woody Guthrie had changed the lyrics of "So Long, It's Been Good to Know Yuh" to help sell Model Tobacco on his radio show of 1940), and Paxton certainly hadn't become rich as a result. But in the earnest 1960s, especially following a 1964 folk singer's boycott of the ABC-TV show *Hootenanny* for its blacklisting of Pete Seeger for his refusal to sign the network's "loyalty oath," selling a song on TV for a commercial end was considered only slightly less damning than selling one's soul to the Devil. That night Guthrie decided to have a little fun at Tom's expense, rewriting Woody's famous Pacific Northwest ballad, "Roll On, Columbia," for use in a deodorant commercial:

> Now for the sake of making a million dollars and TV and all that kind of stuff, I've decided to change the words a little bit, to change the meaning. . . . But

instead of dog food and instead of Columbia being a river, imagine, if you will, [that] *Columbia* was a deodorant. . . . Now, as most of you know, we have a problem in Vietnam. Well, *we* don't have a problem there. The GI's over there have a problem, and the problem is we can't find the Viet Cong. So I've come up with a solution on how to find them. If there's anybody from the military here, I'd be glad to negotiate terms afterward for the sale of this product to the United States Army.

He then began to sing:

> Now in southeast Asia the Viet Cong is bent,
> On spending the millions of dollars we lent,
> So we gave them *Columbia* and followed the scent,
> Roll on, Columbia, roll on.

Harold Leventhal traveled down to Philadelphia to catch Arlo's set at the famed folk-music coffeehouse, the Second Fret. It was the first time that Harold would hear Arlo perform "Alice's Restaurant" in its most recent incarnation. Guthrie had begun to weave the more familiar story elements into the song, seamlessly tying together his Thanksgiving 1965 arrest for littering with his recent and unpleasant visit with the draft board. "It was right then, I felt that he had gotten there, that'd he develop his own material," Leventhal told *Newsweek*. It was during his engagement at the Second Fret that Arlo would write another of his most popular early songs. Following a spoon-stuffing session at a local ice-cream parlor, Guthrie and some of his long-haired friends headed to the nightclub for his second set of the evening. They had planned a shortcut through nearby Rittenhouse Square Park, but, for whatever reason, some of the merry band chose to break off and engage in an impromptu session of the children's game "Ring-around-a-Rosy." The game seemed innocent enough, but as Guthrie would remember it, "just before they got to 'all fall down,' a cop come and arrested them all for disorderly 'Ring-around-a-Rosy' playing." His friends, to everyone's disbelief, were hauled off to the local police station by police officer Joseph Strange, Philadelphia's answer to Officer Obie of Stockbridge. Guthrie told *Melody Maker* a few months following the event, "They busted me in one town for playing ring-a-roses [*sic*] in the park . . . though there were kids all round playing ring-a-roses. So when I was singing that night I told the people all about it and tried to fix a mass protest ring-a-roses-in after the show. But no one came." Perhaps not, but the event inspired Guthrie's tuneful and whimsical "Ring-around-a-Rosy Rag." It wasn't, arguably, a great "protest song," and as Harold Leventhal said of "Alice's Restaurant," the crime may not have been "on a monumental par with the cases of Sacco and Vanzetti or Dreyfus," but Guthrie's young fans really seemed to relate to it as it was all so *absurd*.[54]

Harold Leventhal had arranged for Guthrie to return to Club 47 on two of the popular club's "off-nights," Tuesday, September 20, and Wednesday, September 21. Robert Gustafson of the *Boston Globe* made a short note of Guthrie's upcoming but under-the-radar appearance. He filled in readers of the *Globe* with a skeletal backstory of Arlo's hallowed lineage but assured them that "the word I received is that Arlo is a fine singer and guitarist in his own right." But the shadow of Woody Guthrie loomed large. After attending one of the two engagements at Club 47, Gustafson admitted honestly to the challenge of reviewing the young Guthrie on his own merits. He needed to consciously separate the unformed teenager on stage—singing a twenty-minute-long song that "dragged a few times" about "the desperate crime of littering"—from the long shadow cast by his famous father. "Offspring of performers who choose to become performers face a hazard which others do not," Gustafson wrote, "namely reviewers who inevitably make comparisons between the two generations. Having said that, I know [*sic*] proceed to make such a comparison. Folksinger Arlo Guthrie recently appeared at the Club 47. When I went to hear him, I vowed not to fall into the comparison trap, but I found myself falling all the same." In the end, Guthrie managed to easily win the critic over. Though Gustafson admitted to whispers among colleagues that the younger Guthrie was merely "a carbon copy of his father . . . a good imitator, nothing more," he found little truth to that charge. Though Guthrie did share the southwestern drawl and "understated, dry sense of humor" of his famous father, the *Globe* assured its readers that the "wide ranging repertoire was Arlo Guthrie's, and no one else's." Harold Leventhal was also beginning to book Guthrie into schools, and on October 8 he played one of his first college shows, at the University of Buffalo. Afterwards, he crossed over the border to Canada for a two-week engagement, starting October 10, at the Seven of Clubs in Toronto. Though the Riverboat was Toronto's premier nightspot for folk-music talent, *Hoot* magazine acknowledged that the cash-strapped Seven of Clubs was more willing to host new talent "not particularly known in Canada."[55]

Arlo returned to Great Britain in early December 1966. This time around he wouldn't be visiting as a tourist but as a professional, if still mostly unknown and unrecorded, singer-guitarist on a three-week sortie of the island. The tour, which had been arranged by Harold Leventhal, was set to begin the first week of December at Accrington Town Hall and finish on December 20 in Hemel Hempstead. Journalist Karl Dallas, who had befriended Arlo in the summer of 1965, met up with the musician at several shows en route and marveled at the young Guthrie's progress. When Dallas first met Guthrie in July 1965 the youngster was something of a neophyte; now Dallas compared Arlo favorably to Ramblin' Jack Elliott, the gold standard to which all Woody Guthrie acolytes were measured. Noting that Arlo's guitar playing was more pleasing and complex than Woody's own and his singing voice far "lighter," Dallas found Arlo's take on his father's songs far from imitative. "[Arlo] brings out the essence of the songs by the Oklahoma ballad-maker better than anyone I have heard since the days when Elliott first hit London," Dallas confidently wrote. That may have been so, but Arlo didn't seem particularly interested in trading on his father's legacy, sensing that such commemoration was an artistic dead end. "I don't know if I will sing any of Woody's songs," he told the pop weekly *Melody Maker*. "I don't want people to think I'm trying to make it on his name. But I've got a lot of my own songs that I want people to hear." One of the original songs "that I like very much and people seem to like it, too," he explained, was a twenty-minute opus he called "Alice's Restaurant." Softening his bravado, Arlo offered, "Of course, if people ask me for a song by Woody, I suppose I'll sing them one." "I'm not running the songs down, you understand," he continued. "I think they're great. But I want people to realise that I've got something of my own to say." Though his handful of original songs was received politely throughout the English tour, there was, as expected, a barrage of requests for Woody songs from those gathered to see the son. The interest that Britons had for the songs of Woody Guthrie was genuine, and Arlo, regardless of his protestations, was well prepared to sing a number of his father's songs in concert. Though Arlo had some notion of the Woody idolatry present in Britain, he admitted to underestimating the influence that Jack Elliott had on England's folk scene. "I'd written enough songs for fifteen minutes in a set," Arlo recalled to *Esquire*, "and I did my dad's songs for thirty. All the rest were songs that Jack had recorded that had nothing to do with Dad. Everywhere I went, people would say, 'Oh, that's great—you know Jack Elliott songs.'" In a review of one of his December programs, Dallas wrote in *Melody Maker* that although Arlo managed to succeed entirely on his own merit, "the laconic, relaxed delivery of his patter is very much in the Will Rogers–Woody Guthrie tradition." That night he threaded his set with original material, a trio of Woody Guthrie ballads, and Dylan's "Girl from the North Country." He returned to the United States in time to celebrate Christmas and the New Year.[56]

## NOTES

1. Woody Guthrie, "New People's Songster on Way," *People's World*, June 3, 1947, 5.

2. Ed Cray, *Ramblin' Man: The Life and Times of Woody Guthrie* (New York: W. W. Norton & Company, 2004), 309, 311; Woody Guthrie, "Woody," *Sing Out!*

17, no. 6 (December 1967/January 1968), 10; Guthrie, "New People's Songster on Way," 5.

3. Patricia Bosworth, "Mrs. Guthrie: Kids Know Arlo's Still Searching," *New York Times*, September 28, 1969, D15; Sara Davidson, "Arlo Guthrie," *Boston Globe Sunday Magazine*, June 9, 1968, 20; Bertha B. Cobb and Ernest Cobb, *Arlo* (Boston/ Newton Upper Falls, MA: Arlo Publishing Company, August 1915), 91.

4. Stephen Winick, "I Go by the Name of Arlo," *Folklife Center News* 28, nos. 1–2 (Winter/Spring 2006), 20; Laura Lee, *Arlo, Alice, and Anglicans: The Lives of a New England Church* (Lee, MA: Berkshire House Publishers, 2000), 72–73; Woody Guthrie, *Pastures of Plenty: A Self-Portrait* (New York: HarperCollins, 1990), 205.

5. Joe Klein, *Woody Guthrie: A Life* (New York: Alfred A. Knopf, 1980), 334; "Singing People," *People's Songs* 2, nos. 6 and 7 (July/August 1947), 13.

6. Woody Guthrie, *Pastures of Plenty: A Self-Portrait*, 178–81, 185.

7. Woody Guthrie, "Correspondence," *People's Songs* 3, nos. 1 and 2 (February/ March 1948), 23.

8. Patricia Bosworth, "Mrs. Guthrie: Kids Know Arlo's Still Searching," D15; Joe Klein, "Notes on a Native Son," *Rolling Stone*, March 10, 1977, 53; Sara Davidson, "Arlo Guthrie," 22.

9. Nan Robertson, "Woody Guthrie's Widow: Carrying on the Fight the Folk Singer Lost," *New York Times*, January 27, 1977, 40.

10. Allan Taylor, interview with Jack Elliott, *Shared Experience*, BBC Radio 2, broadcast February 29, 1996; Randy Sue Coburn, "On the Trail of Ramblin' Jack Elliott," *Esquire*, April 1984, 84; Joe Ross, "Ramblin' with Jack," *Folk Roots*, January/ February 1993, 41; Susan Braudy, "As Arlo Guthrie Sees It . . . Kids Are Groovy, Adults Aren't," *New York Times Magazine*, April 27, 1969, 56ff.; "Arlo Guthrie," *New Yorker*, January 6, 1968, 20; Karl Dallas, "Guthrie JNR: Living in the Shadow of a Legend," *Melody Maker*, July 10, 1965, 7; "Woody's Boy," *Newsweek*, May 23, 1966, 113; Ellen Geisel, "Arlo Guthrie (The Story of Reuben Clamzo . . .)," *Dirty Linen*, no. 39 (April/May 1992), 20.

11. Nan Robertson, "Woody Guthrie's Widow: Carrying on the Fight the Folk Singer Lost," 40.

12. Sara Davidson, "Arlo Guthrie," 20–21; Janet Butler, "Arlo Guthrie: Mystic Journey," *American Songwriter*, November 1995.

13. Paul D. Zimmerman, "Alice's Restaurant's Children," *Newsweek*, September 29, 1969, 103; Jeff Tamarkin, "Arlo Guthrie at 50," *discoveries*, no. 111 (August 1997), 47; Doris Willens, *Lonesome Traveler: The Life of Lee Hays* (New York: W. W. Norton & Company, 1988), 228.

14. Woody Guthrie, "Woody Guthrie to Arlo Guthrie" from *Posterity: Letters of Great Americans to Their Children*, edited by Dorie McCullough (New York: Doubleday, 2004), 120–21; Arlo Guthrie, "Despite the Shadow of His Father's (and Possibly His Own) Deadly Disease, a Folk Hero Celebrates Life," *People* 28, no. 10 (September 7, 1987).

15. "Obituary: Miss E. Woodward, Founder of School," *New York Times*, May 12, 1951, 17; "Folk Singer Opposed," *New York Times*, April 13, 1956, 51; Joe Klein, "Notes on a Native Son," 54; Arlo Guthrie to Jim Brown, in *Pete Seeger: The Power*

*of Song* (Genius Products/Ingram, 2008); Arlo Guthrie, "Notes on the Program," *Carnegie Hall Stagebill*, November 30, 1996, 18.

16. Arlo Guthrie, *This Is the Arlo Guthrie Book* (New York: Amsco Music Publishing Company, 1969),

17. Arlo Guthrie, spoken-word introduction to "When a Soldier Makes It Home," Carnegie Hall, November 24, 1990; Harold Leventhal, notes to *Alice's Restaurant* (Reprise RS 6267, 1967).

18. Isaiah Trost, "Coney Island Okie," *Guitar World Acoustic*, no. 24 (1997), 26; Susan Braudy, "As Arlo Guthrie Sees It . . . Kids Are Groovy, Adults Aren't," 56ff. Danny Smith, "A Pilgrim of Peace," *Melody Maker*, May 9, 1981, 36.

19. Paolo Vites, "Ramblin' Jack Elliott," *On the Tracks*, no. 5 (Spring 1995), 28; "Arlo Guthrie," *New Yorker*, 20; Arlo Guthrie, "Foreword," in *Early Dylan* (New York: Little, Brown and Company, 1999), 5.

20. Arlo Guthrie, "House of the Rising Son," *Esquire*, September 1984, 82; "Arlo Guthrie," *New Yorker*, 20.

21. Irma and Mordecai Bauman, *From Our Angle of Repose* (New York: Author, 2006), 199, 222; Isaiah Trost, "Coney Island Okie," 91.

22. "Puerto Ricans Brief Traveling Students on the Homeland," *New York Times*, March 21, 1964, 14; Sara Davidson, "Arlo Guthrie," 22.

23. WBEC radio program broadcast, Pittsfield, Massachusetts, circa autumn 1963.

24. Sara Davidson, "Arlo Guthrie," 22; Barry Robinson, "Despite Her Protestations, Film Makes Folk Hero of Alice," *Sunday Chicago Tribune*, November 16, 1969, sec. 5, 2; Judy Klemesrud, "A Cookbook by That Restaurant's Alice," *New York Times*, July 30, 1969, 44; Laura Lee, *Arlo, Alice and Anglicans: The Lives of a New England Church*, 79; John Stickney, "Alice's Family of Folk Song Becomes a Movie," *LIFE*, March 28, 1969, 48.

25. Barry Robinson, "Despite Her Protestations, Film Makes Folk Hero of Alice," sec. 5, 2; Saul Braun, "Alice & Ray & Yesterday's Flowers," *Playboy* 16, no. 10 (October 1969), 142, 192.

26. Alice Brock, *My Life as a Restaurant* (Woodstock, NY: Overlook Press, 1975), 14; Judy Klemesrud, "A Cookbook by That Restaurant's Alice," 44; Sara Davidson, "Arlo Guthrie," 22; Laura Lee, *Arlo, Alice and Anglicans: The Lives of a New England Church*, 97.

27. Robert Shelton, "Guthrie Honored by Folk Concert," *New York Times*, April 19, 1965, 38.

28. Harold Leventhal, liner notes to *Alice's Restaurant* (Reprise, RS-6267, 1967).

29. Doris Willens, *Lonesome Traveler: The Life of Lee Hays* (Winnipeg, Canada: Bison Books, 1988), 228.

30. Edward Iwata, "Joady Guthrie: Arlo's Brother Tries to Make It on His Own," *San Francisco Chronicle*, January 5, 1986, Sunday datebook, 37; Louise Hoffman, "Joady Guthrie," *Broadside*, no. 174, 10.

31. Karl Dallas. "One of America's Most Interesting Young Folk Singers for Some Time," *Melody Maker*, December 10, 1966, 14; Paul D. Zimmerman, "Alice's Restaurant's Children," 103.

32. Danny Smith, "A Pilgrim at Peace," *Melody Maker*, May 9, 1981, 30; Karl Dallas, "Guthrie JNR: Living in the Shadow of a Legend," *Melody Maker*, July 10, 1965, 7.

33. Karl Dallas, "Guthrie JNR: Living in the Shadow of a Legend," 7; Karl Dallas, "Arlo Guthrie," *Melody Maker*, December 17, 1966, 20; Karl Dallas, "Arlo Doesn't Need the Famous Dad Bit," *Melody Maker*, December 16, 1967, 11.

34. Karl Dallas, "Guthrie JNR: Living in the Shadow of a Legend," 7; Karl Dallas, "Arlo Doesn't Need the Famous Dad Bit," 11.

35. Paul D. Zimmerman, "Alice's Restaurant's Children," 103; Edwin Miller, "Spotlight! The Hollywood Scene," *Seventeen*, February 1969, 56; Arthur Whitman, "The Apotheosis of Woody's Kid," *Chicago Tribune Magazine*, November 10, 1968, 20; Mary Ann Seawell, "Generation of Arlo Guthrie," *Los Angeles Times*, September 17, 1968, C14; "Arlo Guthrie," *New Yorker*, 21.

36. Susan Braudy, "As Arlo Guthrie Sees It . . . Kids Are Groovy, Adult's Aren't," 56ff. Sara Davidson, "Arlo Guthrie," 26.

37. Arlo Guthrie, "Car Talk Junkie Speaks," *Rolling Blunder Review*, no. 18 (Spring 1991), 3; Irma and Mordecai Bauman, *From Our Angle of Repose*, 199, 346–47.

38. "Youths Ordered to Clean Up Rubbish Mess," *Berkshire Eagle*, as reproduced in *This Is the Arlo Guthrie Book*, 39; Saul Braun, "Alice & Ray & Yesterday's Flowers," 142, 122.

39. "Youths Ordered to Clean Up Rubbish Mess," 39.

40. Saul Braun, "Alice & Ray & Yesterday's Flowers," 142, 122.

41. *Berkshire Folk Music Society* (Newsletters), Various 1966–1967.

42. Ray Brack, "Chicago," *Billboard*, January 22, 1966, 30.

43. "Ron," "New Acts: Arlo Guthrie," *Variety*, February 23, 1966, 61.

44. "Night Life: Norwalk Club Features Mamie," *Los Angeles Times*, February 20, 1966, O-15; Jean Heller, "Guthrie's Songs Catch On—But It's Too Late," *Los Angeles Times*, March, 4, 1966, 20.

45. Arlo Guthrie, *This Is the Arlo Guthrie Book*, 29; Sara Davidson, "Arlo Guthrie," 22; Saul Braun, "Alice & Ray & Yesterday's Flowers," 122.

46. Robert B. Semple Jr., "U.S. Award Given to Woody Guthrie," *New York Times*, April 7, 1966, 45; Leroy Aarons, "Songwriter Honored at Last," *Boston Globe*, April 8, 1966, 21; Irwin Silber, "Fan the Flames," *Sing Out!* 17, no. 6 (December 1967/January 1968), 55.

47. Ray Brack, "Chicago," *Billboard*, April 16, 1966, 34.

48. Richard Steele, "Woody's Boy," *Newsweek*, May 23, 1966, 112–13.

49. Jean Heller, "Woody Guthrie Wins Hearts of Hundreds," *Free-Lance Star* (Fredericksburg, VA), April 25, 1966, 2.

50. Mike Gross, "From the Music Capitals of the World: New York," *Billboard*, May 28, 1966, 36; Susan Braudy, "As Arlo Guthrie Sees It . . . Kids Are Groovy, Adults Aren't," 56ff.

51. "Gerdes Folk City: Bucky & Walter/Arlo Guthrie" (advertisement), *Village Voice*, July 7, 1966, 15; Joe Klein, "Notes on a Native Son," 55.

52. Sara Davidson, "Arlo Guthrie," 22.

53. Abbie Hoffman (as "Free"), "Fuck the System," in *Revolution for the Hell of It* (New York: Dial Press, 1968), not paginated.

54. Paul D. Zimmerman, "Alice's Restaurant's Children," 103; Karl Dallas. "One of America's Most Interesting Young Folk Singers for Some Time," 14; Arlo Guthrie, prefatory comments to "Ring-around-a-Rosy Rag," Sanders Theater, November 11, 2001; Harold Leventhal, liner notes to *Alice's Restaurant* (Reprise RS-6287, 1967).

55. Robert Gustafson, "Coffee House Circuit: The Tempo Is Up," *Boston Globe*, September 11, 1966, A43; Robert Gustafson, "Coffeehouse Circuit: Similarities . . . Yes, but No Imitation," *Boston Globe*, October 16, 1966, A18; Roger Lifeset, "Music on Campus," *Billboard*, October 15, 1966, 60; Paula Haberman, "Toronto News," *Hoot* 2, no. 5 (September 1966), 3.

56. Karl Dallas. "One of America's Most Interesting Young Folk Singers for Some Time," 14; Randy Sue Coburn, "On the Trail of Ramblin' Jack Elliott," 84; Karl Dallas, "Arlo Guthrie," 20.

*Chapter Two*

# Wheel of Fortune

On Saturday afternoon, February 18, 1967, Oscar Brand, the folk singer and radio broadcaster for WNYC, was host to a folk-song program in the tony chamber of Carnegie Hall. The free three-hour concert, sponsored by the radio station and billed as the American Music Festival, featured such performers as Len Chandler, John Hammond, Tom Paxton, Jean Ritchie, and Arlo Guthrie. Brand was no stranger. The Canadian had been a contemporary of Arlo's father, and beginning in December 1945 he welcomed such friends as Woody, Lead Belly, the Weavers—and practically everyone else in New York City's small folk-music circle—on his radio program. Brand was also instrumental in arranging one of Arlo's earliest engagements in Canada. Prior to the WNYC festival at Carnegie, Brand brought the young Guthrie to Canada, where the broadcaster hosted an occasional music television program on CTV titled *Let's Sing Out*. It was shortly after that when Brand invited the nineteen-year-old to perform at the American Music Festival at Carnegie. In truth, he didn't think the youngster was all that special. Brand would later reminisce, "I knew he was a kid, I was just doing him a favor by putting him on because, what the hell, he was Woody's kid." The afternoon of the Carnegie concert, Arlo asked Brand, "How long do I have, Oscar?" Brand told him that every performer was expected to adhere to a twenty-five-minute segment. As long as they stayed within their allotted time, performers could choose to perform as many songs as they wished. "Twenty-five minutes is one song," Guthrie frowned. "What do you mean that's one song?" Brand replied incredulously. Following Brand's own set, Arlo managed to perform two original songs in his segment: "I'm Going Home," a slight but pretty autumn song written in the Berkshires, and "Alice's Restaurant." An attending *New York Times* critic described Guthrie's long-winded talking blues as "an amusing but pointed spoken monologue on the vagaries of law enforcement, the selective service draft and their relation to the war in Vietnam." The evening closed two and one-half hours after it began with Brand, Guthrie, and Chandler singing Dick Blakeslee's *People's Songs* classic "Passing Through."[1]

Though the *New York Times* would describe the WNYC audience at Carnegie Hall that afternoon as "large and enthusiastic," the crowd wasn't large enough to launch the cult of "Alice's Restaurant." That responsibility would fall on Bob Fass, a "free-form" radio personality who broadcasted on Pacifica station WBAI-FM in New York City. Fass recalled that it was Ramblin' Jack Elliott, an old friend, who first brought Arlo to the station in the first months of 1967. Elliott, Woody's finest protégé, had returned to New York City for an interim, brought in by owner Sam Hood for a three-week engagement at the intimate Gaslight Café at 116 MacDougal Street in Greenwich Village. That engagement started on or about February 2, but by the 16th Hood added Arlo Guthrie to the bill as Elliott's support. The pairing obviously went well that week, and Arlo was asked to stay on as the Gaslight's main attraction following the conclusion of Elliott's booking. It was late in the evening following one of the shared engagements that Elliott and Guthrie trooped over to WBAI to visit with Fass in the midst of hosting *Radio Unnameable*, his popular late-night radio program. In the weeks and months following that first "on air" appearance with Elliott, Guthrie was a frequent return guest to the program, hanging around the station and playing guitars until all hours of the night with such friends as David Bromberg, Jerry Jeff Walker, and Steve Elliot. Fass recalled, "There were times [Arlo would] come up to WBAI two or three times a week to go on the air. We played 'Alice's Restaurant' a few of those nights, and then the audience wouldn't let us stop playing the tape we made."[2]

The long-standing myth contends that the WBAI recording of "Alice's Restaurant" was an instant underground hit upon its first broadcast in February of 1967, but that wasn't necessarily the case. In the opinion of Mike Jahn, a Manhattan-based music columnist, it was Bob Fass who almost single-handedly made "Alice's Restaurant" "the *thing* for the New York late-night literati." In April of 1967 the residents of an untended street on Manhattan's derelict Lower East Side had grown tired of living among the debris and broken bottles. It was as if the city sanitation department had forgotten them, which it probably had. The area was ignored with intent as the East Village's reputation was that of a high-crime, drug-infested area, with a burgeoning, but non–tax paying, hippie community. In response to the neglect, local activists formed a committee to proactively coordinate a neighborhood "Sweep-In," and the event, to the surprise of many, attracted several hundred volunteers offering to clean their little corner of the East Village. This was the sort of do-it-yourself community action work that the staff of countercultural WBAI was constantly extolling. To help cheer on the sweepers and assist them in publicizing their event, Fass pulled out the tape of "Alice's Restaurant" that he had recorded a few months earlier when Arlo and his friends were at WBAI. He played it often on his midnight to 4:00 a.m. program, for no other reason than, as Fass remembered, the "song was about garbage and the East Village has plenty of garbage." As more and more people heard the song, the more popular it started to become among the moonlighters, hippies, and night-owl radio listeners of New York City and the surrounding areas. It wasn't long after the "Sweep-In" that Fass began to play the entire twenty-minute-long recording *nightly* on his program. The undimming popularity of the song didn't escape the attention of the owners of Pacifica, who, upon seeing their switchboard light up, began to ponder the potential of using "Alice" as a fund-raising tool. The "Massacree," of course, was not available on any commercial LP. Since Arlo was still unsigned and had yet to be brought into a recording studio, and as WBAI seemed to "own" the only tape of the song, broadcasts of "Alice" were only green-lighted when the station's pledge drive ransoms were met. Fass remembered that during one such drive the station's manager decided that "Alice's Restaurant" would only be played if listener contributions totaled $1,000, and such pledge goals were met several times over. Before long the more enterprising music fans with access to reel-to-reel recording decks were recording "Alice" off the WBAI broadcasts, and those tapes were swapped and traded among friends. This was a new phenomenon, as the first rock 'n' roll–era bootleg, Bob Dylan's *The Great White Wonder*, would not start appearing for sale in head shops until the summer of 1969. Harold Leventhal thought the bootlegging of "Alice's Restaurant" had begun even earlier. He remembered that during one of Arlo's engagements at the Gaslight Café, "all the kids brought their tape recorders to record the damn thing." It wasn't the sort of practice that a music business manager could countenance. Leventhal drafted a letter to Fass and the staff at WBAI that, in effect, forbade them to play their recording of "Alice's Restaurant" from that moment forward. On his broadcast of April 26 Fass told listeners, "I just got some bad word. *Radio Unnameable* is no longer allowed to play the version of 'Alice's Restaurant' that we've been playing. The rights have been taken away from us." Later on during the same program Fass sighed to a friend, "I must get six or eight or ten calls a night [from] people either asking me to play ['Alice's Restaurant'] or people asking where they can buy it. People have offered me incredible amounts of money to sell copies of the tape."[3]

Guthrie had appeared at Club 47 in Cambridge, Massachusetts, on March 24, 1967, and was due to return to Boston soon after. The city was to host the three-day-long American Festival of Music '67 at the Commonwealth

Amory, near the campus of Boston University, on the weekend of April 20 through 23. The festival was to offer a slate of performers representing a cross section of America's indigenous music forms: folk, gospel, blues, country and western, and jazz. Pete Seeger, Chuck Berry, Flatt and Scruggs, Muddy Waters, Mahalia Jackson, Thelonious Monk, Tex Ritter, and a score of others were scheduled to perform, but *Billboard* noted that such fresh talent as the Jefferson Airplane and Arlo Guthrie capably held their own among these elder statesman: "One of the many highspots [*sic*] of the festival was the performance of Arlo Guthrie, son of the folk singer-writer Woody Guthrie, who blew the roof off Friday night [21] with 'Alice's Restaurant.'" This sentiment was echoed by a writer from the Boston *Broadside*, who wrote, "Arlo Guthrie gave an epic, twenty-minute rendering of 'Alice's Restaurant.' Let's hope someone taped it for some future illicit listening; in the spirit of his father, it was truly humorous."[4]

Pete Seeger had been friends with Sis Cunningham and her husband Gordon Friesen since 1941. Sis, who played an accordion and sang in a harsh, nasal tone alongside Woody and Pete and others as part of the Almanac Singers in the early 1940s, was now copublisher, with Gordon, of *Broadside—The Topical Song Magazine*. The first issues of *Broadside*, a pasted-up, stapled song sheet and newsletter, ranged from eight to twenty-four pages. The magazine was the first outlet to publish fresh-from-the-front-line protest and topical songs from the pens of such writers as Dylan, Phil Ochs, Tom Paxton, Janis Ian, and Julius Lester. Though each issue of *Broadside* was pasted up informally in Sis and Gordon's modest Manhattan apartment on West 98th Street, the radical magazine had a small but national audience. The editors had gotten hold of a copy of the circulating WBAI recording of "Alice's Restaurant," and a decision was made to transcribe and publish the "lyrics" of the talking blues in the April/May 1967 issue (no. 80) of *Broadside*. Of course, outside of New York, Boston, and Chicago, few subscribers to *Broadside* would have had any idea who this Arlo Guthrie fellow was, though the surname would certainly be familiar. Interestingly, the editors chose to publish only half of the song in *Broadside* 80. They were interested, apparently, only in the political "second" chapter of the song detailing Arlo's trials at the army induction center on Whitehall Street. *Broadside* introduced Guthrie to its readers in the following manner:

(Ed. note: Woody and Marjorie's son Arlo . . . turned professional performer about a year ago and has worked steadily since. He writes much of his own material. One of the pieces most popular with audiences he calls "Alice's Restaurant." . . . Arlo has composed several other "Alice" stories since—in fact it has been suggested he do enough of them to fill up an LP. Below is one of his latest).[5]

Just as the "Alice's Restaurant" bandwagon was beginning to get rolling, Guthrie was due to leave the United States for a month's spell. On Sunday, May 7, 1967, Arlo boarded a plane for Tokyo, Japan. Leventhal had arranged a wearying three-week tour of the island that was to feature one of his most popular clients, the singer-songstress Judy Collins. The tour was set to commence on May 10 in Tokyo and finish, some three weeks later, on May 31 in Higata, with few days off for rest or sightseeing. Both Guthrie and Mimi Fariña, the sister of Joan Baez and wife of ill-fated singer-novelist Richard Fariña, were brought along on the tour as supporting acts for Collins. But with Guthrie being a completely unknown figure in Japan, his laconic stage manner and the language barrier between artist and audience made communication impossible. In Guthrie's own words, his sets in the land of the rising sun were "a disaster."[6]

Thankfully, this wasn't the case back home. The positive response to *Broadside* magazine's publishing of the second half of "Alice's Restaurant" was so overwhelming that, in June of 1967, the magazine chose to feature a photograph of the young, bespectacled Guthrie on the cover of issue 81. They would also, somewhat weirdly, publish the previously omitted first half of the transcript in which Guthrie is busted for littering. The song was becoming a true underground sensation in New York City, and the editors tried their best to provide their national readership with some appropriate context:

> The "song" is proving extremely popular, especially among young people. Radio Station WBAI in N.Y.C. in its recent fund drive got pledges of some $10,000 by playing a tape of the two segments, each time $1,000 was pledged. B'SIDE donated 50 copies of #80 to WBAI which were sold for $2 each. Arlow [*sic*] now has a 3rd "chapter" in which every person in the world is asked to sing "Alice" at a certain time so that the whole world will sing it in unison.[7]

The cult of "Alice's Restaurant" was spreading, and early that summer readers of *Sing Out!* began to write in with requests where they might find "words, music, recordings of songs by Arlo Guthrie." The magazine was the first to break the exciting news that "Arlo plans on cutting his first record in June," but directed all further enquiries to the office of Harold Leventhal. As it had been decided to professionally record "Alice's Restaurant Massacree" in a live setting, the Leventhal staff had already begun to distribute tickets to the session among family, friends, and invited guests. The simple invitation read: "You Are Cordially Invited to The First Recording Session of ARLO GUTHRIE at Columbia Records Studio, 207 E. 30 St. (bet. 2nd & 3rd Ave.). TUESDAY EVE. JUNE 13th at 8:40 pm sharp! ADMISSION WITH THIS CARD ONLY!" The recording was to be prepared under the supervision of Fred Hellerman. Hellerman, the songwriter and singer-guitarist of the legendary Weavers, was a fine record producer and arranger in his own right. The day following his recording of "Alice's Restaurant Massacree," Guthrie traveled to Philadelphia for a return engagement at the Second Fret, beginning June 14 and ending June 21.[8]

The second side of the forthcoming LP would feature all original material wrapped in a mellow instrumental folk-rock blanket. Journalist and rock music critic Richard Goldstein attended one of the sessions that featured Guthrie recording with the session players. Goldstein had no problem finding Guthrie amid the endless parade of suited executives and reporters passing through the control room. The artist was dressed in a "billowing paisley shirt" and dungarees, a set of headphones draped over a ridiculously oversized felt hat. It was the sort of wide-brim hat that would keep "rain off both shoulders," according to the journalist, though Guthrie had earlier told another writer that he wore the oversized floppy hat "to keep my eyes shaded from the glare of the [stage] lights." Guthrie whiled away the studio downtime by playing fragments of jug-band tunes on a washboard and kazoo, but Goldstein noted his manner would turn from playful to serious when listening back "for the ninth time, to a complex rhythm track, nodding at his producer like a patient watching surgeons discuss his forthcoming operation."[9]

That summer Arlo was invited to perform at the seventh annual Newport Folk Festival. The event was to be held over the course of seven days, beginning on Monday evening, July 10, and ending on Sunday evening, July 16. Arlo wasn't scheduled to appear on the main stage at all; he was slotted to perform at the Saturday afternoon topical song workshop, which he did, introducing "Alice's Restaurant" to a small but enthusiastic handful of amused listeners. The phenomenon of "Alice's Restaurant" had not yet gone national; the song was still very much an anthem of the underground New York City music scene. But the song immediately caught the ears of those who had attended the workshop, and their enthusiasm caused George Wein, the festival's promoter, to have Arlo sing the song on Newport's main stage on Sunday afternoon to a crowd of some 3,500 fans. The response to that performance was, according to one report, so "overwhelming" that Wein decided to have Arlo sing "Alice's Restaurant" one last time on Sunday night's program before an audience of 9,500. Towards the finale of that final performance, the entire cast of Sunday's program was behind Guthrie on stage, singing along, on the last chorus of "Alice's Restaurant."[10]

Irwin Silber, the ideologically doctrinaire editor of *Sing Out!* magazine, was mostly disappointed with what he heard at Newport that year. Silber tended to filter events through the prism of his far-left political agenda and was firm in his opinion that the folk singers who crowded the Newport stages had become too insulated from the "struggle" for their own good. Two days prior to the mostly white and gentle Newport event, a riot had broken out in the streets of Newark, New Jersey. The tense insurrection lasted some six days, ultimately leaving 275 people dead, 725 injured, and 1,500 under arrest. Silber seethed that not a single performer at Newport—including Pete Seeger, who, in Silber's estimate, was fast becoming "a latter-day King Lear"—demonstrated enough revolutionary zeal to comment on the unfolding events of Newark. "If there was a moment of truth for Newport at all," Silber wrote, "it was provided by Arlo Guthrie whose socially relevant, existential 'Alice's Restaurant' captured and synthesized the mood of the crowd."[11]

A *Billboard* review of the Newport event also made note of Arlo's triumph, as well as breaking the news that Woody's son was "a recently signed Reprise Records artist," the label a subsidiary of the Warner Bros. conglomerate. Central figures in the signing of Arlo were Mo Ostin, the general manager of Reprise, who came to the company after some thirteen years as controller of the Verve label, and George Lee, the vice president of eastern operations for Warner Bros. responsible for vetting artists from the New York City area. The signing was officially, but belatedly, announced in the September 9, 1967, issue of *Billboard*. Reprise was primarily known as the label formed by crooner Frank Sinatra in 1958. Sinatra was Reprise's biggest star and best-selling artist, the economic heart and soul of the label. But Reprise also boasted an amiable roster of such "adult listening" singers and Sinatra cronies as Don Ho, Sammy Davis Jr., Dean Martin, and Charles Aznavour. In 1967 Reprise was looking to freshen and broaden their catalog by signing more youth-oriented acts. It was teenagers and college students who were now buying LPs in the greatest numbers. In 1967 Reprise brought aboard such FM-friendly rock bands as the Kinks, the Electric Prunes, and the Jimi Hendrix Experience and began making inroads into the folk and folk-rock genres by signing Miriam Makeba, the Jim Kweskin Jug Band, Ramblin' Jack Elliott, David Blue, and Arlo Guthrie. It was no secret that Reprise principally wanted Arlo because they wanted "Alice's Restaurant." They were betting, as were many others, that young Arlo Guthrie might turn out to be the new Bob Dylan. The "old" Dylan was in self-seclusion in Woodstock, New York, having not been seen nor heard from since July 29, 1966. It was on that afternoon that Dylan reportedly fell off a Triumph 650 Bonneville motorcycle—Jack Elliott's motorcycle according to blues singer-guitarist John Hammond—and disappeared from public sight. With the bard of Hibbing, Minnesota, maintaining a prolonged silence, record companies were becoming increasingly anxious to find themselves a "new" Dylan. Arlo Guthrie, the progeny of Dylan's hero Woody Guthrie, seemed to fit that bill.[12]

With work on the *Alice's Restaurant* album completed and Harold Leventhal busy that August preparing sleeve notes for the pending LP release,

*Uncommon Reprise Records publicity image sourced from a 1968 photo session.*
*Photofest.*

Guthrie continued to tour. He was becoming increasingly popular in the
Philadelphia area, playing a cobill with Josh White at the Main Point in Bryn
Mawr on August 3 through 6 and performing later that month at the sixth annual Philadelphia Folk Festival. The latter event, scheduled for the weekend
of August 25 through 27, was held at the Old Poole Farm in Upper Salford,
Pennsylvania. The festival's promoters had asked Guthrie, according to a pre-
event report from *Billboard*, if he might consider conducting "a workshop on
humor in folksongs." On August 27 Guthrie contributed to the "Humor in
Folksongs" workshop with Tom Paxton, Len Chandler, and Tom Paley, also
performing at the "Contemporary Folksong" workshop with Eric Anderson,
Len Chandler, Tom Paxton, and Steve Gillette.[13]

On the eve of the release of *Alice's Restaurant*, Woody Guthrie, the Dust
Bowl balladeer, passed away on October 3, 1967. Shortly before he died,
Harold Leventhal brought along a portable record player and a test pressing
of the LP for Woody to hear. There wasn't much left of Woody, and in the
final days there was no chance of communication with him; no one could say
for sure what Woody thought of his son's eighteen-minute, twenty-second

opus. But what should have been remembered as a poignant "passing of the torch" moment would be recalled by the Guthrie family with gallows humor. Against all odds, Woody had stubbornly clung to life for many years, but directly following his listening of "Alice's Restaurant" he went and died. Only three weeks following the passing of Woody Guthrie, Reprise Records announced in a full-page trade ad published in *Billboard* that with the release of *Alice's Restaurant*, Woody's son, Arlo, would soon be "Breathing New Life into the Guthrie Tradition."[14]

In the weeks following his passing, the prose tributes to Woody Guthrie in newspapers and magazines proliferated. The features examined his life, his genius, his notoriety, his songs, his writings, and the terrible disease that stalked him and cruelly finished him off. As so much of the reportage of Woody's passing was tied to his long battle with Huntington's disease, Marjorie thought the time appropriate to call a family meeting. She was interested in hearing her children discuss what they were feeling at the moment. Huntington's disease was hereditary, and just as Woody had inherited the disease from his mother, who inherited it from her father, who likely inherited it from his father, the three children of Woody and Marjorie had a 50/50 chance of falling victim to the disease as well. Arlo and Nora were stoic and not at all interested in discussing the realities, but Joady was. It was Marjorie's feeling that of her three children, "Joady was the most troubled by the possibility of the disease." So a family meeting was convened, which resulted in a three-hour discussion. It ended when Nora told Joady, "Wouldn't it be terrible if you lived to be 40 or 50 or 60 waiting for Huntington's disease to come and it never came and you never *lived*?" This, essentially, was a mirror of Arlo's feelings. He knew all too well that although his father's life was tragically cut short by Huntington's, Woody still managed to function as a man and as a creative artist for the better part of thirty-odd years. In an essay on the subject of living in the "shadow of his father's deadly disease," Arlo offered that while his father's illness could be viewed as a tragedy, Woody was still around long enough to lead "not just a joyful life, but an important one as well . . . and not just for himself, but for millions of other people." Though he would prefer that the subject not be brought up at all, Arlo bravely told his mother that he wasn't too concerned about the possibility of carrying the Huntington's gene. She remembers him telling her, "Mom, I have the ability to walk into a room and make doors where they do not exist." If pushed on what he would do should he begin to show symptoms of the disease, Arlo flatly answered, "I'll do the same thing my father did."[15]

Two weeks following the release of the *Alice's Restaurant* LP, Arlo consented to a short interview with a writer from the Boston *Broadside*. Though the writer mused that Arlo "was more excited than I was at getting a 'real interview,'" this was mostly wishful thinking on her part. Guthrie was fast becoming an old hand at the art of the absurdist interview. He toyed with the writer, taking her down some Dylan-inspired alleyways. "[I] was born in Coney Island and I went to Nathan's for six years," Arlo began. "I still go to Nathan's and that's all I do. They write my songs and I sing them." He acknowledged that the hamburgers at Nathan's were "too expensive," but remained grateful that the hot dogs were affordable. "If I didn't eat the hot dogs I'd be dead," Arlo offered, "'cause they were the cheapest at the time." When asked his opinion of the new so-called folk and blues style of rock music, Arlo answered, "That's like asking, 'What do you think of Venezuela?' It's groovy if you go there."[16]

Following the October release of the *Alice's Restaurant* LP, Harold Leventhal made arrangements for Arlo to perform at the prestigious Carnegie Hall, situated only a few blocks east of Harold's Manhattan office. Leventhal produced his first concert at Carnegie on Christmas Eve 1955 when he famously reunited the Weavers, rescuing the quartet from the shadows of the blacklist and helping to spark America's nascent folk-music revival. Arlo's Carnegie Hall debut was set for Friday night, November 10. On the weekend prior to his gilded engagement, Guthrie was booked for a three-night residency, November 3 through 5, at the Caffé Lena, Lena Spencer's cozy folk-music coffeehouse nestled in the horse-racing hamlet of Saratoga Springs, New York. That weekend at Caffé Lena, Arlo was interviewed by Bill Blando, a reporter for the Albany-based *Knickerbocker News*. Though Guthrie insisted to Blando that he was "not a protest singer," he agreed to share his thoughts on the Vietnam conflict—and of war in general—with the journalist. "The Vietnam War is wrong because war is wrong," he explained. "War must be eliminated as a means of settling things. It is now at the top of the scale as a means of settling matters. But it's changing, and war will be placed on the bottom of the scale, but that's still not enough. War must be thrown out of the scale." Though Woody Guthrie had passed on less than a month earlier, Blando wrote that the son "carries in him the seed of the hope that Woody fed on." That might have been so, but Arlo insisted that "Woody's music was for another period. I try to explain what's happening today. . . . Some of my songs are like Woody's. Some are about travel, about love, and some are about protest, like 'Alice's Restaurant.'" Surprisingly, Guthrie told Blando that he was planning on retiring the "Massacree." He told the reporter that his forthcoming concert at Carnegie Hall "will be one of the last times I will do it." When asked why he was planning on mothballing his signature song, Guthrie answered, "I don't want to be identified with only one song. There are other songs I want to write and sing, songs I hope will be better."[17]

In a preconcert preview the *New York Times* noted that Arlo, at the tender age of twenty, seemed nonplussed that he was about to transition from "the bare-brick coffee house circuit to the whitewashed flutings of Carnegie Hall." Journalist Richard Goldstein, on assignment for the *Times*, was a fan of the song "Alice's Restaurant" and an admirer of Arlo's whimsical, antiestablishment attitude. But as a music critic he was less enthusiastic about Arlo's talents as a writer of slight "wistful ballads and breezy game-songs." He described the "additional material" that programmed the second side of Arlo's first LP, with the exception of "Now and Then" and "The Motorcycle Song," as "thin and rather ordinary." "Without its title song, this album would be a vaguely unimpressive debut," Goldstein opined. He did allow that it wasn't since Dylan arrived on the scene that "any young performer achieved so personal [of an] approach to the talking blues." Though Arlo wasn't a songwriter of Dylan's caliber by any stretch of the imagination, he wasn't remiss about taking cues from Dylan's playbook. Guthrie perilously shared Dylan's tendency to act aloof or be downright uncooperative with reporters. But Dylan could afford to be indifferent to all the media attention that swirled around him; he was something of a critic's darling from the start, a money-spinning songwriter with a string of successful albums to his credit. Guthrie's aloofness with reporters, on the other hand, was a gamble as he was new to the game. Arlo didn't seem particularly interested in selling tickets to his upcoming Carnegie recital through his *Times* interview. He defensively told Goldstein, "I don't wanna get into where my music is at. . . . My music defines me, and I don't hafta go around defining it." Nonetheless, he did make an attempt to define the term *folk music*, explaining that the form has "nothing to do with the instrument you use. It's the relationship between who's listening and what the singer feels." Although Goldstein noted that Arlo was "supremely conscious" of Woody's reputation as the preeminent balladeer of the American Left, he acknowledged the son stood apart from the father by both "his temper and his time." It wasn't that Arlo was purposefully distancing himself from his father's legacy. He was proud of it and, in some way, thought himself a small part of that legacy. But the simple reality, Guthrie explained, was that Woody had written all those old union-organizing songs in the 1940s. It was now 1967, the world was changing in ways never before seen, and Arlo was determined to be a man of his own time. As Woody had recently passed on following his depressingly long illness, he would not witness the developing worldwide counterculture. The times they *were* a-changin'. In Arlo's blunt estimate, the chasm was generational, and Woody simply "couldn't have written about turning on."[18]

That Friday night Arlo took the stage at Carnegie Hall, where, in one headline writer's assessment, he sang his songs of the "Urban Dust Bowl." The highest priced ticket for Arlo's Carnegie Hall debut was a mere $3.50 since Leventhal wished to fill the house. Harold's strategy was successful; the 2,600-seat concert hall filled to standing room only, with, according to *Variety*, hundreds of others "turned away at the box office." That night Guthrie sang "Alice's Restaurant," but it was important that his other original songs were also received with enthusiasm. One song that met with a great roar of approval was the nonsensical "Ring-around-a-Rosy Rag," the very song deemed "pallid" by Richard Goldstein in the days prior to the concert. Whether you found such songs as "Ring-around-a-Rosy Rag" to be slight or consequential seemed to be a generational thing. "It wasn't a great song," wrote Alfred G. "Al" Aronowitz, a thirty-nine-year-old, blacklisted writer and occasional associate of Bob Dylan, "but it said what young Guthrie's teen-age audience wanted to hear." Aronowitz was at Carnegie that evening to file a report to the *Times*, and he astutely reported that "Woody Guthrie's son isn't trying to take his father's place, he's just trying to find his own . . . singing uncluttered songs that told about actual events and real people." Musically the tone of the evening was a mix of folk and gentle folk rock, with Arlo's acoustic guitar and piano backed by percussion instruments, a cello, and an electric guitar. The band closed the evening with an electric version of "This Train (Is Bound for Glory)," a song not written by, but long identified with, his father. The intent of Guthrie's choice of the final song was lost on no one. The feeling that something special was evolving was evident in the words of the *Billboard* critic who wrote, "Arlo Guthrie, the 22-year old [*sic*] son of the late Woodie [*sic*] Guthrie, has all the earmarks of blossoming into a renowned artist in his own right." The headline of the concert review in *Variety* seemed to perfectly capture the uneasy blending of the counterculture and capitalism: "Hipsters Get a New Hero in Arlo Guthrie Who Pulls SRO $7,800 in N.Y. Debut."[19]

One drawback of the runaway popularity of "Alice's Restaurant Massacree" was that many critics—and fans—chose to focus their attention only on the first side of the LP. In *Time* magazine's three-paragraph review of *Alice's Restaurant*, there's not a single mention of the songs comprising the reverse side of the platter. Dylan's *John Wesley Harding,* released December 27, 1967, and reviewed in the same issue of *Time*, allowed, "like Bob Dylan, Arlo owes some of his direct, throbbing guitar and vocal style to the late Woody Guthrie." *John Wesley Harding* signaled Dylan's return from a self-imposed seclusion, and, remarkably for a modest, mostly acoustic guitar–based album released near the height of the psychedelic era, it climbed to the number 2 position and held it for a full month, staying on the charts for twenty-one weeks. Though Guthrie's chart numbers were more modest, his LP was doing remarkably well. "Its length has kept Alice from wide disk-jockey exposure," *Time* offered, "but Arlo's first Reprise LP is moving steadily up on the charts."[20]

The reviews of *Alice's Restaurant* were beginning to pour in. The *Christian Science Monitor* was charmed by the LP. Contrasting the release of *Alice's Restaurant* with the Mothers of Invention's *Freak Out*, critic David Sterritt wrote, "Mr. Guthrie . . . avoids the big-city rock sound . . . preferring a backwoods-folksy style and a forever-innocent-youth-in-a-big-bad-world image." The original songs on the album's flipside were offered as "light, whimsical numbers, full of love . . . touches of absurdity . . . and peacefulness." *High Fidelity* agreed that the original songs on side B were demonstrative of Guthrie as "master of many styles," hearing traces of Donovan, the Beatles, and jug-band music threaded throughout. In the pages of *Rolling Stone*, then a brand-new start-up underground news sheet, twenty-year-old writer-publisher Jann Wenner raved over the LP. He called Guthrie an "eclectic: he has gathered ideas and snatches of styles from many places—Bob Dylan, Donovan, Tim Hardin, Paul McCartney. The influences include his father and the entire folk milieu of Pete Seeger, Leadbelly [*sic*], Sonny Terry et al, in which he was raised." Wenner was among the first to note the timing of the album's issue; surely it was ironic that Arlo "should be born into his musical career . . . on the eve of his father's death." It was also the belief of *Rolling Stone* that such songs as Arlo's "Now and Then" had "obvious Top-40 potential." The *Los Angeles Times* disagreed, praising "Alice's Restaurant Massacree" but describing the songs on the album's B-side as "routine folk songs, none of them particularly notable." *Hi-Fi Review* chose to ignore side B completely but offered the title song as "one of the funniest, truest, most pointedly intelligent appraisals of our society that has come from anyone, old or young, in a very long time." *Billboard* agreed with that assessment and went into an area that few others had yet dared venture: it described Arlo as "a great artist who may soon even outshine his famous father."[21]

Interestingly, one of the harsher assessments of the *Alice's Restaurant* LP came from Israel G. Young and Paul Nelson, two members of the editorial board of *Sing Out!* Nelson and Young, in agreement with nearly everyone, found the title song to be "an instant as well as a real classic." Nelson was no dyed-in-the-wool folkie with no understanding of pop music. He had battled and rattled members of the *Sing Out!* editorial board with his high praise of the Beatles' *Sgt. Pepper's Lonely Hearts Club Band* and the glories of an electrified Dylan. The problem Young and Nelson found with the reverse side of Guthrie's "somewhat mismanaged debut LP" was simply that "the rock arrangements of six of Arlo's best secondary songs are hopelessly cluttered and out of touch." The review finished with a not-so-well-disguised swipe at Fred Hellerman's production: "We like rock and we think we understand it, two claims that the arranger and producer of this record cannot make."[22]

Though the *Alice's Restaurant* LP was performing well, the staff at Warner Bros./Reprise were no doubt frustrated that no 45 rpm single could be extracted from the popular title song. Perhaps taking a cue from *Rolling Stone*, which mused that "Now and Then" might have "Top-40 potential," that December the company issued the first single from the album, "The Motorcycle Song" backed with "Now and Then" (Reprise 0644), a pair of songs gleaned from the frustratingly rarely played B-side of the LP. *Billboard* made note of the single's first appearance in its issue of December 23, including the release in its "Special Merit Spotlight." Interestingly, the notice ignored "Now and Then" but advised DJs that "The Motorcycle Song" featured "an interesting and commercial original rhythm."[23]

Guthrie was due to return to England almost directly following the Carnegie Hall concert. But prior to setting off for the United Kingdom, Guthrie had agreed to perform with the comedian Flip Wilson and the New Lost City Ramblers on a program at the Brooklyn Academy of Music. That concert, held on Saturday afternoon, November 18, was to benefit the Woodward School Scholarship Fund. Shortly afterwards he flew to London, where he was again met by Karl Dallas. Dallas, writing in the pages of *Melody Maker*, noted that Guthrie's *Alice's Restaurant* album "was sweeping up the album charts" in the United States, which was surely unusual for an LP "having virtually no air plays." This was entirely true. *Billboard* dubbed the *Alice's Restaurant* LP a "new action album" in its November 11, 1967, issue, and one week following its release the disc entered the charts in position 180. By week four the album had climbed to position 140 and was awarded *Billboard* magazine's coveted "Red Star," an honor bestowed on any album on the charts for fifteen weeks or less that registered the "greatest proportionate upward progress this week." By week five (December 16, 1967) the same day as Dallas's *Melody Maker* article, the album had easily climbed into the Top 100 chart (position 92) and was, against all reason, continuing to move steadily up the charts.

Guthrie celebrated the album's success with Dallas in a Soho pub not far from Les Cousins, the London nightclub where he had performed earlier that night. Though they talked a little about the success of *Alice's Restaurant*, Arlo seemed more interested in talking about the current musical scene. He thought Donovan and the Beatles represented the best artists of the new music scene, relating how he and his friends "almost wore our copy out" of *Sgt. Pepper's Lonely Hearts Club Band*, "playing it over and over, discovering new things on it." He much preferred them to a "put-down group" like Frank Zappa and the Mothers of Invention. It was Arlo's opinion that while Zappa was "a sincere guy," he was, ultimately, preaching to the choir, "putting down [what] has already been put down," reaching out only to those audiences already receptive to "the points they are trying to make." In contrast, Donovan and the Beatles were "reaching people who haven't already made up their minds." This was of interest to Guthrie as he was, in a sense, enamored of the long-view "cultural guerrilla tactics" exemplified by Pete Seeger. Producer and ex-Weaver Fred Hellerman was of the impression that Seeger preferred to sing "for the 'non-believers,'" as it were, as he was hoping to find common ground with people with whom he did not necessarily share similar politics. This seemed to make sense to Arlo who, in his own style, would carry on that tradition of bridging the ideological gap. Though the songs of Woody Guthrie and Pete Seeger nourished the fighting spirit of a splintered American Left in the movement's darkest hours, it was becoming clear to some in the movement that the progressive ideals they espoused would only come to fruition when shared by a majority of Americans.[24]

Following his return from his short sojourn to England, Arlo was engaged by managers Paul Colby and Fred Weintraub to perform at the Bitter End. The residency would begin on Wednesday night, December 20, and run through New Year's Day. A writer from the *New Yorker* magazine traveled to Greenwich Village one late afternoon at the beginning of Arlo's run and descended into the cramped "cellar-like" nightclub on Bleecker Street. There he found Arlo, who had played the 2,600-seat Carnegie Hall only a little more than a month earlier, dressed in a white T-shirt, blue trousers, and dark scarf. He was shoeless and standing on the small stage lit only by a "single bulb hanging from a cord." Guthrie was in rehearsal with his band, which included bearded and burly Bob Arkin (the son of actor Alan Arkin, another Leventhal client) on bass and his friend Ed Shaughnessy on tabla and drums. Pianist and harpsichord player Stan Free had not yet arrived at the club. The rehearsals were nothing if not casual. "We'll do it once and if it's groovy, it's groovy," Arlo told the band with no sense of urgency. The *New Yorker* scribe sat in the corner of the club with Arlo's girlfriend, Carol Ann Davis, whom Guthrie had met in England and who had recently crossed over to serve as his personal manager. His brother, Joady, "sitting in the shadows," watched as the band plowed through rehearsals of "The Motorcycle Song," "Ring-around-a-Rosy Rag," "Now and Then," and even a cover of label boss Sinatra's "Summer Wind."[25]

*Variety* sent down a reporter to catch one of Guthrie's Bitter End sets that week, noting that Arlo, if not yet a bona fide star, was "the newest of the big word-of-mouth draws." It was evident to the *Variety* writer that Guthrie was no genuine folk singer from the backwoods of America: "Guthrie is a very hip 'hillbilly' (his intelligence, wit, and sophistication aren't doubted for a second, despite farmer guise and drawl)." He also noted that the young Guthrie's belief system, as reflected in his songs and tales, suggested "fighting absurdity with absurdity," which, all things considered, was a pretty fair assessment of Guthrie's modus operandi. Interestingly, no writer present at the engagement made note that Guthrie's Bitter End sets were being taped by Reprise recording engineer Tony Brainard under the aegis of Fred Hellerman.[26]

In January 1968 Guthrie was scheduled to visit Washington, DC, for a performance at George Washington University's Lisner Auditorium. This was only Guthrie's second proper concert, the first being Carnegie Hall some two months earlier. In his review of the event, Carl Bernstein, then a fledgling reporter for the *Washington Post* and still a few years away from gaining notoriety for his investigation of the Watergate break-ins, waxed rhapsodic over the twenty-year-old offspring of Woody Guthrie. Bernstein was a reluctant "Red Diaper Baby" (he would later reveal in a memoir, and against his father's wishes, that both parents had been members of the Communist Party). But this uncommon American upbringing gave him a unique perspective among music critics working in the fourth estate. In his memoir *Loyalties*, Bernstein recalled the fragile 78s that played endlessly on his father's radio-phonograph console were, invariably, Spanish Civil War songs, Paul Robeson's "Go Down, Moses," and Pete Seeger's version of "Talking Union." The writer also remembered being reluctantly dragged along to the party's all-too-common fund-raising Sunday "picnics," where Pete and Cisco Houston would entertain. Though Bernstein would ultimately reject the left-wing tenets of his parents, he nonetheless possessed some "insider" knowledge of folk music and protest songs in the tradition of Woody Guthrie. In his coverage of Arlo's January 13 concert at the Lisner, Bernstein opined that Guthrie "demonstrated that he is among the finest of this country's young singers and writers. Indeed, he may be the best of the lot." The reporter was also cheered that the younger Guthrie was his own man; rather than sing his father's sepia-tinged Dust Bowl ballads and Columbia River songs, the son chose to draw "on his experiences in the urbanized America of the 60s" when composing his own material. Arlo "has mastered the same traits that made his father's music great," Bernstein wrote. "Guthrie's songs are loaded with irony, wisdom, humor and perhaps, most important, subtlety and optimism."[27]

In the early morning hours of January 17, 198 policeman and 72 patrol cars descended on the center campus of the University of New York at Stony Brook on Long Island. The 5:00 a.m. raid rousted sleeping students out of their beds, and following a flood of conflicting, rumor-stoked word-of-mouth estimates, it was officially announced that the Suffolk County police had swept in and arrested a total of thirty-six people, including twenty-seven Stony Brook students, on narcotics charges, most for the possession of marijuana. The day following the arrests, students on the 850-acre campus, outraged by the "Gestapo" tactics of the police, began to circulate signed petitions in support of those arrested with the declaration, "I, too, have smoked Pot." The same night Guthrie and bass player Bob Arkin arrived at Stony Brook for a campus concert and a little solidarity. Guthrie's performance that night was immortalized, some forty-odd years later, on his wonderful—but mistitled—release *Tales of '69*. Guthrie recalled the atmosphere of the campus concert to the *New York Times*: "I could see the fuzz in the audience who had busted those 26 [*sic*] kids. Every time I mentioned cops, I looked over at them. Everybody else looked over too. Everybody turned their vibes on the fuzz. With all our negative vibrations, we really freaked those cops out."[28]

Guthrie was in the New York City area as he was to take part in a special musical program on the weekend following the Stony Brook incident. On January 20 the cream of the New York City–based commercial folk-music scene would congregate at Carnegie Hall to pay tribute to and offer a sentimental send-off for their comrade Woody Guthrie. Harold Leventhal began to plan the event almost immediately following the early morning telephone call from Marjorie advising him of Woody's passing. The lonesome, stubborn death of Woody Guthrie unleashed the sort of media interest usually reserved for celebrities of more mainstream status. The day following the announcement of Guthrie's passing, the reclusive Bob Dylan telephoned Leventhal. As Harold told Robert Shelton of the *New York Times*, "A lot of people got in touch to say how sorry they were, but only one singer actually suggested that we *do* something—Bob Dylan." The resulting concert, titled "A Musical Tribute to Woody Guthrie," took nearly three months of planning as many touring schedules needed to be reshuffled, but Leventhal had secured commitments from Dylan, Pete Seeger, the actors Will Geer and Robert Ryan, Joan Baez, Judy Collins, Tom Paxton, Odetta, Richie Havens, Ramblin' Jack Elliott, and Arlo. That Dylan had emerged from seclusion to perform at the tribute concert worried many of Guthrie's friends. Dylan's return to the stage and all the attendant press it would bring might threaten to take the spotlight from the man whose life was to be celebrated in prose and song.[29]

Everyone in the cast walked out onto the Carnegie stage together and, as expected, the mere appearance of Dylan was enough to send a charge of electricity through the air. This wasn't the droopy-eyed, wild-haired Bob Dylan of 1966 who dressed Edwardian and sang in riddles. He was conservatively dressed as a country gentleman on hand to pay tribute to Woody. To his credit, he stayed in the background until it was time for him to play his three songs. "At the concert [Dylan] was beautiful," Arlo recalled. "He was nervous at first, but I was more nervous myself, and I didn't pay too much attention to him. He didn't say much, he was quiet." It was whispered among the more revolutionary factions that Dylan's alleged motorcycle accident was no accident at all but the result of a calculated CIA plot. "I don't even know if he had an accident," Arlo told Tony Wilson of *Melody Maker*, referencing the alleged motorcycle spinout. "I don't think he just disappeared. He needed some time. He was getting pushed in every direction by everybody." Journalist Lillian Roxon, reporting on the event for Sydney, Australia's, *Herald*, described, "Woody's son, Arlo, pale, ethereal in a purple jacket and a long curly Louis XVI hairdo." It was Arlo Guthrie who opened the evening's program with a solo Sonny Terry–style harmonica huff on "This Train (Is Bound for Glory)." Following what Robert Shelton of the *New York Times* would describe as Arlo's "wispy harmonica" introduction, Guthrie moved into rocking versions of "Oklahoma Hills" and later "Do-Re-Mi."[30]

Though some of the mossier, more puritanical elements of the folk-music community would scold Dylan and Arlo for their amplification of Woody's classic songs, it's doubtful that either artist cared. Backed by members of the Crackers (later The Band), Dylan managed to garner, in equal measure, both praise and scorn for his steamrolling through two classic, and one more obscure, Woody Guthrie songs. Though all the songs dated from the 1940s, Dylan's versions were refitted with new musical settings that, depending on the newspaper, were alternately described as having been reset in "country-and-western," "rockabilly," and "hard rock" arrangements. "He just did his thing," is how Arlo would remember Dylan's electrifying performances, unbothered by the complaints of the naysayers. The concert closed with the entire cast on stage singing "This Train (Is Bound for Glory)." The song lost a little steam midway through as various members of the cast tried to get a recalcitrant Dylan to sing a verse, but the notoriously obstinate singer wasn't being difficult in this case. "He just didn't know any words," Arlo recalled. "Everybody had a verse. Nobody told him anything. Pete Seeger told him to sing a chorus. The audience dug him there, but it wasn't his crowd."[31]

On Tuesday night, January 23, Arlo made his Southland debut at the Troubadour cabaret, Doug Weston's famed West Hollywood nightclub at 9081 Santa Monica Boulevard near the border of Beverly Hills. The Troubadour engagement, in which Guthrie was accompanied by a bassist and a drummer, was to last through February 4. The *Los Angeles Times* saw Guthrie as much a satirist as singer-songwriter, leading audiences through a slate of "outrageous tales" delivered with a Charlie Chaplin deadpan and "slow-talking way." The critic from *Billboard* made some offhanded mention that Guthrie's cabaret set, no matter how amusing, was all of five combined songs and monologues, including the provocatively titled "Lyndon Johnson Sneak-In Blues" and "The Pause of Mister Claus." It wasn't difficult to understand why many early critics pigeonholed Arlo as a novelty act; his set was primarily assembled around the talking blues of "Alice's Restaurant" and "The Motorcycle Song." "The Motorcycle Song" was disparaged by the *Billboard* critic at the Troubadour as "a foolish, nonsensical waste of time," though Guthrie's young fans would have strongly disagreed. Though it could not have been said of "The Motorcycle Song," there were grumbles that Guthrie's songs were more derivative than original. To those who listened closely to the words, Dylan's poetic sensibilities and free-association wordplay were readily apparent in Guthrie's own songs. It was true that Arlo had, consciously or unconsciously, appropriated some of Dylan's songwriting methodology; both artists threaded poetic imagery and Beat sensibility throughout their purposefully opaque lyrics. In the opinion of the *Times'* Linda Mathews, Guthrie's earliest songwriting efforts were as "deliberately and artfully mangled" as those of Bob Dylan. They differed only in the sense that Guthrie's lyrics were sweet and self-effacing, and, in strong contrast to Dylan, Arlo was far more "fully in control of his wrath."[32]

A stringer from *Variety* was at the Troubadour to report on the second night of Arlo's residency, the top bill of a shared program with the combo Hearts and Flowers, an acoustic-based, country-folk outfit that since 1964 had been an integral part of the West Coast scene. The band would later record Guthrie's "Highway in the Wind" on their 1968 LP *Of Horses, Kids and Forgotten Women* (Capitol). Noting that Guthrie's specialties were "low-key guitar . . . ditties about the FBI, garbage, hard times and life in general," *Variety* agreed with *Billboard* that Arlo's show was overlong, that there were simply too many spoken-word monologues and not enough music. But Guthrie wasn't reading the trades, and on the second night of his Troubadour engagement he trotted out a twenty-odd-minute rendition of "The Alice's Restaurant Multi-Colored Rainbow Roach Affair." This dope-smoking "spy tingler" and sister song to the more popular "Massacree" left the audience in stitches, but one critic moaned that Arlo's seventy-minute-long set had peaked some twenty-five minutes earlier. Following his engagement at the Troubadour, Guthrie and his band traveled to San Francisco, where they had been booked to perform at the Fillmore Auditorium (February 8–10) on a triple bill with John Mayall and the Bluesbreakers and Loading Zone.[33]

The same time that Guthrie was playing Bill Graham's Fillmore, *Alice's Restaurant* had been on the charts for some thirteen weeks straight and was currently sitting at number 37 on the *Billboard* Top 100 album chart. The success of *Alice's Restaurant* was gratifying, and the album's producer, Fred Hellerman, shared his opinion on why this new generation was responding so favorably to Arlo and his music. Hellerman believed that there was "a core of sweetness in Arlo that the kids recognize and respect. So many of us are submerged in hardness. When we come upon genuine sweetness, we reach out and nourish ourselves." That may have been so, but the pragmatic Guthrie understood that the commercial success of the LP was a sweet vehicle that would open new markets to him. He retrospectively told writers and folk-music enthusiasts Kristin Baggelaar and Donald Milton that *Alice's Restaurant* "turned a lot of commercial wheels for me. I didn't change my style very much, but it sure made it possible to work a lot. . . . It also made it possible to entertain a whole new audience, normally middle-of-the-road or country & western, instead of playing to elite college audiences." Guthrie's estimate was premature, for in 1968 he was still performing for college audiences, elite and otherwise. On Saturday night, March 9, Arlo and his band performed in the gymnasium of Fordham University in the Bronx. He was on the bill to support the popular rock band Buffalo Springfield, with the Union Gap opening the night's events.[34]

Near the end of March 1968, the trades announced that the celebrated film director Arthur Penn had purchased the motion picture rights to "Alice's Restaurant." Penn, a slight and intensely focused man, was a Philadelphian who retained that city's fast-talking slang and energy. Bespectacled and often seen in tweedy, rumpled clothes, Penn was intelligent and worldly, having traveled widely and studied abroad. In the early 1950s he settled in Manhattan, where he worked as a television director, soon moving into the area of Broadway production. Twice nominated for that industry's Tony Award in the "Best Director" category, Penn scored his first trophy for the Broadway production of *The Miracle Worker* in 1960. The success of that stage show brought Penn to the attention of Hollywood, where in 1961 he was offered to direct the film version of *The Miracle Worker*, featuring the actresses Anne Bancroft and Patty Duke. In 1967 Penn famously brought the story of *Bonnie and Clyde* to the big screen, cementing enduring careers for leads Warren Beatty and Faye Dunaway and turning a seventy-million-dollar profit on a 2.5-million-dollar investment. Though business required Penn to settle in New York City, he often commuted to his actual home in Stockbridge, Massachusetts, where he was on friendly terms with the all the locals, from the hippie kids he saw riding the back roads on their motorcycles to the local constable Chief William Obanhein. With so many so-called antiestablishment films as *Easy Rider*, *Medium Cool*, and *Blow Up* achieving critical acclaim and bringing in bushels of cash on low budgets, United Artists saw fit to front two million dollars to Penn and producers Hillard Elkins and Joe Manduke to bring *Alice's Restaurant* to the big screen. It was a gamble on the part of United Artists, as Arlo Guthrie, the slight figure around whom the film would be built, had absolutely no resume as an actor.[35]

Though Penn was charmed by the narrative of "Alice's Restaurant" and envisioned it as a serio-comic film, an eighteen-minute, twenty-second monologue—no matter how amusing—would not be enough to carry a two-hour motion picture drama. As a resident of Stockbridge, Penn was intrigued by

Alice and Ray Brock and the gaggle of young "church people" (as they were referred to by the locals) that the couple seemed to easily attract. He was drawn to the alternative world they had created not far from his own more traditional home. Though he wasn't one of them, Penn saw through their mannerisms and costumes and came to believe the youngsters shared a pioneering spirit. "They need new ground to break," Penn told *Life* magazine. "They are not afraid to go out on the farthest edge and live off by themselves." Though Arlo wouldn't necessarily contribute to the screenplay as a writer per se, he did assist the filmmakers in the earliest stage of script development. But there were tensions from the beginning. "Penn and the writer spent a lot of time with me before they did the script," Arlo recalled, "and it represents a lot of things I told them about, but there are things in the script that aren't representative of the way I think." In the end, Penn and coscreenwriter Venable Herndon fashioned a thoughtful screenplay that adequately, if not always seamlessly, threaded the events of the "Massacree" with a parallel story that analyzed the harsh realities of building an Aquarian community on the fringes of an America that had seemingly lost its way.[36]

Just as Penn and Herndon were rolling up their sleeves and preparing their shooting script, Guthrie and Carol returned to England in April 1968 for a brief run of concert dates. They were met by Dylan fan Tony Wilson of *Melody Maker*, whose main interest seemed to be Arlo's assessment of Dylan's mindset at the Woody Guthrie tribute four months earlier. When the conversation finally turned to Guthrie's own doings, the folk singer told Wilson that he was "planning a second album, to be recorded soon." This comment was interesting in that it signaled that Guthrie was already "forgetting" that Reprise was only a few months away from releasing his second album, *Arlo*, recorded "in concert" the previous December at the Bitter End. Guthrie mused that his alternate universe "second album" might be recorded in England, as "there are a lot of good people to work with and good recording studios." He admitted that he much preferred London to New York City, and though he was getting a little bit of fame, his pockets were still empty most of the time. He told Wilson that he and Carol had planned to stay at the swanky Europa hotel when they arrived in London but found the room rates there far beyond their means. The Europa was located in central London and situated not too far from the American embassy near Grosvenor Square. On March 17, a short time prior to Guthrie's arrival, the U.S. consulate was the scene of a riot, with thousands of antiwar demonstrators clashing with police on the steps of the embassy. The wire services sent the story of the melee worldwide, and Guthrie couldn't help but comment, somewhat cheekily, on the recent trouble: "We wanted to stay in the *Europa*," Arlo told Wilson, "so we could throw rocks at the American embassy. But at the *Europa* we had to pay for the rocks." While visiting, *Melody Maker* asked Guthrie to submit to a feature they would run from time to time called "Blind Date." The premise of "Blind Date" was that the staff would play, sans artist identification, the pop singles topping the British Hit Parade chart that week. After each play through, their visiting guest artist would be asked to offer his opinions of the 45s. Guthrie would demonstrate little compatibility with the pop-music tastes of UK record buyers, dismissing all but one of the seven singles, showing fondness only for Chuck Jackson's Motown hit "Girls, Girls, Girls."[37]

As if "Alice's Restaurant" hadn't been enough to cement his reputation as a raconteur of the first degree, Arlo's amusing monologues proliferated, often overshadowing his musical talents. He returned to the United States, and at a concert at Chicago's Orchestra Hall (April 19), there were long and winding tales about getting on and off airplanes to confound the FBI agents tailing him, an extended monologue preceding "Ring-around-a-Rosy Rag," and even a marathon-length version of "Alice's Restaurant Multi-Colored Rainbow Roach Affair," a dope-smoking sister song to the "Massacree." He also took a stab at "Old MacDonald Had a Farm," explaining that the famous children's song was brought by emigrating Jews from Egypt to London and later to America by the Pilgrims. The critic from the *Chicago Tribune* noted that although Arlo (a "Bottecelli [*sic*] figure [who] plays six and twelve string unamplified guitars") may have been the son of Woody Guthrie, his loquaciousness made him "the nephew of the late Will Rogers." "It was a concert of songs introduced, finished, or replaced by a commentary of endless, often nonobjective, digression," the review offered. "The ramblings, like a country stream in summer, usually ended in unexpected places after having made unexpected turns, but they were lovely."[38]

On the misty Saturday afternoon of April 27, some 87,000 people crowded into Sheep Meadow of Manhattan's Central Park for one of the city's biggest antiwar demonstrations. The rally, organized by the National Mobilization Committee to End the War in Vietnam, was to coordinate with similar large-turnout protests against the war in sixteen other cities. Though there were scattered arrests and violence, with tussles breaking out between overwhelmed policemen and exasperated left-wing activists angered that the "imperialist establishment" mayor of New York, John Lindsay, had been invited to speak, things went off mostly peacefully, all things considered. Coretta Scott King, the wife of Rev. Dr. Martin Luther King, would speak on her husband's behalf as the civil rights leader, a staunch antiwar activist, had been assassinated in Memphis earlier that month. The *New York Times* noted a cordon of "50 burly bodyguards . . . formed a hands-locked square" around a van parked near the speaker's platform. Patiently waiting their turn on stage, Pete Seeger and Arlo Guthrie sat in the van, tuning their instruments in the company of demonstration organizer David Dellinger and the militant antidraft counselor Rev. William Sloane Coffin of Yale University.[39]

By April 1968, the trade magazines were reporting that the *Alice's Restaurant* LP had already sold more than 200,000 copies, an impressive feat for a musician still mostly regarded as an "underground" artist. The profits of Warner/Reprise had risen 15 percent from the same period the year before, with sales of LPs from their stable of adult-contemporary artists, Frank and Nancy Sinatra, Dean Martin, and Petula Clark, holding strong. But the new rock-orientated artists of Reprise, led by Jimi Hendrix, Arlo Guthrie, and the Fugs, were scoring impressive numbers of their own.[40]

On May 17 Arlo was scheduled to perform at the Santa Monica Civic Auditorium. The crowd was eager to hear "Alice's Restaurant," but, as per an item in the *Los Angeles Times*, "days before Arlo had been telling friends that he was tired of singing the 20-minute song-story that he made famous, and vice-versa." This tidbit of newspaper gossip wasn't entirely true. He was still performing "Alice's Restaurant," but he had ceased playing the familiar version featured on the Reprise LP. He had started to use the song's memorable musical setting in much the same manner that his father had used the "talking blues," a three-chord guitar progression popularized in the 1930s through the recordings of a performer named Chris Bouchillon. The *Times* fretted that at the Civic Guthrie "tried interspersing unrelated tales between the choruses" of "Alice's Restaurant." To the surprise of columnist Joyce Haber, "no one noticed," and the audience thoroughly enjoyed the different version played that night. Regardless, Haber thought it a mistake for Guthrie not to play his most popular song in concert. "How far would Judy Garland have traveled without 'Over the Rainbow,'" she sulked. In any event, Guthrie missed the career advice as he had already left town, scheduled for a Saturday evening concert (May 18) at the Masonic Temple in San Francisco.[41]

While Guthrie was on the coast for a spring tour, Harold Leventhal was making plans to team him with singer Judy Collins for several dates that summer. But before heading off on that tour Guthrie needed to fulfill a promise made to an old friend. On Saturday afternoon, June 22, Arlo performed at the very first Hudson Valley Folk Picnic at Castle Rock Farm in Garrison, New York. He shared an afternoon bill with Pete Seeger, Don McLean, Elizabeth "Libba" Cotten, Bernice Reagon, and Susan Reed at a riverside concert to benefit the Hudson River Sloop Restoration project. The irrepressible Seeger was determined to raise some $140,000 in cash to build a seventy-five-foot replica of a single-mast sloop that would sail up and down the Hudson to raise public awareness of the river's environmental collapse. "We are giving this boat to the people of the Valley to help them learn to love their river again," Seeger told a reporter from the *New York Times*. They were off to a good start. Six thousand supporters and music fans turned out for the Garrison event, netting the *Clearwater* fund some $12,000.⁴²

The first Arlo Guthrie–Judy Collins concert was scheduled for Friday evening, June 28, at the Saratoga Performing Arts Center in Saratoga Springs, New York. The following night, June 29, a second show with Collins was held at Forest Hills Stadium in Queens, New York. Only 6,000 of the tennis stadium's 14,000 seats were filled, but a *Variety* scribe attributed the empty seats to the steep $7.50 high-end ticket. The price was a bit dear considering that both Judy and Arlo were to perform later that summer, on separate bills, at the Schaefer Music Festival in Central Park, a short subway ride away and for a mere one dollar per ticket. At Forest Hills, *Variety* noted that Guthrie "satisfied in his hipster humorist groove. . . . His stories and songs often have simplicity as a guise for deeper matters; his original material is masterfully contrived but flows with a naturalness that makes him a warm personality." On Friday evening, July 19, the Collins–Guthrie show rolled into the Midwest for a stop at Chicago's Opera House. Though Guthrie's role was to support the top-billed Collins, the programming was strange as he had only recently played a solo concert in the Windy City. This fact was not lost on the critic from the *Chicago Tribune*, who noted "we got the version [of 'Alice's Restaurant'] he gave here last spring instead of the one on the album: Communist plot, noses, and alarm clocks instead of Officer Obie . . ." On July 23, 1968, Guthrie and Collins were scheduled to perform together again at the Blossom Music Center outside of Cleveland, Ohio.⁴³

To no one's surprise, Arlo was invited to perform at the eighth annual Newport Folk Festival, set to take place on the third weekend of July. It was at the previous festival that the relatively unknown musician caused a sensation when he performed "Alice's Restaurant" at a topical-song workshop. This year was different as Arlo would be returning as something of a folk hero. Critic Robert Shelton noted that at Newport '68 "Guthrie was acclaimed for being hip and witty," and though "the old heroes of folk songs, such as the late Woody Guthrie, are still in the pantheon . . . younger talents, such as his son, Arlo Guthrie, are finding room at the top." There were an impressive 12,000 paid admissions to the festival that year, with an additional 2,000 people listening for free from behind the site's curtained fences. Guthrie appeared on Friday night's "Freedom Songs" workshop, where, the *Christian Science Monitor* reported, he "could be heard singing songs by his late father." The "Freedom Songs" workshop was one of the more politically charged events of the festival. *Billboard* reported that at the grim workshop, "condemnation of war, specifically the Vietnam conflict, of economic deprivation, and of racial injustice were heard in material presented by Ms. Baez,

Pete Seeger, Arlo Guthrie, Rev. Kirkpatrick, Bernice Reagon, the Kalideoscope, and by many of the amateurs at the hootenanny."[44]

On Friday evening Arlo performed on Newport's main stage, where the newly minted twenty-one-year-old folk singer rambled and sang on a number of topics ranging "from floods in ancient Egypt to modern governmental procedures—and practically everything in between." *Billboard* noted that Woody's son "did not require the charisma of his father's name and talent to conquer the audience with his deadpan humor and deadly satire. His new, 20 minute talking blues, 'Swim, Swim, Swimmy,' left Friday evening's assemblage shouting for more and left no doubt that he is a mordant Will Rogers, not of the whirling lasso, but of the inspired guitar." The monologue was actually an extended riff on Woody's *Songs to Grow On* recording "Swimmy Swim Swim" (CUB/Folkways no. 4), and not everyone thought Arlo's one-off of the rare single was endearing. *Rolling Stone* correspondent Jon Landau complained, "The routine hit me as being pretty thin and Arlo seemed to be straining for both cuteness and laughs." On Sunday night Arlo was also on stage for Newport's official all-star send-off to his father, "A Tribute to Woody Guthrie." On that program he sang his father's songs with a cast that included Oscar Brand, John Cohen, Agnes "Sis" Cunningham, Ramblin' Jack Elliott, Lee Hays, Sam Hinton, Bernice Johnson-Reagon, Rev. Fred "Brother Kirk" Kirkpatrick, Millard Lampbell, Alan Lomax, Pete Seeger, and others.[45]

That weekend, Arlo was standing on the front porch of Newport's Viking Hotel when two old friends dropped by to visit. The activists Abbie Hoffman and Jerry Rubin had traveled up from New York, where the two had been coordinating "guerilla theater" events to bring attention to their recently established, if loosely organized, Youth International Party. Hoffman and Rubin had sought out Guthrie so they could bring the singer up to date on their plans to bring a "Festival of Life" to Chicago. The plan was to bring thousands of disaffected youngsters and "Yippie" antiwar demonstrators to Chicago the very same week that the Democratic Party would be in town for their national convention. Part of the Yippie strategy was to stage a huge concert in Chicago's Grant Park, the organizers betting that such an event would bring masses of young people into downtown Chicago. They had been trying to get Arlo to agree to appear at the event, but after listening awhile he told them, much as he had at WBAI that past January when they first asked, that he had concerns. Hoffman and Rubin had been unable to secure the proper permits for the use of the park. Guthrie told them that he would not attend and "would, to my best, have other people not attend if the permits weren't granted." His reasoning was that such a gathering was irresponsible as it would likely result in "police violence."[46]

Following Newport, Guthrie continued his tour of the Northeast. There was an August 8 show at the Maisonneuve Theatre of Place Des Arts in Montreal. On Saturday night, August 10, Guthrie performed at the Merriweather Post Pavilion, Columbia, Maryland. On August 14, he headlined a twin bill with Joni Mitchell at the Schaefer Music Festival at the Wollman Rink in New York City's Central Park. Shortly after, he was off to the West Coast, where, beginning Tuesday night, August 20, and through August 25, he had been signed for a residency at the Golden Bear, a popular folk-music nightspot in the California seaside town of Huntington Beach. On August 28, the third day of the Democratic Party convention, Chicago police officers and National Guardsman violently clashed with protestors across the street from the International Amphitheater. Some 700 protestors were arrested and carted away, with nearly 500 requiring immediate medical treatment on the street for tear gas exposure. Guthrie had been right; Chicago had been a trap, and Mayor Daley, as he expected, had sent in the National Guard. He angrily watched the violent images on television along with the rest of America. The following weekend (September 7–8), Guthrie performed at the fifth annual Big Sur Folk Festival, held on the grounds of the Esalen Institute in Big Sur Springs, California. Sharing the festival stage that weekend were Joni Mitchell, Joan Baez, Judy Collins, Mimi Fariña, Richie Havens, and the Charles River Valley Boys. The correspondent from *Rolling Stone* thought Mitchell and Guthrie the "most outstanding singers" of the festival. "Arlo has an excellent voice," the review contended, "not so much from the standpoint of purity, but from the standpoint of authenticity."[47]

The events of Chicago, though expected, left Guthrie in an angry mood. That September a *Washington Post* writer met with him at Harold Leventhal's office in Manhattan. The fascinating article that resulted rarely touched on Guthrie's music at all but focused on the "hippie" mindset of this new generation. Though Woody's music had chronicled the hard times of Depression-era America, Arlo's own music, according to writer Mary Ann Seawell, was directed to a more "affluent generation, concerned that human values not be lost in a machine age." "It's all right to separate church and state," Arlo told Seawell, "but we've separated spirit and person. It's not only wrong to treat people like machines, but also to treat a dog like he's just a dog. We are denying the life flow. We are lost in a world of dead things." Guthrie acknowledged that the nontraditional, nonconformist style of his friends was simply a façade: the intent behind the long hair and the colorful clothing was simply a part of the "struggle to end this kind of faceless existence." He was aware of the hostility that he and his long-haired friends engendered but saw that hatred as misdirected and, perhaps, more than a little sad. "I will be walking down the street and someone will snarl, 'Get your hair cut and go to Vietnam.' These people are reacting not to me," Arlo concluded, "but to something in themselves. Maybe they wanted to do something different when they were young and weren't given the chance." Though many of his folk-singing peers and elders were composing songs urging the nations of the world to "Ban the Bomb," Arlo wasn't terribly worried about the prospect of nuclear annihilation. There was little reason to worry as, if you bothered to look around, *everything* was broken. "Chances are the bomb won't even work," he mused. "Someone's going to push the big button and nothing will happen."[48]

It was time that Guthrie got off the road, if only for a little while. The filming of *Alice's Restaurant* was set to begin the week of October 4, 1968. Though the featured roles of Alice and Ray Brock were assigned to professional actors and actresses (Pat Quinn and James Broderick, respectively), Penn had made the unusual decision to incorporate the talents of the community whose lifestyles he was essaying. Penn bragged to one reporter that 90 percent of the young people featured in the *Alice's Restaurant* cast were "from the community." It was, from the very beginning, an anti-Hollywood production, with an abandoned paper factory in neighboring Pittsfield magically transformed into a professional soundstage for filming interiors. In an inspired masterstroke that no one could have imagined, Penn even convinced police chief William Obanhein, certainly no friend of the hippie kids who nested at the church, to play himself in the film. The burly, serious Obanhein told *Newsweek* that, "in the end, if someone was going to make a fool of me, it had better be me," and, well, the money was pretty good too. Interestingly, the signing of the chief to the cast would facilitate a rapprochement between the forty-four-year-old constable and the kids from the church. Prior to his work on the film, Obie's only contact with the long-haired young people in the community was that of strong-armed deputy of the law ("When Obie picked up Arlo for littering, he was a real Fascist," Alice Brock remembered. "He would handcuff anybody."). But by the time the chief had finished work on the film he had made friends with most of the kids in the cast. The chief was a natural in front of the camera and beamed when telling friends that Penn and the film crew bestowed upon him the title of "One-Shot Obie."[49]

Penn had a far more difficult time coaxing a recalcitrant Guthrie to act. "What was really maddening about him was his passivity," Penn told *Newsweek* scribe Paul D. Zimmerman. Though there would be many aspects of the motion picture that would be out of his control, Arlo was determined to not *act* at all, but to play himself *as* himself. This was, essentially, what Penn wanted as well, but he still needed the novice actor to do it, in the director's terminology, "actively." On screen Guthrie plays most of his role in a sort of neutral state, observing events as they unfolded, almost as a spectator rather than the principle figure in the tale. In scene after scene, Arlo watches the proceedings with a cool detachment that tends to disguise his feelings. This, Arlo argued to Penn, was how he and his friends related to one another. Together, the director and his star were able to agree on a workable model, and for an outright novice, most critics agreed that Arlo managed to acquit himself well. In a surprisingly cerebral interview published in the pages of the otherwise teenybopper magazine *Seventeen*, Arlo sighed, "I'm acting, if you can call re-creating an experience or an emotion you've already had or known acting. . . . I have to be detached in order to keep perspective on my material so I can work out how I feel in relation to it. I'm an entertainer and I function best that way."[50]

Harold Leventhal, credited as the film's associate producer, effectively used his bully pulpit to bring several of his own clients onto the film project. Pete Seeger played himself in a memorable scene in which he and Arlo ser-

*United Artists publicity photograph from the set of Arthur Penn's film version of the "Alice's Restaurant" saga. The film had its world premiere at Boston's Sack Cheri 2 Theater on August 20, 1969, five days following Guthrie's appearance at the Woodstock festival. Photofest.*

enade Woody (in the guise of actor Joseph Boley) at the dying folk singer's bedside. It was a re-creation of an actual event, though Pete later admitted that Penn's restaging of the scene was historically inaccurate. The song that he and Arlo actually sang at Woody's bedside during one visit was "Hobo's Lullaby," not "Riding in the Car" as featured in the film. Fellow Weaver and Almanac singer Lee Hays was brought in to play a small role as a revival tent preacher in the style of the radical Presbyterian minister Claude Williams, Lee's mentor in Arkansas circa 1934. Weavers guitarist and songwriter Fred Hellerman was brought on board as the film's musical director. He had survived the blacklist as a record producer and musician, playing sensitive guitar fills on recordings by such artists as Joan Baez, Judy Collins, and the Chad Mitchell Trio. Having negotiated the deal to bring *Alice's Restaurant* to the big screen, Leventhal was impressed, and relieved, to see Arlo rise to the challenge of his professional responsibilities. Harold was aware that Arlo's public persona as a free-floating musical anarchist was little more than fantasy. "No matter what he says," bragged Leventhal to the *New York Times*, "Arlo can't be a real hippy. He works. . . . He can't live his life, planning to be unplanned. He's got to show up for concerts and recording dates on time. Here's a kid who likes to sleep until 3:30 in the afternoon, who had to make a 7:30 A.M. movie call every day for three months of shooting, and he did."[51]

As the cameras rolled on *Alice's Restaurant*, Reprise Records released Guthrie's second LP, *Arlo,* during the third week of October 1968. Piggybacking on Arlo's media persona as a blithe spirit floating peacefully through the cosmos, the Reprise advertisements promised, "As gently as possible, Arlo dissembles the known world with new tales and songs from Alice's Restaurant. Live, in living color, and to be heard with ultra-high frequency and an open mind." Guthrie's sophomore LP was a live album, the platter's seven tracks having been recorded during his engagement at the Bitter End in December 1967 and early January 1968. *Billboard* found Guthrie "in fine form in this powerful follow-up album to his highly successful *Alice's Restaurant*," the trade magazine citing "The Motorcycle Song" and "John Looked Down" as highlight tracks. "There's plenty of protest in the world, but not enough humor," opined Mary Campbell of the Associated Press. "It's refreshing to have Arlo Guthrie around, blending the two." Though acknowledging that Guthrie's new recording featured no song of the pedigree of the "Alice's Restaurant Massacree," the *Christian Science Monitor* still found the LP a worthy follow-up. The wistful love songs that graced the second side of the *Alice's Restaurant* album were notably absent. Critic David Sterritt found the original songs on *Arlo* "a bit less contented, less peaceful than those on the earlier album," and this was certainly the case. Other than a straightforward recording of Ernest Tubb's "Try Me One More Time," the remainder of the songs were Arlo's alone, performed in a charming hodgepodge of styles and influences. His new compositions blended elements of Woody Guthrie, Bob Dylan, Donovan, Sandy Bull, the *Sgt. Pepper*–era Beatles, and Indian ragas. It was musical and fascinating, but the album suffered from its eclecticism; Guthrie's own distinct voice had not yet emerged. An anonymous staff member at the Leventhal office told the *New York Times* that Guthrie was still in the process of searching for a singular voice. "We have to weather Arlo's enthusiasms," the staffer said. "Today he's doing a hippy Eastern thing. It's a phase. Next week he may be writing Beatle songs. Then the week after he may go on a Donovan toot. . . . Don't forget he's just a baby, musically, a developing 21-year-old baby." The *Christian Science Monitor* was more forgiving, willing to concede that Arlo might forever remain an amalgam of his influences. But the newspaper acknowledged that "Mr. Guthrie is rapidly developing the talent he displayed on side two of his first record for writing compelling lyrics and melodies in more traditional frameworks, and his latest efforts in that direction show a truly extraordinary growth and improvement." *Rolling Stone* thought that the long spoken monologues on *Arlo*, no matter how amusing, would lessen the chance for frequent replays on the turntable. *Rolling Stone* was far more enthused by the musical interludes of "Wouldn't You Believe It" ("The most impressive and moving piece in this collection") and the "musically compelling" "John Looked Down" ("an inexplicable, though, for all I know, brilliant lyric") than with the album's long-winded storytelling.[52]

Interestingly, Guthrie himself wasn't particularly enamored of *Arlo*. Several years following that album's somewhat rushed release, Guthrie chatted a bit about it with Frank Rose, an associate editor of the rock 'n' roll newspaper *Zoo World*. Rose noted that following the success of *Alice's Restaurant*, Reprise was of the mindset that "Arlo should do more talking albums." But Guthrie was a *musician* and not at all interested in being pigeonholed as a maker of "novelty" records, so he begged off. In the end, a compromise was reached, and the album was recorded with "The Motorcycle Song" and "The Pause of Mister Claus" bookending the LP with two monologues of humor and length. In 1974, Rose traveled to the Berkshires to discuss Arlo's then most recent LP *Arlo Guthrie*, which the artist tellingly described to the writer as his "sixth album." It was actually his seventh, but Rose reported that Guthrie "detests" his second Reprise album and chose not to count it as part of his oeuvre. Time and nostalgia would not change the artist's assessment of the LP. Twenty-three summers later, Arlo remarked ruefully to *discoveries* writer and editor Jeff Tamarkin, "The second record I thought was horrible, the live one, in terms of what it was. It could have been a lot better."[53]

The *Arlo* album was, not too surprisingly, less commercially successful than its predecessor. But it was hardly a failure; it entered the charts in the

163 position and began a slow but steady climb. By week three the album had reached position 130 and was awarded the *Billboard* Red Star as an "Action Pick." In its sixth week of release it briefly moved into the Top 100, before edging slowly backwards, dropping from the 106 position to the 150 position. The album's last entry on the charts was at the 172 position on its tenth week of issue. It fared a bit better on the *Cash Box* LP charts, staying in the Top 100 for a full fourteen weeks, peaking at number 40 on week eight. The *Alice's Restaurant* LP, by comparison, was still on the charts fifty-nine weeks after its release.[54]

Arlo enjoyed an odd sort of celebrity. The media adored him. He was, essentially, a nonthreatening hippie, offbeat and eccentric perhaps, but sweet and colorful and funny. His well-publicized exploits kept Middle America up to date on the newest hippie slang, on floppy hats and the latest in ruffled fashions. It also helped that his sardonic humor and bright folk-rock music, while not to everyone's taste, wasn't too offensive or too loud or too raucous to be enjoyed by the extended family. In November 1968, Arlo was the feature of a small photo spread in the *Coloroto Magazine* of the Sunday *New York News*. Describing him as a "21-year-old lanky singer who has a little girl's face with flowing long black hair," there was no *raison d'etre* for the article other than to publish an amusing celebrity photograph of Arlo and girlfriend Carol (her face mostly obscured by the bolt of cotton candy she was eating) riding the bumper cars at Coney Island.[55]

That's not to say that all the press was as adoring. On that same Sunday, in the magazine section of the conservative *Sunday Chicago Tribune*, the young Guthrie was willfully raked over the coals by a thirty-five-year-old reporter named Arthur Whitman. Whitman, clearly immune to Arlo's charm, was maddened by the kid's success and subsequent pop-music deification. He chose to arrange a brief interview with this twenty-one-year-old who, he explained to his readers, "when . . . not slumping around more or less vertically, [is] apt to be completely flaked out." Whitman later worked segments of his interview with Guthrie into an entirely snarky feature titled "The Apotheosis of Woody's Kid." The article was later syndicated under various titles. Whitman's nonenthusiasm for the hero-troubadours of the Aquarian generation was reflected in nearly every paragraph of his essay. Though he allowed that the saga of "Alice's Restaurant" was "occasionally amusing," Guthrie's singing and stage voice was dismissed as "thin and ordinary, like anybody's son singing in the shower. Perhaps because he sings with a hayseed accent that is not his own, he has a tendency to mumble many of the words." Though Arlo could have hardly gauged the writer's intent at the time of the interview, it did seem as if things hadn't gone well from the start. The feature turned even uglier when the reporter wrote, "Despite the fact that young Guthrie is becoming a very high-priced performer, he doesn't feel particularly bad about occasionally forgetting his act." This was a misunderstanding on Whitman's part, as Arlo's casual stage manner was intentional; he was merely channeling the easygoing stagecraft of his father and Ramblin' Jack Elliott. Arlo countered that he wasn't too worried about such criticism, that his fans understood what he was about. "I communicate with people no matter what I do. I know the Source. I know where it's at."

"Where what's at, Arlo?"

Guthrie tried to explain that, in his view, everything was infused with spirit. That everything in the universe, be it a rock, a chair, or a human being, "all have one Source."

"Are you talking about God?" asked Whitman.

"I don't care what you call it, except I'm not a church person," Arlo replied. "To me it's the Source, and when people hear me, that is what it's all about. They know they are hearing the Source, and if there is any of the Source in them, then they will respond to it. Do you understand what I mean?"

"Not really."

"Then I probably can't communicate with you because there isn't any of the Source in you and you're not responding."[56]

It was a maddening time. Guthrie's celebrity was not yet great enough to protect him from the sneers of a populace that looked down on hippies as effete, drug-abusing, draft-dodging, flag-burning, Viet Cong sympathizers. In the hours following a concert in Providence, Rhode Island, writer W. Hedgepath watched in bewilderment as Guthrie ("America's most up-and-coming young anarchist") was refused service at a local luncheonette, taunted by a showboating waitress who had no use for young men who wore their hair long. Later that same night, while in his room of a hotel in which he was a guest, a request for a bottle of wine to be sent to Guthrie's room actually ended in a shoving war between the hotel's bell captain and bartender. The hotel employees weren't fighting about who would *bring* the bottle to Arlo and his friends; they were battling over which of the two wished to serve these "punk Communists" *less*. The confusion in sorting out the true patriots was one of the great tests of 1968. Guthrie wasn't, to the disappointment of some on the Left, a true revolutionary; he was more of a young rebel with an Aquarian design. He suggested to Hedgepath that the "Establishment" that he and his friends and his generation railed against wasn't beyond redemption, that the American experiment seemed worthwhile. "This particular Establishment has got some pretty good ideas," he told the journalist. "I mean the idea of the Constitution is a *gas* as far as I'm concerned. . . . We're gonna get back to that. That's the next part of the scene—to get back to constitutional ideas; not the laws, but the ideas."[57]

It was difficult to gauge Guthrie's interest in political radicalism. His commitments to the causes of the Left were more often than not *assumed* by the radicals, an extension of his heritage. In an article on the popularity of folk rock, writer Herbert Russcol in *High Fidelity* wrote that by 1968 the slate of message and protest song singers was already overcrowded; self-righteous indignation was now passé since "today we are all on the side of the angels." "Of all the young radicals," Russcol wrote, "only Arlo Guthrie . . . seems to have escaped monotony by virtue of a salty humor and a gritty naïf voice." It was true that Guthrie wasn't writing out-and-out protest songs. "My songs are not message pieces," he told Russcol. "I don't want to be that easily understood. I am in my own universe, and other people should take my songs and translate them into their universes. I am not forcing a universal message down anyone's throat." But the fact that he was neither singing nor writing overt protest songs in the style of Pete or Woody was glossed over by those who simply weren't listening closely. He was, after all, a few years younger than such contemporaries as Dylan, Phil Ochs, and Tom Paxton and, as a songwriter, seemed less obsessed about writing singing commentaries on crises gleaned from the newspapers. From the beginning, Guthrie was more interested in writing and singing songs that examined situations from a moral, rather than ideological, view. He was an admirer of the doomed topical songwriter Phil Ochs, who, disillusioned and suffering from depression, ended life by his own hand in April 1976. But Arlo told *Frets* that the celebrated singer-songwriter of such incendiary ballads as "I Ain't Marching Anymore," "Here's to the State of Mississippi," and "White Boots Marching in a Yellow Land" was "a good example of someone who couldn't translate his political action to its moral application." "Once the cause is removed, once the fad dies away, " Guthrie mused, "you have to be left with something for yourself and it has to give you meaning." The 1960s was a time when many young people famously rebelled against the traditions of their parents, and in this regard Guthrie was a man of his time. The tensions of the generations were evident in a profile of Guthrie that appeared in the *Boston Globe* in June 1968. The interview, conducted in the kitchen of his mother's home in Queens, featured a three-way conversation that included Marjorie, her husband Lou Cooper, and Arlo. The chat inevitably steered to the upcoming presidential election. The reporter asked who he was planning on supporting. "I'm not really involved in it," Guthrie answered matter-of-factly. "Most times, to be moral, you have to be apolitical. Now, if you have any moral feelings, you have to be against the war in Vietnam. I support anybody who doesn't support the war." Nonetheless he dismissed Democratic candidates and senators Eugene McCarthy and Robert Kennedy ("They're not great men"), and suggested that he would almost "rather see Rockefeller as President. Because he doesn't really care that much. He doesn't really wanna be President." This last revelation caused his stepfather to groan out loud. Cooper, a left-winger and a veteran of the Abraham Lincoln Brigade (Americans who had volunteered to fight against Franco's fascists in defense of Republican Spain in the 1930s), chided Arlo for his half-warm endorsement of Rockefeller. He taunted that such enthusiasm for the millionaire New York state governor was based solely on the fact that since Arlo's career had taken off, his wayward stepson found himself "in a different income bracket. . . . [T]hat's why you're for Rockefeller," he teased Arlo. "You identify with his tax bracket."[58]

The principal shooting of the *Alice's Restaurant* film wrapped in early December, but there was little time to relax or celebrate. On Saturday night, December 7, 1968, Guthrie returned to the stage for his second Carnegie Hall concert. Trading between guitar and piano and backed throughout by a friend's double bass, Arlo entertained this year's sold-out Carnegie crowd with "The Alice's Restaurant Multi-Colored Rainbow Roach Affair." He also brought along some of the new material (and stories) from the *Arlo* LP, with laugh-filled run-throughs of "The Motorcycle Song" and "The Pause of Mister Claus." Perhaps more surprisingly, he dusted off the old Jimmie Rodgers tearjerker "Mother, the Queen of My Heart," a song gleaned from the Jack Elliott LP *Ramblin' Jack Elliott Sings Songs of Woody Guthrie and Jimmie Rodgers*. Though the material they chose to sing only occasionally overlapped, there was a lot of Elliott to be found in Arlo's stage persona. He didn't shy away from the similarities, and when *Guitar Player* magazine asked him who the greatest musical influence on him was when he was first learning, Arlo answered, "Oh, Ramblin' Jack Elliott probably more than anybody else." To the uninitiated Arlo's concerts may have seemed under- or, occasionally, *un*rehearsed, with the sudden stops and starts, the long spoken asides, and the songs half-played or stopped midway through. This was a totally foreign practice at a pop-music concert, but old-time folkies conversant with Ramblin' Jack would have recognized that Elliott had been employing such stagecraft since the mid-1950s. But to the kids raised on rock 'n' roll who flocked to Arlo's concerts, it was all new and hip and radically different. Twenty-one-year-old Arlo was, importantly, one of *them*. Though Bob Dylan was only twenty-six and still a folk hero to the teenagers, he was no longer one of them. The *New York Times* quoted one eighteen-year-old Guthrie fan that her younger sister, age fifteen, plays "Dylan's records, but she doesn't identify with him. He's a remote figure, married and with kids. He hasn't toured for years. Arlo's her substitute." It was the belief of *Billboard* critic Fred Kirby that at Carnegie, "Guthrie's rapport with the audience was phenomenal throughout and is a key part of his effectiveness as is his direct singing approach and his identification with the attitudes of today's youth."

This opinion was echoed by a writer from *Variety*: "Guthrie has cashed in on the private attitudes of the whole youth thing; the understanding few have swelled to the tuned in many."[59]

## NOTES

1. Allen Hughes, "WNYC Folk Concert Sung in 6 Segments," *New York Times*, February 19, 1967, 71; Kristin Baggelaar and Donald Milton, *Folk Music: More Than a Song* (New York: Thomas Y. Crowell Company, 1976), 158.

2. "Ramblin' Jack Elliott—Gaslight Café" (advertisement), *Village Voice*, February 2, 1967, 33; "Ramblin' Jack Elliott/Arlo Guthrie—Gaslight Café' (advertisement), *Village Voice*, February 16, 1967, 29.

3. Mike Jahn, "Pop Music: Arlo and Alice," *Escapade*, April 1968, 69; Paul D. Zimmerman, "Alice's Restaurant's Children," *Newsweek*, September 29, 1969, 103; "Bob Fass Building Vocal 'Community' over WBAI-FM, N.Y.," *Billboard*, January 22, 1977, 1; Bob Fass on *Radio Unnameable*, WBAI-FM, New York City, NY, April 26, 1967.

4. "Tops in Pop to Appear at Boston Music Fest," *Billboard*, April 8, 1967, 26; "Boston Music Festival Ends with C&W Acts," *Billboard*, May 13, 1967, 28; Neil Nyren, "Review of the American Festival of Music," *Broadside* (Cambridge) 2, no. 6 (May 10, 1967), 23.

5. Arlo Guthrie, "Alice's Restaurant," *Broadside*, no. 80 (April/May 1967), 17–18.

6. "From the Music Capitals of the World," *Billboard*, May 6, 1967, 50; Karl Dallas, "Arlo Doesn't Need the Famous Dad Bit," *Melody Maker*, December 16, 1967, 11.

7. Arlo Guthrie, "Alice's Restaurant Massacree," *Broadside*, no. 81, June 1967, 2–3.

8. Bob Lurtsema, "I Want to Know," *Sing Out!* 17, no. 3 (June/July 1967), 50.

9. Richard Goldstein, "Pop: Arlo Takes a Giant Step," *New York Times*, November 5, 1967, D22; Bill Blando, "Arlo Hoes His Own Row," *Knickerbocker News*, November 11, 1967, B11.

10. John S. Wilson, "Newport Is His Just for a Song—Arlo Guthrie Festival Hero with Alice's Restaurant," *New York Times*, July 18, 1967, 30.

11. Irwin Silber, "What's Happening . . . ," *Sing Out!* 17, no. 5 (October/November 1967), 1.

12. Claude Hall, "Newport Port of Call for All Music," *Billboard*, July 29, 1967, 24; "Talent: Signings," *Billboard*, September 9, 1967, 30; Eliot Tiegel, "W-7 Creates 'Now' Power," *Billboard*, July 20, 1968, 8; "WB's Lee in Talent Hunt," *Billboard*, January 6, 1968, 1, 6.

13. "Folk Fest & Workshops to Adorn Philly Countryside," *Billboard*, August 19, 1967, 23, 53.

14. *Alice's Restaurant* (Reprise 6267) (advertisement), *Billboard*, October 28, 1967, 19.

15. Eugene Scheimann, M.D., "Fight Waged by Family," *Montreal Gazette*, August 25, 1971, 41; Arlo Guthrie, "Despite the Shadow of His Father's (and Possibly His Own) Deady Disease, a Folk Hero Celebrates Life," *People Weekly* 28, no. 10 (September 7, 1987).

16. Bobbi Druse, "Rapping with Arlo Guthrie," *Boston Broadside*, November 1967.

17. "Arlo Guthrie Caffe Lena Star Tonight," *Knickerbocker News*, November 3, 1967, A12; Bill Blando, "Arlo Hoes His Own Row," B11.

18. Richard Goldstein, "Pop: Arlo Takes a Giant Step," D22.

19. Hank Fox, "Woodie Guthrie's Son Is Making It on His Own Talent," *Billboard*, November 25, 1967, 33; "Bent," "Hipsters Get a New Hero in Arlo Guthrie Who Pulls SRO $7,800 in N.Y. Debut," *Variety*, November 15, 1967, 61; Alfred G. Aronowitz, "Arlo Guthrie, 20, Takes Own Road," *New York Times*, November 12, 1967, 85.

20. "Woody's Boy," *Time*, January 12, 1968, 50; John Nogowski, *Bob Dylan: A Descriptive, Critical Discography and Filmography, 1961–1993* (Jefferson, NC, and London: McFarland & Company, 1995), 42.

21. David Sterritt, "They Dress in Hippie Disguises," *Christian Science Monitor*, January 3, 1968, 15; Steven Lowe, "The Lighter Side," *High Fidelity*, January 1968, 100; Jann Wenner, "Records," *Rolling Stone*, November 9, 1967, 20; Pete Johnson, "Popular Records: Chad, Jeremy: Success at Last," *Los Angeles Times*, October 22, 1967, S-37; Peter Reilly, "The Deadly Satiric Aim of Arlo Guthrie," *Hi-Fi Review*, February 1968, 81; "Album Reviews: Folk Spotlight," *Billboard*, November 4, 1967, 46.

22. Israel G. Young and Paul Nelson, "Good News from a Far Country," *Sing Out!* 17, no. 6 (December 1967/January 1968), 42.

23. "Spotlight Singles," *Billboard*, December 23, 1967, 12.

24. Karl Dallas, "Arlo Doesn't Need the Famous Dad Bit," 11; Hank Reineke, "America's Love Affair with Fascism, and What It Did to Our Poets, Singers—From the '50s On," *Soho Arts Weekly*, October 9, 1985, 36B.

25. "Guthrie at End," *Village Voice*, December 21, 1967, 5; "Talk of the Town: Arlo Guthrie," *New Yorker*, January 6, 1968, 18–21.

26. "Brent," "Bitter End, N.Y.," *Variety*, December 27, 1967, 45.

27. Carl Bernstein, *Loyalties: A Son's Memoir* (New York: Simon and Schuster, 1989), 173–74, 210–11; Carl Bernstein, "Arlo Guthrie Shines at Lisner," *Washington Post*, January 15, 1968, D7.

28. Francis X. Clines, "L.I. Narcotics Raid Nets 33 on Campus," *New York Times*, January 18, 1968, 1; Francis X. Clines, "Students Decry Stony Brook Raid," *New York Times*, January 19, 1968, 22; Susan Braudy, "As Arlo Guthrie Sees It . . . Kids Are Groovy, Adults Aren't," *New York Times Sunday Magazine*, April 27, 1969, 56ff.

29. Robert Shelton, *No Direction Home: The Life and Music of Bob Dylan* (New York: Beech Tree Books, 1986), 395.

30. Lillian Roxon, "The Guthrie Concert," in *Bob Dylan: A Retrospective* (New York: William & Morrow 1972), 211; Robert Shelton, "Tribute to the Life and Legend of Woody Guthrie," *New York Times*, January 22, 1968, 31.

31. Tony Wilson, "Dylan's Dilemma," *Melody Maker*, April 13, 1968, 14.

32. Linda Mathews, "Arlo Guthrie on Troubadour Stage," *Los Angeles Times*, January 25, 1968, A10; Eliot Tiegel, "Guthrie Drawing 'Em In," *Billboard*, February 10, 1968, 14.

33. "Fish," "Troubadour, L.A.," *Variety*, January 31, 1968, 69.

34. Jeanne Sakol, "The Hit Generation: Sweet Satire Seen for the Future," *Milwaukee Journal*, April 17, 1968, 2; Kristin Baggelaar and Donald Milton, *Folk Music: More Than a Song*, 158.

35. "'Restaurant' for a Film," *Billboard*, March 30, 1968, 77; Louise Sweeney, "Arthur Penn: 'No Preconceptions,'" *Christian Science Monitor*, August 8, 1969, 4.

36. John Stickney, "Alice's Family of Folk Song Fame Becomes a Movie," *LIFE*, March 28, 1969, 45; Edwin Miller, "Spotlight! The Hollywood Scene," *Seventeen*, February 1969, 42.

37. Tony Wilson, "Dylan's Dilemma," 14; "Blind Date: Arlo Guthrie Singles Out the New Singles," *Melody Maker*, April 20, 1968, 14.

38. Phyllis Dreazen, "Arlo Guthrie's Concert Talk-Fest," *Chicago Tribune*, April 21, 1968, sec. 1A, 6.

39. Michael Stern, "87,000 March in War Protests Here," *New York Times*, April 28, 1968, 1, 72.

40. "WB-7 Sales Up 15%; 7.5 Mil. in Quarter," *Billboard*, April 6, 1968, 3.

41. Joyce Haber, "VV—XXX—PP in Alphabet Game," *Los Angles Times*, May 22, 1968, C17.

42. Nelson Bryant, "Wood, Field and Stream," *New York Times*, July 14, 1968, S24; "Miscellaneous," *New York*, June 24, 1968, 10.

43. "Bent," "Concert Review: Judy Collins/Arlo Guthrie," *Variety*, July 3, 1968, 48; Robb Baker, "Concert: A Spell-Binding Albatross," *Chicago Tribune*, July 21, 1968, A6;

44. Robert Shelton, "Folk Folk Meet at Newport Fete," *New York Times*, July 28, 1968, 64; Robert Shelton, "Folk Music Trends Emerge at Newport Festival," *New York Times*, July 30, 1968, 32; David Sterritt, "Everyone 'Together' in a Free-Form Festival," *Christian Science Monitor*, August 3, 1968, 6; "Festival, Folk Upswing Seen as Newport Lures Whopping 70,000," *Billboard*, August 10, 1968, 10.

45. David Sterritt, "Everyone 'Together' in a Free-Form Festival," 6. Jon Landau, "The Newport Folk Festival," *Rolling Stone*, no. 16 (August 24, 1968), 16; Arnold Shaw, "Festival, Folk Upswing Seen as Newport Lures Whopping 70,000," 10.

46. "Testimony of Arlo Guthrie in the Chicago Seven Trial," http://www.law .umkc.edu/faculty/projects/ftrials/chicago7/Guthrie.html (August 19, 2010).

47. Mary Ann Seawell, "Gentle Arlo's World for People, Not Machines," *Washington Post*, August 9, 1968, C4; "Big Sur Folk Fest Set for Sept. 7–8," *Billboard*, August 10, 1968, 28; "Big Sur Folks' Festival," *Rolling Stone*, no. 19 (October 12, 1968), 1, 8.

48. Mary Ann Seawell, "Generation of Arlo Guthrie," *Los Angeles Times*, September 17, 1968, C14.

49. Paul D. Zimmerman, "Alice's Restaurant's Children," *Newsweek*, September 29, 1969, 104; William Wold, "Arlo's 'Alice.' From Song to Screen," *Los Angeles Times*, July 13, 1969, M20.

50. Paul D. Zimmerman, "Alice's Restaurant's Children," 104; Edwin Miller, "Spotlight! The Hollywood Scene," 42.

51. Susan Braudy, "As Arlo Guthrie Sees It . . . Kids Are Groovy, Adults Aren't," 56ff.

52. Mary Campbell, "Arlo Guthrie Blends Humor with Protest," *Los Angeles Times*, November 25, 1968, C23; Susan Braudy, "As Arlo Guthrie Sees It . . . Kids Are Groovy, Adults Aren't,'" 56ff. David Sterritt, "The Pop Scene: New Guthrie—'Less Contented,'" *Christian Science Monitor*, November 2, 1968, 21; "Album Reviews," *Billboard*, October 5, 1968, 69; Arthur Schmidt, "Record Reviews," *Rolling Stone*, October 26, 1968, 28.

53. Frank Rose, "At Home with Arlo: Conversation in the Berkshires," *Zoo World*, no. 62 (July 4, 1974), 22; Jeff Tamarkin, "Arlo Guthrie at 50: In the House of the Rising Son," *discoveries*, no. 111 (August 1997), 45.

54. Frank Hoffman and George Albert, *The Cash Box Album Charts, 1955–1974* (Metuchen, NJ, and London: Scarecrow Press, 1988), 155.

55. "And Here's Arlo," *Sunday New York News Coloroto Magazine*, November 10, 1968.

56. Arthur Whitman, "The Apotheosis of Woody's Kid," *Sunday Chicago Tribune Magazine*, November 10, 1968, 22.

57. W. Hedgepath, "The Successful Anarchist," *Look*, February 4, 1969, 60–62, 64.

58. Herbert Russcol, "I Gave My Love a Cherry, So Tell It Like It Is, Baby!" *High Fidelity* 18 (December 1968), 58; Marty Gallanter, "Arlo: Bound for His Own Glory," *Frets* 1 (July 1979), 26; Sara Davidson, "Arlo Guthrie," *Boston Globe Sunday Magazine*, June 9, 1968, 26.

59. Michael Brooks, "Woody & Arlo," *Guitar Player*, August 1971, 35; Susan Braudy, "As Arlo Guthrie Sees It . . . Kids Are Groovy, Adults Aren't," 56ff; Fred Kirby, "Arlo Guthrie Folk Singer with Rapport," *Billboard*, December 21, 1968, 14; "Bent," "Concert Reviews: Arlo Guthrie," *Variety*, December 18, 1968, 49.

*Chapter Three*

# I Want to Be Around

Guthrie would begin the last year of the 1960s with a string of solo concerts. On January 10 he was on the West Coast for a solo concert at the University of California, Los Angeles. The following weekend, Manny Greenhill's Folklore Productions brought Arlo to Boston's Symphony Hall for a Friday night concert on January 17. The relaxed spacing of concert dates was intentional. To protect his client from media oversaturation, Leventhal's strategy was to limit Guthrie to no more than twenty-five or so concerts a year and to refuse most offers to perform on television variety programs. That was Harold's original plan, anyway.[1]

One of the most refreshing results of his surprising success was that Arlo was able to fully embrace his father's musical legacy. From the beginning of his career in the basket houses of Greenwich Village, Arlo passionately tried to get audiences, many of whom had gathered only to hear Woody Guthrie songs, to give him a chance, to listen to his own original music and stories without the weight of his legacy. He probably could have carved out a reasonably successful career singing only Woody's Dust Bowl and Columbia River ballads, the children's tunes, and the thousands of other songs his father had written had that tactic been considered. He wasn't blind to the fact that his father was a legend of the folk-singing community, that everyone wanted to hear those old songs, and that everyone from John Steinbeck to Alan Lomax to Pete Seeger to Bob Dylan praised his father. Being the son of a great artist carried both opportunity *and* burden. He acknowledged in an interview with writer Jeff Tamarkin that he was well aware "everybody would come to see me once, because I was Woody's kid. And I knew they would never come back if they were disappointed." He purposefully chose not to build his earliest set lists using his father's vast catalog for material. The strategy worked for him in the long run. It was interesting that, in the early days of 1969, the

majority of kids attending Arlo's concerts weren't starry-eyed Woody Guthrie devotees. They were fans of "Alice's Restaurant" and "The Motorcycle
Song" and of the way that Arlo needled pompous authority and establishment
figures. With the media pressing around him, two Reprise albums under his
belt, and a growing excitement surrounding the motion-picture release of
*Alice's Restaurant*, Arlo had, by any measure, made it on his own terms and
talent. With the pressure and expectations of being "Woody's kid" finally
off his back, he was, somewhat ironically, now able to celebrate his father's
legacy and evaluate his own role as a singer from a tradition. He confidently
told writer Edwin Miller of *Seventeen*, "I feel I'm the first of the second
generation and this is my heritage, growing up with the music of Woody and
Cisco Houston and Pete Seeger and all [of] my father's friends."[2]

Carrying along two guitars and bassist Bob Arkin, Guthrie was due to
perform at Symphony Hall of the University of Cincinnati, Saturday evening,
March 1. Accompanying Guthrie was a *New York Times* freelancer, Susan
Braudy, who was preparing a lengthy feature on the folk singer for a *Sunday
Magazine* supplement. That night he performed before an audience of 3,500
fans. It was Braudy's contention that twenty-one-year-old Arlo was on the
brink of stardom, with critics already suggesting that he "may be moving
into Dylan's place in the hearts of the current crop of teen-agers, expressing
their half-articulate desires and dissatisfactions." It was true that Arlo Guthrie
was accessible in a way that Bob Dylan was not. Jeff Mitchel, a reporter for
the University of Cincinnati's *News Record*, chatted with Arlo the night of
his concert and came away impressed that Guthrie was "truly oblivious to
the fame which was becoming part of his life. . . . Just another guy." This, of
course, could hardly be said of Bob Dylan. Dylan had not been on a proper
U.S. tour since the early winter of 1966, an eternity in pop music. But Guthrie, according to the *Times*, "plays at least one concert a week in colleges
and towns throughout the country." It was acknowledged that Arlo wasn't
positioned to overtake Dylan in popularity anytime soon. Only his first album was a commercial success. Braudy noted that Guthrie's most recent LP,
*Arlo*, "hasn't sold all that well, and the singer-composer himself isn't very
happy with the recording." Following the concert at Symphony Hall, Guthrie
made his way to an underground radio station in Cincinnati, where marijuana
cigarettes were passed around and Arlo played songs off the recent album by
Pentangle, the British folk-rock group, a current favorite of his. When asked
where he was headed next, Guthrie answered, "I'm heading to California,
man, going to get me a 1935 Chevy pick-up truck and drive to Memphis
where I'm making my next record. Groovy musicians in Memphis."[3]

Guthrie wouldn't make it to Memphis, but he did travel to California in
the spring of 1969. On March 15 Arlo sang at a rally in support of the "Pre-

sidio 27," a group of incarcerated military conscripts serving time at a San Francisco stockade for divergent reasons, including AWOL charges resulting from their participation at an antiwar rally on March 14. That April he sang and played at another antiwar rally in San Francisco, but Arlo's decision to go west was more musical than political. In early May *Rolling Stone* reported that Van Dyke Parks was in the studio with Warner Bros./7 Arts staff producer Lenny Waronker, recording Arlo's newest album for Reprise. Parks told *Rolling Stone* that Guthrie had come to the sessions prepared, having "written much more material than would fit on a single disc." Indeed, it seemed as if Arlo's musical batteries had been recharged in Hollywood. Guthrie told *discoveries* that the original "impetus for moving the recording process to L.A. was that I needed to get out of what I thought was the hole of recording . . . in New York." Los Angeles was now the capital of the rock 'n' roll recording industry, with most of the companies on the cutting edge, such as Elektra, having abandoned the gray wash of Manhattan as early as 1965. The hippest session men were in Los Angeles now, and the West Coast was home to the most happening scenes, the hottest bands, and the most talented rock musicians. He told writer Jeff Tamarkin that his decision to record in Los Angeles was for the best; as long as he remained in New York with Fred Hellerman at the production board he would remain "Woody Guthrie's kid." It wasn't that Hellerman hadn't done a great job of helming the first two albums: the ex-Weaver's signature is really only apparent on the songs comprising the B-side of Arlo's debut album. Otherwise the remaining three sides of Guthrie's first two LPs were recorded, neatly and simply, in live-in-concert sessions. But Guthrie told Tamarkin that Hellerman's contributions were handcuffed to some extent as "Fred was [of] my Dad's era and I think they were looking at [the recording process] more from a financial point of view than I would have." Arlo would have really liked to spend more time in recording that first album, believing the songs on side two had not been fully developed. The old guard in charge of overseeing his debut album "simply didn't have the sensitivity to what the songs could have been." From the beginning, Guthrie publicly allowed that he was never pleased with his first two records. In the introduction to a 1969 songbook that consisted primarily of songs from those first two albums, Arlo would famously float the idea that, given the opportunity, he would "spend some time re-writing most of the songs and most positively re-record them."[4]

On his new album, soon to be titled *Running Down the Road*, Guthrie would try to get the sounds in his head on wax. With sales of *Arlo* falling below prognostications, Reprise/Warner Bros. also seemed to be interested in seeing what the new team could come up with. The *Alice's Restaurant* LP was recorded with little sonic ornamentation, but the new album would be, to some degree, a creation of the studio and of the recording process itself. Coproducer Parks explained to *Rolling Stone* that they were keeping the tape rolling, "getting everything down we can. We will be recording steadily for the next several weeks . . . then we'll go back and sort things out." The roster of musicians assembled to contribute their talents to the LP was promising. Clarence White, James Burton, and Arlo's friend and "Spiritual Advisor (Union Scale)" John Pilla were on guitars, with Ry Cooder on mandolin and bass, James Gordon on drums, Gene Parsons on drums and harmonica, Milt Holland on percussion, and Chris Ethridge and Jerry Scheff on bass.[5]

That same month, Guthrie and Pete Seeger, also visiting Los Angeles, were invited by NBC-TV to perform on the *Tonight Show*, the popular late-night talk show hosted by Johnny Carson. In his introduction to the program (broadcast May 27), Carson named Arlo as someone who "speaks, I think, for a great deal of today's youth in his music." That night, supported by his studio band, Guthrie performed two songs ("Ring-around-a-Rosy Rag" and a great electric version of "Running Down the Road," the latter stripped of the psychedelic trappings of the LP version). Moving over to the couch for a chat, Carson began the conversation by noting that the film version of Guthrie's *Alice's Restaurant* was soon due in theaters. Arlo told Carson that the *song* "Alice's Restaurant" had been two years in the making, that after he had written it there was a long process of working it out on stage. He admitted that he originally envisioned the saga of "Alice" as a film rather than a song. "While I was sitting in the jail when some of the incidents that were going down were happening, I said 'Somebody should make a movie of this.' I didn't think it would be a record. I thought it would always be a movie." He described the process of working with Arthur Penn in and around Stockbridge as both "fun" and "terrific." Carson brought up the legacy of Woody, but Arlo admitted that his "greatest influences" were Dylan and the Beatles since "they pertain to *now*, and my father pertained to his time." College campuses and the entire educational system were anathema to him. He told the amiable Carson,

> I couldn't learn anything that I thought would be useful. And this was . . . the thing I didn't like about even grammar school or high school. . . . They put you in a room and say, "Well, you might not like this now, you might not understand it now, but later you're gonna need it." And that's bunk. I *don't* need it. I forgot most of it. I think all the stuff that was really important, I think I could have learned in, maybe, two years

Arlo told Carson that he was presently residing in Greenwich Village, an area increasingly becoming a magnet for stoners and disaffected youth. One consequence of this influx of naïve youngsters to the Village was that, in Arlo's estimate, "the drugs aren't as good." The studio audience laughed, but this was serious business. Things got more interesting, and lightly heated, when the subject of drug abuse and the business of drugs were raised.

> *Arlo:* I think there's more danger in taking drugs now, 'cause you don't know what you're getting anymore. That's the danger in the Village.
>
> *Carson:* You think there's no danger if you know what you're getting?
>
> *Arlo:* Well, it's your own responsibility. I mean, if you wanted to buy some acid when it was legal, and you knew they guy that made it, it was a different thing.
>
> *Carson:* I didn't bring you in to argue with you, but everybody always says when you talk about speed and stuff like that, "Well, it's my body. It's my responsibility, and as long as it doesn't affect you . . ." But the trouble is, when somebody does take acid and drives a car, it *does* affect me. And when they end up in a narcotics hospital or something, or they go "bananas" and they have to be taken in, *that* affects me 'cause I have to pay . . .

Carrying Carson's argument to its logical end, Arlo defensively parried, "In the same way somebody that *doesn't think* affects you. In the same way that *politicians* who *don't think* affect you."

Getting off the topic of drugs, Carson queried Guthrie on his personal interest in political activism. Arlo weakly replied, "I did some things for [Eugene] McCarthy," but admitted his own vision was more revolutionary, though that revolution was more of a spiritual than political nature: "If it's a question of trying to save the old one or build a new one, I'm more for getting the new one started."[6]

On Tuesday night, June 10, Arlo, switching between six- and twelve-string guitars and piano and backed by his band, played a fifty-five-minute set before a full house at the Troubadour in Los Angeles. The Troubadour gigs (June 10–June 15) had, according to a *Variety* scribe, been arranged as a rehearsal of sorts as he and his band were scheduled to go out on a U.S. summer tour starting July 7. Things went very well, and all three versions of "Alice's Restaurant" were given a rest, with such songs from his forthcoming Reprise LP as "Coming into Los Angeles" and Pete Seeger's instrumental "Living in the Country" slotted in with great effect. It was also the week of the Troubadour gigs that Guthrie would meet his future wife, Jacklyn "Jackie" Hyde. Jackie was twenty-four, two years older than Arlo, and working as a temporary waitress at the nightclub. A California girl, she had become friendly with Guthrie's brother, Joady, who had only recently moved to the Golden State from New York. Joady was sitting in the audience one night when he was approached by Jackie, who told him "that she was going to marry his brother Arlo and would he please introduce them." "It was crazy," remembered Guthrie's friend John Pilla to *Rolling Stone*. "All of a sudden they were holed up in a room together and there was nothing that was going to pull them apart."[7]

On July 7 Arlo was to perform in an open-air tent at the Mississippi River Festival held on the Edwardsville campus of Southern Illinois University, a half-hour drive from St. Louis. The festival was a large-scale affair that offered seating for some 1,850 patrons under the tent with a "gently sloping lawn" that could accommodate an additional 10,000 music fans. Primarily conceived as a venue for aficionados of classical music and symphonic orchestras, the festival would help pay the lighting bills through its offering of "pop, rock, and folk music attractions on off nights." The programs of two of those "folk music attractions," Arlo Guthrie and Joni Mitchell, were taped by a local PBS affiliate to be broadcast later that August as *The Sounds of Summer*, with TV personality Steve Allen serving as host.[8]

Guthrie and guitarist John Pilla arrived in Edwardsville from Los Angeles. Flying in from New York City to accompany Arlo for the concert were Bob Arkin on stand-up bass and Paul Motian on drums. Guthrie played the role of stoned-out-freak folk singer throughout the night's performance. "Are you ready for this, man? This is weird," Arlo asked from the stage, tilting into

*Guthrie with Joni Mitchell prior to the taping of the PBS* Sounds of Summer *television program (broadcast August 3, 1969). The actual concert was recorded on July 7 at the Mississippi River Festival on the Edwardsville campus of Southern Illinois University. Photofest.*

a lengthy, crowd-pleasing, spoken-word variant of "The Motorcycle Song" that he subtitled "The Significance of the Pickle." He followed with "Coming into Los Angeles," a rocking song recently recorded about, of all things, dope smuggling. He noted that he had come directly to the concert from Los Angeles where he "just got finished getting harassed out there." He quieted things down with a plaintive reading of "If You Would Just Drop By" on the electric piano before launching into a long, rambling monologue about the Pharaoh of Egypt and his stash of dope seeds.

During his concerts of 1968 and 1969, Guthrie would make offhand references to the predictions of cataclysmic earth events made by the American psychic Edgar Cayce (1877–1945). Cayce's ideas were enjoying recent popularity as his books on prophecy and occult matters were being sold as dime-store paperbacks. Cayce had any number of unusual beliefs. He believed that the souls of human beings, in between various incarnations, would rest on distant planets in the solar system. Cayce also was of the mind that the earth was going to eventually shift on its axis, and this event would set off a cataclysmic series of earthquakes that would create gigantic tsunamis and cause California to disappear in the depths of an ever-expanding Pacific Ocean. It isn't clear if Guthrie genuinely subscribed to these beliefs, but he would discuss several of Cayce's predictions at great length during his concerts. In Edwardsville, Guthrie told his fans from Illinois that they were sitting on potential oceanfront property:

> Edgar Cayce says that the ocean is gonna come . . . a wave is gonna come over the Rocky Mountains, right, and wipe out all of California. All the Rocky Mountains are gonna be islands and . . . what happens once it gets on the other side of the Rockies? Man, there's *nothing* to stop it, right? It was just to get lower and lower 'til it finally gets to Illinois. But it's gonna stop here. You guys are all right. . . . You don't have to do nothing. Just watch it. 'Cause he didn't say *where* in Illinois it was going to stop. But why don't you guys start getting a lot of sand, you know, *cabanas* and stuff like that. Hot dog stands and beaches and the whole. . . . Just set it up! Wait for it to roll in, man! Wouldn't that be groovy?

Arlo and the band then moved into one of his favorite old gospel songs, "Oh, Mary, Don't You Weep," but his mind remained elsewhere. He stopped the song as he began to rethink how the Cayce prediction would affect his fans: "You got to watch out for the Great Lakes though," he mused. "They're going down into the Gulf of Mexico. That could be a drag if you're kinda, you know, in the way."

Prior to performing the flat-picking showpiece "Black Mountain Rag," Arlo went fishing in his pockets for a guitar pick. "I hate reaching in my

pockets on stage, you know," he said in his best Cheech-and-Chong intona-
tion. "Especially when your hands are sweaty, you know? And you got tight
pants. . . . But your pockets always kind of come up with your hand and
anything you got in it kinda falls out. . . . That's a *drag*, man. *Narcs around*."
Arlo's fretting fingers fumbled through the opening notes of the instrumental,
so he brought the song to an abrupt halt. "I come from Coney Island. That's in
Brooklyn. That's in New York. We got a lot of that good country music out
there in west Coney Island. We're gonna do some of it for you here." They
successfully got through their second attempt at the song and moved more
assuredly into two new songs, "Wheel of Fortune" and "My Front Pages,"
both of which would soon be issued on *Running Down the Road*.

Following "My Front Pages," a great new song with Dylan-inspired wordplay and dramatic chord changes, Arlo turned to the band and said, "Hey, I
want to do something that you guys never did." That something was "Stealin'," the old Gus Cannon and the Jug Stompers song, also recently recorded
at the sessions in Los Angeles. The band easily filled in the simple changes,
and before long Arlo segued into his traditional closing song, "Amazing
Grace." Sitting at his piano, Arlo optimistically told everyone assembled that,
like it or not, the new world *was* coming. "I figure we got about ten years,
man, before it all happens," he said.

> Can you dig it? Can you dig it happening, man? Just imagine the day the
> Cat comes down and says, "Hi there." You'll be sitting there saying, "What?
> What?" You can't say "What?" to the Lord, man! You got to say, like, "Ah, I'm
> all right." And he looks you in the eye and then lets you know if you're groovy.
> You oughta know, you should know *now*, man! I mean, there's a lot more room
> in this tent than just for people. You can dig that. So when you sing this song,
> you gotta sing it like he's right there saying, "What's happening?" 'Cause that's
> what he's saying!

The year 1969 was, in fact, turning out to be one of life-changing events.
Earlier that summer Arlo signed on to perform at an event billing itself as the
Woodstock Music and Art Fair Aquarian Exposition, the festival's promoters
bent on featuring the hottest artists and bands of the contemporary-rock scene.
The festival was scheduled to be held on the weekend of August 15 through
17 at Max Yasgur's farm near Bethel, New York, actually some ninety miles
from the village of Woodstock. The promoters were planning on easing into
the weekend with a program of mostly folk music on Friday, the first day of
the three-day event. Saturday's program would feature some of the best rock
artists and bands from the West Coast, with Sunday evening reserved for
several acts of international renown, including Arlo's Reprise label mate Jimi
Hendrix. Arlo and his band were guaranteed $5,000 for their Friday night

appearance, which was slightly better money than was allotted for the Incredible String Band or Indian raga master Ravi Shankar, but a $1,000 less than Richie Havens's fee and only half the fee promised to Joan Baez. As festival promoters feverishly worked through the summer to make the event happen, Guthrie began reading reports that some 100,000 people were expected to attend, and this news gave him pause for concern. Fearing police violence, he admitted to journalist Jan Maas that he was concerned the festival had the real possibility of getting out of hand: "I was questioning whether I should go . . . 100,000 people, wow, man, I don't know if I'm ready to make that because there could be riots and all that stuff."[9]

Guthrie's appearance at Woodstock was at first considered merely one more show on the summer tour, which rolled relentlessly on. On Saturday night, July 12, Arlo and the band performed at the South Shore Music Circus in Cohasset, Massachusetts. One *Boston Globe* correspondent wrote that the Guthrie concert at the South Shore served up a retro evening of good-feeling "singalong [*sic*] anti-establishment" music, conjuring "memories of all night 'hoots,' friends sitting on old mattresses, and candles flickering from the tops of cheap Chianti bottles."[10]

On July 19 Arlo was scheduled to play a solo set at the ninth annual Newport Folk Festival, his third consecutive appearance at the event and his second as a main-stage performer. In the tradition of Newport's eclectic stage booking, appearing with Guthrie on Saturday's program were the New Lost City Ramblers as well as the Everly Brothers, his boyhood heroes. The Everlys were to perform in tandem with their father Ike, a noted "hillbilly" singer who had worked in the 1940s with country-music figures Red Foley and George Gobel. Rounding out the bill was the Canadian songstress Joni Mitchell; the guitar-playing Reverends F. D. Kirkpatrick and J. L. Kirkpatrick; the Rochester, New York–based B.C. Harmonizers; and the crowd-pleasing gospel outfit the Staple Singers. The Newport program guide noted accurately that with *Alice's Restaurant* soon to be released in theaters as a feature Hollywood film, Arlo's "songs have long since ceased to be underground." Pete Seeger, whose own career as an artist often straddled the troublesome chasm between underground folk hero and contemporary popular-music artist, was selected to usher his "old friend" Arlo onto the festival stage. "I said it was an 'old' friend I was introducing," Pete offered. "But . . . I've known him for twenty years, ever since he was born. You know, his father used to tell me, 'I don't want to make kids act more like grown-ups; I'd like to make grown-ups act more like kids.' And it's this wonderful love of fun which Woody passed on to his son Arlo."[11]

It had taken Arlo some twelve hours to travel to Newport from his apartment in New York City, having chosen to visit friends in Great Barrington en route. Even after his arrival on stage, it was clear that Arlo had no plans to work himself, or the wildly enthusiastic crowd, into a froth. "I'm just gonna hang out for a while," Arlo said laconically. Then, gesturing to Seeger, who had stepped off the stage, he said, "I don't know how you follow the *presence* of, you know, like *that cat*. Maybe that's all you can do is follow *it*. I'm not really sure." Thereafter, he launched into "Every Hand in This Land" from the still-forthcoming *Running Down the Road*, his acoustic guitar the only accompaniment. He moved over to his Yamaha electric piano ("Sounds more like a Koto," he laughed, referencing the traditional Japanese instrument) for his second song, a new, gentle song of longing, as yet unissued, titled "If You Would Just Drop By." Acknowledging Newport's ambitious Sunday event program, Arlo remarked, "Tomorrow night's kind of a Lead Belly night. I don't know if I'm gonna be there tomorrow or not." Returning to his guitar, Arlo chose to proactively offer his own tribute to his father's old friend, moving into a somewhat raucous but well-received sing-along of Huddie's "Meeting at the Building." It was back to the Yamaha for still another fractured retelling of the story of Moses, one that not only included footnotes to the scenario at the Red Sea with Pharaoh's soldiers but also to the marijuana-laced brownies that, in Arlo's vision at least, played no small role in helping to move the original events along. He then offered a contemporary parallel to the original story of Exodus, referencing the recent troubles in Berkeley. Two months earlier no-nonsense California governor Ronald Reagan sent 2,700 National Guardsmen to assist local police in violently clearing out the gaggle of hippies, students, left-wingers, and street people who inhabited the community-friendly, but technically illegal, "People's Park" on the campus of UC-Berkeley. The tragedy of it all, Guthrie contended, was that the cops *needed* the hippies; the two groups were, in some strange way, interdependent on one another. "I don't really know, you know, what that's got to do with this song," Arlo admitted. "I was thinking about, like, California, you know? Like when . . . all the *Groovies* get out of California. But when they all leave, man, there won't be no one to bust. I mean, think of it. All the cops, man, out in L.A. with nobody . . . I mean, there's *nobody* on the strip, there's *nobody* hanging out. Just other cops." Then, addressing those from the Golden State in attendance at Newport: "All you cats from California, man. . . . When you go back and start leaving, you know, with everybody else, they might try to get you back. . . . Just like the Pharaoh's cats."

He then moved into a reverent "Oh, Mary, Don't You Weep," urging the audience to sing the song's chorus ("Pharaoh's army got drowned") as a tribute of sorts to Governor Reagan. Afterwards, the usual catcalls for "Alice's Restaurant" soon carried over the seats, but Arlo quickly dismissed the pleas. "I know what I'm gonna do," he answered. Then, following a long pause, he admitted somewhat sheepishly, "I just forgot though." It was at that moment when Arlo looked up at the dusk-filled sky. He couldn't see the moon through the bright stage lights, but he knew it was there. "Can you dig it? In a few hours, man, some cat's gonna be stepping out of his 'thing' on the moon," he continued, referencing Neil Armstrong's historic moon walk. "I mean there, up there right? Walking around, picking up dirt. I guess it's groovy, all those astronauts hanging out up there, looking back on the Newport festival, right? Seeing all those cats looking at them." He then played "Wheel of Fortune" from *Running Down the Road*, the only song in his repertoire that had some basis in the extraterrestrial with its reference to biblical Ezekiel, who, of course, "saw the wheel." As the sky at Newport passed from dusk to darkness, Arlo went "old school" with a piano-backed version of "Amazing Grace" and closed with Dylan's "Walkin' Down the Line" ("I always like to, kind of, sing songs of people that ain't around," Arlo remarked, slyly referencing Dylan's self-imposed exile from Newport's hallowed grounds) and his own "Highway in the Wind." The attending scribe from *Billboard* made note that the "audience would probably have kept [Arlo] going half the night, trying to get him to sing 'Alice's Restaurant,' had it not been for the Newport curfew regulation." Following his latest triumph at Newport, Guthrie set off for the Main Point in Bryn Mawr for a four-night residency beginning July 25.[12]

That same month Arthur Penn was overseeing the final edit of *Alice's Restaurant*. United Artists was scheduled to release the film in New York City on August 20, and Penn, already elbow-deep in preproduction of *Little Big Man* with Dustin Hoffman, was rushing to meet the deadline. Though filming had officially ended the previous December, Penn and film editor Dede Allen were still cutting the film seven months on. Penn's vision of the film morphed as he screened and rescreened the footage. The original events of the "Massacre," in the filmmaker's admittance, now constituted "only three reels of the 12." Though Arlo would remain the connecting thread, the heart of the film now focused on the troubled marriage of Alice and Ray Brock. The dissolution of their real-life marriage would neatly mirror the failing Aquarian experiment of the brood of disaffected youngsters who surrounded them. James Broderick, the actor who played Ray Brock in the film, befriended many of the "church" kids on the set. He shared with *Newsweek* mixed feelings regarding both the finished film and the troubled young people he met while working on it. "It's a very sad movie," he explained, admitting that although he had come to really love and care about the kids he had met at the church, "I feel very sad about them. They have their life up there. It's what they want. There's a lot of peace, but somehow it's sad." Penn's artful meshing of fictitious drama with acute reality caused more than a few episodes of psychological torment for Alice Brock, who worked as an extra on the film and was reportedly paid $12,000 by the producers "for her name and story." The film's production put the "real" Alice under severe emotional strain, with doctors telling her she was "perilously close to a severe nervous breakdown." It was little wonder as throughout the filming she mostly stood off camera as the tumultuous—and sometimes unhappy—events of her life with Ray were re-created by strangers before her eyes. "The same week Arthur was shooting the scene in which Ray and I get married a second time, in real life we were getting divorced," Alice remembered. "I spent the whole time they were shooting the movie reacting like crazy—crying, laughing."[13]

The one person who remained relatively unscathed by the emotional tumult of the Penn film was Arlo himself. Though he was on tour throughout most of the summer he did take some time off to meet with United Artists music arranger Garry Sherman. It was under Sherman's direction that Guthrie was to record incidental music, mostly instrumentals, for the film's soundtrack. Through residuals on album sales of his first two LPs on Reprise, and a generous paycheck as a composer and principal actor of a feature Hollywood film, Arlo was afforded the opportunity to live his dreams in a way his friends simply could not. In his biography of Woody Guthrie, author Joe Klein made the succinct point that "Alice's Restaurant" would bring "Arlo more fame and commercial success by the age of nineteen than Woody had achieved in his entire life."[14]

On August 2 Guthrie performed at Castle Hill in Ipswich, Massachusetts, the top bill of a program that would also feature the Pentangle, an influential British folk-rock band and a favorite of Arlo's. On August 10 Guthrie traveled south to the Storrowton Theater at Exposition Park, West Springfield, Massachusetts. The next day Guthrie and the band were in New York City for two shows with Melanie at the Schaefer Music Festival in Central Park. It was also around this time that Guthrie was a guest on Dick Cavett's erudite talk show on ABC television. Sharing the guest couch with the British actor Nicol Williamson, the Cavett program featuring Arlo was broadcast August 12, 1969, three days prior to his scheduled appearance at the Woodstock festival.[15]

The roads leading to Max Yasgur's farm near Bethel were so inaccessible that Guthrie and the band had to abandon their Checker touring cab and be brought into the event via helicopter. On August 15, shortly before midnight and at the conclusion of Melanie's set, Arlo strolled onto the Woodstock stage accompanied by guitarist John Pilla, bassist Bob Arkin, and drummer Paul Motian. There was some backstage scuttlebutt that Guthrie and his band might not perform at all—and in this case it wouldn't be due to fear of police violence, scheduling conflicts, or stage fright. The weather forecast warned that a particularly nasty storm was closing in. The promoters, concerned for the safety of both the artists and audience, were considering canceling or postponing the music for an interim. Michael Lang, one of the architects of the festival, recalled that after some hemming and hawing the staff "decided to go for it." There were already a half-million people surrounding the stage. But a slight problem had arisen. Lang discovered that Arlo, thinking that he was "off the hook" from performing due to the impending storm, "had dropped acid. He wasn't up for going on. But we talked him into it." Arlo has long told the story that his iconic but somewhat diffident performance at Woodstock was due to an overconsumption of champagne. Cases of the bubbly beverage had reportedly been stacked backstage by the promoters for a celebratory uncorking at the festival's end. Whatever the cause, there was certainly some chemical element shaping Arlo's performance that evening.[16]

Most of Guthrie's Woodstock set has been preserved as a forty-minute line recording, but it is thought that the extant tape is probably short of complete. The tape begins with technical gremlins sabotaging an otherwise normal version of "Coming into Los Angeles" and continues with a program comprised of the usual songs featured on his summer tour of 1969: "Wheel of Fortune," "Every Hand in the Land," "Walkin' Down the Line" ("We're gonna do a Bobby Dylan tune, man. . . . Maybe you'll do it with us?"). He closed on a gospel note with "Oh, Mary, Don't You Weep" and "Amazing Grace." As would be the case with many of the Woodstock performances, Arlo's set was only occasionally transcendent and, in truth, a bit of a mess. His voice was exceedingly reedy, and on occasion his singing was totally off key. Of course it's likely that no one in attendance really noticed. Lang thought that Arlo's set had gone along pretty well, all things considered, with Guthrie in full raconteur mode carrying "on a kind of one-sided conversation with the audience." The recording allows that there was a certain revival-show spirit swirling about that night, Paul Motian's high-hat cymbal chiming throughout and Arlo's spiraling vocal declarations adding luster to an otherwise routine retelling of his "Moses" monologue. Of course, thanks to the successful *Woodstock* three-LP set and film that would follow in 1970, Arlo is probably best remembered among a general rock-music audience for the memorable commentary that followed his performance of "Coming into Los Angeles." It was an off-the-cuff aside that seemingly left no hippie-speak phrase unexpressed: "Hey, it's far out, man. I don't know if you. . . . I don't know, like, how many of you can dig how many people there are, man. Like I was rapping to the fuzz, right? Can you dig it, man? There's supposed to be about a million and a half people by tonight. Can you dig that? The New York State Thruway is closed, man! Yeah! *Lotta freaks*!" Following Joan Baez's angelic closing set on Friday, Arlo grabbed a guitar and excitedly wandered troubadour-like through rows and rows of rain-soaked young people who hadn't arrived early enough to get anywhere near the stage to hear the music.[17]

To say that the Woodstock festival was a life-changing event for Guthrie would sell the moment short. Three months after the experience he gushed to the *New York Sunday News* that, from the moment he walked on stage, "it was probably one of the most wonderful moments of my life. . . . I don't know how the festival could have been better than it was." He recalled his amazement that although a half-million people had gathered together, everyone was able to "get along together without one black eye, one cut lip. I mean, everybody came out, more people than have ever gathered before for any rally, and there were no guns, no helmets, no clubs—and no trouble." The state and local police, greatly outnumbered by the concertgoers, had left the revelers for the most part to fend for themselves. "If people want to know why there are riots and why there aren't," Guthrie concluded, "this should answer them." The experience of Woodstock also reinforced his belief that it was the kids of America who were trying to save the soul of the country. He told writer Jan A. Maas, "A lot of adults think that kids are trying to tear down the country. But actually the kids see society crumbling already and want to do something about it. I mean, this is their country and they dig it. This is the only country in the world where you got mountains and forest and deserts and oceans and all these people mixed together. Kids really dig this and it makes them so much more patriotic than adults."[18]

Two nights following his Woodstock set, on Sunday night, August 17, Guthrie performed before a standing-room-only crowd at the Cape Cod Melody Tent in Hyannis, Massachusetts. In a *Billboard* column published several weeks following that concert, the entertainment weekly teased, "Bob Hughes, Mirasound engineer, recorded Arlo Guthrie at the latter's sold-out concert last month at the Cape Cod Melody Tent, Hyannis, Mass. The material will be included in Guthrie's next Warner Bros.-7 Arts album." Members of the Grateful Dead, who had played a famously awful set on Saturday afternoon at Woodstock, were also on hand at the concert as spectators. The Dead and assorted other friends and hangers-on gathered into Arlo's dressing room prior to the show and had, as far as Guthrie could recollect, "a pretty good time."[19]

Though Penn's *Alice Restaurant* was set for release on Wednesday, August 20, 1969, United Artists staged the film's world premiere one night earlier at Boston's Sack Cheri 2 Theatre. Though his commitment to *Little Big Man* left Penn unable to attend the gala opening, producer Hillard Elkins and wife Claire Bloom, the actress, were on hand to enthusiastically sell the movie to the press. It was fortunate that someone was there to help cheerlead the movie's release as the film's star seemed to be in a desultory mood, unwilling to smile or engage in the promotional ballyhoo. Tightly clutching a fragile,

*Rare 1969 United Artists advance newspaper advertisement to promote the forthcoming* Alice's Restaurant *movie. Author's collection.*

long-stem red rose that someone had given him, Guthrie told the bank of crushing reporters and autograph seekers, "This is it. No more movies, no more promos. I'm into music, not this stuff." Alice Brock appeared to be a bit more compliant, smiling for the cameras and cross-promoting her forthcoming Random House tie-in tome *The Alice's Restaurant Cookbook*. The street in front of the theater was cordoned off for an hour-long folk music concert and block party that would precede the screening, and some 1,500 fans pushed into the area for the concert and the chance to get a glimpse of a celebrity face or two.[20]

The critical reaction to the film was almost entirely favorable. Charles Champlin, writing in the *Los Angeles Times*, thought the film "less consistently successful in its own terms" than its natural cousins, *Easy Rider* or *Midnight Cowboy*, but admitted that it was nonetheless "a fresh, captivating and important piece of those untraditional times." Of Guthrie's performance, Champlin assured readers that the young folk singer "more than holds his own with the professionals . . . and his laconic style is almost hypnotically fascinating on screen." Vincent Canby of the *New York Times* called Penn's film "a funny and loving elaboration" of Guthrie's ballad. But Canby also suggested that the relationship of Arlo to his communal "family" in

Stockbridge was less interesting than the re-created fly-on-the-wall bedside visits with his dying father. Canby wrote, the "movie . . . touches obliquely, but with real perception, on the ties that bind—and the times that separate— father and son." The differences between Woody and his son were only the temper of the times. "Woody worked to modify the system," Canby wrote, perhaps not appreciating the full breadth of the elder Guthrie's revolutionary fervor, but "Arlo ultimately ignores it." Writing in the *New Yorker*, Penelope Gilliatt offered that in showcasing "one of the gentle radicals who seem to be changing America," Arthur Penn delivered "a purely conceived film, clown- ish and sad, beautifully put together." For the handful of critics that filed mixed or negative reviews, their main complaint was the perceived "struc- tural weaknesses" of the film. There were also criticisms that the screenplay strayed too far from the storyline of Guthrie's original talking blues and that the Alice and Ray drama was superfluous and unnecessary.[21]

On August 23, *Billboard* published one of the earliest advertisements for the release of *Running Down the Road* in the popular eight-track cassette format:

> Arlo Guthrie is about to become The Thing to talk and write about. His movie, "Alice's Restaurant," will be this year's movie-to-see. Reprise will cash in with another subversive album by our favorite long-haired creep. The LP's called "Running Down the Road," and is in the "Alice's" mood. A fancy display promotes both the restaurant and the new LP, and will soon be cluttering up otherwise decent shop windows across the land. Extensive underground ads in such media as *Rolling Stone* and *Village Voice* and (if it doesn't get busted) *Screw*. All the while, Arlo will be calmly cutting his own radio commercials.[22]

The Guthrie tour rolled on even as the first promotional copies of *Running Down the Road* were hitting the turntables of radio stations and music crit- ics. There was an August 24 show at the Rockpile in Toronto, and on August 25 Guthrie and the band performed at the "Musicarnival" in Warrensville Heights, Ohio, a suburb of Cleveland.

The consensus was that *Running Down the Road* was Guthrie's most ambitious and imaginative album to date. The newspaper adverts promised that the LP was a "gently subversive new album by Arlo. . . . It's just out this month and should get the Feds on Arlo's tail again." The album was certainly different from its predecessors. On the eve of the LP's release, Arlo told *Newsweek*, "I record because it's fun. . . . I have a lot more instruments to play with, buttons to push, knobs to turn. The studio is a big expensive toy." The album was decidedly slicker and more musically satisfying than either of its predecessors. *Rolling Stone* praised producers Lenny Waronker and Van Dyke Parks for their oversight of "something more than just another

Arlo Guthrie album." The dope-smuggling anthem, "Coming into Los An-geles," was heralded as "the best tune he's written" and offered proof that Guthrie "can tell a story in a song, instead of . . . a half-hour rap while his guitar gently vamps." This may have been so, but most of Arlo's original material on the LP was ignored by the *Rolling Stone* writer; the critic tended to reserve his praise for the great reworkings of Woody's "Oklahoma Hills," John Hurt's "My Creole Belle," and Gus Cannon's "Stealin'." Though the title song was "magnificently produced, with explosions of electric violin and ravaged feedback," *Rolling Stone* thought the song was slight and simply didn't "match up to its showcase." The magazine also hinted that the album's handsome gatefold design was a statement of a sort. The photograph featured a remarkable Henry Diltz photograph of Guthrie capably handling a Triumph motorcycle. This was the same brand of cycle that Dylan had reportedly *failed* to maneuver properly on a wet mountain road near Woodstock a few years earlier. *Sing Out!* thought *Running Down the Road* was "Arlo's best record to date," offering a "selection of fine songs well-sung and with a tight and excellent backing group." The magazine was happy that, this time around, there was no "long rap" on the album to distract listeners from the beautiful music settings. The *New York Times* believed Guthrie was not, "at this point in his career, a particularly original composer," though they found his songs "pleasant enough, touched with an appropriate awareness of rock and blues." Though the melancholy "Oh, in the Morning" was singled out as the "best" original song, the *Times* was more impressed by Guthrie's covers of other people's material.[23]

Shortly after the release of *Alice's Restaurant* to U.S. theaters, Guthrie found himself listening to an AM radio station, surprised to hear a barrage of hit singles featuring tasteless covers of popular songs. "They weren't even bubblegum," Guthrie mused. "They were worse—it was like *Henry Mancini Plays Alice's Restaurant*. It was worse than anything I ever heard." He called Lenny Waronker and Van Dyke Parks and told them that he had a great idea and wanted to get together for an impromptu recording session. "I went into the studio and said, 'Listen, let's do a funky 'Alice,' and get it out so that the combination at least will be something funny." In Guthrie's estimation, the resulting recording, which featured Cajun Doug Kershaw on violin, was noth-ing short of terrific. "We did a great 'Alice's Rock & Roll Restaurant.' One of the lines was: 'You can eat anyone you want,' and the rest was like that." The single of "Alice's Rock & Roll Restaurant" backed with "Coming into Los Angeles" was released circa November 1969, but the 45, unfortunately, bore little resemblance to what Arlo had originally conceived. He was, in fact, embarrassed by the issue of the Reprise single: "When the record finally came out it was absolutely cut, edited, snip, snap, beeped, and absolutely diluted and there was nothing left. It was absolutely terrible. . . . I tried to pull it back, obviously." But it was too late. The record had already been shipped to radio stations. Guthrie recalled that he all but pleaded with Reprise, "Listen you guys, I don't like the record. I want you to go to the people you gave it to and take it back. They said: 'Right.'" The irony of it was that Arlo's original intention of recording a tasteless single for the Top 40 charts was, in some bizarre way, perversely successful. He was told that the record was "doing well" in England of all places, "which is unfortunate. . . . I'm ashamed that other people have to listen to it if *I* don't like it." The single even slipped briefly and belatedly onto the U.S. *Billboard* Top 100 singles chart in January 1970.[24]

On Wednesday, September 24, Marjorie Guthrie was in Manhattan, scheduled to address a meeting of the World Congresses of Neurological Sciences. She had formed the Committee to Combat Huntington's Disease some two years earlier, working with customary energy and goodwill to bring public attention—and much-needed funding—to the study of the disease. She admirably used the last years of her life educating both medical professionals and stricken families about the nature of the illness while canvassing for research funding. On hand to listen to his mother's speech was her eldest son who, as the press would continually point out, had a 50/50 chance of succumbing to the disease that laid waste to his famous father. During the news conference that followed, Arlo surprised everyone with two announcements. He mentioned that he was soon to wed Jackie Hyde, the waitress he had met earlier in the summer at the Troubadour. He then went on to explain that neither he nor his prospective bride-to-be would be worrying about the disease when planning their life together. Many in the medical profession thought this was a poor decision for those at risk of carrying the Huntington's gene as the disease was hereditary. But friends and family told one journalist that Arlo and Jackie were absolutely certain that, should they decide to have children, their offspring would be free of the disease. Thelma Tharp of the *Sarasota Herald-Tribune* reported that Arlo and Jackie, initially out of simple curiosity, had been dabbling in mysticism and spiritualism but were now "devotees" of these science-religions, "attending séances, and personal development classes." The Guthries had a medium friend who "assured" the young couple "they have nothing to fear from H.D." The news of Guthrie's interest in astrology was so widespread that it wasn't long before one occult magazine splashed the headline, "Moonchild Arlo Guthrie: Tell Them to Get Ready, the Spaceships Are Coming." The family wasn't sure what to make of Arlo's new interest. Marjorie had good-naturedly weathered most of her son's enthusiasms but said forthrightly that she was hoping he would soon outgrow this "occult phase." His sister, Nora Lee, wasn't a believer either, but she confessed that her brother's interest in the occult had, at the very least, allowed him to expand "his interest in intellectual matters, reading, and conversation."[25]

On the Sunday afternoon of September 28, Guthrie performed a solo concert to a crowd of some 3,000 fans on the football field of Tufts University in Medford, Massachusetts. The concert was a casual affair with people milling about and campus activists setting up collection boxes so concertgoers could donate a dollar to help raise funds in bringing busloads of student protestors to the moratorium against the Vietnam War in Washington, DC, set for November 15. It was an easygoing afternoon with concertgoers listening to the music while sitting on blankets, drinking wine, and blowing hundreds of soap-water bubbles into the air. The wind began to carry the bubbles toward the stage, causing Guthrie to interrupt his performance to ask, "What's that flying around here? I'm starting to feel like Lawrence Welk." Shortly afterward, the *Boston Globe* reported that Guthrie "challenged the crowd 'to blow bubbles with smoke in them. It makes it more fun to bite the bubbles.'" Things got even more interesting when a skywriting plane flew overhead, sketching out a giant white-lined "Peace" symbol in its wake. "That guy's a freak flying around up there," Arlo offered while looking skyward. "We'll just wait for the Air Force to come out and get him."[26]

The air force wasn't the only power in the sky, of course, and Guthrie's interest in astrology and the occult sciences continued to deepen. He would sometimes go on television and attempt to explain some of the more unusual beliefs that he had adopted. He straight-facedly told British television personality David Frost, "This world, the earth, was brought in from another solar system, before there were dudes on it or anything. . . . They stuck it in here. That's why it's so different than all the other worlds." The Frost audience tittered, but to Guthrie this was serious, if occasionally inarticulate, business. Then, on October 8, 1969, with the stars and planets in alignment, Arlo Davy Guthrie wed Jackie Hyde. Their autumnal marriage was held outdoors on the grounds of Arlo's new 250-acre property in the Berkshires of Washington, Massachusetts, purchased outright with his "Alice's Restaurant" monies. The houses on the property were in midrenovation, the couples' newly purchased bathtub and storm windows on prominent display on the porch. In contrast, the leaves on the trees that surrounded them from all sides had all turned bright orange, red, and yellow, and though it had rained the night before the sky was now perfectly blue. This favorable weather was no accident. As Arlo and his bride-to-be were still in the thrall of Eastern mysticism, the wedding date of October 8 had been "carefully selected" by a medium friend as ideal. One of Guthrie's friends in attendance told *Time* magazine, "It was the kind of wedding where nothing could go wrong. If it did, it was incorporated into the proceedings." For Alice Brock, the wedding day was a working day. She volunteered to handle the catering, working out of Arlo's kitchen to serve a buffet of lasagna, turkey, fruit salad, and curried shrimp across a series of rented card tables. The Guthries had invited some 150 friends and relatives to the ceremony at their hillside idyll, as well as a cabal of newsman and photographers. ("Today you're not photographers," Arlo told them. "You're guests—right?") Puppies seemed to be everywhere, barking and mixing playfully amongst the guests. "One of my mystical friends told me that one of these puppies will some day save the life of one of my children," Arlo told a reporter that afternoon. "I don't know which one it is, so I have to take care of all of them."[27]

Marjorie Guthrie would arrive a little late for her son's wedding. The Guthries had chartered a bus to whisk some forty-two guests from New York City to Washington County. But the old bus arrived behind schedule and wasn't quite up to the task of climbing the final hill to Arlo's home, so everyone had to exit the vehicle and make the final ascent on foot. Arlo met the bus at the bottom of the hill. "I feel like a flower child," Marjorie told her son as she stepped off the bus in a mustard-colored dress accentuated with an orange shawl and an assortment of flowers. "You look like a flower child," Arlo smiled. Then again, nearly everyone gathered that afternoon looked like a flower child. Though a few elderly guests were dressed more traditionally, most of those invited, arriving on motorcycles and in microbuses, wore blouses, gowns, boots, and beads. In this instance, both bride and groom wore white: Arlo in bell-bottom trousers and a long-sleeved, ruffled shirt; Jackie in a long gown of white silk with a long train trimmed in lace. Both wore crowns of stephanotis trimmed with plastic ivy leaves upon their heads. Prior to the ceremony the folk singer Judy Collins sang Leonard Cohen's "Suzanne," and Marjorie Guthrie read aloud a poem that Woody had written that "she had saved for this day." It read, in part, "May your gladness ripen as a yellow sweet fruit and the radiance of your thinking invigorate the world / May you never include the word 'enemy' in your vocabulary / May you attain." The poem was signed, "Woody Guthrie, the soul doctor."

As some friends blew on conch shells, the couple was wed by Justice of the Peace Donald M. Feder of neighboring Becket, who good-naturedly took the unusual ceremony in stride. Following the traditional first kiss and the declaration that the couple had been officially pronounced husband and wife, everyone gathered sang "Amazing Grace," Arlo's favorite hymn. On the receiving line, Officer Obie happily kissed Jackie in congratulations but steadfastly refused to buss Arlo's cheek.[28]

The fact that Arlo Guthrie, the cosmos-floating poster boy of the flower-child generation, would be married in what was essentially a traditional wedding ceremony surprised many. It was a time when many young people were rejecting the time-honored concept of marriage. But Guthrie was little troubled about getting hitched the old-fashioned way. "It didn't matter to me one way or the other," he explained. "And seeing as how it didn't mean anything to me or my wife, and it *did* matter to our parents and all of her friends and all of that weirdness, we decided, 'Well, let's get married.'" It was *love* itself that was exalted, and there could be no shadings of that. It had to be all encompassing, and the only way you could truly "get it together" was if you were able to love everything and everyone without condition. He told David Frost that it was important that "you love the tree, and you love the cat, and the dog, and your brother, and your sister, and you love Spiro"—that would be Spiro Theodore Agnew, Nixon's vexing vice president and professed enemy of the counterculture. Guthrie admitted that evolving one's self to this high level of attainment was difficult, that it was a process that he himself was still working out. "Spiro's a tough one," he admitted. "But I'm getting there, Spiro. Don't worry about it."[29]

There wouldn't be time for a honeymoon. Guthrie had already committed to a three-month solo tour and was due in Washington, DC, for a concert only two days following the wedding. On Friday night, October 10, he was scheduled to perform at Georgetown University's McDonough Gym, the top bill of a card that would also feature the rock bands Tractor and Mountain. The demand for tickets was so great that promoters could only accommodate the crowds by staging two separate concerts that night, the second scheduled to begin at 10:30 p.m. The newspapers had been running the story of Guthrie's recent marriage, causing the elated Georgetown promoter to gush to the *Washington Post*, "It's fantastic. He'll be spending his honeymoon with 10,000 people." To everyone's surprise, Guthrie arrived at the Washington, DC, national airport the afternoon of the concert alone, carrying only his guitar and a small suitcase. "Jackie's at home feeding my dogs," Arlo told reporters. "If I canceled it would be three months and I can't cancel the whole tour." But the logistics of staging two separate concerts was too overwhelming for the promoters, and at 11:00 p.m., a half-hour following what should have been the start of the *second* concert, Mountain was still performing their *first* set of the evening with Guthrie not yet having appeared on stage. The thousands of fans who had crowded the lobby expecting entrance to the second show began to insist entrance to the gymnasium, while others angrily demanded refunds. Things were more relaxed on the second night. On Saturday evening, October 11, Guthrie returned to the University of Cincinnati for his second concert at the school in a space of eight months. This time the event was moved from Symphony Hall to the Xavier Fieldhouse, where Guthrie was to be preceded on the program by Santana, a little-known-outside-the-West-Coast rock band that had just cut its first album for Columbia. On Sunday, October 12, Guthrie would appear as the top bill on a program with the Youngbloods, at the recreation hall of Pennsylvania State University, in University Park.[30]

In the autumn of 1969, Arlo Guthrie was spinning gold. The *Boston Globe* noted that the *Alice's Restaurant* LP was still "doing super for Reprise," with sales pushing past one million dollars. The soundtrack album to the film was also doing well, and the shelves of bookshops sagged with a host of *Alice's Restaurant*–related titles. There was Alice Brock's *Alice's Restaurant Cookbook*, released that October with a first printing of 50,000 copies, which included a flexi-disc recording of Guthrie and Brock "performing" "Italian-Type Meatballs" and "My Granma's Beet Jam." Grove Press published a cartoon version of *Alice's Restaurant* (Grove Press Special GS-1), which featured the complete text of the official recording of the "Massacree" with accompanying illustrations by the artist Marvin Glass. Doubleday Publishing Company was also at work typesetting Arthur Penn and Venable Herndon's screenplay of the *Alice's Restaurant* film and readying its publication in early 1970. Perhaps most importantly, the Amsco Music Publishing Company of New York published *This Is the Arlo Guthrie Book*, a collection featuring sheet music and such assorted Guthrie ephemera as photographs, letters, essays, and poems. The songbook, most importantly, included lead sheets—and even the occasional guitar transcription—of twenty songs: eighteen of Guthrie's compositions from the *Alice's Restaurant*, *Arlo*, and *Running Down the Road* albums, his arrangement of Gus Cannon's "Stealin', and one yet unreleased song, "If You Would Just Drop By." There was plenty of material in the tome to interest the nonmusical fan as well, not least of which were a score of rare and candid Guthrie family photographs and images of Arlo playing and hanging out with such friends as Pete Seeger, Doug Kershaw, and Ramblin' Jack Elliott. There was also a copy of "A Letter Read to the Draft Board" (dated March 8, 1966), a collection of Arlo's poetic musings from early winter and spring of 1969, and, most intriguingly, a reproduction of his eighth-grade report card from the Woodward School. In one of the few reviews of *This Is the Arlo Guthrie Book*, *Sing Out!* offered the well-meaning but empty platitude, "Taken as a whole, the songs offer some insight into where Arlo has been and where's he's going. It's going to be an exciting trip. Get the book and come along." The improbable financial success of the *Alice's Restaurant* machine caused Gregory McDonald of the *Boston Globe* to ask glibly, "Kinda makes you feel like litterin', don't it?"[31]

The *Alice's Restaurant* LP (300,000 copies sold by autumn 1969) and Arthur Penn's film adaptation were, in fact, bringing in bushels of cash. (The motion picture would eventually gross in the excess of six million dollars.) If one was hoping to book Arlo Guthrie for a concert engagement, the Leventhal office was asking for, and getting, a flat fee of $3,000 per show as well as a

*Guthrie listening to the speeches and songs delivered at the Moratorium against the Vietnam War in Washington, DC, November 15, 1969. Earlier that morning, Guthrie had performed Woody's little-known ballad "I've Got to Know" as well as "This Land Is Your Land" before a sea of some 250,000 antiwar demonstrators. Author's collection.*

percentage of the box office take. Guthrie wisely left most of the financial planning to Harold, who years earlier had been charged with belatedly putting the publishing and copyrighting of Woody's song catalog in order. Just as Arlo Guthrie began to practice vegetarianism near the close of the 1960s ("Which I don't mind, as long as he's healthy," his mother would tell the *New York Times*), Harold was investing a chunk of his young client's *Alice's Restaurant* earnings in the cattle-ranching industry. On the surface it seemed an incongruous compromise of principle, but, as Marjorie Guthrie recalled, her son, the "ardent vegetarian," thought it pretty funny. It's tempting to suggest that Guthrie's recording of his father's obscure grassland-to-slaughterhouse cattle-ranching ballad "Lay Down Little Dogies" (*Washington County*, 1970), was, at least in part, a sly wink to his own financial stake in the business. Starting with his concerts of 1971, Guthrie would put a contemporary ecological spin on "Dogies," introducing Woody's ballad about hitting the "old beef trail" as something resembling an "animal recycling song."[32]

Guthrie, along with 250,000 others, traveled to Washington, DC, on November 15 to take part in the Moratorium against the Vietnam War. Climbing on the speaker's stage early that chilly morning in overcoat and cowboy hat, Arlo told everyone gathered,

> It's kind groovy to. . . . You know. It's kind of far out and groovy to be here, man. I was up in Canada yesterday and they all wanted to be here, you know . . . and I see some Canadian flags. It's nice to have you guys here, too. We're talking about the whole world, right? So . . . I don't see any Mexican flags, must be some around though. I don't have much to say. I mean, it's kind of [all been] said already. I don't even think anybody had to show up. You know, as soon as they put them machine guns at the Capitol, I think the point was made.

The first song he sang that morning was "I've Got to Know," a little-known song of his father's first published in *Sing Out!* in October 1950. It was a perfect song for the occasion, Woody's plaintive original lyric (only slightly modified by Arlo for this performance) asking, "Why do your war boats ride on my waters? Why do your death bombs fall from my skies? Why don't your ships bring food and some clothing? I've got to know. I've got to know." Pete Seeger told writers Studs Terkel and Calvin Trillin that it was his belief that "I've Got to Know" was Woody's response to the well-known southern gospel song "Farther Along," which complacently comforts listeners that the promise of heaven is reward enough for all the unfairness and deprivations weathered on earth. This was the sort of sentiment that really stuck in the craw of such radicals as Woody and Pete, the latter of whom disparaged the hymn's original verses as saying, in effect, "God knows everything, so don't worry. . . . Just take things as they come." Following "I've Got to Know," the crowd began to shout for "Alice's Restaurant," but Arlo gently shook his head and firmly answered, "No," instead reflecting on what his father would have thought of the Moratorium. "I'm kind of thinking that my old man would really dig to be here. Not only would he dig it, but I'm sure he is . . . maybe [his spirit is in] one of your little kids out there. Maybe not." He laughed nervously, dismissing that notion with a shake of his head. "We're gonna do some verses of a song that he wrote that aren't usually sung very much. . . . At least they're not taught in the school." He sang "This Land Is Your Land," but with 9,000 armed troops surrounding the government buildings it certainly didn't appear that way.[33]

Less than two months following the mass protest gathering in Washington, DC, Arlo began to reevaluate his involvement, offering an opinion that "the Moratorium has more or less outlived its usefulness." After witnessing soldiers positioning machine guns on the steps of the U.S. Capitol that November, and with memories of violent confrontations between U.S. citizens and National Guardsmen in the streets of Watts in 1965 and Chicago in 1968 still fresh in mind, Arlo seemed less enthusiastic about the effectiveness of mass protest events; these large gatherings all seemed to beget violent confrontations. He told a reporter from the *New York Times*, "I think demonstrations will probably become a lot more violent. . . . Violence doesn't have a saturation point. That's what's useful about it."[34]

On Friday night, November 21, Arlo performed at the Aragon Ballroom in the heart of Chicago's uptown district. He was becoming increasingly at ease blending some of his father's material into his shows, as he did that evening with "Grand Coulee Dam" and "I Ain't Got No Home." The actor Will Geer, an old friend of Woody's, told Ed Robbin, a former editor of *People's World*, that he believed that the success of "Alice's Restaurant" allowed Arlo to reclaim his father's songs without the onus of riding "on his father's coattails." It was important that Arlo find his own voice when starting out, and now that he had clearly made it on his own terms he could willfully reclaim his father's legacy. The transition wasn't always an easy one. The Chicago concert was met with middling enthusiasm, Arlo's inclusion of a number of Woody Guthrie songs notwithstanding. He ignored repeated cries for "Alice's Restaurant Massacree," suffered through "several false starts and miscues," and even remarked over the house system to guitar-playing accompanist John Pilla, "We're blowing it tonight." The music critic from the *Chicago Tribune* wasn't going to argue with Arlo's harsh self-assessment, noting the "elusive quality—charisma, whatever, that holds an audience spellbound wasn't there."[35]

The year 1969 ended with a Christmas weekend concert at Carnegie Hall. This year Carnegie was a stripped-down affair, with Guthrie trading between six- and twelve-string guitar and piano, with John Pilla assisting on second guitar and bass. The Carnegie holiday show had, for the third year straight, sold out, bringing in an impressive gate of $12,850. Critics from both the *New York Times* and *Variety* thought Guthrie had "matured" as a songwriter and performer in the last year, with both commenting on his remarkable ability to intimately transform the "concert hall into a living room." He sang a lot of his new material that night but, as always, would revisit favorite songs such as Dylan's "Don't Think Twice, It's All Right" and his father's gorgeous paean to the Northwest, "Roll On, Columbia."[36]

The 1960s technically ended at the stroke of midnight, January 1, 1970. A Toronto newspaper had earlier assembled a list of celebrity newsmakers, asking them to submit, in the form of a hundred-word telegram, their predications on what the new decade held in store. Guthrie answered in 111 words: "Replying to your wire for 100 words. Man, I don't know what is going to happen in the 1970s." Then he typed and retyped the word *Love* ninety-two times. He would share a far more articulate vision of the future during his lengthy interview with the *New York Times*, published a week and a half later. The conversation touched on his usual hot-button topics, from the failures of the educational system to the ascendance of youth culture. There was a brief discussion of the recent Moratorium in Washington, DC, and of the activities of the antiwar movement ("If Dick Nixon says the silent majority is supporting the war, let them all go"). Though the revolution was surely coming, only the kids understood that the big change wouldn't arrive via a political missile. The true revolution was a spiritual awakening. "We're all God's kiddies," Guthrie continued. "No more nationalism, countryism, land-of-the-free-ism. It's world-of-the-free-ism, universe-of-the-free-ism. We're thinking big." When asked for a timetable of the revolution, Guthrie answered, "You want a date? O.K., 1983."[37]

For others 1983 was far too long a wait. That January Arlo traveled to Chicago, where he was to appear as a witness for the defense in the celebrated, and often anarchic, trial of the so-called Chicago Eight. The eight (Rennie Davis, David Dellinger, John Froines, Lee Weiner, Tom Hayden, Abbie Hoffman, Jerry Rubin, and Bobby Seale) had been charged by government prosecutors for "conspiracy to incite a riot" during Chicago's hosting of the 1968 Democratic national convention two summers earlier. It wasn't too long before the "Chicago Eight" became the "Chicago Seven" when Bobby Seale was separated from the others following a series of bitter confrontations with the bench. The remaining defendants, with the tacit support of their counselors, the radical activist attorneys William M. Kunstler and Leonard Weinglass, saw the trial as a free-speech subterfuge; they planned on discrediting government prosecutors, Chicago mayor Richard Daley, and the city's nightstick-wielding police force with a spirited defense strategy. The defendants, with the exception of fifty-four-year-old pacifist David Dellinger, were all in their late twenties or early thirties. Having been the first generation to come of age during the advent of television, the defendants were extremely media savvy and planned to use their notoriety and time in the spotlight to engage in some absurdist political theater. It was to that end that the defense brought in a slate of politically sympathetic celebrity figures, including the writer-poets Allen Ginsberg and Ed Sanders, the comedian Dick Gregory, and the folk singers Pete Seeger, Judy Collins, Phil Ochs, and Country Joe McDonald. The defense team and their colorful, outrageous clients were famously but unwittingly abetted by their principle target of ridicule, the stern Judge Julius J. Hoffman. Judge Hoffman was, as the *New York Times* would note, "74 years old and a firm enforcer of courtroom protocol."[38]

Arlo was scheduled to appear at the Federal Building in Chicago on the Thursday afternoon of January 15. He arrived dressed to the nines, the stodgy *New York Times* noting Guthrie's attire of "grey, wide-lapeled, pin-stripe Edwardian suit and an orange, red and white paisley shirt." Upon taking the stand, Arlo was asked by Kunstler to state his occupation. He answered, "I am a musician. I am an actor and a writer." He went on to explain that he had performed in America, Europe, and Asia and had made several record albums. Kunstler then brought from the defense table copies of the LPs *Alice's Restaurant* and *Running Down the Road*, holding them across his chest. He asked Guthrie to identify the platters. The aggravated chief counselor for the prosecution, Thomas A. Foran, swiftly rose to his feet to object, "What in Heaven's name is the relevancy of these records? We've been through all this before." When Kunstler asked Arlo if it was his father, Woody Guthrie, who wrote "This Land Is Your Land," Arlo's reply was cut off by Foran's swift "objection, your Honor." Kunstler moved on, knowing full well the fact was now part of the record. Arlo recollected the circumstances of his meetings with Abbie Hoffman and Jerry Rubin, telling the court about the first time he heard of their plans. "Abbie wanted me to come down and sing at a 'Festival of Life' in Chicago," Arlo answered, admitting to some reluctance in signing on. "What I said to Abbie was that it would be rather difficult, you know, for me to get involved in that kind of thing, because we had had a lot of trouble before with festivals and gatherings because of police violence. Abbie asked me if I had any song or kind of theme song for the festival, and I said 'Yes,' 'Alice's Restaurant.'" He confirmed that he offered the Yippies his talking blues to be used as a "theme" of the festival. Kunstler proceeded to ask Arlo to relate the story of "Alice's Restaurant" and, since Judge Hoffman had repeatedly clamped down on singing in the courtroom by earlier defense witnesses, it was understood that Arlo would have to relate the gist of the "Massacree" without benefit of guitar accompaniment. It was ironic that Guthrie was asked to perform "Alice's Restaurant" in the courtroom, as Judge Hoffman had, in effect, silenced the singing voices of a parade of defense witnesses. But as "Alice" was, of course, a mostly talking song anyway, Guthrie reasoned, "I was about the only singer who could get through some of his own material at the trial and still [have it] sound really like it did originally when we sang at the riots." Though it had been some time since Guthrie had sung the recorded "draft" version of the song, the spell of "Alice's Restaurant" was cast even in the solemn courtroom setting. The *Los Angeles Times* noted, "In the past, outbursts of laughter have been met with rebukes, but Thursday laughter flowed everywhere, unchallenged and unchecked." The sheer outrageousness of the litterbug tale seemed to amuse everyone, including the usually grim government prosecutor Thomas A. Foran. When Arlo got to the part of the song about how the garbage had piled up at the church, the *Times* noted that the taciturn U.S. attorney "tried, but failed, to swallow his laughter. Guthrie assured Foran, 'I thought it was funny too.'" Things went on ordinarily enough until Arlo got the point of the "Massacree" when he was at the Draft Induction Center on Whitehall Street and "went to see a psychiatrist." Upon hearing this revelation, and obviously getting into the spirit of the courtroom mischief, Judge Hoffman interrupted. He asked Arlo directly, "Did you pass?" Hoffman's snarky attempt at humor reportedly sent everyone sitting in the courtroom to burst into laughter. Though Guthrie responded to Judge Hoffman's query, his answer was, sadly, lost to stenographers in the courtroom transcript. Nonplussed, Arlo continued on with the "Massacree" until he finally got around to the song's chorus and began to sing, "You can get anything you want . . ." That's when the song got clamped down. Hoffman protested immediately, "Oh, no, no. . . . No, I am sorry." There would be no singing in Hoffman's courtroom. Kunstler argued that the song was directly relevant to the case as that was what the witness had "sang for the defendants." Having earlier established in his testimony that the film *Alice's Restaurant* was currently playing in Chicago cinemas, Hoffman's answer was curt. He told the defense attorney that there would be no singing in his court since he didn't "want the theater owner where this picture is shown to sue me." "We'll represent you, your Honor," Kunstler replied.[39]

The United Press International (UPI) correspondent covering the trial filed a report stating Guthrie had "charmed everybody in the courtroom including U.S. District Court Judge Julius J. Hoffman," and that seemed to be the general consensus of most in the media. Following his testimony, Arlo was met on the steps of the courthouse by a swarm of camera crews and newspapermen. He likened the trial of the Chicago Seven to an episode of the popular television drama *Perry Mason*. "The good guys are in trouble. The bad guys have the evidence. But the good guys are going to win—like they always do."[40]

Several days following his courtroom appearance, Arlo was scheduled to perform as a guest of country-music legend Johnny Cash on the singer's popular TV show on ABC. The *Johnny Cash Show* was proving to be a surprise hit for the network brass at ABC, getting off to a much-publicized start the previous season when Cash secured the services of the reclusive—and rarely seen on television—Bob Dylan for the series's first program, broadcast June 7, 1969. Though long an anathema to both folkies and rock 'n' rollers, the role of country music in fashioning contemporary music would be reevaluated when Dylan's best-selling Columbia LP of self-penned country and western–styled songs, *Nashville Skyline*, first hit record shops in February 1969. Guthrie was scheduled to appear on the sixteenth episode of that first season, sharing the stage of Nashville's famed Ryman Auditorium with Johnny's guests Bobbie Gentry and Jose Feliciano. On January 20, four days prior to the program's airing on Saturday evening, January 24, a writer from *Variety* visited Guthrie during rehearsals. There was a sentiment amongst folkies that country and western music was the exclusive province of the reactionary right wing. Guthrie thought otherwise. He told *Variety*, "Country music is becoming popular because it is becoming relevant to a nation—not just a state or two. . . . The psychedelic, teeny-bopper stuff is about dead already, and most of the radio stations are just playing trash, if you ask me. . . . But I think the trend over the next few years will see music get simpler and more relevant." Guthrie also mentioned how country music and his father's own music were intertwined and how, while "attending boarding school in the Berkshires," he would tune in at night to the Nashville radio stations. "When I first started singing for money," he recollected to *Variety*, "all I did was country stuff." With all those credentials lined out, it's of interest that Guthrie chose *not* to sing any country and western songs on the program. It's not that he didn't *intend* to, but at the last moment the show's producers red-penciled the song he wished to sing. The long-haired Guthrie had planned to sing Merle Haggard's proestablishment anthem "Okie from Muskogee." This great Merle Haggard song had earned the rough-and-tumble country singer both an album and single of the year award from the Academy of Country Music in 1969. The song was immediately embraced by the segment of Americans regarded by Richard Nixon as "the Silent Majority," those who looked down their noses in disgust on the unwashed hippies and the counterculture and the drug scene. Guthrie made certain at the rehearsals that he played the song absolutely straight. The song was performed entirely in Haggard's barroom honky-tonk style, "with a country band behind me, a little dobro, a little bass, regular straight country funk, and the audience loved it."

The problem wasn't with the song but with the artist *singing* the song. Pete Seeger recalled that the performance caused a dilemma for the staff of the Cash program, for its context, not its content. "Arlo looking and being what he is," Seeger would write, Haggard's "words take complete new meanings. It was so hilarious that Johnny Cash and the entire crew were rolling in the aisles with laughter. But it got cut from the show before going on the air." Guthrie would later tell his friend Karl Dallas, "It was an absolutely fascist song, but when I did it I tried to do it with a straight face. I walked in with a grey pinstripe suit and a cowboy hat and started to sing that thing in the middle of the Bible belt. They cracked up. They went absolutely wild." But the producers thought that Guthrie's version, no matter how amusing, was a bit too much for their core audience to reasonably digest. There was an attempt at compromise, a suggestion that if Guthrie were to lighten his performance, perhaps mug and laugh it up, they might consider allowing the performance to be broadcast. "They wanted to make it a satire," Arlo told *Guitar Player*, "but I think the humor is in the song. They weren't interested in what I had to say, but that's cool, that's their trip." That night Cash brought out Arlo, whose pale and triangular face was topped this evening by a crown of curly black hair pressing out from under the brim of a beige cowboy hat. He sang a version of his ever-evolving "The Motorcycle (Significance of the Pickle) Song," "Highway in the Wind," and a gentle new song, "Gabriel's Mother's Hiway Ballad #16 Blues." The program ended with Cash and Guthrie singing the chorus of "Alice's Restaurant" as the credits rolled.[41]

One month later Arlo and Jackie traveled to England. Arlo was to appear at the London Pavilion on Monday, February 9, having agreed to attend a press screening of the *Alice's Restaurant* film, soon to be released to theaters in Great Britain. So many new things were happening to Guthrie that it seemed as if the film was already something from the distant past. Though Arlo wasn't unwilling to promote the motion picture overseas, his experiences with the ballyhoo surrounding the earlier U.S. premiere were mostly sour. He no longer wished to be consumed by the film, agreeing only to promote it in England on his own terms. But United Artists was insistent that he needed to actively "sell" the film to European cinemagoers, telling him that it was essential he did so as most folks on the old continent didn't really understand the concept of the draft. It was Guthrie's idea that in each city he visited, United Artists would put up the money to stage a party of sorts. This would enable Guthrie to not only mingle with members of the press but also with friends, hangers-on, hippies, street people, stoners, and political types, anyone he chose to invite along. Though it seemed a good idea at the time, Guthrie discovered that the antiwar movement sweeping through Europe wasn't the same as the one back home. In the United States, the protests weren't necessarily ideological. The greatest percentage of those in the United States who opposed the war in Vietnam were not bomb-throwing revolutionaries or communists or Ho Chi Minh disciples; the movement was comprised of people of conscience, people of faith, pacifists, and ordinary Americans who thought their country's foreign policy was misguided or illegal. In Europe, the protest movement was ideological and obsessively anti-American in tone. At the press parties, Guthrie's involvement in an expensive Hollywood film was decried by those on the European Left as an outright capitulation to "capitalistic imperialism." Instead of bringing friends and comrades together, the press parties only highlighted the left-factionalism of the movement in England. "Over there the groups were the Che guys, and the Mao guys, and these guys and those guys," Guthrie recalled, and the only middle ground they were able to find was when they decided that "they would all come down on me." Occasionally a mainstream newspaperman would stop by to chat with Arlo about the film, or music, or about the changes in his life. "Now I'm married, my wife is expecting a baby, and I'm absolutely gassed about that," he told *Melody Maker*. "Things are different for me now." Guthrie hadn't planned any concerts in England this time around. Though he admitted he would "love to come back and do some of the same clubs I did before," Guthrie acknowledged that his overseas sorties were rarely profitable. "I never made any money yet in England," he sighed, "and I don't expect I will." He did agree to perform on the popular BBC television music program *Beat Club*, however.[42]

On April 8, 1970, the wire services were reporting that Arlo Guthrie, twenty-two, was "practicing lullabies." Jackie and Arlo were at home in Washington, Massachusetts, celebrating the birth of their first child, a seven-pound son named Abraham. The child and mother were resting comfortably at nearby Fairview Hospital in Great Barrington, where a hospital spokesman relayed the news that both were doing "very well" and that Arlo had been "at the hospital when his child was born." It was a momentous moment for the Guthries, as it would be for any young family. Arlo would later share interesting thoughts on the arrival of his son on a television talk show. He recalled being at the hospital and staring through the protective glass into the row of newborns in the maternity ward. He wasn't surprised that Abraham seemed to recognize him, as Arlo believed that the newborn had already chosen who his parents were to be. Guthrie explained that this was the way it had been for him too, that it was of his own choosing to "make it down" to earth in 1947 following the end of World War II. "I started thinking before I was a kid," Guthrie would philosophically muse to a somewhat puzzled David Frost. "I was up about eight miles in the air. I was hanging out and looking at the world and I said, 'Wow, the war is over. I might as well make it down. . . . So I waited around until one night I caught my parents . . . and I made it down. Now it was possible for me to make it down 'cause they were really in love." He went on to explain that not everyone could "make it down" to earth under the same circumstances, but it was important that he made it down his own way as "in order for me to continue and do my 'number,' I had to go through those channels. I had to live my life. I had to go to the schools I went to. I had to meet the people I met . . . and here I am." Guthrie would reference this belief in one of his best songs, "I Want to Be Around," a bright folk-rocker that closes out his *Washington County* LP. He told Frost that he wrote the song shortly after Abraham's birth when he was "thinking about my kid." "It's not really complicated," Guthrie haltingly allowed. "It's just very hard to explain."[43]

With the ratings winner *Johnny Cash Show* on summer hiatus, ABC television test-piloted a new music and variety program. The replacement show, awkwardly titled *Johnny Cash Presents the Everly Brothers Show*, ran on three consecutive Saturday nights in July. Much in the spirit of the Cash program, the guests of brothers Phil and Don Everly, the 1950s rock-and-country-singing teen idols, were performers who most successfully bridged the disparate worlds of rock 'n' roll and country music. Guthrie appeared on the show's middle episode (broadcast July 15), along with Marty ("El Paso") Robbins and the singer-songwriter Jackie DeShannon. Arlo sang "I Could Be Singing" from his forthcoming *Washington County* LP and paid homage to John Lennon and Paul McCartney by teaming with the Everlys on a duet of the Beatles' "Hey Jude," then a popular song riding high on the Top 40 charts. The show's finale featured Arlo, Phil, and Don singing a medley of Woody Guthrie songs, including "Grand Coulee Dam" and "So Long, It's Been Good to Know Yuh."[44]

On July 22 Guthrie returned to the Schaefer Music Festival at Wollman Rink in Central Park, where he was the top bill in a concert with the Manhattan Transfer. He opened the evening with Merle Haggard's satirical "Okie from Muskogee," now an integral part of his set list, as well as a number of new songs including a cool piano-based rocker titled "Fence Post Blues." One critic from *Billboard* thought Arlo somewhat more "introspective" than usual.[45]

That summer the McGraw-Hill Book Company issued the very first literary biography of Woody Guthrie. Henrietta Yurchenco, an ethnomusicologist, college educator, radio personality, and lifelong leftist, had written a slim but welcome volume titled *A Mighty Hard Road: The Woody Guthrie Story*. Yurchenco had known Woody since the early 1940s, when he, Pete Seeger, Lead Belly, Burl Ives, and Alan Lomax were frequent guests on her radio program on WNYC. With the assistance of her friend Marjorie Guthrie, Yurchenco aimed at the young readers market. Arlo was drafted to supply the book's introduction, and he delivered two short paragraphs to McGraw-Hill. The first explained how "Woody's musical training came from the songs he heard as a kid. Songs about the people who lived before him. Songs about outlaws and lovers and about everything else that was going down when they were written." In the second paragraph, Arlo offered that in 1970 such artists as the Beatles and Bob Dylan were doing much the same as Woody had in the 1930s and 1940s. "Where they get the words and ideas they use to write (these) songs is something they might not even know," Arlo conceded, but "Woody said they came from YOU!"[46]

That summer Guthrie was again teamed with Judy Collins for a series of tandem concerts. On Friday night, July 31, he appeared as the support act for Collins at her Hollywood Bowl concert. Though he would perform some new material and "Coming into Los Angeles," there were a lot of "cover" songs in the set list: Kristofferson's "Me and Bobby McGee," Haggard's "Okie from Muskogee," and no fewer than three from the pen of Bob Dylan. Robert Hilburn of the *Los Angeles Times* could appreciate Arlo's refusal "to rely on his early successes" such as "Alice" or "The Motorcycle Song" to carry him through a performance, but the critic believed that Guthrie's audience was far too willing "to overlook his often repetitious melodies and sometimes uneventful lyrics." Guthrie and Collins were also booked for a multiple-night residency at the Carter Barron Amphitheatre in the suburbs of Washington, DC. The first show of the four-evening double bill began on Thursday evening, August 20. On the final night Guthrie talked at length about the country's "dope crisis." "Anybody can get *on* a plane with marijuana," Guthrie mused. "It takes a pro to get *off* a plane with it." On August 27 Guthrie and Collins ended their month-long tour with a concert at the Garden State Arts Center in Holmdel, New Jersey.[47]

Pete Seeger, Arlo Guthrie, Seals and Croft, and the Evolution Revolution, a quartet of performing chimpanzees, were guests of the Smothers Brothers for their summer ABC-TV replacement show broadcast August 12. Seeger performed "Sailing Down My Golden River" and followed with a cheery, whistling song in tribute to North Vietnamese leader "Uncle" Ho Chi Minh. The latter song, no doubt, rankled network censors, who only a few years earlier had controversially sliced his far more allegorical "Waist Deep in the Big Muddy" from an earlier Smothers Brothers broadcast. Arlo's appearance was less confrontational. He chose to sing "Coming into Los Angeles," "Me and Bobby McGee," and his sly and winking, but otherwise straight, cover of Haggard's counterculture-bashing "Okie from Muskogee."[48]

On Saturday evening, September 12, the Hollywood Bowl hosted a belated West Coast version of 1968's "Musical Tribute to Woody Guthrie." To the disappointment of many, Dylan chose not to participate, but the roster was still impressive: Joan Baez, Ramblin' Jack Elliott, Peter Fonda, Arlo Guthrie, Richie Havens, Country Joe McDonald, Odetta, Earl Robinson, Pete Seeger, and Will Geer. The concert would again benefit Marjorie's Committee to Combat Huntington's Disease. A coproduction of Harold Leventhal and Sight and Sound Productions, the concert was not as well staged as the earlier benefit at Carnegie Hall, nor would the event attract the same level of media attention. The *Los Angeles Times* noted there were "some awkward moments when performers, hampered by the briefest of rehearsals, didn't know what song to sing next or which microphone to use." But that was part of the evening's charm, with the music making and song swapping loose and informal. Guthrie would tell one TV personality that the Hollywood Bowl show was purposefully "set up so that we had all the performers on the stage at the same time . . . and microphones in front of everybody so that if you wanted to sing or play with whoever was up there, you could do that." Arlo opened the evening, chugging away on a Sonny Terry–style harmonica solo of "This Train (Is Bound for Glory)" and performing a near-rock version of "Oklahoma Hills," with Ry Cooder accenting the lead line with his expert bottleneck guitar playing. The concert closed, as always, with the entire cast and audience singing "This Land Is Your Land." That same day Reprise Records took out a full-page advertisement in *Billboard* to announce that the newest Guthrie album, *Washington County* (from "whence he hails these days"), was due soon from the label's "album machine."[49]

On September 22, the eve of the release of *Washington County*, Arlo was a guest (preceded by the "prize winning cats from the recent Westminster Cat Show") on the popular and erudite TV interview program *The David Frost Show*. Guthrie's segment began with a solo acoustic performance of "Coming into Los Angeles." Following the song, Guthrie moved onto the seat beside Frost, and the interviewing began in earnest. Referencing Guthrie's participation in the recent concert at the Hollywood Bowl, Frost asked him if there were any songs of his father's that were personal favorites. "I like the ones that are still relevant," he answered. "I like any kind of art that is, more or less, eternal." He cited the ballad "Tom Joad" as one favorite, suggesting that Woody's song was perhaps more relevant in 1970 than the far better known "This Land Is Your Land." Though Frost prompted Guthrie to perform "Tom Joad," Arlo begged off, agreeing only to perform the ballad's final verse as the lyric demonstrated how the struggle against injustice was continuous. It was Arlo's belief that "Tom Joad" clearly established his father's awareness that he wasn't just "somebody that came in in 1912 and went out in 1967." In his songs Woody managed to leave a "part of himself that is eternal. . . . That he's become part of that struggle, and that until it's done, *he's* not done." Frost asked Guthrie to further extrapolate on the true nature of that struggle.

Arlo explained that Woody's songs documented an era in the United States when "the masses" were militant, striking and demanding more from the bosses, fighting for fair wages and benefits. It was true that those who fought on the front lines for such workingman ideals won some of those battles. The problem was that their radicalism began to fray once they slipped into a comfortable self-existence. They became complacent, and, in Guthrie's estimation, "forgot [what] they went through. . . . All the unions that are around today started like that, pretty much, and the cops were beating them up and the governors were sending in the troops." What was most disturbing to him was that in 1970 it was "these same guys [who] are putting down the kids for doing the same thing." The struggle was continuous and without end as "people change sides very quickly." He insisted that Woody "wasn't concerned with unions because he liked *unions*. . . . He was concerned [that] unions became a mechanism for the evolvement of mankind." Though *Look* magazine had already attached the title of "successful anarchist" to Arlo, the younger Guthrie begged off on any such labeling: "I'm not a Democrat or a Republican or a liberal or a this or a that," he told Frost. "I agree with a lot of the things that specific people say—not many. But if it seems to me that it really helps, I'm for it. And if it doesn't seem to me that it does anything except prolong these times, I'm not for it."

In a new song from *Washington County*, "I Could Be Singing," Guthrie sang confidently that "the new world is coming together." This idea that the world was going to change soon, and for the better, was not some sort of "We Shall Overcome"–type abstraction. It was already happening, he assured Frost: "The world is starting to move very quickly, because we're trying to get somewhere. All of a sudden, we have an idea of where it is that we want to go. And that came about with all the drug scenes and all of that, and we've slowly, kind of, *evolved*. We saw what was possible." There were people, and governments, trying to derail these changes, but Guthrie was certain that history would not be on their side.

> A lot of people [are] saying, "Well, it's moving too fast, put on the brakes," not realizing that the world doesn't stop. It doesn't stop for Spiro. It doesn't stop for "Tricky Dick." It doesn't stop for *any* of those guys. The world goes on. The things they suppress they really can't hold down, so they send in the troops: which is the same thing that was going on twenty years ago . . . except it was a different specific.

The conversation with Frost began to muddle somewhat when Guthrie attempted to explain the concept of "evolving God." "We're going into an era of the world that is not confined by the traditional culture," Guthrie offered. "It's more. . . . Like a moth is attracted to a lightbulb, most of the young kids are feeling a kind of attraction [to] a higher rate of exchanging energy. . . . We are evolving God." It was at this point that Frost asked his guest to explain such terminology as "exchanging energy," resulting in a somewhat winding, convoluted discussion. Guthrie attempted to explain that young people really don't have to talk to one another in words, that their rate of "exchanging energy" was so great that they already knew what each other was thinking, that their communication was mostly silent, that the process of speech itself was a roadblock to an exchange of energy. "Since we're on television," Frost pointed out, "that might be a bit boring." Guthrie's "evolving God" reference, on the other hand, was never really explained to his satisfaction.

When the subject of America's urban unrest was brought up, Guthrie answered defiantly:

> When a whole bunch of black dudes is burning up the town, it's their town they're burning and they're burning it 'cause they don't like it that way. . . . Right? 'Cause it's been that way for a long time and it's a drag. So they're burning it down. When you send the troops in and stop all that, what you end up with is more angry people and a little more "weird" town, a bad place to be. I would almost rather that we wipe all these towns out that are real bummers for people to live in, and we started using all the money we're spending on airplanes and war and stuff like that and really build some places for people to *live*. Then we wouldn't have people wanting to burn it down anymore.

"The real anger and anguish," Frost countered, "comes when people burn down *other* people's places."[50]

The night, following his hour-long chat with David Frost, Arlo was on the television sets of America again, this time as a returning guest on the *Johnny Cash Show*. This time Guthrie would share the Ryman stage with celebrities Ray Charles and Liza Minnelli. The segment began with Cash strumming and singing through a single verse and chorus of Woody's "Oklahoma Hills," the camera pulling back to reveal the composer's son strumming along off screen. The cameras closed in on him, but Guthrie appeared less enthusiastic about being on the program this time around, his face solemn and bordering on grim. In contrast to his previous appearance, Guthrie wasn't plying the tools of a method actor. He had forsaken the cowboy hat and western jacket worn at his first appearance in January. Under a flowing crown of curly hair, Guthrie looked very much a man of his time, stylishly attired in a bright blue satin shirt. Directly following "Oklahoma Hills," Arlo performed two new songs from the forthcoming *Washington County* LP: his own "I Could Be Singing" and the mountain gospel song "Valley to Pray." He performed the former on acoustic guitar with Cash's studio band backing him off screen, and the latter while sitting behind a grand piano, the Statler Brothers and

Carter Family Singers singing along on the chorus. He finally cracked a smile at the very end of his segment.

The recent spate of Guthrie sightings on television was no accident. The promotional department of Warner Bros./Reprise was setting the stage for the release of *Washington County*. Released at the tail end of October, the album entered the *Billboard* LP chart on November 7 in position 180. By the second week the LP had moved an incredible 113 places, slipping into position 67. The upward trend was more incremental afterward, and five weeks following its release, *Washington County* would peak at position 33, though sales remained strong. It would remain in the Top 200 for seventeen weeks, staying on the charts through the very last week of February 1971. *Washington County* fared well on the *Cash Box* charts too, peaking in position 29 and staying on for a fourteen-week ride.[51]

The critical reception to the lovely and folksy *Washington County* LP was mostly positive. Lynn Van Matre of the *Chicago Tribune* welcomed the new album as a soothing antidote to the "grating electronic accompaniment" that "marred" *Running Down the Road*. "Arlo's doffed the mantle of hip, groovy, like-wow younger generation spokesman and has gone back to more or less being a folk singer. . . . After all the ruffles and motorcycles, Arlo's back on the folk trail in his blue jeans, and they fit him very well." *Billboard* opined that "Guthrie continues to be one of the most in tune artists of today's youth" with *Washington County* sure to be "another winner." *Billboard* also selected the first single from the LP, "Valley to Pray," as an "Action" record, with stirrings of a regional, if not national, breakout. The "Valley to Pray" 45 was poised to crack the *Billboard* Hot 100 singles chart, sitting in position 102. The single made its debut on the *Cash Box* chart on October 31, where it stayed for four weeks, peaking at position 84. But not every outlet was enjoying Guthrie's return to the country. *Rolling Stone* blasted the album as "the nadir of the abyss . . . mediocre mass-manufactured-sounding 'country rock.'" They couldn't have been more wrong.[52]

## NOTES

1. Paul D. Zimmerman, "Alice's Restaurant's Children," *Newsweek*, September 29, 1969, 103; *Billboard*, December 21, 1968, 16.

2. Edwin Miller, "Spotlight: The Hollywood Scene," *Seventeen*, February 1969, 54.

3. Jeff Mitchel, "Music Echo: Arlo, Santana at X," *News-Record*, October 7, 1969, 18; Susan Braudy, "As Arlo Guthrie Sees It . . . Kids Are Groovy, Adults Aren't," *New York Times Sunday Magazine*, April 27, 1969, 56ff.; Jeff Mitchel, "Arlo," *News-Record*, February 28, 1969, 8.

4. "Random Notes," *Rolling Stone*, May 3, 1969, 4; Jeff Tamarkin, "Arlo Guthrie at 50," *discoveries*, no. 111 (August 1997): 45; Arlo Guthrie, *This Is the Arlo Guthrie Book* (New York: Amsco Music Publishing), 1969, 4.

5. "Random Notes," *Rolling Stone*, May 3, 1969, 4.

6. *The Johnny Carson Show*, broadcast May 27, 1969.

7. "Fish," "New Acts," *Variety*, July 2, 1969, 60; Joe Klein, "Notes on a Native Son," *Rolling Stone*, March 10, 1977, 55; "A Joyful Happening," *Time*, October 17, 1969, 66.

8. Thomas Willis, "Mississippi River Festival Opens Friday at Edwardsville," *Chicago Tribune*, June 15, 1969, sec. 5, 9–10; "Weekend TV Key," *Pittsburgh Post-Gazette*, August 2, 1969, 23.

9. Michael Lang with Holly George Warren, *The Road to Woodstock: From the Man behind the Legendary Festival* (New York: Ecco/HarperCollins), 2009, 83; Jan A. Maas, "Troubadour for Our Times," *New York Sunday News*, November 16, 1969, 13.

10. Nathan Cobb, "Arlo at South Shore Makes You Smile," *Boston Globe*, July 14, 1969, 15.

11. *Newport Folk Festival—1969* (program), ed. James K. Rooney (Concert Hall Productions, 1969), 22.

12. Craig Stinson, "Newport's Folk Festival Scores with Varied Acts," *Billboard*, August 9, 1969, 32.

13. Louise Sweeney, "Arthur Penn: 'No Preconceptions,'" *Christian Science Monitor*, August 8, 1969, 4; Paul D. Zimmerman, "Alice's Restaurant's Children," 104; Saul Braun, "Alice & Ray & Yesterday's Flowers," *Playboy* 16, no. 10 (October 1969), 142.

14. Joe Klein, *Woody Guthrie: A Life* (New York: Alfred A. Knopf, 1980), 442.

15. "Arlo at Ipswich," *Boston Globe*, August 2, 1969, 10; "Television Previews," *St. Petersburg Independent*, August 12, 1969, 9B.

16. Michael Lang with Holly George Warren, *The Road to Woodstock: From the Man behind the Legendary Festival*, 191–92.

17. Michael Lang with Holly George Warren, *The Road to Woodstock: From the Man behind the Legendary Festival*, 192; Thelma Tharp, "Arlo Guthrie's Gamble," *Sarasota Herald-Tribune/Family Weekly*, April 12, 1970, 28–29.

18. Jan A. Maas, "Troubadour for Our Times," 13.

19. Michael Steinberg, "Under the Marquee," *Boston Globe*, August 17, 1969, 28A; Fred Kirby, "From the Music Capitals of the World: New York," *Billboard*, September 6, 1969, 34.

20. Peter Z. Perault, "Alice's Restaurant World Premiere Attracts 1500," *Boston Globe*, August 20, 1969, 29.

21. Charles Champlin, "'Restaurant' Based on Guthrie Song," *Los Angeles Times*, August 26, 1969, D1; Vincent Canby, "Our Time: Arlo and Chicago," *New York Times*, August 31, 1969, D1. An overview of the critical reception that greeted the release of the *Alice's Restaurant* motion picture can be found in the "Alice's Restaurant" entry in the American Film Institute's *filmfacts* 12, no. 13 (1969), 289–93.

22. "8-Track Tapes—Ready *Now*—100% Fill from the Tape Company That Delivers Today" (Warner Bros. advertisement supplement), *Billboard*, August 23, 1969.

23. Paul D. Zimmerman, "Alice's Restaurant Children," 102; Chas. Burton, "Record Reviews," *Rolling Stone*, December 27, 1969, 58, 60; Warner Bros./Reprise Records advertisement, *Sing Out!* 19, no. 4 (Winter 1969/1970), 30; Mickey Friedman, "Record Reviews," *Sing Out!* 19, no. 5 (March/April 1970), 47; Don Heckman, "Nyro, Donovan, Zappa and More," *New York Times*, November 9, 1969, D36.

24. Karl Dallas, "Arlo—Trying to Escape from Alice's Restaurant," *Melody Maker*, February 21, 1970, 9.

25. "Arlo's Mother Pleads for Disease Cure," *New York Times*, September 26, 1969, G21; Thelma Tharp, "Arlo Guthrie's Gamble," 28–29. Arlo Guthrie, "Despite the Shadow of His Father's (and Possibly His Own) Deadly Disease, a Folk Hero Celebrates Life," *People Weekly* 28, no. 10 (September 7, 1987); Joe Klein, "Notes on a Native Son," *Rolling Stone*, March 10, 1977, 55.

26. David Taylor, "3000 Fans 'Bubble' over Arlo," *Boston Globe*, September 29, 1969, 15.

27. Fred Ferretti, "Arlo Guthrie Weds in Berkshire Meadow," *New York Times*, October 10, 1969, 34; "A Joyful Happening," 66.

28. Fred Ferretti, "Arlo Guthrie Weds in Berkshire Meadow," 34; "A Joyful Happening," 66.

29. *David Frost Show*, broadcast September 22, 1970.

30. B. J. Phillips, "Arlo Solo—Without His Bride," *Washington Post*, October 11, 1969, E1; Jeff Mitchel, "Music Echo: Arlo, Santana at X," *News-Record*, October 7, 1969, 18.

31. Gregory McDonald, "Rap-Up," *Boston Globe*, November 19, 1969, 49; Gregory McDonald, "Arlo Always Liked Playing Solo," *Boston Globe*, March 18, 1970, 14; Bob Atkinson, "Book Reviews," *Sing Out!* 19, no. 6 (June/July 1970), 41.

32. Patricia Bosworth, "Mrs. Guthrie: 'Kids Know Arlo's Still Searching,'" *New York Times*, September 28, 1969, D15; Saul Braun, "Alice & Ray & Yesterday's Flowers," 120.

33. WBAI (Pacifica Radio) Moratorium live broadcast, November 15, 1969; *Night Cap—Conversation on the Arts and Letters* with Studs Terkel and Calvin Trillen, Arts Network (cable), broadcast May 7, 1983.

34. Mel Gussow, "Arlo: Kids Want to Be Free," *New York Times*, January 11, 1970, 81.

35. Lynn Van Matre, "Arlo Lets 'Em Down," *Chicago Tribune*, November 23, 1969, sec. 1A, 6; Ed Robbin, *Woody Guthrie and Me: An Intimate Reminiscence* (Berkeley: Lancaster-Miller, 1979), 125.

36. Mike Jahn, "Love Tales Sung by Arlo Guthrie," *New York Times*, December 27, 1969, C14; "Jeff," "Arlo Guthrie, Carnegie Hall, N.Y.," *Variety*, December 31, 1969, 34.

37. "Newsmakers," *Los Angeles Times*, January 4, 1970, A; Mel Gussow, "Arlo: 'Kids Want to Be Free,'" 81.

38. J. Anthony Lukas, "Song by Guthrie Barred at Trial," *New York Times*, January 16, 1970, 10.

39. J. Anthony Lukas, "Song by Guthrie Barred at Trial," 10; "Arlo Guthrie's Tune Livens Chicago Trial (AP)," *Sarasota Journal*, January 16, 1970, 2; "Chicago

Court Entertained by Guthrie (UPI)," *Times-News* (Hendersonville, NC), January 16, 1970, 3; Richard T. Cooper, "Guthrie and 'Alice' Liven Chicago Trial," *Los Angeles Times*, January 16, 1970, 4; Karl Dallas, "Arlo—Trying to Escape from Alice's Restaurant," 9.

40. J. Anthony Lukas, "Song by Guthrie Barred at Trial," 10.

41. "Guthrie Analyses Country Music," *Variety*, January 21, 1970, 53; Pete Seeger, "Johnny Appleseed, Jr.," *Sing Out!* 20, no. 2 (November/December 1970), 23; Michael Brooks, "Woody and Arlo," *Guitar Player* 5, no. 5 (August 1971), 35.

42. "Caught in the Act," *Melody Maker*, February 14, 1970, 14; Karl Dallas, "Arlo—Trying to Escape from Alice's Restaurant," 9; Susan Brewster, "The Coop Interview: Arlo Guthrie," *Coop/Fast Folk Musical Magazine* 1, no. 8 (September 1982), 26.

43. "News of the Day," *Los Angeles Times*, April 8, 1970, part 1, 2; "Singer Arlo, Lullabyist," *Washington Post*, April 10, 1970, C4.

44. "Television Previews: Arlo Guthrie Guest of Everlys," *Eugene Register-Guard*, July 15, 1970, 7E.

45. Fred Kirby, "Arlo Guthrie, Central Park, New York," *Billboard*, August 1, 1970, 22.

46. Henrietta Yurchenco, assisted by Marjorie Guthrie, *A Mighty Hard Road: The Woody Guthrie Story* (New York: McGraw-Hill, 1970), 7; Douglas Martin, "Henrietta Yurchenco, 91, Pioneer Folklorist," *New York Times*, December 14, 2007, A39.

47. Robert Hilburn, "Collins, Guthrie at Bowl," *Los Angeles Times*, August 3, 1970, sec. IV, 1, 18; Tom Zito, "Guthrie, Collins in Superb Concert," *Washington Post*, August 21, 1970, B1.

48. "TV Previews: Pete Seeger on Smothers Show at 10," *Eugene-Register-Guard*, August 12, 1970, 8B; "Television," *New York Times*, August 12, 1970, 83.

49. "Tribute to Guthrie Will Be a Benefit," *Los Angeles Times*, August 30, 1970, D13; Robert Hilburn, "Tribute to Woody Guthrie," *Los Angeles Times*, September 14, 1970, E1; "The Mo Ostin Experience" (advertisement), *Billboard*, September 12, 1970, 7.

50. "Television," *New York Times*, September 22, 1970, 91.

51. Frank Hoffman and George Albert, *The Cash Box Album Charts, 1955–1974* (Metuchen, NJ, and London: Scarecrow Press, 1988), 155.

52. Lynn Van Matre, "Sound: Neil Young's Strange Vocal Gymnastics," *Chicago Tribune*, October 18, 1970, sec. 5, 4; "Album Reviews," *Billboard*, October 24, 1970, 57; Pat Downey, George Albert, and Frank Hoffman, *Cash Box: Pop Singles Charts, 1950–1993* (Englewood, CO: Libraries Unlimited, 1994), 147; Ed Ward, "Record Reviews," *Rolling Stone*, November 26, 1970, 38.

## Chapter Four

# Somebody Turned On the Light

On January 20, 1971, Guthrie traveled to Houston, Texas, in a show of support for Pacifica station KPFT-FM. The underground countercultural radio station was planning to resume broadcast operations following not one but *two* bombings of its transmitter the previous year, each blast effectively knocking the station off the air for long stretches of time. Guthrie had a reason to take the first bombing of May 12, 1970, personally. KPFT was in the midst of a broadcast of "Alice's Restaurant" when the first bomb went off, violently suspending the talking blues. KPFT staffer Linda Todd told a UPI reporter, "Our transmitter was just leveled. It was very well done. It went off right on the dot at 11 P.M. exactly. We were playing 'Alice's Restaurant' and Arlo Guthrie was yelling '*Kill, kill, kill*' on the record just as we went off the air." If the crime itself wasn't bad enough, local authorities didn't seem all that motivated to find those responsible. Following a second bombing on October 6, the beleaguered station manager, Lawrence Lee, told members of the press that KPFT would not be revealing "the location of the new transmitter." The plight of KPFT soon went nationwide, and as this was a classic free-speech issue there was an outpouring of support among media colleagues. One hundred members of the National Educational Radio Network, fifteen commercial and noncommercial TV networks, and the Canadian Broadcasting Corporation were planning to converge on Houston to cover and celebrate the station's January 20 relaunch.[1]

That afternoon, Guthrie, surrounded by a sea of KPFT supporters and reporters, stepped up to the microphone. "We were doing a rehearsal, *kind of*, before," Guthrie drawled,

> and I was kind of thinking about the fact that I've never been blown up . . . but I've been bombed before. So I thought about it, like, "Wow, that's far out."

I mean bombs are an old tradition. They have quite a long history and I was thinking about all the, kind of, historic bombings that went on in the world. . . . I mean . . . *suppose* they *always* had bombs. I mean, Cain could have bombed Abel. They could have bombed Christ. It would have been a little different. . . . It's amazing to me. . . . Everybody in this room pretty much knows. . . . I mean, you could look at a guy. . . . I mean, you could look at yourself first, right? And you could say, "Wow, I'm the guy that gets *bombed*, man. People go around and they *bomb* me." And you can recognize the bomber. . . . The thing that's so incredible is that you couldn't have a . . . *bomber* without the *bomb-ee*. . . . That may be where the trouble lies, [but] I'm not really sure about that. It's like. . . . Cops recognize robbers and robbers recognize cops. . . . What a great union there is between those people and people who are absolutely indifferent. So I was sitting in West Palm Beach yesterday—this is in Florida—and I said, "Wow, I'm gonna go over to Houston. What am I going to do there?" I mean, maybe somebody will bomb me. . . . I didn't have any songs about bombs or nothing like that, so I had to write one. . . . I'd like you to sing it with me, 'cause it's kind of [a] "mass" bomb song.

Playing a gentle chord progression on his twelve-string guitar, Guthrie tilted into his new song written for the occasion:

> You get bombed
> I get bombed
> All God's children get bombed.
> When I get to Houston
> Pull out my strings
> Walk to the station, you can hear me sing . . .
> You get bombed
> I get bombed
> All God's children get bombed.

The song recognized that the "bomb-ees," rather than the bombers, were the true American patriots, that the staff at KPFT was holding the moral high ground. American revolutionary Patrick Henry, "with his long hair blowing in the morning breeze . . . said 'Give me liberty, or bomb me, please,'" is aligned with the radio rebels and not the cowardly bombers. The song concludes with the warning to the bombers, "Remember the story 'bout the mob Christ calmed / He said, 'You stone that lady, and you'll all get bombed.'"[2]

Guthrie's gentle strum-through of the "Bombing Song" would be featured on the third installment of WNET-TV's program *The Great American Dream Machine*, a ninety-minute-long news "magazine of the air," hosted by writer-broadcaster Studs Terkel. The focus of nearly half of the program was the twin bombings of station KPFT "to the accompaniment of acute municipal indifference." "Arlo Guthrie is a sort of subversive angel: he would joy-ride with Lucifer," opined critic John Leonard in his review of the PBS documentary, but he regretted that not even Woody's son "was capable of snatching joy from the jaws of tedium" of *The Great American Dream Machine*.[3]

Soon after, Arlo traveled to Chicago for two shows at the Quiet Knight at 953 West Belmont. The nightclub was owned by Richard Harding, the former owner of Poor Richards, the venue where Guthrie had gotten his Midwest start in the early winter of 1966. He was scheduled to perform on the weekend of January 23 and 24, and it was during that engagement that Harding introduced Guthrie to an aspiring Chicago-area songwriter-guitarist named Steve Goodman. Goodman promised to buy the reluctant folk singer a beer if he would listen to him audition a song or two. One of those songs was "City of New Orleans," titled after a passenger train linking Chicago and New Orleans that was now threatened with being taken off the line. Though Goodman was as yet unrecorded, his pleasant train song had achieved some small notoriety in the Chicago area due to occasional airplay of a tape recording the songwriter had made for the *Midnight Special* program on WFMT. Goodman was hoping that Guthrie might use his celebrity status to deliver the song to his friend Johnny Cash, but as Arlo wasn't planning on seeing the country-music star anytime soon, he wisely decided to keep the song for himself.[4]

Though *Washington County* was still on the *Billboard* charts in the early winter of 1971, sales were beginning to trail off, and the album's last sighting was on February 27. That same month Reprise chose to issue a single of a non-LP song of Guthrie's titled "Ballad of Tricky Fred," an uncharacteristic funky rock song in the style of Warner Bros. label mate Little Feat. (The band had been in the studio in late summer 1970 recording their first album, and their drummer, Richie Hayward, was a featured player on both the *Running Down the Road* and *Washington County* sessions.) Propelled by horns and Ry Cooder's funky lead guitar, the single starts off with a bang, Guthrie warning, "Oooh, mama, there's a gun at your back!" But this was one of the rare occasions when Guthrie's lyric was totally subservient to the rollicking music; the listener never really learns what was going down when blackjack-dealing "Tricky Fred" is brought down by police brandishing "tear gas and bully clubs." As Warner Bros. publicist Barry Hansen (a former columnist for the *Little Sandy Review* and "Dr. Demento" of radio fame) would note, "Only the climax of the tale is told here, leaving the details to your imagination. The effect is cryptic, but electric." The single didn't receive all that much attention, but the editors at *Billboard* thought it had potential, writing, "Clever rhythm material, penned and performed by the artist, should bring him to the best selling charts in a hurry." This single would be one of the more unusual releases of Guthrie's career, as the B-side of the 45, "Shackles and Chains," a tuneful cover of the old hillbilly song, had also yet to be issued on LP. Warner

Bros. would eventually include "The Ballad of Tricky Fred" on *The Days of Wine and Vinyl* (PRO 540, 1972), one in a series of handsome and collectible "Loss Leader" gatefold album sets. Hansen mused that "The Ballad of Tricky Fred" had been previously left off "Arlo's albums not because of any shortcomings, real or imagined, but perhaps because its sound is a bit different from that which Arlo fills his consistently best-selling LPs."[5]

Guthrie's popular song "Coming into Los Angeles" wasn't faring so well either. In the early hours of Thursday morning, March 11, a Philadelphia DJ was fired on the air for spinning the 45. Steve Leon, an overnight DJ on station WDAS-FM, was removed from the control room when a wary "station executive," identified as either a brother-in-law or his own father (there were differing reports), deemed that the song, with its blatant reference to "bringing in a couple of keys," was an obvious glorification of drug smuggling. Several months earlier, the Federal Communications Commission (FCC) had sent out a vaguely worded "public notice" to radio station mangers that any song glorifying drug use should be excised from their playlists, effectively forcing station mangers to nervously and overcautiously act as their own censors.[6]

That March Arlo was scheduled to set out on the first half of an extensive cross-country tour, supported by the country-bayou-rock band Swampwater. The musical partnership traced its beginnings to the previous autumn, when Guthrie shared a brief tour with an up-and-coming singer named Linda Ronstadt. Following her tenure as the vocalist of the folk-rock band the Stone Poneys, Ronstadt had recently transformed from rock 'n' roller to tuneful country-singing chanteuse. Swampwater was engaged as the singer's instrumental support, and the band easily delivered the down-home musical goods for her, capably providing Ronstadt with all the necessary country and western trimmings. But the greatest strength of the Louisiana-based outfit was their mesh of danceable Cajun and bayou rhythms with fiddle- and pedal-steel guitar–driven country-rock. The musicians, including Gib Guilbeau on fiddle and John Beland on guitar, were so multitalented that, in Guthrie's estimation, they were capable of switching "all their instruments around and still sound great, or they could get up on stage with anybody and sound as if they had been playing with that same person for years." Guthrie would recall that "the best thing" about the autumn 1970 tour with Ronstadt was not the gigs themselves but "rather before the gigs as we were tuning up and after the gigs when we were sitting around and playing together." To offset the monotony of a string of one-night stands (or, in Guthrie's term, as the "road got longer"), he and members of Swampwater would break out their instruments and jam together whenever circumstance allowed. It was Guthrie's estimation that some of the best and freshest music of the tour was made backstage prior to shows or in otherwise grim hotel rooms. At the final show of the tour in Sacramento, and with Ronstadt's blessing, Guthrie and Swampwater decided at the sound check that they would perform a total of five songs together that night, the ones they had worked out to satisfaction during their motel-room sessions. The experiment went almost *too* well as the Guthrie-Swampwater segment was received so rapturously that, to maintain the night's high-energy momentum, the concept of top bill/support act had to be abandoned. As Arlo recalled, "Linda did some songs, and I did some, and then to everyone's surprise, Swampwater did some songs and the place was bouncin' around and having an incredible time, and it was about the most best and beautiful time I ever had on stage." The excitement couldn't last long. As Guthrie later remembered, "Linda and I worked together a lot . . . and we shared the band. The problem was that they didn't work unless Linda or I worked." This would become a pressing problem when Ronstadt began to tour with a lighter-touch, less mossy band that would later evolve into the Eagles. Guthrie enjoyed working with Swampwater, and their subsequent U.S. tour of 1971 would be remembered by fans as one of the greatest. But Guthrie knew from the beginning that he would be unable to carry the responsibility of keeping the band gainfully employed. He told writer Marty Gallanter that "it wasn't really feasible [economically] because I didn't work enough for them to support themselves."[7]

The first leg of the 1971 Arlo Guthrie–Swampwater tour began with a half-rehearsal, half-performance at the Miami Beach Convention Hall on March 26. Several days later, on Wednesday evening, March 31, Guthrie and the band (abetted by *Washington County* producer John Pilla on guitar) were on stage at Carnegie Hall. Swampwater opened the night's set with a fiery showcase of Gib Guilbeau's fiddle-driven bayou-flavored country-rock. Arlo's concert segment, on the other hand, was by most press accounts, including that of *New York Times* critic Mike Jahn, "more easygoing than usual, though that might be hard to imagine." This sentiment was echoed by the *Village Voice* critic, who thought the concert wonderful but took Arlo at his word when he scoffed on stage, "I'd just as soon be picking in my living room." There was a general feeling that the musical program was unfolding spontaneously on stage. *Billboard* scribe Nancy Erlich thought that Guthrie and Swampwater were natural compatriots: "At Carnegie Hall . . . they sounded as if they had been spending many days together playing music for the love of it, which they had." Nearly everyone agreed that, to their surprise, Guthrie's segment of the concert was as much a country and western revue as a program of folk songs. Songs by Merle Haggard ("Okie from Muskogee"), Dylan ("Don't Think Twice, It's All Right" and "You Ain't Going Nowhere"), and Kris Kristofferson ("Me and Bobby McGee"), were all given a respectful Nashville treatment, with Jahn noting that Arlo was showing "a bit of the influence of Jack Elliot [*sic*] in some of his country songs." He didn't ignore his own material, of course. The recently controversial "Coming into Los Angeles" was performed, as was the whimsical "Ring-around-a-Rosy Rag." But there was a palpable feeling among the crowd that Arlo's mind was elsewhere, that he would have rather been anywhere but on stage. "I might not do this anymore. It's too weird," Arlo would tell the audience at one point during the concert. Jim Dickinson, Swampwater's piano player, would later tell a journalist that the Carnegie Hall gig had been a difficult one for Guthrie. Dickinson mused that Arlo was of the mind that he had failed to "communicate with the kids" due to the constant catcalls of "a bunch of fried-out 'Ripple winos' in the audience."[8]

On Friday evening, April 2, Guthrie and Swampwater rolled into Boston for a performance at Symphony Hall. The sight and sound of southern musicians assisting the Coney Island–born Guthrie on such instruments as pedal steel guitar and fiddle caused the critic from the *Boston Globe* to wryly suggest, "One had to blink his eyes a few times to reassure himself he wasn't watching 'Hayloft Jamboree.'" But though Guthrie may have "gone country" in musical style, his political sensibilities remained unchanged. Following his performance of "Okie from Muskogee," Guthrie surprised fans when he described Merle Haggard as "a political Neanderthal who writes incredible songs." The *Globe* reviewer seemed to agree with his press colleagues in New York City that Arlo's segment of the program "came across a bit too mechanical," winning the crowd over "more on Charisma than on merit." On Saturday, the band traveled to Hartford, Connecticut, for a show on April 3 at the Bushnell Memorial Auditorium. The *Hartford Courant* described the hour-long concert as a "low key evening of country style music," with Guthrie mostly deferring "from his extended raps, a former trademark." The set list wasn't all that different from the Carnegie Hall and Boston gigs, but Guthrie did slot in an early cover of Steve Goodman's "City of New Orleans," which the *Courant* described, with astute premonition, as "a superb train song." There was also, as in Manhattan, a continual back-and-forth banter between Guthrie and an increasingly vocal audience. The Hartford crowd was only blessed with a single encore, and though there were cries begging for "Alice's Restaurant" and a handful of other old favorites, Guthrie responded with disinterest, "Good luck. . . . That stuff is on the albums. If you want that stuff, you know where to find it." Afterwards, the tour rolled on with shows in White Plains, New York (April 10); Denver, Colorado (April 15); Seattle (April 16); Corvallis, Oregon (April 17); San Jose, California (April 19); and Pasadena, California (April 23).[9]

A month following the end of the first leg of the Arlo Guthrie–Swampwater tour, the trades reported that Arlo had "recorded several of his recent concert appearances for his first live concert LP for Warner Bros./Reprise. Lenny Waronker of Warner Bros./Reprise supervised the recording sessions." There was obvious interest from the label that Guthrie's fifth album might be a live recording, and several concerts were taped with that intent in mind. The proposed album with Swampwater would not, unfortunately, see the light of day. On the eve of the release of his 1972 follow-up to *Washington County*, the studio-crafted *Hobo's Lullaby*, Guthrie recalled, "We were originally going to do a live album. We taped a lot of live gigs and started working on it, and wound up with this somehow."[10]

Arlo's music continued to appear in the most unusual places. On Sunday evening, April 18, TV viewers tuning into the Paul Newman–narrated feature *Once upon a Wheel* on ABC-TV were treated to an exciting soundtrack that included the Association, Cher, Kenny Rogers and the Fifth Edition, Wilson Pickett, James Taylor, Neil Young, and Arlo Guthrie. The one-hour documentary examined the history of such motor sports as the Indy 500, drag racing, NASCAR, and the Formula 1 racing scene. The program was partly sponsored by the Coca-Cola Company, and for a brief time following the broadcast fans of the program could send away six bottle caps and $2.75 in cash for a "special offer" cassette tape or eight-track cartridge of the film's soundtrack.

On July 14, Woody Guthrie's fifty-ninth birthday, Marjorie and Arlo pulled into Woody's dusty hometown of Okemah, Oklahoma. In the past the majority of Okemah's residents weren't terribly anxious to claim Woody as one of their own. This was a very insular community, politically conservative and overwhelmingly Christian. Woody's alleged communist sympathies (and the ideology's attendant atheism) had made him anathema to most; few townspeople were aware that Jesus Christ, who tended to the needs of the poor and drove the bankers from the temple, was one of Woody's heroes. Those in Okemah determined to not see the town embrace their native son argued that to celebrate Woody's legacy would be an insult to the memory of three young men from the community who had died in Vietnam. It was a struggle that was to be repeated time and again. Was Woody Guthrie an American patriot or a treasonous subversive? There were some local people who thought it was time to embrace Woody's legacy, and as early as September 1965, the General Study Club of Okemah began to examine how the town might celebrate Woody's significant contribution to American culture. To that end they arranged to have Woody's sister, Mrs. Hulett (Mary Jo) Edgmon, a lifelong resident, share some memories of her brother at a meeting of the local study club. But Guthrie's fans and defenders soon learned that resistance to any sort of acknowledgment was still too great. The Guthrie family tried again, sometime around the time of Woody's passing in 1967, with Marjorie offering to donate some LPs and books to the Okemah Public Library. The offer of materials was rebuffed.[11]

Then, on the occasion of Woody's fifty-ninth birthday, there was a small fracture in the impasse. Mrs. V. K. Chowning, Okemah's librarian, spearheaded a committee to organize a memorial concert that would feature the popular country and western singer Jimmie Driftwood. The concert was to be staged at Okemah's Mummer's Theater, and Chowning quietly invited Marjorie to the event. On July 14 she arrived in town, along with Arlo, his wife Jackie, and their one-year-old son Abraham (whom Arlo would identify to the press only as "Creepers"). The committee, in the description of the Times Wire Service, hosted a "secret luncheon" with the Guthrie family. "We're not ashamed about having them here," Mrs. Chowning said, apologizing for the veil of secrecy, "but we're doing it quietly and asking people not to tell about it until they're away and safe." Marjorie and Arlo met with a number of residents sympathetic to their efforts, and these "discussions resulted in the establishment of the Woody Guthrie Okemah Memorial Committee." That same afternoon Arlo traveled to his father's boyhood home, known by the locals as the New London house, and stood on what remained of the rickety front porch. He surveyed the sleepy little town where Woody remained, sadly, an unwelcome guest. In the end the library accepted the Guthrie family's gift of books and record albums, promising to place them on a special "Woody Guthrie shelf," and Arlo would share the Mummer's stage that night with Driftwood and other local musicians, performing before an audience of 2,500 fans—not necessarily locals—who wanted to share their support. It was a beginning. In October 1972 the committee would achieve its first big victory when Okemah's town council, by a vote of four to one, chose to have the legend "Home of Woody Guthrie" painted on the town's brand-new 105-foot water tower. The lone vote of dissent was cast by board member Allison Kelly, who was, to no one's surprise, a banker.[12]

The second leg of the cross-country Arlo Guthrie–Swampwater concerts (with "Special Guest, Ry Cooder," a Reprise/Warner Bros. label mate, assisting on mandolin) was scheduled to begin in late autumn. The first four shows were at the Main Point, in Bryn Mawr, Pennsylvania, beginning October 28 and lasting through Halloween. Afterwards, the tour visited the Proctor Theater, Troy, New York (November 2); Maryland's Frederick Community College (November 6); and the Music Hall in Cincinnati, Ohio (November 7).

It was then on to Florida. On Thursday evening, November 11, Guthrie and the band performed at the Fort Hesterly Armory in Tampa. Though the show was scheduled for 8:00 p.m., Guthrie didn't amble out on stage until nearly 9:30, making fans in attendance at the far-from-sold-out gig restless from the outset. A local music critic from the *St. Petersburg Times* thought the concert a mixed success and the long wait for the main artist to show "a drag." Describing Guthrie's strengths as his "nasal twang and simple renditions of other people's hits," critic Mary Nic Schenk was dismayed that his foggy stage "conversation with the late teen, jean-clad audience centered (mostly) on dope." The surviving audience tape of this concert confirms that, at times, Arlo's druggy monologues would not have been out of place in a vintage Cheech and Chong routine. Musically, his shows were still demonstrating a strong country and western flavor, with Ry Cooder's superb mandolin playing bringing a tasteful bluegrass sensibility to the proceedings. But Arlo was also beginning to slot his program with material that would be featured on the upcoming Reprise album due out in early summer of 1972. "This is a tune from our next hit album," is the way that Arlo introduced Tampa to his moody "Days Are Short," a lovely original that his friend Hoyt Axton would later cover on his own album *Less Than the Song* (A&M SP-4376, 1973). Better yet was Arlo's sleepy introduction to his exciting bluegrass instrumental "Mapleview 20% Rag." "We're gonna do you a picking thing called the '20% Rag,'" he drawled.

> About twenty percent of this is mine and the other eighty percent, I guess, I stole from other people, you know? But that's not why it's called the "20% Rag." I guess I *could* call it that because of [that], but I didn't. . . . I got a manager whose name is Harold. And Harold called me on the phone when I was home. He said, "Arlo, you're not working enough." So here we are. Here we are in Tampa. We was just sort of picking when he called, you know, and I told him that it didn't make any difference whether we was picking here in Massachusetts or picking in Florida. It's just that twenty percent of picking at home doesn't add up to a whole lot for Harold. That's why this is called the "20% Rag."

The Guthrie show next rolled into the Jacksonville Civic Auditorium (November 12) and the Jai Alai Arena in Fronton, near Miami (November 13), before turning westward.[13]

There were gigs at Marquette University in Milwaukee (November 19), followed by shows at the Grand Rapids, Michigan, Civic Auditorium (November 20), and the University of Missouri, in Columbia (November 21). By the end of November the band was on the West Coast for a Saturday-evening show at California's Long Beach Auditorium (November 27). They next made their way to the Pacific Northwest, where on Monday night, December 6, the band was to perform at McArthur Court, a basketball arena at the University of Oregon–Eugene. This was their third-from-last engagement on the wearying "20 percent" tour that had the band on the road for seven weeks straight in thirteen states. Guthrie's contract with the University of Oregon stipulated that he would receive a $7,500 guarantee or 75 percent of the box office gross. Ticket sales had been relatively brisk, and some 3,700 fans gathered at McArthur Court, at three dollars a ticket, for a gross receipt totaling $11,000, bringing Arlo's share to a cool $8,200. Though the money was better than anticipated, the box office take wasn't enough to boost Arlo's mood; he was looking forward to the tour's end. He brushed off one reporter looking for a preconcert interview, telling him flatly, "I don't like interviews. . . . Because they always lead to interpretation of things I said, and I don't like interpretation of any kind." He was, obviously, defining "interpretation" only in the most literal sense. He couldn't have been referring to his interpretations of other artist's songs, as nearly three-fourths of the songs he performed at his 1971 concerts were written or made famous by others. Though he declined to be interviewed, he did admit that he had no problems with newspapermen reviewing his show. "There you can write what you think," he allowed. Swampwater's Jim Dickinson believed that following communication problems at last March's Carnegie Hall concert, Harold Leventhal was strategically booking Guthrie into small colleges rather than concert halls. It was Dickinson's view that Arlo was growing increasingly dissatisfied with big venues as the rock 'n' roll crowd he now attracted had different expectations, and Guthrie had "trouble relating to . . . large audiences."[14]

If Guthrie's "message," especially relating to use of recreational drugs, was misinterpreted, it was not difficult to see why. That night in Eugene, during his spoken-word introduction to "Coming into Los Angeles," Arlo observed, as he had on every tour stop in 1971, "Anybody can get on a plane with dope, but only a professional can get off." It was a stock line, told in his usual slow, slightly stoned drawl, and everyone laughed at the outrageousness of it all. But Dickinson thought the press, as well as the majority of fans, were misinterpreting the intent of the message. "Arlo's trying to mellow people out, to bring 'em down," he said. "He's trying to help. That business before 'Coming into Los Angeles . . .' He's trying to tell the kids *not* to smuggle dope on a plane." If that was the intention, the message was lost among the kids out for a chemically enhanced night's party. The crowd convened at McArthur Court was a particularly rowdy one, with newspaper reports noting that the students had engaged in such unsanctioned activities as "extraneous noise, alcohol consumption and marijuana smoking." The resulting chaos compelled the none-too-pleased fire marshal of Eugene to suggest that all future concerts at the venue should be canceled due to "numerous flagrant violations of the safety rules at Monday night's Arlo Guthrie concert."[15]

The *Eugene Register-Guard* noted Guthrie's "selection of music for Monday night's concert gave evidence of his desire to give depth to that well-established image, both in terms of what he played and what he didn't play." What he didn't play, much to the disappointment and derision of those gathered, were the songs he was best known for, "Alice's Restaurant" and "The Motorcycle Song." As with the spring tour, the rowdy and well-oiled audience called out repeatedly for the Arlo Guthrie songs they wanted desperately to hear. But Arlo continued to answer, with some frustration, "If we'd wanted to do our records for you, you could have sat at home and heard that." In the end it all worked out somehow, with most leaving satisfied and the crowd calling back the band for two encores, the second of which was Goebel Reeve's haunting "Hobo's Lullaby," the working title of the forthcoming album. The 1971 tour would soon conclude with final shows at the Capitol Theater, Lawrence, Kansas (December 8), and at Austin's Armadillo World Headquarters in Texas (December 10).[16]

On July 1 Congress ratified the Twenty-Sixth Amendment to the Constitution, granting the country's eighteen-year-old citizens the right to vote. The amendment was signed, with a weak smile, by President Richard Nixon, who understandably saw a youthful voting-age demographic as unfavorable, if not downright adversarial, to the policies of his administration. The president had reason to fret as opponents to America's war in Vietnam were actively registering the new influx of draft-age voters, hoping to unseat hawkish legislators in the upcoming 1972 elections. The recording industry was among the groups leading the effort to get newly minted voters to go out and register. Some artists were recording public service announcements intended for radio broadcast, and a few even recorded jingles for the effort. Arlo's contribution was a succinct solo piano-backed song titled the "Voter Registration Rag," which challenged, "You're sitting around / Nothing to do / While the future of the country / Is up to you." Guthrie's promotional spot was sent to radio stations and later included on the Warner Bros./Reprise "Loss Leader" omnibus *Burbank* (PRO 529, 1972).[17]

Citing the tangled legalities, contracts, and rights of putting together the set, *Chicago Tribune* music critic Lynn Van Matre noted that tapes of the Guthrie tribute concerts at Carnegie Hall 1968 and the Hollywood Bowl 1970 "took a while to get the music to the people, on two records . . . on two labels." In an odd partnership necessitated, no doubt, by Dylan's commercial value, Columbia Records released *A Tribute to Woody Guthrie, Part One* (Columbia KC 31171) on January 12, 1972, with Warner Bros. following with the weaker-selling and Dylan-less *A Tribute to Woody Guthrie, Part Two* (WB K 46144) that April. The *Chicago Tribune* thought the two LPs a "magnificent folk feast," but there was little unanimity in that opinion. The somewhat doctrinaire folk singer Michael Cooney wrote in *Sing Out!* that the set was abysmal, fretting that the plugged-in Dylan and Arlo were in competition "for 'Farthest-Out Screaming Rock Arrangement'" of a Woody Guthrie song. Sharing Cooney's general lackluster enthusiasm for the albums, Paul Nelson, writing in the pages of *Rolling Stone*, acknowledged that the set was a disappointment and that "the less said about the LPs, the better." But Nelson had a different take; he thought that most of the waxed efforts on the Guthrie tribute concerts sagged under the weight of their "lifeless, safe, sanctimonious, and uninteresting" performances. But it was Nelson's view that the contributions of Dylan and Arlo stood apart, that they were among the *best* the set had to offer; their performances were, like the best of Woody's art, challenging and controversial. The critic from *Gramophone* agreed, writing, "only Woody's son Arlo and, notably, Bob Dylan remind the listener of Woody's unpretentiousness and gusto." Shortly after the release of *A Tribute to Woody Guthrie, Part Two*, Arlo (thinly disguised, for contractual reasons, as "Arloff Boguslavki") appeared on a single cut of Earl Scrugg's new album *I Saw the Light with Some Help from My Friends* (Columbia KC 31354): Guthrie provided vocals for the gloomy country song "A Picture from Life's Other Side," an old favorite of Woody's.[18]

That spring Reprise was in the process of putting the final touches to Guthrie's fifth album, *Hobo's Lullaby* (Reprise MS 2060). Though Guthrie had been playing Steve Goodman's "City of New Orleans" at his concerts since early spring of 1971, his attempts at recording the song in the studio hadn't worked out well. He wasn't exactly sure what was wrong. He had changed the song since first learning it from Goodman; Guthrie recalled taking "City of New Orleans" home with him and working on it, on and off, "changing a few of the musical lines and a few of the words so that it would be easier for me to sing." But it still wasn't working. Guthrie recorded at least five different versions of "City of New Orleans" at sessions for *Hobo's Lullaby*, and though he was fond of *parts* of each version, he wasn't really satisfied *in total* with any of them. "We could have taken parts of each of the versions," he recollected, and pasted them all together, "but I don't like to that sort of thing. I don't know what took so long, but it was a really hard song to get down." The new album promised to be Guthrie's most eclectic to date. One song he was considering for inclusion on *Hobo's Lullaby* was the old Herbert "Happy" Lawson standard, "Anytime," a staple of Ramblin' Jack Elliott's sets. Though Guthrie was familiar with the song through Jack, he only set about learning it when he and Elliott found themselves sitting and playing guitars together one night in 1969. "I knew that there wouldn't be many of my own songs on the album, and I wanted to include some that were at least influenced by some of my friends," Guthrie told a Warner Bros. publicist. "So this one's for Jack."

Guthrie also acknowledged that it was Elliott's emotive reading of Woody's "1913 Massacre" at the Hollywood Bowl concert of 1970 that inspired him to record the wrenching ballad for *Hobo's Lullaby*. Guthrie's good friend Hoyt Axton contributed two songs to the album, "Lightning Bar Blues" and "Somebody Turned On the Light." Guthrie had been visiting with Hoyt in Oregon, where friends of Axton's had assembled to assist the extroverted, burly singer-actor out on a children's film that he was planning. Though nothing ever came of the movie, Hoyt playfully suggested to Arlo at that time that he record one of his originals; Axton had, of late, the musical Midas touch, charting a couple of songs. Guthrie remembered Hoyt teasing him, "'You know, I'm getting a lot of airplay on 'Joy to the World' and 'Never Been to Spain.' Arlo, *you* should do some of my songs.' Hoyt figured that if I'd do one of his songs, he'd make me a star," Guthrie laughed. The first song he chose was Axton's traditional country "Lightning Bar Blues." Following his recording of that song, Guthrie told *Circular* he had come across Hoyt's mysterious "Somebody Turned On the Light," "which we thought was an even better song. So, rather than choose between them, we decided to do both. I don't think that either one of them's [*sic*] going to make me a star," Guthrie mused, "but they're both good album cuts."[19]

Arlo admitted that "Shackles and Chains," which had already been issued as the B-side to "The Ballad of Tricky Fred," was similar to "City of New Orleans" in the sense that he and the studio musicians had recorded and re-recorded the song on various occasions, but never to satisfaction. "Shackles and Chains" was one of the songs recorded live by Warner Bros. during the spring leg of Guthrie's 1971 tour with Swampwater, but, according to Arlo, neither he nor anyone else involved cared for *that* version. The song was later reworked in the studio, but Guthrie sighed that he "didn't really think that it should be on the album, but everybody else did. I still don't know if I like it too much." He first heard the novelty song "Ukulele Lady" on the Jim Kweskin Jug Band Vanguard LP *Jug Band Music* (VRS 9163, 1965), and when he decided to record the song for his own project, he sought out the advice of Kweskin producer Fritz Richmond, who agreed to "come down and help us figure it out." The first of the two self-penned Guthrie songs was the bluegrass instrumental "Mapleview 20% Rag," featuring Doug Dillard on five-string banjo and Byron Berline on fiddle. The entertaining "Harold Leventhal Gets Twenty Percent" stage tale notwithstanding, Guthrie claims to have named the song after a saloon near his home in Washington, Massachusetts, which the singer would visit on occasion for a bottle of cold beer and to shoot a little pool. Guthrie's own "Days Are Short" was one of the album's highlights, but Arlo admitted that the provenance of the song was a little mysterious: "I don't know too much about this one, even though it's one of mine." He remembered that the song came very quickly to him, a "real early-in-the-morning tune." Goebel Reeves' "Hobo's Lullaby," which closes the album, was one of Woody's favorite's, though no recording of his father singing the song has ever surfaced. Arlo Guthrie's haunting, lonesome version is an amalgam of the melancholy versions waxed by such Woody disciples as Pete Seeger, Cisco Houston, and Jack Elliott.[20]

Perhaps it was merely the usual prerelease nervousness, but Arlo seemed concerned that *Hobo's Lullaby* would not appeal to either FM radio programmers or casual fans: "This is a weird kind of album," he cautioned his own publicist. "It's not the kind of thing that you can just stack on the changer and play while you're working on something in the kitchen—there are too many things on it. There are a couple of songs that, if you're just playing the album for background, you'll want to move the needle over. Which bothered me for a while. But the songs are so important and so valid that it might persuade you to not play the album at all, if that's the kind of mood you're in. I don't think that it's the kind of album that people will play a whole lot. But I think that when they do play it, it'll be important to them."[21]

As Reprise was readying the LP for release, Guthrie went out on the road for a short sortie that May. There were dates at the John Fitzgerald Kennedy Center in Washington, DC (May 4); the Mosque Auditorium, Richmond, Virginia (May 5); the University of Mississippi in Oxford (May 6); and Milwaukee, Wisconsin (May 7). Near the end of the month, Reprise began to send out the first promotional copies of *Hobo's Lullaby* to radio stations and music critics. On May 27 *Billboard* offered a welcome and bright preview, noting, "It's been a long time since LP releases and Guthrie's latest was worth the wait." The magazine cited "City of New Orleans," "Days Are Short," "Ukulele Lady," "Hobo's Lullaby," and "Anytime" as possible breakout songs.[22]

On Wednesday, May 24, Guthrie, along with 150 other protestors, was in Washington, DC, for a sit-down demonstration in the Capitol's marble corridor, passing out a "petition for redress of grievances" to Carl Albert, the Democratic speaker of the House. The protestors called for an "immediate cessation of air, ground, and naval operations in Indochina." Though a peaceful assembly, with the strains of John Lennon and Yoko Ono's "Give Peace a Chance" and the civil-rights anthem "We Shall Overcome" filling in the air, the police were called in, and nearly one hundred of the demonstrators were arrested on charges of unlawful entry.[23]

*Hobo's Lullaby* entered the *Billboard* chart, with a "Red Star," in the 152 position on June 10, 1972, and began its long ascent throughout the summer and into autumn. It entered the *Cash Box* chart a few weeks later (June 24) in position 136 and similarly climbed steadily up that chart through the second half of summer. The success of the album was partly the result of the fact that Reprise successfully extracted a 45 rpm single from *Hobo's Lullaby*, "City of New Orleans" backed with "Days Are Short." The 45 resonated with radio listeners, scoring immediately as an "Action" single on the *Billboard* charts. By July 22, the single had a regional breakout in the Los Angeles market and was only one click away from cracking into the Top "Hot 100" nationally. On August 5, "City of New Orleans" made its debut on the *Cash Box* singles chart, where it would ultimately peak in position 16, staying on the charts for a full sixteen weeks. Three weeks following its release, "City of New Orleans" was swiftly moving up the *Billboard* charts as well. Once the song crossed over from FM stations and entered into rotation on pop music–oriented AM radio, the single broke into the Top 10 of *Billboard's* "Easy Listening" chart in September.[24]

The company was planning on sending Guthrie on a two-month-long summer tour of amphitheaters and music sheds to help push sales of *Hobo's Lullaby*. The cross-country tour began on July 10, his twenty-fifth birthday, at the Garden State Arts Center in Holmdel, New Jersey, and ended some six weeks later on August 19 in Santa Barbara, California. Just prior to setting off on that tour, Guthrie brushed the lightly settled dust from his guitar with two solo acoustic appearances. On Wednesday evening, June 28, he teamed with guitarist Doc Watson for an informal concert at Boston Common for that city's "Summerthing" festivities. Then, on Friday night, July 7, Guthrie was in Manhattan sharing the stage at Carnegie Hall with Pete Seeger, Oscar Brand, Mimi Fariña, Richie Havens, Carol McComb, the bottleneck blues guitarist Robert Pete Williams, and James Taylor. The *raison d'etre* for the Carnegie gathering was to generate funds for the Newport Folk Foundation. The Newport Folk Festival was not staged in either 1970 or 1971 due to financial issues and mounting security concerns. Oscar Brand, a trustee of the Newport Folk Foundation, needed to raise some $30,000 if the Newport event was to return in 1972, and he enlisted his singing friends to freshen the committee's piggybank. Seeger opened the evening with a few sing-along numbers before ceding the stage to the assembled cast. James Taylor, near the height of his popularity with *Sweet Baby James* and *Mud Slide Slim and the Blue Horizon*, was the night's biggest attraction, but he would not eclipse Guthrie and Seeger as the standard-bearers of the folk-music continuum. Arlo and Pete closed the evening of gentle acoustic music with what the *New York Times* described as a "joyous finale."[25]

The summer tour officially kicked off with the New Jersey show, and on the following evening, Tuesday, July 11, Guthrie performed at the Blossom Music Center in Cuyahoga Falls, Ohio. His appearance at the Blossom was slotted into the schedule at the last minute when the easy-listening duo of Richard and Karen Carpenter unexpectedly canceled their concert at the venue. The atmosphere was far stormier, literally and figuratively, at Arlo's July 12 concert at the Music Pavilion at Ravinia Park, in Highland Park, Illinois. It was, for starters, a rowdy, relatively nonattentive crowd, and Arlo wasn't the sort of performer who suffered an indifferent audience. Things quickly took a bad turn when some unruly concertgoers began to toss firecrackers on the lawn area circling the pavilion. Things turned more hostile when an increasingly agitated Guthrie suggested to the audience that they "shut up" when the rumble and din got completely out of hand. Then a sudden thunder-and-lightning storm swept through Ravinia, causing all sorts of electrical gremlins to ripple through the microphones and sound system. Several songs into the concert, the skies completely opened, causing waterlogged patrons watching from their lawn seats to flood under the roof of the amphitheater. With the situation disintegrating rapidly on and off stage, the band took an unplanned ten-minute intermission. Upon his return to the stage, a contrite Guthrie told everyone that the raucous atmosphere in the pavilion was making it difficult for the band to hear themselves, but if everyone could "quiet down, we might be able to make it." One critic from the *Chicago Tribune* noted the "thinly disguised hostility between Guthrie and the crowd" was primarily the fault of a "portion of the audience—most of whom had come out of the rain—but couldn't or wouldn't listen." The band closed their abbreviated second set with Dylan's "You Ain't Going Nowhere" ("Clouds so swift / The rain won't lift") and beat a hasty retreat. Those who had come for a pleasant night of Arlo Guthrie music dutifully clapped and whistled. They were waiting for the star to return for the customary encore and were confused by the abrupt curtailment of the concert. But when it became clear that Arlo had no intention of returning to the stage, scattered boos could be heard bouncing off the seats of the rain-soaked venue.[26]

Arlo had a few days to recharge his batteries: the next scheduled gig was a Sunday afternoon show at the Merriweather Post Pavilion in Columbia, Maryland, on July 16. On the evening of July 14, Woody Guthrie's sixtieth birthday, Arlo was resting peacefully in his hotel room. Sleepy and "beginning to yawn," he turned on the television for company. On the screen he saw South Dakota senator George McGovern standing behind the lectern on the stage of the Democratic National Convention in Miami Beach, addressing a room that brimmed with fervent supporters. Guthrie watched and listened for an interval, but as McGovern's speech rattled on and on, reprising familiar themes, Arlo admitted to "getting sleepier and sleepier." But his imminent slumber was soon arrested. McGovern was nearing the end of his emotional address, having accepted his party's nomination in the upcoming presidential election against incumbent Republican Richard Nixon. The theme of McGovern's oration was that it was time for America to "come home" to its best values, to turn away from the Nixon administration's "secrecy and deception in high places," and from "military spending so wasteful that it weakens our nation." He implored Americans to come together to fight off the scourge of poverty, prejudice, and the special privileges of the elite. As the senator's speech continued to build to a rousing climax, McGovern cried to frenzied loyalists, "Come home to the belief that we can seek a newer world, and let us be joyful in that homecoming, for this 'is your land, this is my land, from California to New York island, from the redwood forest to the gulf stream waters, this land was made for you and me.'" Arlo later recollected, "I sat bolt upright in bed . . . I mean, it just blew me out. . . . I was so amazed."[27]

Though Guthrie had been doing his part for voter registration, he really hadn't been active for any of the presidential candidates. Many of Guthrie's friends were supporting McGovern. The candidate, after all, had been bravely campaigning for an American withdrawal from Vietnam and amnesty for draft evaders. Though Guthrie would have preferred to keep his options open, the McGovern speech forced him to reevaluate his position. McGovern's surprising use of a line from his father's most famous song was a watershed moment for the Guthrie family. Woody's songs, after all, were better known by those on the outside of Washington's halls of power. Guthrie still wasn't sure that McGovern was the man to beat Nixon in November; he would have preferred that Senator Edward Kennedy of Massachusetts had stayed in the race. He told one friend that he would first need to look McGovern "in the eye and see what sort of a man he is" before supporting his candidacy, though he admitted his platform "sounds OK to me."[28]

That July the American Greeting Card Company announced it had licensed the images and lyrics of such rock performers as Jimi Hendrix, Melanie, Three Dog Night, Donovan, Rod Stewart, the Bee Gees, and Arlo Guthrie to grace a series of colorful posters and greeting cards, a marketing plan to offset rival Hallmark's proposed "Sounds of Love" series to be introduced in the early winter of 1973. The Guthrie poster, number twenty-six in the series and measuring 26-by-35 inches, featured an impressionistic soft-focus image of Arlo standing in a field with a verse of his obscure "Meditation (Wave upon Wave)" striped across the bottom in bright pink lettering.[29]

The 1972 summer tour rolled on with visits to Forth Worth, Texas (July 17); Rochester, Michigan, (July 19); Milwaukee, Wisconsin (July 21); Saratoga Springs, New York (July 23); and the Temple University Music Festival in Ambler, Pennsylvania (July 25). On Wednesday night, July 26, Guthrie played New York City's Schaefer Music Festival at the Wollman Rink. This time around, Guthrie wasn't headlining the Central Park concert; he was tapped to support Harry Chapin, the Long Island–born songwriter then enjoying great commercial success on AM radio for such hit singles as "Taxi" and "W*O*L*D." The combination of Guthrie and Chapin on a double bill proved so popular that the demand for tickets necessitated an extra show to be added, the first beginning at 7:00 p.m. and the second following at 9:30 p.m.[30]

With the first half of his summer U.S. tour completed, Guthrie flew to London. On Saturday evening, July 29, he performed at the glass-enclosed Crystal Palace Bowl in London's Hyde Park, the headliner of the Garden Party rock festival. The event was, in the words of a Warner Bros. publicist, "Arlo's first major U.K. appearance." This was somewhat true. Although Guthrie had previously visited Great Britain on several occasions, his brand of musical Americana hadn't really caught on with English record buyers. The times had changed, and Britons were less interested in American country and western music. To one British critic attending the Garden Party, the booking of a folk singer with a country steel-guitar backing shouldn't have worked at a rock festival, and in fact it almost didn't. Guthrie himself recalled the Crystal Palace event as "terrible," and one postconcert notice groused that while Woody's son was not "the phenomenal talent he was touted to be," it generously allowed that Guthrie's style was "the antithesis of overbearing. The songs were taken leisurely and sung in a voice of no great emotional distinction besides a humorous twang." One song performed, and recalled by many in attendance as a highlight, was his father's chilling "1913 Massacre," a ballad first introduced to British folkies in 1955 via the Jack Elliott recording of *Woody Guthrie's Blues*. It was one of the times during the concert where the artist and the audience shared a moment: "I think Woody would have really liked to hear the way his '1913 Massacre' went down . . . at the rock festival," Guthrie remembered. "That would have really blown his mind to have seen the way that many people would shut up and listen to a song like that." The following day, Arlo made an unscheduled, but well-received, appearance at the eighth annual Cambridge Folk Festival. His friend Karl Dallas remembered Guthrie showing up at the festival on Sunday, July 30, where the folk singer unpretentiously "jammed all day for free in the middle of the field with anyone who felt like picking or singing along with him." The Cambridge organizers, made aware of Guthrie's unscheduled visit, sought him out, asking that he perform as a guest on the main stage. He obliged, later recalling the Cambridge event as "really great. That's what a festival ought to be." The American guitarist Happy Traum, also performing at the Cambridge event, remembered Guthrie's "beautiful surprise set" that included at least one priceless moment: Steve Goodman and Arlo singing "City of New Orleans" together on stage.[31]

Though Guthrie had expressed some wariness regarding the commercial prospects of *Hobo's Lullaby*, the album's surprising success allowed him to suggest that its inspired mosaic programming had been intentional from the start. He told *Melody Maker* that the songs from *Hobo's Lullaby* were *not* on the LP by accident; they were "on the album for a definite purpose, so that when it was over and you've done listening to it you have some sort of idea where I was at." The success was especially pleasing as, this time around, no one from the Reprise staff had obsessed about breaking a hit single from the sessions. The success of the "City of New Orleans" single was a happy accident, according to Arlo: "The funny thing is that in the past when I've done albums, we've planned for this song or that song to be a single and it's never happened. So this time we said, forget singles, that's not my scene, we'll just make an album."[32]

Guthrie returned to the United States as he was due to continue his summer tour out west. Shows were scheduled for San Diego's Civic Theater (August 17), the Hollywood Bowl (August 18), and Santa Barbara, California (August 19). The concert at the Hollywood Bowl was a cobill with Pete Seeger, and a few days prior to the show both artists appeared on the popular NBC-TV program *The Johnny Carson Show*. Following his chat with Las Vegas "Rat Pack" entertainer Joey Bishop, Carson introduced Arlo and the singer moved into "City of New Orleans." Promoting the Hollywood Bowl engagement, Carson noted grimly that rock concerts were routinely making the nightly news telecasts; the stabbings at a music festival in Altamont was still fresh in the mind. Guthrie protested that recent rock 'n' roll festivals grabbing the headlines were "nothing like Woodstock. It's bigger than any that's been. But it was also the *nicest*. . . . That's the strange thing. [We've] had a lot of the small ones with trouble and people getting hurt. The incredible thing about Woodstock was that there was a million people . . . and nobody got a black eye." Carson asked Arlo if he was optimistic about the future, or if the ongoing cycle of political and social violence had dimmed the Aquarian vision of his friends and colleagues. Guthrie reflected before answering that the future was *still* bright: "People know that it can get done, you know? That's something they didn't know. *We* didn't know a couple of years ago. Everybody sort of knew what should be done, but no one really knew if you could do it. . . . People, I think, are getting on the ball. They know the things that have to be done, and know that it's possible to do. So I feel pretty good." The subject of political activism caused Carson to ask whether or not Pete Seeger's music had a strong influence on him. "Not musical so much as personal," Guthrie allowed. "The great thing about Pete is that his concern for humanity is so great that it [has] outlasted all of his critics through the years. I mean, he's still working." For the enlightenment of the studio audience, Carson acknowledged Seeger's weathering of a number of political storms that effectively blackballed him from the entertainment industry. Arlo nodded and continued, "His concerts were picketed and so forth and so on. But he's outlasted them all, and that's inspiring for me, anyway." It wasn't long before Carson shifted the conversation from Pete Seeger to Woody Guthrie. Arlo conceded that "I'm not as valid for my time as [Woody] was for his, you know? And that's cool. I can dig that. But he did an incredible thing for his time that. . . . I don't know, maybe. . . . Dylan did it here, that same kind of thing. The Beatles did it, sort of, for the world. But I'm having fun doing what I'm doing. It's really great."[33]

Following the conversation with Arlo, Carson brought out Pete Seeger, who performed the gentle "Living in the Country," followed by the not-so-gentle "Last Train to Nuremburg," his withering assessment of the state of the nation circa 1972. The show closed with Arlo and Pete teaming for a run-through of the old Bob Nolan/Sons of the Pioneer yodeling song "Way Out There," their version gleaned from an old Cisco Houston LP. The singing and yodeling was so infectious that Joey Bishop, whose milieu was a nightclub lounge on the Vegas Strip, was moved to tell Carson, "I imagine to the average person, you and I don't look like the kind of guys that would *dig* this, right? But I think this is really, really beautiful."[34]

This view was apparently not shared by Richard Cromelin, the cranky music critic of the *Los Angeles Times*. In Cromelin's view the Seeger–Guthrie Hollywood Bowl concert of August 18 was neither beautiful nor transcendent. Cromelin wasn't one of Guthrie's bigger fans in any case, decrying the "cutesy-poo style with which he is saddled" and lamenting that Arlo's solo turns at center stage were, at best, "uneven." It's possible that Cromelin was simply taken back by Guthrie's casual stage presence and musical eclecticism. Guthrie's Hollywood Bowl set was programmed with the usual material by Dylan and Jimmie Rodgers, but he also chose to perform a generous sampling of songs from the new album, "Ukulele Lady" and "1913 Massacre" among them. Cromelin believed the format of the show, which featured Seeger and Guthrie casually trading off songs, was the evening's undoing. The "result of their constant alternation at the microphone," Cromelin sulked, "was a feeling of disjointedness and the inability of either to establish a complete, coherent personality."[35]

In a signal that *Hobo's Lullaby* had caught the press by surprise, belated reviews of the best-selling LP were still appearing as late as November 1972. Though it had been some time since an Arlo Guthrie album had received a favorable notice in *Rolling Stone*, this changed with the release of *Hobo's Lullaby*. The magazine's Janet Maslin wrote, "Spirited production, intriguingly off-balance arrangements and especially well chosen material combine here to synthesize a genuine modern folk epic." *Rolling Stone* was especially intrigued by the way Guthrie had chosen to scale down, rather than amp up, the tempos of many of the songs included on *Hobo's Lullaby*. On Dylan's original guitar recording of "When the Ship Comes In," the song was played on *The Times They Are A-Changin'* LP at a "medium bright" tempo, in the terminology of the song's publisher, M. Witmark and Sons. But on the Guthrie album, the song was rescored for piano as "slow and almost dirge-like," according to Maslin. Goodman's "City of New Orleans" was also dialed back when compared to Goodman's own more robust version, the song far more melancholic than originally conceived by its composer. Though Guthrie's thin singing style often brought forth complaints among critics, Maslin found "Arlo's singing is more than a match for the unfailingly fine material. He remains nasal as ever, but distinctively so, and he musters just the right degree of expressiveness for the countrified old-timey vein he seems to favor at the moment. He does a beautiful job, and one that really deserves to be heard."[36]

Of all the reviewers, only Maslin and Ira Mayer of the *New York Times* noted that *Hobo's Lullaby* was the first album of Arlo's to feature primarily cover songs. Only two songs, the bluegrass instrumental "Mapleview 20% Rag" and the moody "Days Are Short," were self-penned. This trend would not continue; the next two albums, *Last of the Brooklyn Cowboys* (1973) and *Arlo Guthrie* (1974), featured five and seven original songs, respectively. Mayer, referencing his earlier review of Guthrie's Carnegie Hall "living room" concert of March 31, 1971, wrote, "Guthrie said he preferred playing in his living room to doing live concerts. Though the tastefully elaborate settings with which he has surrounded himself here [on *Hobo's Lullaby*] are far from what you'd expect in his (or anybody else's) living room, they certainly do make you feel at home." Though only the title song and "1913 Massacre" were performed as stripped-down acoustic guitar affairs, *Hobo's Lullaby* still managed to retain a general mood of folksiness due to John Pilla and Lenny Waronker's polished, elegant production. *Hi-Fi News & Record Review* wrote, "Although the sleeve lists a heady cast of contributors, the music is kept simple, unpretentious and ultimately effective." *Gramophone*, generally impressed by the album's "country-rock," noted, "the virtues of Arlo's music are those of good selection and pleasing arrangements, rather than any special quality of interpretation." The more austere *Sing Out!* thought the arrangements and production of *Hobo's Lullaby* "a bit too lush" but otherwise found it a "fine album," the song selection both "tasteful and widespread." Writing in the rock magazine *Creem*, Robert Christgau described the LP as "one of the best of those exploring-the-folkie-sensibility records," awarding the LP a score of B+. *High Fidelity*, on the other hand, was the lone dissenter, dismissing *Hobo's Lullaby* as an "undistinguished collection."[37]

The success of the "City of New Orleans" single was instrumental in pushing album sales of *Hobo's Lullaby*. As early as July, the Warner Bros. *Circular*, the weekly in-house newsletter of the record company, was tracking the momentum of the 45 with enthusiasm. "Arlo Guthrie's new single, 'City of New Orleans,' continues to break ground," the news sheet bragged, noting that the single had been added to playlists "in Augusta, Atlanta, Denver, Lowell, Houston, Des Moines, Omaha and it's charted on KJR in Seattle, not to mention being #9 in San Diego and #28 on KHJ." But this would only be the beginning. By the end of September the single was positively catching fire, with Warner Bros. celebrating Guthrie as the label's "big winner" of the moment. The "City of New Orleans" single, *Circular* bragged, had risen to number 26, "with a star," on the *Billboard* charts, as well as "number 31 with a bullet in *Cash Box* and 26 with a square in *Record World*." The record company also boasted that the single was receiving "untold major AM play" in the important markets of Cleveland, Atlanta, Philadelphia, Milwaukee, San Francisco, Los Angeles, Chicago, and New Orleans.[38]

By October 9, *Hobo's Lullaby* was the fourth best-selling new release LP under the Warner Bros./Reprise banner. The album had bested sales of the recent albums by such popular label mates as the Doobie Brothers, T. Rex, Seals and Crofts, and Van Morrison. Only Alice Cooper's *School's Out*, Jethro Tull's *Thick as a Brick*, and Black Sabbath's *Volume 4* were keeping Guthrie from claiming the top spot. On October 28, twenty-one weeks following its release, *Hobo's Lullaby* peaked on the *Billboard* album charts in position 52. Sales were buoyed by radio play of "City of New Orleans," which had moved into position 18 on the *Billboard* overall Top 40 chart by the end of October (and into number 4 on the "Easy Listening" chart). In the news item "Arlo Breaks into Top 20," the Warner Bros. publicity department crowed that the "City of New Orleans" single was "currently listed at #18, #18, and #23 in *Billboard*, *Record World* and *Cash Box* respectively." *Hobo's Lullaby* would be, following *Alice's Restaurant*, Guthrie's second best-selling album, remaining on the *Billboard* album charts through mid-January of 1973, some thirty-two weeks following its release. It did nearly as well on the *Cash Box* album chart, remaining for some twenty-six weeks and peaking at position 35.[39]

That October, Don Fouser, a PBS television producer in association with New York City's WNET-TV, unleashed *VD Blues* on an unsuspecting public. This informational program on the subject of venereal disease was primarily targeted to an audience of teens and young adults. To offset the sensitive nature of the topic, *VD Blues* masqueraded as a television variety show featuring celebrities, musical performances, and comedy sketches that gently educated viewers about the dangers of syphilis. To get the message across, Fouser assembled an all-star cast to support TV personality and host Dick Cavett. "I just said to myself, 'Who's hot,' and called 'em up," Fouser told Carol Kramer of the *Chicago Tribune* press service. With "City of New Orleans" riding high on the AM charts, Arlo was definitely a "hot" property (as was the program's other musical guest, Doctor Hook and the Medicine Show). Interestingly, Arlo was not only brought aboard due to his celebrity status. He was also there to shine a light on a little-known facet of his father's musical legacy. In 1949 Woody's friend, the folklorist Alan Lomax, had arranged for the underemployed elder Guthrie to write and perform a dimly remembered cycle of songs on the dangers of venereal disease for a government radio program. One of Woody's songs, "Child of VD," came to the attention of those putting together the WNET program when, in the course of developing the show, a "music agent told Fouser he had a tape of old songs written by Woody Guthrie and never published." Fouser made arrangements to bring Arlo onto the project and perform his father's long-forgotten song. *VD Blues* was broadcast, amid some mild protest, on Monday evening, October 9.[40]

Guthrie spent the latter part of November on tour. The ten concerts began on November 13 at Brown University in Providence, Rhode Island, and ended on November 26 at the Veteran's Memorial Hall in Columbus, Ohio, with a number of college and music hall dates in New Jersey, New York, Ohio, Alabama, and Georgia in the interim. In December, Reprise tried to recharge softening sales of *Hobo's Lullaby* by issuing a second single culled from the album, "Ukulele Lady" backed with "Cooper's Lament" (REP 1137). "Cooper's Lament" was an odd choice as the song was a recent recording not included on *Hobo's Lullaby*. Warner Bros. publicity championed "Cooper's Lament" as "a more than worthy follow-up to 'City of New Orleans,'" noting the "newly-recorded" song was a lament only "in a very broad sense of the word . . . not so much a song of sadness as one of peace on earth and good will to men." Though "Cooper's Lament" would not chart, the "City of New Orleans" single was still showing some energy, even beginning to demonstrate international appeal. That December the single made it to number one on the Austrian Top 40 chart, causing the sales staff at Warner Bros. to offer a "hearty Glückwünsche to Mr. G."[41]

Though Brownie McGhee and Sonny Terry were on cool personal terms in the late stage of their blues-singing careers, they were interdependent and chose not to break up their popular and successful act. In the latter half of 1972, the aging bluesmen were signed to A&M Records, with their first LP for the label due out in January 1973. That album, *Sonny & Brownie* (A&M SP 4379), was recorded at the Paramount Recording Studios in Hollywood, California, and featured contributions from such revivalist friends as John Hammond, John Mayall, Arlo, and Sugarcane Harris. Guthrie contributed to three of the album's twelve tracks, supplying acoustic guitar accompaniment to Curtis Mayfield's "People Get Ready" and a bluesy piano to "Mighty Mo" Maurice Rodgers' "God and Man." But Guthrie was most notably present on the album with his contribution of guitar and secondary vocals to a plaintive rendering of Randy Newman's sardonic slave trader ballad, "Sail Away."[42]

Guthrie's *Hobo's Lullaby* was still sitting on the *Billboard* album charts as late as January 1973, and it wasn't too surprising that Reprise was pushing for a fast follow-up. On February 5, a Warner Bros. newsletter reported, "Arlo Guthrie has finished recording all the tracks for his [next] album, with the able assistance of musicians Ry Cooder, Jim Keltner, Jesse Edwin Davis, Gene Parsons, Grady Martin, George Bohannon, Lee Sklar, and Richie Hayward." That information was leaked to the trades a month later when, on March 3, *Billboard* reported that Guthrie had wrapped up the recording. The new album, as yet untitled but eventually issued as *Last of the Brooklyn Cowboys*, was principally recorded at the Buck Owens Studio in Bakersfield and at the Warner Bros. studio in North Hollywood. The studio had been recently converted into a facility with twenty-four-track capability, and the production team planned on taking advantage of the new sonic tools at their disposal. *Last of the Brooklyn Cowboys* found Lenny Waronker and John Pilla once again at the helm, with no fewer than three engineers (Lee Herschberg, Donn Landee, and Bobby Hata) overseeing production. The *Circular* noted that although all the songs were in the can, "the arduous task of the final mix remains." Though a final track listing had yet to be chosen, songs considered for inclusion were five Guthrie originals ("Last Train to Glory," "Old Time Cowboy Song," "Cooper's Lament," "Week on the Rag," and "Uncle Jeff"), as well as such old-timers as "Gypsy Davy" and "Miss the Mississippi and You." Other intriguing titles suggested as candidates for programming were versions of Mississippi John Hurt's "Louis Collins" and something called the "Café Harris Rag." Though both songs were recorded at the sessions, they would remain, frustratingly, unissued. John Pilla reported that the album was expected to be out in April of 1973 and would serve as "a perfect accompaniment for springtime." It was also announced in early March that Guthrie would go out on a month-long cross-country tour in the spring in support of the forthcoming LP.[43]

The spring shows of 1973 were mostly programmed with songs featured on *Hobo's Lullaby* ("Anytime," "City of New Orleans," "When the Ship Comes In") and the forthcoming *Last of the Brooklyn Cowboys* ("Gypsy Davy," "Lovesick Blues"). On April 10 at Boston Music Hall, Guthrie and his country-rock accompanying band played their usual two-hour-long concert. The set list included a performance of "Shackles and Chains," a popular bluegrass song Guthrie had gleaned from mandolin player Frank Wakefield. The song had been culled from *Hobo's Lullaby* and released as a single a year earlier, the B-side of the otherwise forgotten "The Ballad of Tricky Fred." The "Shackles and Chains" single did not enjoy even mild chart success.

Guthrie told his Boston audience, "It sold about seven records. Everybody in the band bought a copy and my mother wanted two."[44]

On April 14 *Billboard* reported the release of the new Guthrie album, his sixth for the Reprise label. The album debuted April 28 on the *Billboard* album chart in position 164 with little fanfare, inching slowly but steadily to position 87 on its seventh week of release. But it would slip to position 94 on week eight, and was off of the *Billboard* Top 100 album chart by week nine. On July 14, the album's twelfth week of release, *Last of the Brooklyn Cowboys* would enjoy its last showing on the *Billboard* chart in position 145. The LP would fare somewhat better on the *Cash Box* chart, rising as high as position 63 and enjoying a full fourteen-week run on the album chart.[45]

Reprise issued a single of "Gypsy Davy" backed with "Lovesick Blues" to bolster sales of the slow-out-of-the-gate *Last of the Brooklyn Cowboys*. The single would debut on the chart on the seventh week of the LP's run on the *Billboard* Top 100. Much as the single of "City of New Orleans" had earlier, "Gypsy Davy" was faring best on *Billboard's* "Easy Listening" chart, the record moving from position 40 on June 9 to the position 23 in less than a month. But airplay of the song soon dropped off, and the single fell completely off the charts by July. Though sales of *Last of the Brooklyn Cowboys* were sluggish, *Hobo's Lullaby* too had taken some time before catching fire with the public. The sales staffs at Warner Bros. were still hoping that the LP would enjoy a breakthrough, though a company memorandum conceded, "Arlo's 45, 'Gypsy Davy,' hasn't exactly crashed onto the charts." Though the single and album were performing well in some markets ("Gypsy Davy" was "proclaimed a Pop smash by WTIX [New Orleans]," and the LP "termed 'Hottest in Release' by our men in Hartford"), it was clear that the Warner Bros. accountants were not, this time around, banking on a national breakout. "We'll soon see," they wrote, guardedly.[46]

If *Last of the Brooklyn Cowboys* wasn't hitting the turntables of the mass record-buying public, it was far from an artistic failure. Janet Maslin of *Rolling Stone* saw *Last of the Brooklyn Cowboys* as an "outgrowth" of *Hobo's Lullaby*, though "less mercurial, without any [of the] obvious highs or lows" of that LP. With the album's appealing mixture of original compositions, fiddle tunes, ragtime piano solos, and songs written or popularized by Jimmie Rodgers, Woody Guthrie, Woody's cousin Jack Guthrie (a recording artist for Capitol Records in the 1940s), Hank Williams, and Bob Dylan, Maslin thrilled that Guthrie had assembled a sonic "collage touching diverse corners of Americana, [treating] each song with a wonderfully unifying diffidence, and finally [binding] it all together with proof—via his own original material—that's he's truly part of the album's wonderfully vivid panorama." The *Los Angeles Times* heralded *Last of the Brooklyn Cowboys* as a "worthy follow-up to *Hobo's Lullabye*." Guthrie's "vocals are warm and arrangements in harmony with his mood on this collection of new and old, original and borrowed tunes," the *Times* reported. The review cited John Pilla and Lenny Waronker's production and Arlo's own "Cowboy Song" as album highlights. Ed Ward in *Creem* wrote that *Last of the Brooklyn Cowboys* was "easily his best record to date." The lone complaint of David Clark of *Records and Recording* was with the album's "shortness—17 ½ minutes on one side, 19 on the other. We could have had a couple of Arlo's own numbers in the extra time one normally expects." For others, however, the value of the album was subverted by its touch-all-the-bases eclecticism. Harvey Andrews of England's *Folk Review* cried, "Good God! Such a diverse hotchpotch of material has never before come my way in one album." But in the final summation, Andrews conceded, "I cannot for the life of me explain why I enjoyed it so much. . . . Arlo has a way of playing on weaknesses." In a more unpleasant summation *Stereo Review* agreed that *Last of the Brooklyn Cowboys* was "more fragmented than usual" and suggested the new LP offered evidence that Guthrie, paradoxically, was "a performer who tends to make good songs sound mediocre and mediocre songs sound good." Though England's *Country Music Review* thought the album made for "extremely good listening," they warned country and western fans to carefully consider before adding the LP to their personal library: "The fact that the contents are so varied prompts me to suggest one gives the album a listen before actually purchasing."[47]

Near the end of August, Warner Bros./Reprise (partnering with Elektra and Atlantic Records) announced that a series of albums featuring their best artists were to be remastered and made available in September as "Quadradiscs," that is, albums mixed in Quadraphonic, four-channel sound. The format was geared to the audiophile and home-stereo enthusiast with discretionary income. To reach this small but significant consumer group, the companies combined to run both full and double-page spreads in *Rolling Stone*, *New York*, and *Stereo Review* to exult the glories of Quadraphonic sound. That said, *Billboard* thought that *Last of the Brooklyn Cowboys* didn't make full use of the Quadraphonic medium, finding only "Cowboy Song" and the songs that Arlo recorded with Buck Owens' Buckaroos ("Gypsy Davy" and "This Troubled Mind of Mine") as the tracks most demonstrative of the format's four-track potential: "On both tunes . . . the separation is good, tense, and exciting; you're literally part of the band itself. The left rear fiddle work of Don Rich is outstanding. This is probably the best example of what can be done with country music in quadrasonic [*sic*] that's on the market today."[48]

Shortly after the Quadraphonic release of *Last of the Brooklyn Cowboys*, Guthrie was the featured guest of hosts Seals and Crofts on the September 28 episode of the popular NBC television music show *Midnight Special*.

NBC broadcast his rocking performances of "Gypsy Davy" as well as "Bling Blang," a little-known but delightful children's song of his father's that Woody had recorded for Moses Asch but that had not to date been issued. The tuneful "Bling Blang" would be featured on Guthrie's next Reprise LP, due out in early summer 1974. During the taping Guthrie chose to share an amusing story with the *Midnight Special* television audience. Though Guthrie already had accumulated enough anecdotal evidence that suggested he had long been a target of government eavesdropping, it wasn't until March 1970 that the U.S. Army admitted to covertly collecting information on the political activities of select private citizens. In February of 1971 an undercover agent testified before Congress, confirming that army counterintelligence officers had, quite illegally, monitored the comings and goings of U.S. citizens that they viewed as potential troublemakers. The army had compiled dossiers on the "usual suspects" of the folk-singing crowd (Pete Seeger, Judy Collins, Joan Baez, Phil Ochs, and Arlo Guthrie) but also on selected "mainstream" politicians, journalists, writers, and ex-servicemen—practically anyone and everyone who dared go public with their criticisms of the foreign and domestic policy follies of the Johnson and Nixon administrations. Such revelations by military intelligence officers were, of course, merely fodder for an amusing Guthrie monologue. The night of the *Midnight Special* broadcast, Guthrie related,

> [It was] in nineteen-sixty-something-or-other that I got a call from somebody on the *New York Times* wondering how I felt about having my phone bugged. I didn't *feel* anything, you know? So I just called up on the telephone, just picked up the phone, 'cause I *knew* that "they" were there . . . and I told them that I was building my house and I was right in the process of building my dog door. . . . It was 16" high and 14 ¾" wide, and I wanted to know what the *smallest Commie* on file was, to make sure that he couldn't get in. . . . But they didn't call me back or nothing. . . . Just really a shame, 'cause I figured [with] all the taxes that I was paying them they ought to, at least, give me a call.

Guthrie had actually performed a third song during the *Midnight Special* taping, his father's haunting "Deportee (Plane Wreck at Los Gatos)." But Woody's mournful poem, inspired by an indifferent news report regarding the tragic crash of an airplane carrying home a number of Mexican migrant workers, would not escape the scissors of NBC editors. Arlo reflected that it wasn't the message of the song itself that caused its excision. He figured that it was most likely the spoken-word introduction that he added as prelude. "It must be strange to grow up in this country," Guthrie opined, "and not know what a grape looks like." The network feared that Guthrie's sly introduction was an endorsement of the recent call by Cesar Chavez and the United Farm

Workers Union (UFW) for a consumer boycott of Californian grapes following a statewide grower's decision to bargain with the appeasing Teamsters
Union rather than the more militant UFW.[49]

Guthrie was to set out for a month-long tour to begin in Chicago on October
18 and finish in San Diego. The autumn shows were similar in design to the
spring concerts, but Guthrie was writing new songs all the time, and he began
to introduce some of this material to his Midwest and Pacific coast audiences.
The songs were more intimate this time around, as Guthrie was playing the
shows primarily solo, with the occasional augmentation of John Pilla's second guitar. It was raining outside when the musicians walked out on stage for
the concert at the Berkeley Community Theater on Tuesday night, November
11. Though there were some empty seats in the house, the Berkeley crowd
welcomed the prodigal son with such a momentous ovation that it caused
Guthrie to quip, "You shouldn't clap until you hear the tune. . . . That's how
Nixon got elected. We clapped before we heard the tune." He played a lot
of material from *Hobo's Lullaby* and *Last of the Brooklyn Cowboys*, but he
also surprised the audience with a new song, "Me and My Goose," a morbid,
modern take on the old country and western faithful-dog weeper "Old Shep."
He also seemed to make peace with "Shackles and Chains," a song composed
by the former governor of Louisiana, Jimmie Davis. Guthrie had protested the
inclusion of "Shackles and Chains" on *Hobo's Lullaby*, but since the tuneful
song seemed to resonate with concertgoers, it was occasionally performed at
his concerts. It's possible that Guthrie wasn't as much troubled by the song
than by the history of the song's composer. Jimmie Davis had been a popular
figure on the country and gospel music circuit of the 1930s and 1940s, but
as governor of Louisiana he served as an unrepentant segregationist; it was
with this acknowledgment that Guthrie acknowledged that night in Berkeley
that Davis "wasn't one of [Louisiana's] best governors, I guess, but he wrote
some pretty nice tunes." One critic, writing of the concert in *Rolling Stone*,
couldn't help but notice that the Arlo Guthrie on stage in Berkeley "showed
a maturity and confidence that, taken in combination with his two recent and
excellent albums, made him look more and more like one of our important
singer/songwriters instead of the son of one."[50]

Two nights prior to the tour's conclusion, Arlo and Pilla performed at the
Civic Auditorium in Santa Monica on November 16. Guthrie opened with
"Oklahoma Hills," moving quickly into his monologue detailing the events
and arrests in Philadelphia that inspired his "Ring-around-a-Rosy Rag."
Six weeks prior to the concert, the beleaguered vice president of the United
States, Spiro Agnew, had resigned under the weight of tax evasion charges
and for his alleged involvement in the Watergate break-in, when members of
Nixon's staff were accused of burglarizing and wiretapping members of the

rival Democratic National Committee. Spiro, with his bombastic and amusing alliterative taunts of political enemies, was a favorite target of those on the New Left and often the subject of Arlo's mild ridicule. That night in Santa Monica Guthrie introduced "I Could Be Singing" (from *Washington County*):

I wrote this next song a long time ago about Spiro. [It's sort of an] "I told you so" kind of song. Things have a way of working out sometimes. I was just getting to like [Spiro]. It wasn't that he was *cute. . . .* Wasn't "*cuddly.*" That's not the word either. He was sort of *far out . . .* and when you boil everything down [that] Spiro says to *something* that makes a little sense, it sort of comes out "Yes, I'm a crook, but I never let [unintelligible]." Actually, this song isn't really about Spiro. Just mentions him in one of the verses. . . . I didn't want to waste a whole song on him.

The nation was still to witness the second act of the contemporary political drama unfolding in Washington. In July 1973 the famous Oval Office tapes of President Richard Nixon had been subpoenaed by Congress. Citing the president's "executive privilege," the White House refused to surrender the tapes, though Nixon's pledge that he was unaware of the events of the Watergate break-in held no water with Guthrie. "You know, it took me awhile to write a Watergate song," Guthrie told the crowd at the Civic,

'Cause in the beginning I thought, "This is pretty funny, I'm gonna write a funny song." Well, it got past the point of being funny real quick. So I said, "Hey, I better write one of those satirical ballads." But it got past that part. . . . Every time I thought I had got to a place where I could write a song about it, it kept moving on and getting worse and worse. So I never wrote a song about Watergate. Until about three or four weeks ago when I forgot all about Watergate and I wrote. I wrote this song the day before Spiro resigned.

Though an overt protest song in style, the lyrics to "Presidential Rag" were neither revolutionary nor incendiary, but simply morally indignant. Through seven inspired verses, Guthrie masterfully skewered Nixon's dismissive contention that the illegal wiretaps and shadowy activities of the Watergate burglars was a Capitol Hill scandal-sheet non-starter; that no political espionage was involved and that there were no rogue elements on the fringes of his administration. But in July 1973 existence of the infamous, and potentially damning, Watergate tapes came to light, causing the increasingly entangled president to refuse to release the recordings to an investigating Congressional committee. With its insistent and tumbling piano-backed rhythm, Guthrie's missive ridiculed Nixon's dogged deferment of culpability in the scandal as, at best, woefully inadequate. He reasonably suggested that as America's highest office-holder, the president could not be exempt from accountability for appointing and protecting administration officials whose actions ran contrary to the nation's laws and values.

Guthrie's "Presidential Rag" was only the first of a series of new songs performed that were being prepared for Arlo's forthcoming seventh Reprise album, *Arlo Guthrie*. Other new songs this evening were his own "Nostalgia Rag" and "Me and My Goose," as well as his father's "Deportee (Plane Wreck at Los Gatos)," which had recently reblossomed as a protest anthem.

The *Los Angeles Times* critic Richard Cromelin argued that Arlo's new songs were more Randy Newman or Tom Lehrer than Woody Guthrie, though he begrudgingly admitted that "Nostalgia Rag" worked "modestly" and allowed the artist to be one of the few singers able to bring Woody's songs "to life with chilling effect." Though Cromelin allowed that the younger Guthrie was "charming," he thought his two-hour acoustic set "suffered from an encroaching monotony." "Both the pace of the show and Arlo's approach to each song were maddeningly even, as if designed to let nothing stand out one way or another," wrote Cromelin, who seemingly would have preferred sitting through an evening of cabaret rather than folk singing. "His voice does have an endearing quality about it, but is otherwise unremarkable and extremely unvaried. He puts no demands on it as he treats every line he sings very carefully and safely. Sometimes voice and music work well together, but one is always aware that it's a result of limitation, not choice. He can do justice to a good song, but can't make undistinguished material anything more than ordinary." The audience that evening would not have agreed with Cromelin's estimate, and the critic fairly noted, with some puzzlement, the "wild enthusiasm" that Guthrie stirred in his fans. His fans recognized Arlo's casual stage manner and unpretentious singing style as his greatest strength.[51]

## NOTES

1. "Bits of Show Business," *Milwaukee Journal*, January 12, 1971, sec. 2, 8; "Explosion Levels Radio Transmitter," *Rome News-Tribune*, May 13, 1970, 16.

2. *Great American Dream Machine* (PBS-WNET TV), program no. 3, February 1971.

3. John Leonard, "TV Review: Dime-Store Display of Imagination," *LIFE*, February 19, 1971, 16.

4. "Swinging Things," *Chicago Tribune*, January 22, 1971, B2; Ron Stevens, notes to "City of New Orleans," *Sing Out!* 21, no. 3 (March/April 1972), 20.

5. "Special Merit Spotlight," *Billboard*, February 20, 1971, 62; Barry Hansen, notes to *The Days of Wine and Vinyl* (Warner Bros. PRO 540, 1972).

6. "Philly DJ Out—Lyrics Cited," *Billboard*, March 27, 1971, 4; Ben Fong-Torres, "Radio: One Toke behind the Line," *Rolling Stone*, April 15, 1971.

7. Marty Gallanter, "Arlo: Bound for His Own Glory," *Frets* 1, no. 5 (July 1979), 28; Arlo Guthrie, liner notes to *Swampwater* (RCA Records, 1971).

8. Mike Jahn, "Arlo Guthrie Gives a Concert Marked by Country Songs," *New York Times*, April 2, 1971, 32; Ira Mayer, "Riffs," *Village Voice* 16, no. 16 (April 22, 1971), 43; Lloyd Paseman, "Folksinger Demonstrates He Takes Work Seriously; Arlo Guthrie Performs for UO Audience," *Eugene Register-Guard*, December 7, 1971, 1; Nancy Erlich, "Arlo Guthrie, Carnegie Hall, New York," *Billboard*, April 10, 1971, 20; "Jeff," "Concert Reviews," *Variety*, April 7, 1971, 54.

9. Ernie Santosuosso, "Arlo Guthrie on Stage at Symphony Hall," *Boston Globe*, April 3, 1971, 17; Bruce Kauffman, "Easy at the Bushnell. . . . Arlo," *Hartford Courant*, April 4, 1971, 6B.

10. "From the Music Capitals of the World: New York," *Billboard*, May 15, 1971, 24; "The Evolution of Arlo," *Circular* 4, no. 19 (May 16, 1972), not paginated.

11. "Guthrie Recognized by His Hometown," *Los Angeles Times*, July 15, 1971, sec. 1, 25; "Bits of Show Business," *Milwaukee Journal*, October 5, 1972, sec. 2, 15; Times Wire Service, "Fans Defy Town, Plan Guthrie Memorial," *St. Petersburg Times*, July 15, 1971, 9A; Associated Press, "Okemah Honors Woody," *Daytona Beach Morning Journal*, July 15, 1971, 8.

12. "Guthrie Recognized by His Hometown," sec. 1, 25; "Bits of Show Business," sec. 2, 15; Times Wire Service, "Fans Defy Town, Plan Guthrie Memorial," 9A; Associated Press, "Okemah Honors Woody," 8.

13. Mary Nic Schenk, "Music Review: Sound New, Message Isn't," *St. Petersburg Times*, November 15, 1971, 3D.

14. Lloyd Paseman, "Folksinger Demonstrates He Takes Work Seriously; Arlo Guthrie Performs for UO Audience," 1.

15. Lloyd Paseman, "Folksinger Demonstrates He Takes Work Seriously; Arlo Guthrie Performs for UO Audience," 1.

16. Lloyd Paseman, "Folksinger Demonstrates He Takes Work Seriously; Arlo Guthrie Performs for UO Audience," 1.

17. "Registration Effort Expands," *Billboard*, April 8, 1972, 6.

18. Michael Krogsgaard, *Positively Bob Dylan: A Thirty-Year Discography, Concert & Recording Session Guide, 1960–1961* (Ann Arbor, MI: Popular Culture Ink, 1991), 78; Lynn Van Matre, "Sound: It's a Feast of Folk in Memory of Woody," *Chicago Tribune*, April 23, 1972, sec. Arts and Fun, 9; Michael Cooney, "Record Reviews: The Woody Guthrie Tribute: Another View," *Sing Out!* 22, no. 2 (March/April 1973), 43; Paul Nelson, "Record Reviews," *Rolling Stone*, July 20, 1972, 50; Tony Russell, "Folk Song," *Gramophone*, November 1972, 989.

19. "The Evolution of Arlo Guthrie," *Warner Bros. Circular* 4, no. 19 (May 15, 1972), not paginated.

20. "The Evolution of Arlo Guthrie," *Warner Bros. Circular*, not paginated.

21. "The Evolution of Arlo Guthrie," *Warner Bros. Circular*, not paginated.

22. "Album Reviews," *Billboard*, May 27, 1972, 53.

23. Marjorie Hunter, "Prominent Foes of War Arrested," *New York Times*, May 25, 1972, 20.

24. Pat Downey, George Albert, and Frank Hoffman, *Cash Box: Pop Singles Charts, 1950–1993* (Englewood, CO: Libraries Unlimited, 1994), 147.

25. Bruce Sylvester, "Guthrie and Watson Bring 'Country Folk' to Boston," *Boston Globe*, June 29, 1972, 25; George Gent, "2 Concerts to Sing Folk Festival Blues," *New York Times*, July 6, 1972, 42; Don Heckman, "Taylor Leads Good Vibes at Folk Festival Benefit," *New York Times*, July 8, 1972, 16.

26. *Youngstown Vindicator*, June 2, 1972, 16; Lynn Van Matre, "Ravinia's Rain Clouds Arlo's Joy," *Chicago Tribune*, July 13, 1972, sec. 2, 6.

27. Karl Dallas, "Arlo Looks Back," *Melody Maker*, August 12, 1972, 43; *Baltimore Sun*, July 13, 1972, B7.

28. Karl Dallas, "Arlo Looks Back," 43.

29. "American Greetings Card Corp. Bows 2 Pop Hits-Inspired Card Series," *Billboard*, July 8, 1972, 12.

30. "Kirb.," "Concert Reviews," *Variety*, August 2, 1972, 43.

31. Michael Watts, "Arlo Guthrie," *Melody Maker*, August 5, 1972, 29; Karl Dallas, "Arlo Looks Back," 43; *Warner Bros. Circular* 4, no. 28 (July 17, 1972), not paginated; Karl Dallas, "Guthrie's Survival Course," *Melody Maker*, July 27, 1974, 24; Happy Traum, "The Eighth Annual Cambridge Folk Festival," *Sing Out!* 21, no. 5 (September/October 1972), 13.

32. Karl Dallas, "Arlo Looks Back," 43.

33. *The Johnny Carson Show*, broadcast August 17, 1972.

34. *The Johnny Carson Show*, broadcast August 17, 1972.

35. Richard Cromelin, "Seeger and Guthrie Share Bowl Stage," *Los Angeles Times*, August 21, 1972, sec. 4, 17.

36. Janet Maslin, "Records," *Rolling Stone*, July 20, 1972, 50.

37. Ira Mayer, "Arlo Guthrie: Hobo's Lullaby (Reprise MS 2060)," *New York Times*, August 27, 1972, D19; Tony Russell, "Folk Song," *Gramophone*, November 1972, 989; Bob Norman, "Record Reviews," *Sing Out!* 21, no. 5 (September/October 1972), 38; Fred Dellar, "Current Pop," *Hi-Fi News & Record Review*, September 1972, 1683; Robert Christgau, "The Christgau Consumer Guide," *Creem* 4, no. 6 (November 1972), 15; Henry Edwards, "The Lighter Side," *High Fidelity* 22, no. 9 (September 1972), 108.

38. "Dots and Dashes," *Warner Bros. Circular* 4, no. 28 (July 17, 1972), not paginated; "Dots and Dashes," *Warner Bros. Circular* 4, no. 38 (September 25, 1972), not paginated.

39. "Dots and Dashes," *Warner Bros. Circular* 4, no. 43 (October 30, 1972), not paginated; Frank Hoffman and George Albert, *The Cash Box Album Charts, 1955–1974* (Metuchen, NJ, and London: Scarecrow Press, 1988), 155.

40. Carol Kramer, "VD Blues: Taking the Worry Out of Being Close," *Chicago Tribune*, October 8, 1972, sec. 10, 2; Joe Klein, *Woody Guthrie: A Life* (New York: Alfred A. Knopf, 1980), 350.

41. "Fast Spins," *Warner Bros. Circular* December 11, 1972, not paginated; "Items," *Warner Bros. Circular* 4, no. 48 (December 11, 1972), not paginated.

42. "Random Notes," *Rolling Stone*, December 21, 1972, 7.

43. Sam Sutherland, "Studio Track," *Billboard*, March 3, 1973, 30; "Studio Watch: Recording in Hollywood, North and Otherwise," *Warner Bros. Circular* 5, no. 5 (February 5, 1973), not paginated.

44. Bruce Sylvester, "Tall Tales and Country Rock by Arlo Guthrie," *Boston Globe*, April 13, 1973, 29.

45. Frank Hoffman and George Albert, *The Cash Box Album Charts, 1955–1974* (Metuchen, NJ, and London: Scarecrow Press, 1988), 155.

46. "Watergate Tentacles Tighten, Stock Market Plummets," *Warner Bros. Circular* 5, no. 21 (May 28, 1973), not paginated.

47. Janet Maslin, "Record Reviews," *Rolling Stone*, June 21, 1973, 64; Robert Hilburn, "Pop Album Briefs," *Los Angeles Times*, August 12, 1973, sec. Calendar, 41; Ed Ward, "Records," *Creem* 5, no. 3 (August 1973), 66; David Clark, "Rock," *Records and Recording*, July 1973, 80; Harvey Andrews, "Record Reviews," *Folk Review* 2, no. 11 (September 1973), 27, 29; Noel Coppage, *Stereo Review*, September 1973, 90, 94; "On Record," *Country Music Review* 2, no. 8 (October 1973), 29.

48. "Quadradisc" (advertisement), *Billboard*, August 25, 1973, 12–13; "Top Album Picks: Quadrasonic," *Billboard*, September 1, 1973, 48.

49. John Hall, "Former Agents Testify Army Snooped on People in All Walks of Life," *Wilmington Morning Star* (Wilmington, NC) from UPI, February 25, 1971, 2.

50. Steve Moore, "Performance," *Rolling Stone*, December 20, 1973, 88.

51. Richard Cromelin, "Arlo Guthrie at S.M. Civic," *Los Angeles Times*, November 19, 1973, part IV, 14.

## Chapter Five

# Presidential Rag

In the early winter of 1974 Harold Leventhal telephoned Pete Seeger at the folk singer's home in Beacon, New York. He asked Pete, "Listen, how about you and Arlo doing some concerts together?" Seeger replied, "Sure." Harold then rang Arlo at his home in the snow-covered Berkshires, asking if he would be willing to go out on a short tour with Pete. He too agreed without hesitation. Guthrie had been sharing concert stages with Pete Seeger from the very beginning of his career; though separated by nearly thirty years in age, they had played together at benefits, peace rallies, television programs, festivals—even on the occasional "Together in Concert" double bill—but the two had never been paired for a proper tour. Seeger was already considered the grand old lion of American folk music, though in the early winter of 1974 he was only fifty-four years of age. Pete was far more of a political radical than Arlo, and his radicalism was never more evident than in the 1960s and 1970s, a time when he effectively used his music as a tool in the struggle for civil rights, against American involvement in the war in Vietnam, and for environmental concerns. Pete firmly remained a man of the Old Left. He had come of political age in the early 1940s when the Communist Party of the United States of America was touting communism as "twentieth-century Americanism." To his admirers, Seeger was an authentic American patriot, a dissenter of conscience whose New England ancestors had roots in America's founding. Seeger maintained that he could trace his lineage to settlers who came over on the *Mayflower* and "participated in the good and bad decisions which formed this country." Though he had drifted out of the Communist Party "around 1950," Pete's radicalism remained intact, and he remained a lifelong target of blacklisting and picketing by right-wing groups. But the charge that he remained a "secret" communist or, at the very least, a "fellow traveler," dogged him throughout his career. In his book *The Incompleat*

*Folksinger*, Seeger nimbly side-stepped his accusers, answering their "question of patriotism" with this definition of the term *left-extremist*: "Someone who stands up to defend the Bill of Rights, the Declaration of Independence, and the Sixth Commandment (Thou Shall Not Kill)."[1]

Leventhal knew that getting Pete and Arlo together for a series of concerts wasn't going to be easy. Though Arlo was the younger man, he was, by his own admission, content to idle the days away on his farm in Washington County. Seeger, in contrast, was indefatigable, a man on a mission; Harold noted that Pete was rarely at home in upstate New York but out on the front lines tirelessly fighting the good fight and "traveling all over the country doing benefits." Leventhal learned early on that it was best to reroute Arlo's more traditional touring schedule to align with Pete's, as Seeger's calendar morphed weekly as he would agree to perform at hastily staged benefit concerts, political rallies, and *Clearwater* environmental events. But the schedule soon fell into place, and by the early winter of 1974 Leventhal had arranged the first four official Pete Seeger and Arlo Guthrie "Together in Concert" programs, with the first to be held on Friday night, March 8, at Carnegie Hall. Afterwards, the musicians were to fly directly to the Chicago Opera House for a Saturday concert the next night, followed by a show at Montreal's Place des Arts on the 17th and, finally, at Boston's Music Hall on the 30th. Plans were made for Warner Bros./Reprise to record all four concerts for possible release on LP.[2]

The concert at Carnegie served as the template for what would follow. Seeger and Guthrie walked onto the stage and immediately moved into "Lonesome Traveler," a song written by their mutual friend Lee Hays. The song had been popularized by the Weavers in 1950, appearing as the B-side of a Decca single with Woody Guthrie's "So Long, It's Been Good to Know Yuh." The song's inclusion as the opening volley of the Seeger–Guthrie concert was, consciously or unconsciously, a sign of continuity. The Weavers had sung the song at their very first engagement at Carnegie Hall on Christmas Eve 1955, and here it was again, this time with Woody's son singing along. The musicians moved into a spirited guitar and banjo duet of a new Seeger song, "Well May the World Go," before Arlo ceded the stage to Pete, who sang Malvina Reynolds' haunting "God Bless the Grass." "We've got three generations of Guthries and Seegers out there in the audience, and I hope three generations of all of you out there . . . am I right?" Seeger queried, moving seamlessly into his generation-bridging rendition of "Declaration of Independence" with "Get Up and Go." For his part, Arlo traded easily between his own original songs ("Me and My Goose," "Presidential Rag") and songs popularized in the early days of the folk-music revival (Gus Cannon's "Stealin'," Lead Belly's "On a Monday," and his father's "Deportee [Plane

Wreck at Los Gatos].") Occasionally Guthrie would make eye contact with friends and relatives sitting in the first few rows of Carnegie's plush seats. He dryly noted, "There are a lot of people here tonight who don't usually get together in a joint like this." The show ended with a rousing finale of "This Land Is Your Land," everyone in the house on their feet singing along on this third encore of the evening. In a review of the show, Ira Mayer, a critic from the *Village Voice*, made note that Arlo, a bigger "star" at the box office than Pete, appeared "detached and casual" most of the night. Whenever Pete performed a solo turn, Guthrie sat "cross-legged on the floor, a few feet from Seeger, as if to receive the torch." In the end Leventhal's vision of shepherding the "Seeger-Guthrie Union" out of the 1940s and into the 1970s had been a resounding success. "Some in the audience must have felt a haunting sense of déjà vu," the *Voice* review closed. "It is another time, but the need for Seegers and Guthries of whatever generation remains."[3]

Not everyone thought the pairing of Seeger with Guthrie was for the best, but all agreed the Carnegie concert brought young and old together. Both *Variety* and *Billboard* noted, with more than a little surprise, that the double bill managed to attract an unusually multigenerational audience. Carnegie Hall was filled to the rafters with grandparents, parents, teenagers, school-age children, old lefties, and hippies, all of whom sang and clapped throughout the concert. Only members of the passive rock generation, most of whom had crowded into the venue only to hear Arlo Guthrie, seemed uncomfortable singing along with "Uncle Pete," regardless of how many times the grey-bearded folk singer would exhort them to do just that. Both critics from *Billboard* and *Variety* saw the Carnegie event as an evening with Pete Seeger with augmentation by Arlo Guthrie rather than a true collaboration. They were of the opinion that the seasoned folk-singing legend eclipsed "Guthrie on stage, telling longer anecdotes and generally controlling the ambience of the sets." Though Seeger's credentials as the most eminent American folk-music troubadour were unassailable, *Billboard* made note that twenty-six-year-old Arlo Guthrie "has emerged in recent years as a far more mature and sensitive musician than his initial, happy freak image might have suggested." Though *Variety* thought the evening of mostly old songs was little more than a celebration of "moldy nostalgia," the trade magazine noted the collaboration had been "etched by Warner Bros., which should find a ready market for the package. It was a folkie's evening, but wearing for others."[4]

It was on to Chicago. The weekend before the concert at the opera house, the *Chicago Tribune* offered a recent interview with Seeger, the article mentioning Pete's travels in the 1940s with Woody Guthrie. The article noted, not without irony, that in 1974, a "good portion of the younger generation familiar with Seeger in fact, is far less familiar with Woody than it is with his son Arlo Guthrie." *Tribune* music critic Lynn Van Matre thought the pairing of Seeger and Guthrie made for "a pleasant evening rather than a tremendously exciting one," finding Arlo "rather subdued," choosing to forego not only his best-known material but his "usual 'youth culture' rags." It's true that the Arlo fans weaned on the folk-rock offerings of his Reprise LPs were unprepared for the set list, peppered throughout with gentle readings of folk songs from the "Popular Front" era by Woody, Cisco Houston, the Weavers, and Lead Belly. With Guthrie on the bill, many of the younger fans had understandably assumed the concert would feature a rock 'n' roll segment and, as such, found themselves unprepared for a gentle evening of pastoral song leading, mostly led by the ministerial Seeger.[5]

The final Seeger and Guthrie winter concert at Boston's Music Hall on Saturday, March 30, was perhaps the best of all, with everyone getting into the hootenanny spirit. "Seldom do you see such a diverse concert crowd," wrote William Howard of the *Boston Globe*, "street freaks, students, families, middle-aged couples, and more than a few old folks who had brought along their grandchildren." The cross-generational appeal of the music that welded together "the Seeger-Guthrie union" was affirmed, with the *Globe* noting, "Few other artists whose ages differ by nearly 30 years can work as well together."[6]

Following the success and press attention brought by the "Together in Concert" events, Leventhal returned to his schedule book and planned two more Seeger–Guthrie double bills later that summer at Tanglewood, in the heart of the Berkshires, and in Denver, Colorado. In the meantime, with Reprise readying Guthrie's seventh LP for the label, *Arlo Guthrie* (Reprise MS 2183), for a May 5 release, Guthrie was off on a solo spring tour to begin on April 19 in White Plains, New York, finishing in Winston-Salem, North Carolina, on May 5.

Guthrie was due back in New York City on May 9, having agreed to perform at Phil Ochs' "An Evening with Salvador Allende" benefit at the Felt Forum. The previous fall, on September 11, the democratically elected president of Chile, Salvador Allende, was overthrown in a bloody military coup orchestrated by a general of the Chilean army, Augusto Pinochet. Allende, a gentle doctor and lifelong Marxist who helped cofound Chile's Socialist Party in 1933, made fast enemies with the Chilean elite shortly after assuming the presidency in November 1970. Nationalizing many Chilean industries, including the country's lucrative but foreign-owned copper mining and banking industries, Allende's earliest successes in implementing his socialist experiment were soon reversed by a series of worsening economic downturns. The discontent enabled Allende's powerful enemies—the military, the Christian Democrats, and the Roman Catholic Church among them—to unite and orchestrate his downfall.

Following the coup, the brutality and horror of the military's cleansing of those they accounted as their enemies was made graphic when thousands of political opponents were rounded up and detained at Estadio Chile, a football stadium in Santiago. Among those taken prisoner was Victor Jara, a teacher, artist, and folk singer who was an architect of the *Nueva Cancion Chilena* movement, a union of leftist singer-songwriters. Jara had befriended Phil Ochs in 1971 when the American folk singer, along with friends Jerry Rubin and Stew Albert, visited Chile and sang to the hardscrabble copper miners of the Andes. Jara was, in Phil's estimation, the Woody Guthrie or Pete Seeger of Chile, a defender of the nation's poor and a loyal, if sometimes critical, supporter of the Allende government. In the grim aftermath of Allende's ousting, later revealed to be orchestrated with the covert assistance and blessing of the U.S. Central Intelligence Agency, Jara was identified among the prisoners held at Estadio Chile. The military brutally tortured and executed him in front of thousands of frightened and horrified comrades and friends.[7]

After learning of the military coup in Chile and the subsequent cold-blooded murder of his friend Victor Jara, an angry Phil Ochs enlisted the assistance of sympathetic political friends and founded "Friends of Chile," based in New York City. His plan was to host an "An Evening with Salvador Allende (on Film)," a multimedia concert planned for the Felt Forum, a 4,600-seat theater in the basement of the Madison Square Garden complex in midtown Manhattan. The proceeds from the benefit would assist Chilean refugees. To that end, Ochs secured commitments from Pete Seeger, Arlo Guthrie, Melanie, Gato Barbieri, Dave Van Ronk, the actor/filmmakers Dennis Hopper and Melvin Van Peebles, Julian Beck's Living Theater, former U.S. attorney general Ramsey Clark, Daniel Ellsberg, and Allende's daughter, Isabel Tambutti. Ochs also, and most famously, convinced Bob Dylan to bring along his guitar and sing three or four songs. The last-minute announcement of Dylan's participation helped fill those seats that had remained empty only days before the event, but the majority of Dylan fans attended to see their hero perform and were not necessarily political. The *Village Voice* reported that most in attendance had bought their tickets months before Dylan was added to the bill, and the sold-out audience was mostly comprised of "faces familiar from decades of left-wing politics . . . [and] a surprisingly large contingent of Latin activists, primarily Puerto-Rican . . . [who had] certainly not paid $7.50 a ticket for a chance to hear Dave Van Ronk."[8]

The May 9 concert began with Ochs bringing the entire cast on stage. Predictably, there was an explosive reaction when the crowd spied Dylan standing alongside the ensemble, but Ochs, who had been drinking all afternoon, chastised the crowd for their "star-fucking excitement," reminding them that they were gathered for a political end, not to see Bob Dylan. If this was true it would be a good thing as Dylan was as intoxicated as Ochs, the two old friends having begun a reckless session of drinking some three hours earlier. Arlo, sharing a dressing room with Pete Seeger that night, recalled to *Rolling Stone* that "they finished the beer before I got there, and were starting on the wine."[9]

Following some prefatory comments, Ochs brought out Seeger, who was already scheduled to perform elsewhere. With Guthrie seconding on guitar and vocals, Pete performed Jose Marti's "Guantanamera" and the old gospel song "Oh, Mary, Don't You Weep." But it was Seeger's chilling solo rendition of Jara's last poem, "Estadio Chile," written shortly before the singer was tortured and murdered by Pinochet's soldiers, that stilled the rambunctious room and sobered the crowd, reminding everyone why they had gathered together that night.

Following a wistful song by Dave Van Ronk ("He Was a Friend of Mine"), a stirring performance by the La Victoria Dance Company, and Dennis Hopper's recitation of the Rudyard Kipling poem "If," Guthrie strolled out on stage alone with an acoustic guitar. "Hello. I'm gonna sing you some weird songs," he began. The usual catcalls for "Alice's Restaurant" and other popular Guthrie songs echoed throughout the theater, causing Arlo to ask, "Are you guys doing this or me?" Guthrie chose to open with Ernest Tubb's "Try Me One More Time." "Now the first thing I'm gonna sing you is this old cowboy song," he explained.

> This is directed to our president, 'cause I think before we start thinking about anywhere else, we ought to know who's talking. And if it's us talking, [we] got to have something to talk about *here*. Seeing as how nothing's happening here—too much—we got to start something. You know, a lot of people are worried that Richard Nixon is gonna stay in office longer than he's supposed to. A lot of people are worried he'll get kicked out, some are worried he'll stay in. . . . If he wants to run again, this is the song he ought to learn. I used to sing this song about Lyndon Johnson, but it works a hell of a lot better for Richard Nixon.

He followed with his father's "Deportee (Plane Wreck at Los Gatos)":

> The next song I sang on that *Midnight Special* show on the NBC network. Never got on the air though. I think part of the reason was the introduction, you know, because sometimes I say weird things before I sing songs. And all I said about this one was that it must be strange growing up in the United States, being a kid, and not knowing what a grape looks like. Doesn't sound too subversive. It was enough to can the song though.

Guthrie next moved to the piano. He explained that he had been sitting around one day playing ragtime on the piano when the next song suddenly "jumped up and wrote itself down." He moved into "Presidential Rag," his withering, uncompromising indictment of Richard Nixon and the state of the nation. Guthrie signed off following the song, but the audience was on their feet and wouldn't stop calling for his return to the stage. Ochs tried to settle everyone down, finally admonishing, "Hold it. Hold it. What we're trying to do here is an experiment in aesthetics and politics. We're trying to get across a political message. Arlo will be back later. The mere fact of you yelling 'More!' is part of a kind of worship, the same kind of fan worship you have for Dylan."

Guthrie would return to the stage following Melanie's performance of "Ring the Living Bell." Sitting at the piano, the folk singer delicately unfolded a slip of paper. "Now I'm gonna do something very strange," he offered. "This is something I have never done before. As a matter of fact, somebody handed me this poem—or this song—oh, not too long ago. I just picked it out of my pocket. So I'm gonna sing it for you. It's gonna be sort of weird. Now this is a poem about Victor Jara and it's written by an English poet named Adrian Mitchell. So here it goes . . ." It was a beautiful ballad, a simple but evocative retelling of the story of Jara's sparkling life and of his subsequent cold-blooded murder. The song was performed somewhat tentatively, and there were rough spots; Guthrie had not yet fully worked out a melody to fit the meter of the lyric. But it was a song that perfectly caught one element of the tragic story of the crimes committed in the wake of the Chilean political drama. Guthrie would return to the stage a third time to sing, this time at Dylan's insistence, a fractured reprise of "Deportee (Plane Wreck at Los Gatos)" alongside the drunken troubadour. The night ended with the entire cast on stage for a chaotic sing-along of "Blowin' in the Wind."

Journalist Frank Rose, who would subsequently write of the Chile concert in great detail for *Zoo World* and the *Village Voice*, offered, "Dylan aside, you'd have to say that Arlo Guthrie was the star of the show," a view plainly supported by the low-fidelity audience tapes that were soon traded among collectors. "Guthrie blended an acute political sensibility with an equally highly developed sense of humor," Rose offered, "resulting in a performance which was as enjoyable as it was relevant to the purpose of the evening."[10]

In the weeks following the Chile benefit, the effect of the event on Guthrie's political sensibilities began to focus. Though there were few people in the world he admired more than Pete Seeger, he *wasn't* Pete Seeger. He began to intimate that only so much could be accomplished through political benefits such as the most recent one in support of Chilean refugees. He was becoming increasingly suspicious that his singing at such affairs was merely a salve to the mostly left-wing audiences who already shared his concerns. It wasn't that political benefits were worthless enterprises. The best ones helped stimulate a dialogue on issues, and their capacity for fund-raising was important. But he told Rose, "It occurred to me that the only real value of doin' that concert [for Chile] was to get money and hopefully to get some guys out of prison. . . . I'm almost inclined to believe that aside from that there's nothin' that we can do in Chile that's so important as to make it different here, because the things that happened in Chile started *here*." The real problems were by-products of self-interested American foreign policy—and those of the world's other superpowers. In Guthrie's view there would be no "cure" for the ongoing troubles in Chile and Southeast Asia without first dealing with issues at home. The secret bombings of Cambodia, Watergate, "the Brazilian things," the wheat deal, the milk deal, were all a "direct result of the decadent society" in the ascendant. It was also Guthrie's view, one not generally seconded by many on the American Left, that the United States was not a singular repository of such decadence. "It doesn't matter to me what political system it is because they're all decadent as far as I'm concerned. They all have guys up there who like tellin' other guys what to do."[11]

Arlo's seventh album, *Arlo Guthrie*, made its first appearance on the *Billboard* charts on June 1, 1974. Preorders had allowed the album to enter the *Billboard* chart in the 201 position, moving to 192 following its first week of release. Though *Arlo Guthrie* would begin to slowly climb the charts in subsequent weeks, the movement of the LP was glacial. Five weeks following its release, *Arlo Guthrie* had moved only twenty-seven slots into position 165. This, disappointingly, would signal the LP's best placing on the *Billboard* chart. The album then began a slow downward trend. In the ninth week it slipped to 176, and soon totally disappeared from the *Billboard* Top 200. The album fared a little better on the *Cash Box* chart, rising to position 136 before vanishing after a seven-week ride. The results were disappointing, as the earliest notices seemed promising. *Billboard* described the contents as being "as fine a variety of material as Guthrie has ever offered on one set," noting the tuneful songs could play equally well on FM and AM stations. Though AM interest didn't pan out at all, *Billboard* was able to cite *Arlo Guthrie* as an "FM Action Pick," as the album was intergraded into the playlists of FM stations offering progressive programming.[12]

The influence of Pete Seeger on Guthrie's recent political activities was increasingly self-evident. On Monday night, June 17, Arlo returned to Carnegie Hall, where he appeared alongside Seeger, Judy Collins, Mary Travers, the actors Ossie Davis and Elliott Gould, Michael and Robert Meeropol (the sons of Ethel and Julius Rosenberg), and Morton Sobell (a scientist accused and convicted of spying for the Soviets). The solemn memorial event for Ethel and Julius was designed to generate funds to benefit the National Committee to Reopen the Rosenberg Case. Guthrie would also sing alongside Seeger at a June 26 concert at the Palace Theater, in Albany, New York, to benefit the "Stop the Grapes" strike fund. Cesar Chavez, the president of the United Farm Worker's Union of America, was on hand that night to stir up support for striking farmworkers in the grape and lettuce industries.[13]

Throughout the summer of 1974 reviews of *Arlo Guthrie* trickled in from the usual outlets. As was becoming increasingly the case, the reviews of his most recent mosaic album of Americana were mixed and occasionally harsh. On the support side was England's *Gramophone* reviewer, who suggested that Guthrie was a "star in the literal sense but without any of the superficial trappings enjoyed by so many other stars." *Melody Maker* agreed, musing that the release of a new Arlo Guthrie LP was rarely met with the enthusiasm of a new Rolling Stones or Bob Dylan disc, which was too bad as the singer consistently issued excellent albums. The music weekly noted that Guthrie had really matured as a songwriter. Citing Arlo's "Hard Times," a sepia-tinged "anthem for the New Depression" as one perfect example, *Melody Maker* suggested "Arlo's understanding of his own heritage is so profound that his own songs immediately sound like classics." Though *Stereo Review* was also of the mind that Guthrie "has never turned out a bad album," they sighed that "all of them, like this one, have had their small failings" but acknowledged Arlo's "great touch with campy old things." Critic Cameron Crowe, writing in the *Los Angeles Times*, offered that the success of "Alice's Restaurant," Guthrie's "whimsically anti-establishment . . . novelty tune," was a blessing that came at some cost. Following the runaway success of that first LP, "Guthrie has succeeded in releasing four superbly well-crafted efforts which have gone relatively unnoticed." There were negative notices as well. Though Janet Maslin had praised both *Hobo's Lullaby* and *Last of the Brooklyn Cowboys* in the pages of *Rolling Stone*, the new *Rolling Stone* music critic, Bud Scoppa, had little positive to say about Guthrie's recent albums. Though Scoppa allowed that *Last of the Brooklyn Cowboys* was as eclectic and "occasionally brilliant" as its predecessors, he deemed that record was nonetheless a misfire, and "*Arlo Guthrie* suggests not that the earlier album was an easily correctable miscalculation, but that things are becoming progressively more unglued." *Rolling Stone* found fault with nearly everything: Guthrie's choice of material, the album's arrangements (particularly Nick De Caro's use of strings on several tracks), and even the contribution of the Southern California Community Choir on the spirituals. Interestingly, *Rolling Stone* thought the only "salvageable tracks" on *Arlo Guthrie* were three Guthrie originals: "Won't Be Long," "Last to Leave," and "Hard Times." In the end Scoppa fretted, "Throughout *Arlo Guthrie* there's too much going on, and the heap of superfluous touches underscore rather than conceal the album's meagerness." *High Fidelity* agreed that De Caro's string arrangements were "a little syrupy" and suggested that Guthrie might consider a live album next time out as "in a studio context such as this, the result is slightly antiseptic." *Country Music Review* expressed their desire that Arlo "stick to hard and fast country material, which he does so well, and stop trying to cut across into rock." Robert Christgau, writing in *Creem*, gave the album a surprising B+ but not without noting the irony that "the two spirituals that make you wonder why he's fooling around with the Southern California Community Choir turn out to be about Israel."[14]

Surprisingly, Guthrie didn't appear stung by some of the harsh criticism. In fact, he agreed that parts of the album were overproduced. Less than ten days following the unfair drubbing in *Rolling Stone*, the singer told England's *Melody Maker*, "What can I tell you? The album's really got too much droop on it for me. It's something that I had to try; just one of those kind of things." He admitted while there were some cuts that he wasn't thrilled with, "I don't want you to say that I don't like the whole album . . . that would be stupid." He suggested that future recordings would be stripped-down affairs and that *Arlo Guthrie* was, in a sense, a transitive album, the last of his Los Angeles session-men albums. But he wasn't apologizing, telling *Melody Maker* that the album was solely of his design, and "by doing it now, by getting it out of the way, I've got some time to do what I think would be better later." Earlier in the interview, Guthrie chatted a little about his recent stateside concerts with Seeger; he described those events as featuring "lots of old songs, some new ones, the kind of songs that old Seeger audiences would really appreciate." It's possible that singing with Seeger in a relaxed setting helped revitalize his interest in old-time music, as Guthrie suggested that on his forthcoming LP he might forego the extravagant trimmings of his recent productions and "write some simpler kind of stuff."[15]

Guthrie and John Pilla were in England to perform at the tenth annual Cambridge Folk Festival, scheduled for the weekend of July 27 and 28. Though Arlo promised that he would primarily play the old tunes, as "Cambridge is more of a traditional festival," he wasn't averse "to sneak a couple of mine in there if it feels right." Harvey Andrews in England's *Folk Review* thought Guthrie's appearance was a "disappointment . . . that a more intimate atmosphere is more suitable for him." Though Andrews would have been unaware, Arlo's visit to Great Britain wasn't a proper tour; he and Pilla had planned on playing Cambridge and just enough gigs in small clubs throughout northern England and Scotland to "have part of our trip paid for." Arlo traveled to Greece in early August, and it was there, on the morning of August 9, 1974, that he first heard the news that on the previous evening Richard M. Nixon had resigned as the president of the United States.[16]

On August 12, Guthrie and Pete Seeger celebrated Nixon's resignation with a show at the Tanglewood music shed near Lenox, Massachusetts. In the audience that night was Constance Seeger, Pete's eighty-nine-year-old mother, a very dignified and proper concert violinist. *Rolling Stone* reported that she told her wayward banjo-playing son that while she enjoyed the show, she asked Pete if he might "teach Arlo not to sing so nasally." "But mother," Seeger answered, "I've been trying to learn to sing like that all my life." Following Tanglewood, Guthrie set off for concerts at the Mississippi River Festival at Southern Illinois University, Edwardsville (August 13), and at the Pine Knob Music Center outside of Detroit (August 14).[17]

The thirteenth annual Philadelphia Folk Festival was scheduled for the weekend of August 23 through 25, and though the commercial "folk boom" had, in principle, passed, the teeming crowds that attended the festival a year earlier forced the township officials of Upper Salford, Pennsylvania, to limit this year's attendance to some 6,500. In an attempt to sate the thousands of disappointed fans who would be left out of the event, the local PBS television station, WHYY, agreed to tape the festival for a series of TV specials to be broadcast the following January. There were some complaints that the Philadelphia gathering, for all its notoriety, was hardly a "folk" festival anymore. This year's schedule included a slate of male singer-songwriters, most of whom were signed to major labels: Arlo Guthrie, Tom Rush, John Prine, David Bromberg, Steve Goodman, Bruce Cockburn, and Leon Redbone. Though they had passed through the folk-music revival at the beginning of their careers, few sang traditional music anymore. "What this country needs," declared the decidedly unplugged Irish folk singer Mick Moloney, peering over the bank of electronic equipment on the festival stage, "is an influx of Luddites." Guthrie was scheduled to perform on the 23rd. Depending on one's definition of the term *folk music*, Guthrie performed only a single traditional number at the festival, the old whaling song "Reuben Ranzo." Guthrie likely gleaned the work song from the singing of the first *Clearwater* crew, as this "halyard shanty" was often sung as the sloop's crew performed the long drag on the rope to raise the main sail. Guthrie acknowledged that although the song's character was actually named *Ranzo*, he chose to sing "Ramzo, me boys, Ramzo." He suggested the downside of the simple word change was that it made the otherwise innocuous shanty sound "sort of dirty." In the introduction to his scathing indictment of Nixon, "Presidential Rag," Guthrie quipped, "Pete Seeger used to say when he couldn't get songs on the air, people used to ask him, 'Pete, do you really think those folk songs really do anything?' He said, 'I don't know, but they're keeping me off the TV.'"[18]

Following the Philadelphia event, Guthrie traveled to Saratoga Springs, New York, for concerts at the Saratoga Performing Arts Center (August 25) and to the Blossom Music Center in Cuyahoga Falls, Ohio (August 28). On August 30, he performed before a sold-out house at the Filene Center of Wolf Trap Farm Park, an outdoors performing-arts center in Vienna, Virginia, a suburb of Washington, DC. The concert differed little from the usual set list of 1974, which included "The Motorcycle (Significance of the Pickle) Song," Dylan's "Don't Think Twice, It's All Right," his father's "I Ain't Got No Home" and "Deportee (Plane Wreck at Los Gatos)," "Mother, the Queen of My Heart," "Presidential Rag," "Me and My Goose," "Goodnight, Irene," and even a little solo bluegrass banjo picking on "Washington County." As he finger-picked the guitar intro to the now rarely aired "Alice's Restaurant," a "premature applause" rippled throughout the venue. Guthrie good-naturedly chastised his capital city fans, warning them not to assume things: "That's how we elected Richard Nixon in the first place. . . . We clapped before we heard the tune."[19]

Several days later Guthrie, with John Pilla accompanying on bass and second guitar, was scheduled to perform a series of shows at the Quiet Knight, Chicago's premier folk-music nightclub. Guthrie's residency was to begin Wednesday, September 4, and last through Sunday. Acknowledging that Arlo wasn't the only entertainer whose stage act might be "affected by the departure of Richard Nixon," the music critic of the *Chicago Tribune* noted that the singer "might just pick at the carcass for a while." The set that night was a very relaxed affair, and Guthrie surprised everyone by having hometown hero Steve Goodman collaborate on the encores.[20]

There was a second reason for Arlo's visit to Chicago. *Billboard* reported on September 14 that he was to appear with his friend Hoyt Axton "in a 60-minute *Soundstage* special" to be produced in Chicago by WTTW, the local PBS affiliate. Plans were made for the program to be "distributed to some 240 public service stations nationally." *Soundstage* was an offshoot of an earlier Windy City area music program, *Made in Chicago*, which was first telecast in 1973 and featured such artists as Jim Croce, Gordon Lightfoot, Curtis Mayfield, and Seals and Crofts. The success of that show led WTTW to inaugurate *Soundstage*, and it attracted an all-star slate of performers, including Michael Bloomfield, Harry Chapin, Dr. John, Jose Feliciano, Maria Muldaur, Randy Newman, the Pointer Sisters, Muddy Waters, and Johnny Winter. Though the PBS program couldn't compete for talent with such deep-pocket network shows as *Midnight Special* and *In Concert*, the musicians who appeared on *Soundstage* wouldn't need to cede the control of their music to the whims of a Hollywood producer. Ken Ehrlich, the executive producer of *Soundstage*, suggested, "I think we began right from the start to establish a reputation of treating performers like people instead of that old, 'get-on-and-get-off in two minutes thing." To more firmly establish that point, Ehrlich continued, "The Arlo Guthrie show [to be broadcast] in December is a good example of what we try to do. We just talked to him and said, 'Who would you like to do a show with?' He said, 'Hoyt Axton, Steve Goodman, and Jack Elliott.'" In the end, and try as they might, WTTW "couldn't reach" the migratory Ramblin' Jack, but Axton and Goodman enthusiastically signed on, and the resulting program was something special.[21]

It was apparent that the *Soundstage* budget didn't allow for a set of any great note. The setting for the Guthrie program was a framed ramshackle structure, an assortment of wood planks crossed and sticking out over the stage at irregular angles. Arlo, wearing a garish blue floral-print jacket and brown cowboy hat, a mop of brown curls sticking out from under the brim, strode out with his guitar and sang "Try Me One More Time," noting that he had been out of the country when he first learned that Nixon had resigned. With John Pilla on electric bass, Guthrie moved to the piano for his next three songs, "Son of Week on the Rag," "Presidential Rag," and "City of New Orleans." The studio audience responded with respectful applause, though they appeared to hold most of their enthusiasm in check. Guthrie then introduced Chicago's own Steve Goodman. The two friends performed a marvelous twin-guitar version of "Boomer's Story," a song that Guthrie had learned from his friend Ry Cooder, who in turn had learned it off a record by Cisco Houston. Following a solo three-song set by Goodman, Guthrie brought out Axton, a gregarious man of good humor, who instantly connected to the crowd by proactively asking for their forbearance as "I've been up since the middle of March." Hoyt, a bear of a man who towered over the slight figures of Guthrie and Goodman, had the two join him for a run-through of his song "Boney Fingers," which he suggested recently charted as "36 with a bullet . . . in Kansas City." Following two additional solo originals by Hoyt, the three friends closed the program with sing-alongs of Dylan's "Walkin' Down the Line," "Reuben Ranzo," and Lead Belly's "Goodnight, Irene."

Following the *Soundstage* taping, Guthrie performed at an ambitious event called the West Virginia Bluegrass Folk Festival. The festival, which took place on the weekend of September 13 through 15 at Cold Stream Campgrounds, Capon Bridge, West Virginia, featured an unusual teaming of traditional bluegrass and country artists with a slate of urban singer-songwriters thrown in for good measure. The traditional bluegrass artists included Doc and Merle Watson, Roy Acuff and the Smoky Mountain Boys, the Carter Family, Uncle Josh, the Dillards, Jim Eanes, and Vassar Clements. Representing the new acoustic-based young artists were Arlo, John Prine, Steve Goodman, Doug Kershaw, and John Hartford. The rowdy event was taped by WNYC in New York City, and Guthrie's set was broadcast in its entirety. Arlo was no longer enamored of playing large-scale rock or bluegrass festivals. He told WNYC,

I like to be able to really be loose and free on stage, but the audience makes it super difficult these days to really get that kind of scene going. If you're playing super funk you can get on stage and [though] people are throwing Frisbees around, drinking Ripple in the back, you can still do it, because that's what you're there to do, to get everybody grooving or boogieing. I'm not trying to pull that scene off. The kind of stuff that we're doing . . . requires an incredible union with the audience. And if the *audience* isn't there, it's then very difficult for *me* to get there.[22]

Guthrie was due back on the road in October for a month-long tour of the U.S. Pacific coast and western Canada. On Saturday night, October 19, the tour kicked off with a performance at the Santa Monica Civic Auditorium, but the press resulting from that engagement was somber. Three fans had ingested "windowpane," described in the local paper as "a clear, crystal form of the hallucinogenic drug" LSD. One died from an overdose, with the other two hospitalized and seriously ill. Though his earliest songs and stage monologues suggested that Guthrie was something of a "stoner," he admitted that lifestyle was mostly in the past. In the winter following the birth of his son, Guthrie recalled getting high with some friends around the family's woodburning stove when he startled himself with the thought, "Suppose something happens to the kid? Who's gonna drive him to the hospital through five feet of snow?" Guthrie remembered to *People* magazine, "Nobody raised his hand, so I quit." Following a concert at Massey Hall in Toronto on November 7, Guthrie made it down to the Riverboat nightclub to "sit in" with old friend Mimi Fariña, also in town for a gig. After visiting California, Washington, Arizona, New Mexico, Missouri, Minnesota, and Kitchener, Canada, the autumn tour concluded with a November 16 concert at the Civic Center in Ottawa.[23]

There was one final date before he could rest at home for his usual holiday break. On Tuesday evening, November 26, Guthrie appeared alongside Buffy Sainte-Marie, Harry Belafonte, and the Skitch Henderson Orchestra at the First Americans Gala, actor Marlon Brando's benefit for the American Indian Development Association. The event was held in the tony Starlight Ballroom of the Waldorf-Astoria hotel in Manhattan and attracted such patrons as Ethel Kennedy, George Plimpton, Bette Midler, and Dick Cavett. But the *Los Angeles Times* suggested the $125-a-plate dinner was little more than a glitzy bust, with "half of New York's beautiful people mingling with 30 impoverished Indians."[24]

On the morning of February 27, 1975, sleepy-eyed early risers tuning in to the popular NBC-TV program *The Today Show* were treated to a musical wake-up call from Pete Seeger and Arlo Guthrie. The two musicians were on the show to perform the songs of Woody Guthrie and chat with Barbara

*Guthrie accompanies Pete Seeger in this candid backstage photograph from 1975. Photofest.*

Walters about the newly published *Woody Sez* (Grosset & Dunlap), a collection of Woody's columns written May 12, 1939, through January 3, 1940, and first published in *People's World*. Marjorie Guthrie was pleased that Pete and her eldest son got along so well as the serious and remote Seeger shared many of Woody's traits. "There was a simplicity to Woody," Marjorie shared to one reporter. "He was not suave or sophisticated. He was a graceless, artless kind of reticent guy. Woody was like Pete Seeger is: they love the world and identify with all the people but they have a very hard time loving people independently."[25]

In the early winter of 1975, Guthrie was at Warner Bros. Recording Studios in North Hollywood overseeing the final mixes of the forthcoming *Together in Concert* double album with Pete. The set had been assembled at Shaggy Dog Studios, Stockbridge, Massachusetts, from the master recordings of the four March 1974 concerts. Following the mixing session, Guthrie told *Rolling Stone* that he and his wife and children were off to Hawaii for a family holiday. But before leaving, Arlo stopped by Oakland's Focus Cable TV Studio to tape a segment of the locally popular *Went Like It Came* program.

He was joined on the program by such old friends as Bonnie Raitt and the hippie-clown Wavy Gravy (Hugh Romney), along with Werner Erhard, the controversial guru and founder of the EST movement. Following the taping, Erhard invited everyone on the program to a small wrap party at his mansion on San Francisco's Russian Hill. Guthrie sat alone in a corner, apart from the others, and watched as Erhard's "eerily blissful minions" served their guests persimmon pudding and sake. The *Rolling Stone* stringer who accompanied the cast to the residence asked a noticeably wary Guthrie his thoughts on the scene. Arlo suggested to the writer, "Leave yer hat on."[26]

In March Harold Leventhal arranged for an additional three Seeger and Guthrie "Together in Concert" concerts. The first was held at the Berkeley Community Theater on March 5; their easygoing camaraderie and cross-generational appeal, so apparent back east, was easily replicated out west. One writer noted, "The range of ages in the crowd was certainly the most diverse I have ever seen anywhere. Children and babies in arms contrasted heavily with grey-haired Berkeley radicals."[27]

That winter also saw the NBC-TV broadcast of *The Hoyt Axton Country Western Boogie Woogie Gospel Rock and Roll Show*. Hoyt, who had recently hit the big time with Three Dog Night's cover of his song "Joy to the World," hosted an all-star lineup of friends from the country and rock music worlds. The celebrity guests included Rita Coolidge, Loggins and Messina, Kris Kristofferson, Tanya Tucker, Doug Dillard, Charlie Rich, Linda Ronstadt, Harry Nilsson, Buffy Sainte-Marie, Ringo Starr, Billy Swan, Paul Williams, and Arlo. The program fared best during the show's many musical interludes, but things got a little silly when the musicians were drafted into performing in comedy sketches. In one segment, Guthrie and Axton, toting guitars, arrive at the schoolhouse of dowdy principal Buffy Sainte-Marie. The two guitar players were, according to the script, scheduled to perform at an elementary school pageant, where they were required to wear sandwich boards championing the perfect union of peanut butter and jelly on white bread. A television critic from the *Los Angeles Times* described the comedy segments as scenes from an amateurish Axton home movie, no doubt "more fun to make than . . . to watch."[28]

On Saturday night, March 15, Lead Belly's niece, Tiny Robinson, and Blue Labor Records rented out Hunter College's Assembly Hall in Manhattan for "A Tribute to Leadbelly—all of Leadbelly's songs sung by his friends." On hand were Pete Seeger, Arlo ("For Woody"), Sonny Terry and Brownie McGhee, and the Lunenberg Travelers. Guthrie sang Lead Belly's "Redbird," "Pigmeat," "Lord Lord Lord," and "On a Monday" and also collaborated with Seeger and the ensemble on the evening's closing songs: "Midnight Special," "Meeting at the Building," and "Goodnight, Irene." One reviewer on hand wrote, "Mr. Guthrie managed, above all, to capture Leadbelly's style, especially on the piano: not quite an impersonation, it was an affectionate portrait." Tomato Records released the evening's concert on a two-LP set in 1977.[29]

On March 25, Guthrie and Seeger were in Washington, DC, for a standing-room-only concert at Constitution Hall. The *Washington Post* noted that the evening's program had more "political overtones" than usual. Seeger had been troubled by the tensions between the People's Republic of China and the Soviet Union, the former charging the latter with being counterrevolutionary. This embarrassing public chasm between the world's two largest socialist societies, popularly termed the "Sino-Soviet Split," troubled old-guard left-ists such as Seeger. When later questioned by a *Village Voice* writer about with whom his worldview aligned, Seeger diplomatically referenced a rally at Madison Square Garden in support of Puerto Rican independence. "Did you notice the cries of *Unidad, Unidad* that went up when people got sectarian?" Seeger answered. "Those are my sentiments." In a symbolic gesture to bring both sides together, the *Washington Post* reported that "delegations from the Chinese liaison mission and the Russian embassy were on hand as invited guests of the performers," though the former comrades were "seated, diplomatically, 10 rows apart." That night, in the spirit of antisectarianism, Seeger sang both a Russian folk song and the Mao-era revolutionary marching song "The Three Rules of Discipline and the Eight Rules of Attention." But for all of Pete's best ideology-mending intentions, the *Post* allowed, "the loudest response, which came from the younger members of the audience, seemed to be for Guthrie's solos." Guthrie and Seeger's final concert of their brief winter reunion was on March 28 at Philadelphia's Academy of Music.[30]

That April, Warner Bros. publicists announced that Guthrie would be featured on "a special concert segment of NBC's resurrected Smothers Brothers show." The brothers, whose TV series had come to a well-publicized end after numerous battles—one involving Pete Seeger—with network censors at rival CBS, had coaxed Guthrie, as well as Kris Kristofferson, Rita Coolidge, Don McLean, Billy Swan, and Mickey Newbury, to perform on their new program. For his segment, Guthrie performed Dylan's "Walkin' Down the Line," an as-yet unreleased Dylan song recently slotted on the *Together in Concert* LP. The Smothers Brothers program was broadcast on Monday evening, May 5.[31]

On Saturday, April 19, the year-and-a-half-long national celebration of the American Bicentennial was officially launched. Nixon's successor, President Gerald Ford, was scheduled to speak at a bicentennial ceremony in Concord, Massachusetts, not far from the site where the legendary "shot heard 'round the world" was fired. Though the Ford event would attract a crowd of some

100,000 spectators, the official ceremony was preceded by what newspapers termed an "anti-establishment vigil." Some 25,000 to 30,000 protestors were expected to gather at the stroke of midnight on April 19 and stay until 8:00 a.m. on the morning of the Ford event. This outdoor "town meeting" was to demonstrate support for "The People's Bicentennial," whose countercultural platform was designed to "send a message to Wall Street" with calls to democratize "the American economy." The committee was also demanding the cessation of U.S. militarism abroad. Scheduled to appear at the alternative celebration were such speakers as Harvard's Nobel Prize–winning Dr. George Wald, Richard Chavez of the United Farm Workers Union, the ecologist Barry Commoner, and a gaggle of sympathetic union leaders from Boston. The speeches were augmented with musical performances by folk singers Pete Seeger, Phil Ochs, U. Utah Phillips, and Arlo.

The protest event was marred from the beginning by a gentle but steady rain, which forced the crowd to shield themselves from the cool night air and precipitation with blankets and tarps. The *Christian Science Monitor* suggested that in the same manner of those at the Ford ceremony awaiting the arrival of a faux Paul Revere, the economic democracy activists "were waiting for Arlo Guthrie." The event organizers acknowledged that large numbers of young people attending the event were simply curious teenagers out for a good time; the "local townies" flocking to the event were not necessarily aligned politically. They merely wanted to party through the night. This was confirmed by the *Boston Globe,* whose reporters roamed through the crowd to interview those in attendance. They found that many shared the sentiment of one eighteen-year-old who admitted, "All I came to do was to hear Arlo Guthrie." In the end not too many of those attending would even get the chance to hear the folk singer. He ambled on stage around eight in the morning, hours after most of the soaked and chilled crowd had wandered home in weary disappointment. Things got uglier in the afternoon when a number of People's Bicentennial protestors chose to stay on for the official Ford ceremony, catcalling and disrupting the president's speech. Guthrie found it deliciously ironic that President Ford delivered his speech on the east end of the Old North Bridge, as that was the same side of the river occupied by British troops in 1775. It was shortly after the event that Guthrie sat down at his piano and wrote the beautiful "Patriot's Dream."[32]

On Saturday evening, May 3, Guthrie returned to a standing-room-only Carnegie Hall for his annual concert. This year Guthrie played solo, without Pete Seeger or a band for accompaniment, on a two-hour program. Switching between a six-string guitar and Carnegie's grand piano, the show served up the usual mélange of Lead Belly, Hoyt Axton, and Bob Dylan songs interspersed with his own "The Motorcycle Song" and the chart-topping single

"City of New Orleans." In his between-song monologues, *Variety* noted that Guthrie, "a folksinger-spokesman for today's youth," had a lot to say on the subjects of "war, police and Federal 'spying.'"[33]

On Tuesday, July 1, Pete and Arlo performed at the Saratoga Performing Arts Center in Saratoga Springs. In a preconcert interview with the Newburgh *Evening News*, Seeger told reporter Jon Halvorsen that he first met Arlo when Woody and Marjorie brought him to the Seeger cabin in Beacon, when the boy was "barely out of his diapers." Though Seeger was fifty-six and Guthrie twenty-seven, Pete acknowledged that since the two musicians enjoyed listening to each other sing and play, "it's very easy for us to perform together." The evening's concert, a folksy night of acoustic guitar, banjo, and solo piano, was to be filmed by the local Schenectady PBS affiliate WMHT. Fifteen songs from the concert were included on the PBS special *Arlo Guthrie and Pete Seeger in Concert*, which first aired on July 16, 1977.[34]

Otherwise the summer tour rolled on with little fanfare. There were two solo shows at Washington Park, Illinois (July 12) and at the Merriweather Post Pavilion, Columbia, Maryland (July 19). He shared another bill with Seeger on July 20 at the Pine Knob Music Theater, Clarkston, Michigan, before moving onto Milwaukee for a sold-out solo concert (July 22) at Uihlein Hall, a performing-arts center in the city's downtown area. Sitting at the venue's impressive grand piano that night, Guthrie teased his image as a roaming troubadour by offering, "Here I am, carrying my nine foot grand across America in a Conestoga wagon to sing folk songs." Though Guthrie could rock when the occasion called for it, there was little doubt that he was best able to communicate in a more folksy, relaxed setting. One critic attending the show wrote, "In days when tons of equipment and large bands are the rule, it's nice to see an exception like Arlo Guthrie."[35]

Guthrie and Seeger were scheduled to perform on the evening of Friday, July 25, at the Wollman Rink in Central Park. The tandem concerts of Guthrie and Seeger in New York City were always something of a homecoming, with the musicians performing before, in the estimation of *Village Voice* writer Tom Smucker, "what was largely an audience of old-lefties and old-lefties' children." Though Smucker guiltily admitted that he wasn't as confident as the perennially optimistic Seeger that America's better days were still ahead, he acknowledged that Guthrie's appearance with the old lion of folk music emphasized the survival of certain "aspects of family and tradition and self-definition" in these waning days of Manhattan's *Popular Front*–era left-wing culture.[36]

That summer Reprise released the two-album set *Pete Seeger & Arlo Guthrie: Together in Concert*. Paul Nelson, a longtime fan of Seeger's and a former coeditor of the *Little Sandy Review* and *Sing Out!* contributed a short review in *Rolling Stone*. The album *was* something of an anachronism, and though packaged with gloss and featuring better production, Nelson described the set as a natural cousin of such 1950s-era Folkways platters as *With Voices Together We Sing* and *Pete Seeger and Sonny Terry at Carnegie Hall*. As the new release featured the same vague internationalism and left-wing motifs as its forebears, Nelson believed the album's contemporary political content "invariably seems cultist and safely condescending, its humanism trite and softly sentimental. Still, there is great sweetness and innocence here and some of the music is truly timeless." Though Nelson's soft spot for the LP was apparent, his nostalgic pang for the Moses Asch era of record production was not shared by Mike Jahn of *High Fidelity*. In a mean-spirited appraisal of the album and the artists, Jahn fumed, "Seeger wore out his welcome twenty years ago, yet persists in singing the liberal line and delivering monologues so condescending they sound like the perorations of a Cub Scout leader on the subject of camp-fire building." Guthrie hardly fared better, with the critic decrying the singer's "slipshod" performances on *Together in Concert*. "He here delivers some of the most ragged vocal performances ever taped for posterity, butchering a variety of worthy songs." England's *New Music Express* didn't necessarily mind the left-wing politics of the set, but with Seeger's valentines to "Joe Hill" and a marching Red Chinese Army, the *New Music Express* critic rued, "I doubt there has ever been a greater show of commitment that was so irrelevant to anything going on today." The critic from *Hi-Fi News & Record Review* believed the album was worth a listen but admitted, "I am left with the feeling that the 'magic' more likely rests in being at the concerts than sitting here in England hearing this disc, track by track." *Gramophone*, on the other hand, thought *Together in Concert* "a masterpiece," with *Stereo Review* and *Folk Review* also more impressed than not.[37]

That summer Guthrie visited a local roadhouse a mile or so from his home in the Berkshire woods. The band that night was Shenandoah, an accomplished combo that played a muscular mix of rock 'n' roll, country, and blues. Guthrie remembered, "I just went in to hear them, and the thought struck me that, with a little work, they could play the same circuits I was playing." Shenandoah wasn't a side project for its members; they were a working band who had already attracted a small but devoted following in the area. Though they weren't earning much of a living, they were, in Guthrie's words, "at least surviving" solely on their music. Shenandoah was formed by rhythm guitarist David Carron, who had been born in nearby Pittsfield, and his friend, David Grover, a brilliant, nimble-fingered lead guitarist whose father served as president of the Berkshire Folk Music Society. Shenandoah's bassist, Dan Velika, had earlier played with Carron as two members of the rock band Quarry. Shenandoah's drummer, Terry Hall, was also a local boy, having attended Stockbridge's Indian Hill School. Guthrie had earlier consented to perform at a benefit concert near his home, and he asked the band that night at the roadhouse if they would consider playing a set on the program. They agreed, and after playing at the benefit, without the aid of a rehearsal, the band agreed to accompany Arlo on several songs during his own program. Things went so well that Guthrie and Shenandoah "agreed to rehearse and go on the road." It would prove to be a long-lasting, and inspired, musical association. The partnership of Arlo Guthrie and Shenandoah, with occasional changes in band personnel, would endure through the next twelve years.[38]

Guthrie returned to the road, still as a soloist, in early August. The short week-long sortie was scheduled around his near-annual appearance at the Mississippi River Festival on August 6. Next Guthrie performed at the Civic Center, Charleston, West Virginia (August 8); the Temple University Music Festival, Philadelphia, Pennsylvania (August 9); and the University of Delaware in Newark (August 10).

That September it was announced in the trades that rockers Billy Preston and Arlo Guthrie would be featured spokesmen for the Craig Car Stereo Company. The advertisements, according to *Billboard*, would feature both artists prominently in magazine print ads and were also planning to license the artist's "songs . . . as beds in radio spots." The fact that Guthrie would shill for a car stereo company was seen as something of a sellout. The announcement was greeted by antagonism by those who would have preferred that he follow his father's example, which they believed, erroneously, was to shun all forms of commercialism. Guthrie would have none of it, telling Joe Klein shortly following the kickoff of the advertising campaign, "I did a Craig car stereo ad . . . just to piss those people off." The truth was that the people who self-righteously invoked the spirit of Woody Guthrie as the symbol of all things anticommercial were simply misinformed. In the days when he was something of a minor radio personality, Woody Guthrie sang on-air praises of a number of products such as Model Tobacco.[39]

Though the first frost of autumn had already fallen on the Berkshires, Guthrie agreed to perform at a Sunday afternoon outdoor concert on October 5, with proceeds to benefit the Worthington, Massachusetts, Health Association. Though Worthington (population 800) was somewhat wary of "the prospect of some 5000 cars jamming the two or three access roads" into their little town, the town's elders were firmly in support of the benefit. They were, in fact, staffing the planning committee for the planned five-hour-long event, which would also feature Shenandoah and another well-known Berkshires resident, singer-songwriter James Taylor.[40]

On November 5, Guthrie performed at the Westchester Premier Theater in Tarrytown, New York. The next night he would appear as a surprise guest of Bob Dylan's Rolling Thunder Revue at the Civic Center in Springfield, Massachusetts. Guthrie hadn't planned on playing with the revue. In a week's time he was to head off on tour—his first with Shenandoah in tow—for several dates in the Deep South and a short residency in Chicago. It was Guthrie's pal, Ramblin' Jack Elliott, on tour with the Rolling Thunder Revue, who telephoned, inviting him to join them. Arlo sang two songs on the program with Roger McGuinn, formerly of the Byrds, backing on harmonica. Writer Larry Sloman, following the Dylan tour as a correspondent for *Rolling Stone*, noted that the revue's closing song, "This Land Is Your Land," was "wonderful, Arlo back on to do a chorus of his father's song and getting the loudest ovation of the night."[41]

The following day, with no Rolling Thunder concerts scheduled, the cast, and the camera crew who followed them everywhere, pulled into Mama Frasca's Dream Away Lodge, a hideaway on the timbered summit of October Mountain in nearby Becket. Described by playwright Sam Shepherd as "small bar/diner–former brothel somewhere in the extreme boondocks of Massachusetts," the lodge had long been a favorite spot of Guthrie and his friends. The Guthries would often bring their children to the restaurant for a meal and to visit with Mama Maria Frasca, a colorful, vibrant, and much beloved local character. Italian born, Mama was warm, friendly, and generous with everyone. Though she was nearing octogenarian status, Mama was a renaissance woman who busied herself by running her restaurant business, dispensing old-world "natural healing" treatments to customers in need, and singing and playing Italian folk songs on her green-painted guitar. Guthrie suggested to photographer Ken Regan that Mama's lodge would serve as an interesting filming locale for Dylan's film project. Celebrity visitors were no strangers to Mama's, as many performers from nearby Tanglewood would visit the lodge and be welcomed in the same informal manner as all the regular guests. The restaurant did proudly display a photograph of Mama standing alongside the great Liberace. Dylan and Joan Baez arrived at the lodge sometime after the camera crew had set up and begun taking light readings, and though Mama showed no particular kinship with the remote Dylan, she was completely taken with the smiling and sunny Baez. The camera crew hustled to get the surreal meeting down on film, and some scenes shot that afternoon, which included Guthrie sitting alongside Frasca and Baez, playing soft mandolin fills on the melancholic "Mama's Lament," which was later incorporated into Dylan's art-house film *Renaldo & Clara*. In 1976, Mama, along with Guthrie, John Pilla, and a couple of members of Shenandoah, would cut a very rare 45 single together ("Mama's Lament" and "God and Mama") for Reprise Records (Reprise MX 1575). The two songs were recorded at Stockbridge's Shaggy Dog Recording Studios under the supervision of Pilla's Route 183

Productions and published by Guthrie's Howard Beach Music, Inc. The record was sold for one dollar at the lodge; Mama, characteristically, donated all proceeds from the vocal-guitar-mandolin recording to a local church.[42]

Following his adventures with Dylan and the Rolling Thunder Revue, Guthrie traveled to the Deep South for shows at Southeastern Louisiana University in Hammond (November 12); Gusman Auditorium, Miami, Florida (November 13); and the Civic Auditorium, Jacksonville, Florida (November 15). Afterwards, he was scheduled to return to the Quiet Knight in Chicago for a five-night residency beginning on November 18. These were the earliest of the Arlo Guthrie and Shenandoah shows. Shenandoah, a four-man ensemble at present, would perform their own brief set before accompanying Guthrie as he paged through a set that included "Gypsy Davy," "The Shade of the Old Apple Tree," and "This Land Is Your Land."[43]

Following his traditional December break, Guthrie returned to the road in January 1976 for a series of shows on the West Coast. On January 22, he and Shenandoah appeared at the Boarding House in San Francisco. There had been a drop-off of Guthrie's songs played on FM radio in recent years, resulting in a noticeable decrease of young people in attendance. The house that night was crowded, but the beginning of a demographic shift was evident. The floor wasn't filled with the usual tie-dye hippies who normally populated his West Coast concerts. In their place, in the estimate of one *Billboard* writer, were "an unusually high percentage of well dressed suburban liberals in their thirties and early forties."[44]

Things were changing. In fact, *everything* was changing, sometimes in unexpected ways. On Friday night, January 30, Guthrie and the band performed at a sold-out concert at the Lane County Fairgrounds in Eugene, Oregon. On the night prior to the concert, Guthrie was resting at Eugene's Valley River Inn when he was visited by a reporter from the *Eugene Register-Guard.* Their conversation touched on a number of topics of interest to Arlo, not the least of which was his reawakened interest in spiritual matters. Talking of the recent past, Arlo recollected to the reporter, "I wrote some songs and I sang some songs and I changed some scenes, but there was something bigger 'n me, and I would have been a fool not to recognize that." That something "bigger," he went on to explain, was God. "I don't mind being a fool as long as I'm God's fool," he continued. "The job of musician is to create an atmosphere where the person who's listening can perceive deeper into himself. I think good music helps tune the soul. Tuning the soul is like tuning an instrument so that it's more receptive to the one who's making the music. The creator makes the music and he makes it better on souls that are tuned."[45]

Guthrie's interest in religious and spiritual matters was nothing new, but reports of his recent immersion into the teachings of Franciscan Catholicism certainly were. He told writer Joe Klein that he first met his monk friend and teacher, "Brother Michael," almost by accident "on one of those little airplanes that fly into Pittsfield. We met in the air, so to speak." Brother Michael was a member of a small hermitage based not far from Guthrie's Washington County home. That hermitage was affiliated with a much larger Franciscan province based across the country in Santa Barbara, California. The Guthrie family was, at first, confused by Arlo's sudden interest in Catholicism; he and sister Nora would occasionally spar on theological issues. But since he didn't proselytize with evangelical zeal, most saw it as a phase he would eventually pass through. A lengthy feature on Guthrie's "conversion" written for the Franciscan magazine *St. Anthony Messenger* suggested that "justice, morality, compassion, the little against the big, light against dark—this is what Arlo Guthrie writes and sings about today." Though that sentence was entirely true, Arlo countered that, in a sense, these

> have always been the things I wrote about. . . . I have lots of songs I wrote about Jesus before I figured out who he was. . . . I wasn't the one who figured out who Jesus was. I'm not Catholic or Franciscan or Christian because I wanted to be. I was compelled by God to follow the direction he was leading me in.

Guthrie insisted that although his immersion into the teachings of St. Francis was going to be a long process, he was a willing and devoted student committed to the long run. Shortly afterwards there was a report that Guthrie had been admitted into the Secular Franciscan Order during "a simple ceremony in Springfield, Massachusetts." It was also during this long interval of study that Guthrie was, on occasion, accompanied on the road by Brother Michael and Brother Jonathan of the Good News, a Berkshires-based monastic order. The *Messenger* wrote:

> When they travel together, Arlo and his Franciscan friends try to arrive early in the city where a concert is scheduled. Dressed in traditional Third Order habit without cowl, Arlo joins the brothers in simple apostolic tasks, walking the streets, visiting the sick in hospitals and homes.[46]

The year 1976 wasn't totally consumed by matters of the spirit. Guthrie would also actively support the campaign of a political figure seeking the Democratic Party's nomination as its presidential candidate. Fred R. Harris, who had served as a Democratic senator from Oklahoma for nearly ten years, was no stranger to the Guthrie family. As early as 1971 the liberal-minded lawmaker sponsored a bill in the state legislature that proposed that the birthday of Woody Guthrie be commemorated as a holiday. That proposition was voted down.[47]

Arlo recollected that he first agreed to assist the Harris campaign following a meeting with the senator in a New Hampshire saloon. "I was sitting in a bar. That's how it got started," Arlo told a UPI reporter. "I said I would do it so here I am." Harris was something of a populist candidate; his campaign championed working-class interests, and he ran as a strong supporter of Native American rights. Harris's base wasn't particularly wide reaching, but it appealed to progressive-minded Americans; his campaign would attract the support of such liberal-left performers as Guthrie, Pete Seeger, Harry Chapin, Tom Paxton, and John Hall of the band Orleans. Arlo wasn't always articulate when talking to the press on why he threw himself so genuinely into the Harris candidacy, but it was clear he was taken by the candidate's interest in spreading a "diffusion of economic and political power" throughout the working class. "On the Presidential level, there hasn't been that much to excite me in the past," Arlo told the *Eugene Register-Guard*. "I think Fred Harris comes closer to being able to stimulate the country. . . . So we can get on cases we should be on and get off ones we have been on." With the harsh lessons of Vietnam and Chile fresh in his mind, Guthrie offered, "We support the wrong guys for the wrong reasons and they lose and we end up with no foreign policy at all. Now that's dumb."[48]

On Sunday evening, February 22, Arlo and Harris were in New Hampshire for the country's first primary race. Some 1,500 fervent supporters—and Guthrie fans—crowded "into a church hall on the southern end of Elm Street" for the free beer and hot dogs and a chance to catch a glimpse of such celebrity Harris supporters as Boston Red Sox pitcher Bill Lee and actor Mike Farrell of the television drama series *M\*A\*S\*H*. The air was so rife with possibility at the "statewide rally" that even broadcast legend Walter Cronkite stopped by to gauge the moment, catching Arlo just as the singer was preparing for his first encore of the night. The *Chicago Tribune* splashed a large news photo of Guthrie singing "This Land Is Your Land" as Fred and his wife, LaDonna, sang along in the background. But in the finally tally, Harris finished a disappointing fourth in New Hampshire, capturing less than 9,000 ballots, a mere 11 percent of the total.[49]

The result left them undeterred. On February 26, Guthrie, Shenandoah, and Tom Paxton were at Boston's Orpheum Theater for another fund-raising event. On March 2 voters were to go to the polls for the crucial Massachusetts primary, and over 3,000 fans crowded into the Orpheum for the Harris benefit. It was mostly a business-as-usual concert, with tickets priced at $5.50 to $6.50 and Guthrie doing very little overt politicking from the stage, only bringing on Harris prior to the "This Land Is Your Land" finale. "If you elect me president of the United States," Harris told the crowd that night, "you and I, together, will make ol' Woody Guthrie's song come true." The last words

# Arlo Guthrie
### and Friends
## in a benefit concert for
# Fred Harris for President
## Orpheum Theatre
## 8 p.m. Thursday February 26<sup>th</sup>
## tickets $5.50 in advance
## $6.50 at the door

on sale at:

Out-of-town (Harvard Square)

Strawberries (Boston & Cambridge)

Ticketron

Factory Sound (Boston & Brookline)

*This handbill advertises a benefit concert for Democratic senator Fred W. Harris of Oklahoma, an ill-fated progressive candidate in the 1976 presidential primary race. That spring Guthrie was scheduled to perform twenty-three concerts on behalf of the Harris campaign. Ronald D. Cohen.*

that night belonged to neither Guthrie nor Harris but to a beleaguered campaign staffer who implored those exiting the theater that they needed to "go out there on March 2 and put Fred Harris on the road to the White House."

In the middle of the Harris campaign, Guthrie needed to set off for California to honor a previous commitment. On March 12, he was scheduled to perform with Seeger, Odetta, John Hartford, Jane Fonda, and the activist singer Holly Near at Will Geer's seventy-fourth birthday celebration at the Santa Monica Civic Auditorium. It was only in recent years that Geer, an old friend of Woody's dating back to the late 1930s, had at last emerged from the blacklist to find surprising success as Grandpa Walton on the popular Depression-era CBS television drama *The Waltons*. The Geer event, a benefit for the Theatricum Botanicum, the actor's blossom-enshrouded Shakespearean outdoor theater nestled in the hills of Topanga Canyon, was a welcome respite from the Harris campaign, which was exciting but proving to be a lost cause. By March the field of Democratic candidates was rapidly thinning. Senators Birch Bayh of Indiana and Terry Sanford of North Carolina, and Pennsylvania governor Milton Shapp, were all forced to drop out as, according to an item in the *Chicago Tribune*, they had been "unable to raise the small individual donations needed to qualify a campaign for federal matching funds." Things weren't looking rosy for Senator Harris either. He, too, was failing to solicit enough monies to keep his candidacy afloat; the *Chicago Tribune* reported that Harris was relying more and more "on the audiences his folksinger friend Arlo Guthrie draws than his own brand of populism." Undeterred, Guthrie agreed to stage some twenty concerts to benefit the campaign. Each check written out to purchase tickets for Arlo's shows would be matched by federal funds. Signed waivers would be distributed among concert attendees so box office cash sales would go towards the same end.[50]

The first two of Guthrie's twenty-three planned Harris benefits had been set for Springfield, Massachusetts, and Willimantic, Connecticut. The *New York Times* reported that the Harris team would brief Arlo on the "local situation" prior to his shows. This adjournment was to assist Arlo in his relating of "national issues to my audience—unemployment, for example, or pollution." Though he dutifully plugged on with the benefits, Arlo was increasingly aware, even early in the tour, that the campaign was a lost cause. On March 20, Arlo and Shenandoah were to perform their third Harris benefit at the field house of Rockland Community College near Suffern, New York. There was a problem as only 700 attended that show, at a nominal four or five dollars per ticket. The light turnout was, in Arlo's estimate, due to the fact that the show had been poorly promoted and the concert venue, the school's field house, was makeshift. Though he had committed to some twenty more benefit concerts, Arlo candidly sighed to the *Times*, "Fred doesn't have much of a chance, but he's [*sic*] does have a program, and a good one, and I'd like to get kids involved." But for the most part, Arlo rarely engaged in any political hard sell from the stage. The national finance director of Harris for President, William Rosendahl, was fine with that situation as Arlo *was* bringing the kids out, and the campaign committee still held to the slim hope that the Guthrie concerts might net $400,000 in receipts, which would surely be enough to carry them through to the Pennsylvania primary on April 27. Following the Rockland concert, the band was due in Baltimore on Sunday evening for their fourth benefit show at Johns Hopkins University on March 22, then on to Heinz Hall in Pittsburgh for a benefit on the 25th.[51]

But it was becoming an increasingly tough slog for Harris. On March 25, the battle-scarred candidate admitted to a UPI reporter that he was pinning his hopes on the chance that the benefits staged by Seeger, Guthrie, and Paxton might raise enough cash to allow him to finish as a strong contender in the Pennsylvania primary. But just as the Oklahoman was optimistically looking forward to a strong showing in the New York primary on April 6, his campaign's support structure was crumbling; there were reports that the telephones of his campaign office in New York had already been disconnected. On Thursday, April 8, a beleaguered Harris returned to Washington, DC, for a hastily arranged news conference. Though not a great surprise to the pundits, Harris announced his withdrawal from the race, admitting with disappointment, "Neither I nor my campaign have come to the attention of enough people." Promising his supporters that he would remain in the race as an independent presidential candidate, his full-time staff was reduced from thirty to six. Arlo would continue with his fund-raising concert efforts, but as the concerts weren't generating the amount of cash needed to qualify for federal matching funds, Harris's prospects seemed grim. In the end Harris chose not to run as an independent candidate as promised.[52]

Free of the political campaigning, Guthrie and Shenandoah played a two-hour show at Cain's Ballroom in Tulsa on May 8. Though Fred Harris hadn't been able to muster a lot of energy, his campaign troubadour certainly could, and Guthrie was welcomed by the Oklahomans as one of their own. A critic from *Billboard* marveled that Guthrie's "performance carried such an impact that two encores were called for with the bulk of the audience stomping the floor for a third when the house lights were finally brought up."[53]

On August 20, Guthrie and Shenandoah played an early evening concert at the Schaefer Festival in Manhattan's Central Park. Prior to his appearance, Arlo consented to a telephone interview with music critic John Rockwell of the *New York Times*. The biggest news was that a new album, titled *Amigo*, was to "be released any day now." It had been two years since *Arlo Guthrie* had been released to a somewhat cool critical and commercial reception. But he insisted that the long gap between studio albums had nothing to do with the disappointing sales of *Arlo Guthrie*. "I haven't done a record recently because I just never got around to it," he mused. Though he admitted that he "didn't do as much" touring in 1975, he already had been on the road for most of 1976, and his energy level remained surprisingly high. He had been sharing concert stages with Shenandoah to great response, and he was more politically active than at any other time in his career. He told Rockwell that he had done, or was considering, benefit concerts for conservation and anti–nuclear energy groups and the American Indian movement, as well as for the recently reconstituted Black Panther Party. He wasn't concerned that political activism was less prevalent on college campuses. "There are fewer people than there were in the '60s," Guthrie explained, "but those who are there are a lot more dedicated . . . and they're making changes that are reaching the Congressional level." Though Rockwell hadn't yet heard *Amigo*, the album would feature a number of original but Dylan-influenced songs. Guthrie offered to Rockwell, perhaps preemptively, that he wasn't bothered by comparisons to Dylan. "I was more influenced by Dylan's songs than by my father," he explained. "They made an impact on me the same way my father's songs made an impact on Ramblin' Jack Elliott, and even Dylan." The process was cyclical. Guthrie knew all too well "where Dylan got his ideas—nothing wrong with people knowing where I get mine."[54]

Arlo's eighth, and final, album for Reprise was *Amigo* (MS 2239), his finest studio recording to date. In late 1976, following the release of *Amigo*, the majority of artists recording for Reprise had been shuttled over to the parent-company Warner Bros. label. The reviews for Guthrie's swan song were, for the most part, positive. But the new Guthrie LP was partly lost to the acclaim in the wake of Dylan's own dramatic return to form: the bard's back-to-back releases of *Blood on the Tracks*, *The Basement Tapes*, and *Desire* left critics swooning at their typewriters but cool to artists deemed mere mimics of the great man. For whatever reason, it was the rare critic in 1976 that chose *not* to gauge the value of *Amigo* against the merit of Dylan's most recent work. Terry Atkinson of the *Los Angeles Times* believed that while the original songs on *Amigo* aspired to the heights of Dylan's *Blood on the Tracks*, Guthrie's original songs offered "watery sentiments" rather than blood: "There is the Guthrie who is uniquely himself, and there is the Guthrie who is merely another Dylan imitator." The *Times* critic thought the strongest material on *Amigo* was the self-penned songs that flashed with humor and *not* the album's many love songs. Janet Maslin, writing in the *Village Voice*, also made note that Dylan's lyrical exoticism was omnipresent throughout *Amigo*: such lines as "She is dressed up like a bandit, with a hundred sparkling rings" (from the enchanting "Darkest Hour") were clearly lifted from the Dylan playbook.

But Maslin noted that Arlo was more elusive than most of his musical peers in that he was not a "confessional songwriter." He possessed, on stage and on record, a "rare capacity for establishing intimacy without ever revealing anything specific about himself." To help illustrate her contention, Maslin chose to single out Guthrie's "Walking Song." Wrapped in an "irresistible" reggae-rhythm groove, the track was surely deserving of AM radio play, but Maslin maintained there remained "an odd air of privacy" about the song. It was mysterious, "as if only the singer and his mate were meant to understand what this walking is all about." Maslin rightly crowned *Amigo* the artist's "most self-assured effort thus far," singling out John Pilla's "vigorous" production and Arlo's ability to "adapt" the methodologies of both Woody and Dylan to create music uniquely his own.[55]

The notoriously opinionated *Village Voice* critic Robert Christgau, who was among the few critics who didn't really care much for Dylan's *Desire*, agreed with Maslin that *Amigo* was a winner. Christgau honored the album with his coveted "Pick Hit": "Side one is his best since the 'Coming into Los Angeles' side of *Running Down the Road* in 1969, and there's been a lot of good since then," he wrote. Though Christgau had routinely disparaged Arlo's reedy vocal style, he now argued that his thin and nasal singing voice actually *worked* for the artist; "this release has me pulling out my old Arlo albums and discovering how ideally the limitations of his voice have always suited his wry and complex understanding of things." Kit Rachlis of *Rolling Stone* thought his "fragile, twangy voice is too idiosyncratic to be maudlin," and that *Amigo* provided the perfect snapshot of Guthrie as an astrological Gemini, "who believes that it is possible to be both a radical and a patriot, a humorist and a romantic." Acknowledging that Arlo had partly built his career as one of the "best interpreters" of material by both his father and Dylan, Rachlis enthused that on the new album he finally exorcised their formidable "ghosts" by composing his own fine set of original songs. Even the acerbic Mike Jahn, who had savaged the previous year's *Together in Concert* in *High Fidelity*, saw *Amigo* as a welcome return to form. The mainstream rock-music magazines also took notice. Pointing out that the LP release was a "bicentennial" milestone of sorts, *Circus* critic Ken Tucker wrote, "Guthrie's *Amigo* makes that event more than a pathetic cliché: here's an American to celebrate." *Crawdaddy* saw the album in much the same light, with critic Gary Lambert writing, "the finest cut of all is 'Patriot's Dream,' a stunningly beautiful call for America to rediscover its lost revolutionary vision."[56]

Though *Amigo* wasn't showing up on many radio playlists, the good press notices should have kick-started sales. But the album peaked in position 133 on the *Billboard* chart and stalled. It was maddening, especially as Guthrie regarded *Amigo* as his personal "favorite album." But the folk singer ac-

*With Pete Seeger and Judy Collins during the taping of the PBS* Soundstage *program "Woody Guthrie's America," first broadcast on WTTW in Chicago on October 31, 1976. Photofest.*

knowledged that the new album was turning out to be his "least popular." "I thought technically [*Amigo*] was exquisite and emotionally very satisfying," Guthrie opined. "The album that most people like who buy my albums is *Washington County*. That seems to be the favorite of everyone, but they haven't heard *Amigo*." In answering the charge that Guthrie's albums were too mosaic in their programming and rarely thematic, Arlo told the *Christian Science Monitor*, "Two people can see the same thing [differently]. One can call it versatility and the other lack of continuity. We only have so much we can do. I'm not filled with thousands of songs bursting and then being able to choose the ten best. I don't write that much."[57]

In the autumn of 1976, Woody Guthrie was poised to become part of the national conversation as United Artists readied their Hollywood feature-film adaptation of *Bound for Glory*. On October 31 Chicago's PBS station WTTW and *Soundstage* broadcast "Woody Guthrie's America." It was a wonderful program, the antithesis of much of the Woody Guthrie hoopla that would ensue as the United Artists media machine geared up for the film's release. Much as Millard Lampell had done with the Guthrie tribute concerts of 1968 and 1970, the *Soundstage* producers skillfully wove Woody's best-known songs, performed by Pete Seeger, Fred Hellerman, Judy Collins, and Arlo

Guthrie, with emotive readings of Guthrie's prose by host Studs Terkel. The songs were performed both solo and in various configurations. Pete, Fred, and Arlo started things off with "Oklahoma Hills," with the trio later playing "The Sinking of the Reuben James." Arlo, solo on the guitar, sang "Dust Storm Disaster" and his father's little-known "East Texas Red," about a notorious railroad brakeman who rode the rails on the "Southeast Texas Gulf." Arlo also sang a duet with Collins ("Roll On, Columbia"), and was part of the full-cast renderings of "Union Maid" and "This Land Is Your Land."

There was suddenly a spate of Woody Guthrie–related books and recordings, all hoping to ride the coattails of the movie's publicity campaign. Woody's *Bound for Glory* was brought back into print as a mass-market paperback, but, more importantly, his unpublished *Seeds of Man* appeared, its publication causing the novelist-poet-critic James Dickey to rhapsodize about Woody as "the best spokesman in word and music that the American proletariat has ever had." Harold Leventhal and Marjorie Guthrie were the principal players behind publication of the wonderfully illustrated and assembled *The Woody Guthrie Songbook* (Grossett & Dunlap). Though United Artists was planning to issue a soundtrack album featuring David Carradine's counterfeit warbles through the Guthrie back catalog, one of the more interesting LPs released in the wake of the *Bound for Glory* storm was *Woody Guthrie's "We Ain't Down Yet"* (Cream Records CR-1002), an album whose presentation closely mirrored Millard Lampell/Moses Asch's 1956 effort *Bound for Glory: The Songs and Story of Woody Guthrie* (Folkways FP 78/1). The original Folkways album featured Woody's own recordings interlaced with recitations of his prose by the actor Will Geer. The Cream album, on the other hand, featured a slate of contemporary artists singing Guthrie's songs in modern pop-music settings. The roster of talent included Arlo, Seals and Crofts, Peter Yarrow, Hoyt Axton, John Hartford, Ramblin' Jack Elliott, and Doug and Rodney Dillard. Filling in for Will Geer on the recitations for the new LP was the actor Jess Pearson, though Geer himself contributed to the new LP as well. The actor read an excerpt from Woody's "Letter to Will Geer," a fragment of personal correspondence in which the folk singer warns the actor "all sorts of Hell is settin' in to make a national calamity." Geer's recitation was blended on the LP with a bluegrass version of "Goin' Down the Road (Feeling Bad)," featuring Arlo and the Dillards. Though the original Folkways album was musically skeletal, Woody's dusty guitar playing and railroad-wailing mouth organ offering a suitably authentic monochrome sound, the musical arrangements on the Cream LP were, perhaps, a little too slick. Critic Robert Hilburn, writing in the *Los Angeles Times*, thought the musical performances were "tenderly affectionate, but hardly distinguished," with the "heavy-handed" oratory of Pearson's narration—occasionally in-

*Guthrie was featured on the popular ABC-TV drama* Rich Man, Poor Man—Book II, *broadcast October 19, 1976. This episode, "Chapter IV," was written by Millard Lampell, who earlier had performed in the 1940s with Pete Seeger, Woody Guthrie, and others as part of the Almanac Singers. Photofest.*

tercut with excerpts of speeches from Senator Robert F. Kennedy and Dr. Martin Luther King—adding little more than "extremely sentimental, syrupy touches." That November *Woody Guthrie's "We Ain't Down Yet"* was awarded "Recommended LP" status by *Billboard* magazine.[58]

On October 19, Guthrie appeared as himself, singing a fragment of "Alice's Restaurant" on the fourth episode of the popular nighttime television drama *Rich Man, Poor Man—Book II*. This episode of the popular television drama series starring Peter Strauss was cowritten by series creator Irwin Shaw and Millard Lampell, one of Woody's old buddies from the Almanac Singers who had become a radio and TV writer, although blacklisted through the 1950s.

Woody wasn't the only Guthrie to be celebrated that autumn. On November 5, Arlo was at the statehouse in Boston, where he received a citation from Governor Michael Dukakis and the Massachusetts House of Representatives. The proclamation cited the fifth of November as "Arlo Guthrie Day" throughout the Commonwealth. Guthrie wasn't exactly sure what to make of the honor, telling the *Boston Globe*, "I just took it with a grain of salt, and I'm sure the governor and legislators did the same thing. . . . It's something to do and you might as well enjoy it." That night he and Shenandoah performed before a standing-room-only audience at Boston's Orpheum Theater. When a stage monologue was interrupted by fans shouting out requests for "Ring-around-a-Rosy Rag" and "Massachusetts," Guthrie pondered for a moment before answering, "It's my day. I'll do what I want."[59]

On December 5, United Artists released *Bound for Glory* to theaters in the United States. Though the reviews were, at best, mixed, the film would go on to receive four Academy Award nominations. But the film did not resonate with cinemagoers, and the box office receipts were dismal. Those who actually *knew* Woody weren't charmed by David Carradine's mute and humorless portrayal, not recognizing much of Woody's persona in his performance. In her characteristic cheeriness, Marjorie Guthrie told Joe Klein, freelancing for *Rolling Stone*, that she was "so pleased with it, especially when you consider how Hollywood might have distorted his life." For the most part, Arlo tried keeping his personal feelings regarding the film to himself. There was a lot of money invested in bringing his father's famous novel to the screen, and many of the film's principal players were friends. His manager, Harold Leventhal was, after all, one of the film's producers, and other old friends of the family, such as the blacklisted cinematographer Haskell Wexler, had photographed the film. But once *Bound for Glory* had run its theatrical and commercial course, Arlo was free to vent his frustrations. As a guest on television's *Mike Douglas Show*, he was asked how accurate the portrayal of his father's life was in Hal Ashby's film. "Not very," Arlo replied somewhat acidly. "I think it was great for some people . . . like my age or younger, who didn't know anything about the Depression. In that sense, it was nice, historically." But Arlo was clearly disappointed with Ashby's selection of Carradine for the lead role. It wasn't so much that the rangy actor shared none of Woody's physical characteristics; it was more that the actor portrayed Woody as unrelentingly grim, demonstrating nothing of his father's "survival" humor. Arlo believed that somebody who didn't understand that facet of Woody's personality "shouldn't have done that part. So I wasn't happy with it." He also admitted to his frustration that "I didn't have anything to do with it, and I really wanted to. But everybody said, 'Well, he's just a singer. What does he know about that stuff?'"[60]

Two days following the New York release of *Bound for Glory*, Marjorie Guthrie, Arlo, and two bluegrass musician friends, Doug and Rodney Dillard, crowded into a Manhattan television studio to tape a segment of the popular ABC-TV program *Good Morning America*. Though the promotion of *Bound for Glory* was the *raison d'etre* for their involvement, everyone had his or her own reasons for being there: Marjorie to promote the agenda of her Committee to Combat Huntington's Disease, her son and his two bluegrass friends on hand to perform one of Woody's songs from *We Ain't Down Yet*. Guthrie, for his part, no longer seemed interested in performing on television. After the *Good Morning America* producer blocked out their segment and lined out what was expected of each participant, Guthrie told his mother, "You know, Pete Seeger had the best idea of how to do these things. . . . You just nod your head and agree to everything they say, then go out there and do what you want." Things went along well until the host used Marjorie's plug of the Huntington's committee as the excuse to ask Arlo what were the chances of him coming down with the disease. He explained that his chances were 50/50, as they were with all the children of Huntington's patients. "And do you think about that?" Arlo was pressed. "Only when people ask me about it," he replied flatly.[61]

That Christmas, the Guthries had an additional guest at their Great Barrington farmhouse. Joe Klein, on assignment to write a portrait of Arlo for an upcoming issue of *Rolling Stone*, had accepted Arlo's casual offer to visit him at home to gather material for the profile during the Christmas holiday. The resulting article, "Notes on a Native Son," earned the political writer the ASCAP Deems Taylor Award of 1978 for his brilliant and insightful essay that offered a rare glimpse into Guthrie's private life, including his recent immersion into Franciscan Catholic studies. "Remember when I said that I became a Catholic because my mother was Jewish and my father was Protestant?" Guthrie asked Klein. "Well, I wasn't kidding. See, from my mother, I got the whole Jewish mind thing, you know, asking questions. From my father, I got the idea that the answers to the questions don't make a goddamn bit of difference. Well, what do you call someone like that? A Catholic!"[62]

One morning near Christmas Guthrie traveled through the snow to a small recording studio in neighboring Stockbridge. He had agreed to appear, along with the Boston-born actor Leonard Nimoy—Mr. Spock of TV's *Star Trek*—and Massachusetts governor Michael Dukakis, in a promotional film titled *A Special Place*. The film, helmed by a freshly minted film director named Robert Radler on commission from the Commonwealth of Massachusetts, was designed to promote statewide economic and industrial development. Guthrie's involvement was a source of some small controversy among local green activists. They were puzzled by his participation as the singer was on record as not being particularly predisposed towards industrialization of rural areas. But Guthrie signed on regardless, offering as explanation that he thought the filming might be "fun." He devilishly told Joe Klein, "I think I'll wear a suit. . . . That ought to blow their minds." It helped that Guthrie wasn't expected to actively pitch for industrial development, only to sit at a piano and lip-synch to his studio recording of his gorgeous song "Massachusetts" from *Amigo*. In the end, he would play-act his performance a total of four times from multiple different camera angles. *A Special Place* would win an honorable mention award at the twenty-first American Film Festival in May 1979.[63]

## NOTES

1. Harold Leventhal, notes to *Pete Seeger & Arlo Guthrie: Together in Concert* (Reprise Records 2R 2214, 1975); Tom Smucker, "If Every Concert Were a Benefit, Pete Seeger Would Be Frank Sinatra," *Village Voice*, October 18, 1976, 78; David King Dunaway, *How Can I Keep from Singing: Pete Seeger* (New York: McGraw-Hill, 1981), 300; Pete Seeger, *The Incompleat Folksinger* (New York: Simon and Schuster, 1972), 462, 485.

2. "Random Notes," *Rolling Stone*, March 14, 1974, 30.

3. Ira Mayer, "Generations without a Gap," *Village Voice* 19, no. 11 (March 14, 1974), 56–57.

4. Sam Sutherland, "Talent in Action," *Billboard*, March 23, 1974, 20; "Kirb.," "Concert Reviews," *Variety*, March 13, 1974, 62.

5. Lynn Van Matre, "Pete Seeger: Plucking a Banjo of Brotherhood," *Chicago Tribune*, March 3, 1974, E8; Lynn Van Matre, "Pete and Arlo: A Pleasant Bit of Art with Politics," *Chicago Tribune*, March 11, 1974, sec. 2, 17.

6. William Howard, "Guthrie, Seeger at Music Hall," *Boston Globe*, April 2, 1974, 40.

7. Marc Eliot, *Death of a Rebel* (Garden City, NY: Anchor Books), 206–7.

8. Geoffrey Stokes, "Art & Politics: A Certain Tension," *Village Voice*, June 6, 1974, 62–63; Frank Rose, "I Don't See Any Stars. Do You See Any Stars?" *Village Voice*, May 16, 1974, 74.

9. "A Little Booze, Song and Dance, and One Loud Anthem for Chile," *Rolling Stone*, June 20, 1974.

10. Frank Rose, "Talking Chile Blues," *Zoo World*, June 20, 1974, 14–15.

11. Frank Rose, "At Home with Arlo Guthrie: Conversation in the Berkshires," *Zoo World*, July 4, 1974, 22–23.

12. "Top Album Picks," *Billboard*, May 25, 1974, 65; "FM Action Picks," *Billboard*, May 25, 1974, 33; Frank Hoffman and George Albert, *The Cash Box Album Charts, 1955–1974* (Metuchen, NJ, and London: Scarecrow Press, 1988), 155.

13. "Concerts," *New York*, June 17, 1974, 34; "Memorial Benefit Scheduled to Clear Rosenbergs' Names," *Lewiston Evening Journal*, June 12, 1974, 15; "Pete Seeger to Perform in Benefit," *Schenectady Gazette*, June 18, 1974, 8.

14. Derek Grant, "Popular Reviews," *Gramophone*, November 1974, 978; Steve Lake, "Arlo's Fresh Chapter," *Melody Maker*, August 17, 1974, 47; Noel Coppage, *Stereo Review*, September 1974, 93; Cameron Crowe, "Pop Album Briefs," *Los Angeles Times*, July 21, 1974, sec. Calendar, 60; Bud Scoppa, "Record Reviews," *Rolling Stone*, July 18, 1974, 64; John Rockwell, "The Lighter Side," *High Fidelity &*

*Musical America* 24, no. 10 (October 1974), 124; Alan Pettifer, "On Record," *Country Music Review* 3, no. 5 (September 1974), 34; Robert Christgau, "The Christgau Consumer Guide," *Creem* 6, no. 3 (August 1974), 13.

15. Karl Dallas, "Guthrie's Survival Course," *Melody Maker*, July 27, 1974, 24.

16. Karl Dallas, "Guthrie's Survival Course," 24; Harvey Andrews, "Reviews Records," *Folk Review* 4, no. 1 (November 1974), 19, 20; Joe Klein, "Notes on a Native Son," *Rolling Stone*, March 10, 1977, 52.

17. Joe Klein, "Notes on a Native Son," 52.

18. "Philly Fest on WHYY-TV," *Billboard*, September 7, 1974, 20; John S. Wilson, "Can Rock and Pop Be Folk Music?" *New York Times*, August 29, 1974, 24.

19. Joseph McLellan, "Funny—Even Profound," *Washington Post*, August 31, 1974, C5.

20. Philip Van Huesen, "Arlo Doesn't Forget, but He's Memorable," *Chicago Tribune*, September 6, 1974, sec. 2, 5.

21. "General News: Hoyt-Arlo Special," *Billboard*, September 14, 1974, 4; Pat Colander, "Soundstage: Where It's Happening in Chicago," *Chicago Tribune*, November 10, 1974, O3; Jay Sharbutt, "Television: 'Soundstage' Is All a Matter of Taste," *Free Lance-Star* (Fredricksburg, VA), November 12, 1974, 21.

22. "Folksong Festival" (WNYC) broadcast from the *West Virginia Bluegrass Folk Festival*, September 14, 1974.

23. "The Southland," *Los Angeles Times*, October 21, 1974, sec. 1, 2; Mark Goodman, "Aloha, Arlo," *People*, June 13, 1994, 68; "From the Music Capitals of the World: Toronto," *Billboard*, December 14, 1974, 56.

24. Sally Quinn, "Indian Benefit: A Vanishing Breed?" *Los Angeles Times*, December 5, 1974, 122.

25. "Radio and TV," *Lewiston Evening Journal*, February 26, 1975, 18; Woody Guthrie, *Woody Sez* (New York: Grosset & Dunlap, 1975), xix; John Grissim, "Woody Guthrie: Return of the Dust Bowl Poet," *Rolling Stone*, no. 229 (December 30, 1976), 16, 20.

26. "Random Notes," *Rolling Stone*, February 27, 1975, 22.

27. Todd Tolces, "Caught in the Act: America," *Melody Maker*, March 22, 1975, 47.

28. Colleen Clark, "Country: Nashville Scene," *Billboard*, February 22, 1975, 48; James Brown, "Hoyt Axton Hosts Variety Special," *Los Angeles Times*, May 20, 1975, E18.

29. Ian Dove, "Seeger and Guthrie Salute Leadbelly," *New York Times*, March 17, 1975, 38.

30. Tom Smucker, "If Every Concert Were a Benefit, Pete Seeger Would Be Frank Sinatra," 78. Alex Ward, "Seeger, Guthrie: Soft Politics," *Washington Post*, March 26, 1975, B16.

31. *Warner Bros. Circular* 7, no. 4 (April 14, 1975), not paginated; "Smothers Brothers Set Special Concert," *The Day* (New London, CT), May 3, 1975, 18A.

32. Nick King, "People's Bicentennial Gambles on Angry Patriots," *Boston Globe*, April 14, 1975, 3; Gary McMillan, "People's Rally Jams Concord," *Boston Globe*, April 19, 1975, 1, 5; Gary McMillan and Nick King, "Rally More Like a Party with

Raspberry for Ford," *Boston Globe*, April 20, 1975, 61; Melvin Maddocks, "Two Nations Indivisible," *Christian Science Monitor*, April 21, 1975, 1; Rudy Abramson, "Pageantry and Tumult: Ford, Concord Join in a Historic Salute," *Los Angeles Times*, April 20, 1975, A1.

33. "Kirb.," "Concert Reviews," *Variety*, May 7, 1975, 336; Jim Fishel, "Talent in Action," *Billboard*, June 7, 1975, 39.

34. Jon Halvorsen, "Seeger, Guthrie in Benefit," *Evening News*, June 30, 1975, 7B.

35. Ron Legro, "Relaxed Arlo Guthrie Sings a Good Show," *Milwaukee Sentinel*, July 23, 1975, 10; Michael Miller, "Guthrie: Traveling Light & Versatile," source unknown, 1975.

36. Tom Smucker, "Pete and Arlo: All in the Family," *Village Voice* 20, no. 31 (August 4, 1975), 89.

37. Paul Nelson, "Record Reviews," *Rolling Stone*, August 28, 1975, 74; Mike Jahn, "The Lighter Side," *High Fidelity & Musical America* 25, no. 8 (August 1975), 111; Mick Farren, "Platters," *NME*, June 28, 1975, 18; Tony Jasper, "Folk," *Hi-Fi News & Record Review*, September 1975, 117; Derek Grant, "Popular Records," *Gramophone*, August 1975, 371; Noel Coppage, "Recordings of Special Merit," *Stereo Review*, September 1975, 97; Mike Sager-Fenton, *Folk Review* 4, no. 11 (September 1975), 30.

38. Marty Gallanter, "Arlo: Bound for His Own Glory," *Frets* 1, no. 5 (July 1979), 29.

39. "Craig 1 Mil Promo Push," *Billboard*, September 6, 1975, 57; Joe Klein, "Notes on a Native Son," 56.

40. Ernie Santosuosso, "Arlo Guthrie to Top Bill at Outdoor Concert," *Boston Globe*, October 3, 1975, 20.

41. Larry Sloman, *On the Road with Bob Dylan: Rolling with the Thunder* (New York: Bantam Books, 1978), 119–20.

42. Sam Shepherd, *Rolling Thunder Logbook* (New York: Penguin Books, 1977), 64; Larry Sloman, *On the Road with Bob Dylan: Rolling with the Thunder*, 119–20; Rick Hampson, "Most of All They Remember Mama," *Lewiston Evening Journal*, October 17, 1978, 29.

43. Lynn Van Matre, "Music: Nothing's Changed about Arlo Guthrie," *Chicago Tribune*, November 21, 1975, sec. 3, 7.

44. Jack McDonough, "Talent in Action," *Billboard*, March 27, 1976, 46.

45. Ken Van Osdol, "Arlo Guthrie: Music . . . Tunes a Soul," *Eugene Register-Guard*, February 1, 1976, 4c.

46. Joe Klein, "Notes on a Native Son," 57; Judy Ball, "On the Road with Arlo Guthrie," *St. Anthony Messenger* 87, no. 9 (February 1980), 18–19.

47. Rob Fleder, "What's Happening," *Sing Out!* 20, no. 5 (May/June 1971), 29.

48. Ken Van Osdol, "Arlo Guthrie: Music . . . Tunes a Soul," 4c; Charles Mohr, "Harris's Fate Is Linked to Defeating Bayh," *New York Times*, February 29, 1976, 42; "Report from America: Balladeer's Son Does Political Gig," *The Dispatch* (Lexington, KY), April 8, 1976, 5.

49. Edward Jones, "Politicking along Elm Street—Clue to Presidential Prospects," *Free-Lance Star* (Fredericksburg, VA), February 23, 1976, 1; "4 Democratic

Candidates Discuss Economic Issues in Boston," *Boston Globe*, February 23, 1976, 7; Douglas E. Kneeland, "Pace of New Hampshire Campaigning Slows before the Primary Tomorrow," *New York Times*, February 23, 1976, 29; "Pulling Out All the Stops to Win the First Primary," *Chicago Tribune*, February 24, 1976, not paginated.

50. Charles Mohr, "Harris's Fate Is Linked to Defeating Bayh," *New York Times*, February 29, 1976, 42; James Coates, "Ford Camp Errs; Reagan's Not Broke," *Chicago Tribune*, March 20, 1976, sec. 1, 6.

51. James Feron, "Concert by Arlo Guthrie Aids Harris Campaign," *New York Times*, March 21, 1976, 42; George Anderson, "Talk of the Triangle in Entertainment," *Pittsburgh Post-Gazette*, March 23, 1976, 9.

52. United Press International, "Udall Vows to Badger Carter in Wisconsin," *Pittsburgh Press*, March 25, 1976, 8; Associated Press, "Harris Withdraws from Primaries," *Lewiston Morning Tribune*, April 9, 1976, 3A.

53. Richard Fricker, "Talent in Action," *Billboard*, May 29, 1976, 36.

54. John Rockwell, "Arlo Guthrie's Band Politically Active," *New York Times*, August 19, 1976, 48.

55. Terry Atkinson, "Brief Reviews of Pop Albums," *Los Angeles Times*, October 17, 1976, sec. Calendar, 77; Janet Maslin, "Arlo Guthrie Lives Up to His Name," *Village Voice*, November 15, 1976, 97.

56. Robert Christgau, "Christgau's Consumer Guide," *Village Voice*, November 1, 1976, 79; Kit Rachlis, "Record Reviews," *Rolling Stone*, January 27, 1977, 65; Mike Jahn, "The Lighter Side," *High Fidelity & Musical America* 27, no. 1 (January 1977), 143; Ken Tucker, "Longplayers," *Circus* 145 (December 14, 1976), 16; Gary Lambert, "Capsule Reviews," *Crawdaddy*, November 1976, 80.

57. Ward W. Smith, "Arlo: Too Busy for Stardom," *Christian Science Monitor*, March 30, 1978, 19; Mary Campbell, "Arlo Guthrie Asks Refugee Family In," *Harlan Daily Enterprise*, August 24, 1979, 6.

58. James Dickey, "Woody Guthrie: Who Touches This Touches a Man," *New York Times*, October 3, 1976, 212; Woody Guthrie, "Letter to Will Geer," from *Woody Guthrie's "We Ain't Down Yet"* (Cream Records, CR-1002, 1976); Robert Hilburn, "Woody Guthrie Born Again in LP Reissues," *Los Angeles Times*, December 14, 1976, G1; "Billboard's Recommended LPs," *Billboard*, November 13, 1976, 75.

59. Steve Morse, "Arlo Guthrie Has His day," *Boston Globe*, November 8, 1976, 16.

60. *Mike Douglas Show*, September 17, 1980.

61. Joe Klein, "Notes on a Native Son," 52–53.

62. Joe Klein, "Notes on a Native Son," 57.

63. Joe Klein, "Notes on a Native Son," 56; Ward W. Smith, "Arlo: Too Busy for Stardom," 19.

*Chapter Six*

# Last to Leave

With the exception of a Warner Bros.–generated "Best of" collection to be released in late summer, 1977 would mark the first year since 1971 that Guthrie did not deliver a new studio or concert recording to the label. There was lots of wearying touring, as ever, starting with a spring trip with Shenandoah to the West Coast. Though he remained a popular concert attraction, Guthrie's engagement with the media was more incidental, and there were far fewer in-depth interviews of consequence published. One exception was Joe Klein's prize-winning article published in the March 10, 1977, issue of *Rolling Stone,* the first nationally circulated story of the folk singer's immersion into Franciscan Catholic studies. Indeed, Guthrie seemed more enthused talking about God than talking about music, though both of these interests were intertwined and always had been. He told the *Washington Post,* "I'm limited by life, by the work I have to do: by mothers, fathers, sisters, brothers. The world is a restrictive place—except for those who go at it with pride or lust or envy. Spirit is, however, not burdened by such things." The mainstream newspapers hinted that Guthrie's sudden interest in God was tied to the fact he was reaching his middle years, the period when he would find out if he carried the gene for Huntington's disease. Though Woody would not begin the first stage of his hospitalization years until age forty, his symptoms had begun manifesting, undiagnosed, years earlier. Arlo was to turn thirty in 1977. It wasn't only the media that fretted about the frightening possibility. His family and friends were concerned, too. Pete Seeger told *Rolling Stone* that Arlo was "an expert at being a human being in spite of all the pressures he's had to live with. I mean—and I suppose there's no way to say this that doesn't sound tacky—I don't see how the guy manages to live so normally with that disease hanging over his head."[1]

On Monday, June 27, Guthrie, Massachusetts governor Michael Dukakis, and actor Leonard Nimoy were to appear together at the Museum of Science in Boston. The occasion was the world premiere of Robert M. Radler's promotional film *A Special Place*. As the movie project was a state-funded promotional vehicle, the *Boston Globe* noted that "the ceremonies preceding the film were possibly more austere than the revels that used to precede premieres" at Hollywood's Grauman's Chinese Theater. But that didn't mean there was a shortage of celebrity worship. Some 1,200 "Trekkies," fans of the popular TV series *Star Trek*, filled the three tiers of the museum to overflowing in order to catch a glimpse of "Mr. Spock." Guthrie seemed bemused by the hoopla, telling the crowd that he had arrived in style: "A helicopter come 'n picked me up this morning. There's been a lot of helicopters flying 'round my part of the state lately. Don't know what they're looking for. Can't be us farmers." Guthrie's song "Massachusetts" was moodily threaded throughout the film, and at the press conference Arlo admitted it had been conceived as a musical "reply" to John Denver's "Rocky Mountain High." That syrupy single, extolling the virtues of Colorado, would make the *Billboard* Top 10 chart in 1973. There was some history there. Denver's fiddle player, John Martin Sommers, allegedly appropriated the tune of Guthrie's own "Uncle Jeff" (from 1973's *Last of the Brooklyn Cowboys*) for his song "Thank God, I'm a Country Boy." Denver would record and issue the Sommers song on his *Back Home Again* album of 1975, which would hit number one on both the *Billboard* country and pop music singles charts.[2]

That summer Guthrie continued to tour with Shenandoah (mischievously dubbed the "Rolling Blunder Revue"), with Pete Seeger occasionally in tow. On Saturday, July 2, Seeger and Guthrie performed two shows on the main stage at Milwaukee's "Summerfest event." That afternoon they were visited by a film crew from the Italian television news magazine *Odeon* for broadcast on Italian TV in September. Guthrie and Seeger would resume their on again–off again summer tour of amphitheaters with a concert at the Blossom Music Center in Cuyahoga Falls, Ohio, on August 1.[3]

On July 10, 1977, Arlo turned thirty years of age. In the weeks following that milestone, Paul Richard, a writer for the *Washington Post*, decided the time was right to seek out Guthrie for a midcareer assessment. Though Arlo had recently taken ownership of a touring coach that he named the "Blunder Bus" (a reference to the seventeenth-century firearm, not to his own "Rolling Blunder Revue"), Richard found the singer in "another bland motel room" somewhere on a never-ending road. The Arlo Guthrie that the writer spoke with that afternoon barely resembled the skinny, brooding, and inarticulate teenager that a generation embraced in 1967. More full faced and mustachioed, and presently the responsible father of three children, Guthrie sat cross-legged on his motel bed and reflected on the changes in his life. The chat would inevitably return to such familiar subjects as religion (he described himself as "Catholic-Jewish"), and Huntington's disease ("The textbooks say my chances are 50-50"). But mostly the *Post* feature painted Guthrie as an anomaly: someone who had lived his entire life, both personally and professionally, "at the center of the fringe." Guthrie didn't seem to mind that in commercial terms his musical career seemed to have veered off course. It was his view that his career was simply *different* from that of label mates and colleagues in the music industry. "I'm in the midst of an enjoyable situation," he offered. "Nobody knows what to do with me, with me or with my product. I can tour ten months a year, and sell my concerts out, but try to find my records. I'm never on the radio. I'm half in and half out [of the business]." He acknowledged that as a songwriter he wasn't, and could never be, another Woody Guthrie or Bob Dylan. "Woody, like Dylan," Arlo tried to explain, "was a singer driven by the muse. I'm not like that." His songwriting was more occasional than when he started out, but in contrast he was more pleased with his new songs. "Every poet flashes at some time in his life," Guthrie went on. "And then he sees the infinite. The perception is a gift." When asked if he had seen the "infinite," Guthrie corrected, "I'm a musician, not a painter. I've *heard* it."[4]

The problem was that it was becoming increasingly difficult getting *others* to hear it. Beginning August 16, Guthrie and Shenandoah were scheduled to perform a three-night residency, two sets a night, at Paul Colby's Other End in Greenwich Village. Janet Maslin, writing in the *New York Times,* noted that while sheer likeability was Arlo's principle asset, his easygoing charm and affability sometimes disguised the fact that he was "also a serious and sophisticated folk artist whose work deserves much more attention than it generally receives." It was frustrating to Maslin that "the material he performs most winningly in concert" was the songs recently featured on *Amigo.* Though that album had, in Maslin's analysis, "failed to find an audience," it was "Mr. Guthrie's finest album." Though the accountants at Warner Bros. were less likely to dub the poor-selling *Amigo* as the artist's finest LP, the company was making plans on putting together its own vision of what constituted Guthrie's finest work. The summer of 1977 witnessed the release of *The Best of Arlo Guthrie*, a nine-song collection spanning the artist's decade-long partnership with the label. Arlo speculated that Warner Bros. was promoting the album as a "Best of" rather than a "Greatest Hits" collection, as I "really [don't] have any hits to choose from." *The Best of Arlo Guthrie* (Warner Bros. BSK 3117) was released in August 1977. A safe but satisfying compilation, it was most noteworthy for its inclusion of the previously unreleased "Motorcycle (Significance of the Pickle) Song." Though the album was packaged handsomely, there were few production credits included on the sleeve or labels. In his half-warm review, *Village Voice* music critic Robert Christgau suggested that this previously unissued version of "The Motorcycle Song" was "rescued from Arlo's unnecessary live collaboration with Uncle Pete."[5]

In late November 1977, Guthrie sang the ballad of "Victor Jara" for a "radical chic" crowd of 800 at Manhattan's Ethical Culture Society on Central Park West. The program, titled "The Night of the Empty Chair," was a two-hour-long affair to benefit Amnesty International and dedicated to those "artists and writers who have been imprisoned, tortured, or killed for their beliefs." The night's program, which had been filmed for broadcast on PBS in January 1978, was a somber one, with serious readings by the writers Studs Terkel, Arthur Miller, and Robert Penn Warren and the actor Richard Widmark. The music was supplied by Paul Simon, Patti Smith, Guthrie, and New York Philharmonic conductor Leonard Bernstein. It was a blending of music and politics, and when a reporter from the *Washington Post* suggested there were few "light moments" in the program, Guthrie snipped that he "refused to judge the show as entertainment." "That's not the point," he cautioned.[6]

In February and March 1978 Guthrie and Shenandoah were on the road for another long string of tour dates in the South, the Midwest, and Texas. His February 18 outdoor concert at the University of Florida's Lake Alice Field in Gainesville attracted, according to the *Ocala Star-Banner*, not only Guthrie's most devoted fans but an assortment of sleeping dogs, "the usual drunks," and a motorcycle gang. That spring Woody's old friend, the actor Will Geer, passed on at age seventy-six on April 22. His friends, including actors, musicians, and representatives of the actor's union, honored his memory with a "Farewell to Will Geer" commemoration on May 12 at the Health and Hospital Worker's Union Hall of the Rev. Martin Luther King Jr. Center at 310 West 43rd Street. "There was a lilt to his voice," Arlo told a writer from the *New York Times*, "and it made you want to listen." Recalling the actor as one of Woody's most staunch admirers, Arlo recalled Geer as a man of spirit who loved the music not only for its "fun" aspect but for its "realness; he liked people who sang songs that meant something to him." Following an evening of warm testimonials and heartfelt remembrances, Guthrie and Pete Seeger sang "Kisses Sweeter Than Wine," "This Land Is Your Land," and "So Long, It's Been Good to Know You" to those in the packed union hall. Marjorie Guthrie, on stage at the concert's end, called out to Geer's ex-wife, Herta Ware, "With or without Will in front of us, we know he's with us, right?" Ware, the white-haired granddaughter of Communist Party U.S.A. founder Ella Reeve Bloor, smiled and cheered, "Forever!"[7]

There *were* new struggles to be fought, and the most important for many was the fight against nuclear power and nuclear weapons. On May 21, two days before the first meeting of the United Nations Special Session on Disarmament, Guthrie was at the Hollywood Bowl in Los Angeles, part of Peter Yarrow's four-hour-long event "Survival Sunday." Three months in the organizing, the event was, in Yarrow's words, "a cross between a concert and a teach-in" and "supported demonstrations nationwide protesting the proliferation of nuclear weapons." Performing before an audience estimated at 12,000 to 14,000, Arlo shared the stage with a long lineup of guests: Peter, Paul, and Mary; Harry Chapin; Richie Havens; Holly Near; Tom Paxton; Minnie Riperton; the Starland Vocal Band; the comedian George Carlin; and speakers Cesar Chavez, Daniel Ellsberg, Daniel Berrigan, Allard Lowenstein, Senator Eugene McCarthy, and the actor Herschel Bernardi.[8]

Tom Smucker, a leftist journalist and longtime Pete Seeger fan, was among the first to note that Arlo wasn't simply carrying the torch of his father but of his father's comrades as well. Reporting on the annual Hudson River Revival (June 17–18), a benefit for the sloop *Clearwater*, for the Manhattan-based *Village Voice*, Smucker mused that there were few performers who could hitch Ed McCurdy's "Last Night I Had the Strangest Dream" with "Amazing Grace," as Arlo had that weekend. Guthrie enjoyed playing the relatively small *Clearwater* event; he had, after all, performed at the sloop's first fundraiser in 1968. "I loved the old folk festivals," he told the *New York Times*, but offered that he wasn't particularly unhappy to see the era of the large-scale festival pass: "They got out of hand. The first year they'd have 30,000 people. The next year, 50,000. And on up. They became too expensive to put on." Smucker fretted that he "used to worry that Arlo might not have an audience when all the hippies disappeared. But it was clear [at the revival] . . . that he's really going to carry on for Pete Seeger, and that developing anti-nuke, ecology (and etcetera, I hope) movement is going to become his audience." These sentiments were shared by Sunday's crowd, which was not all that surprising; the *Clearwater* event was, in inspiration and design, an activist's festival. The problem with the annual fundraiser was that it attracted an audience of mostly middle-class whites; there were, in Smucker's terminology, too few "rough-looking kids . . . nonwhites and non suburbanites . . . the kind of people who aren't sure that anti-nuke and ecology nuts care whether they have jobs." Interestingly, Arlo shared some of Smucker's concerns. He acknowledged that while it was important to support ecological activism, it was equally important to remember "that basically people still have to work. They've got families they want to feed." Guthrie's position on this matter occasionally brought criticism from those on the Green Left. His appearance in the film promoting industrial development in Massachusetts was met with disbelief, even outright hostility, by many with whom he was usually politically aligned. But instead of reflexively rejecting industrial development, Guthrie thought it would be better if activists, companies, and the working people of Massachusetts got together to discuss what factories were best suited to the surrounding areas. Though Guthrie would always support "Green" efforts and causes, he acknowledged, "You can't knock out the important thing, which is that people have to work."[9]

The "developing anti-nuke" movement that Smucker saw smoldering would ignite on a national stage the following weekend. On June 24 and 25, members of the antinuclear coalition the Clamshell Alliance hosted a weekend rally in the eighteen-acre marshlands surrounding the twin nuclear towers at Seabrook, New Hampshire. Formed in July 1976, the Clamshell Alliance was at the forefront of the fight to ensure that the twin 1,150-megawatt reactors built at Seabrook would not go online. Stressing civil disobedience as a tool in the resistance to the nuclear ambitions of New Hampshire's Public Service Company, they first made local news after staging two nonviolent occupations at the site in August 1976, the protests resulting in 198 arrests. A demonstration in April 1977 led to an incredible 1,414 arrests, which brought national attention to the antinuclear movement. The weekend rally planned for late June attracted a slate of speakers and musicians lending support to the cause. On Sunday, June 25, Arlo Guthrie and Shenandoah, Pete Seeger, Jackson Browne, and John Hall of the band Orleans performed at Seabrook. Seeger sang a great new song he learned from folk singer Charlie King of Voluntown, Connecticut. King had rewritten the words of a traditional song from the Pacific Northwest, "The Old Settler's Song," transforming the tune into an antinuclear ballad titled "Acres of Clams" in recognition of the efforts of the Clamshell Alliance. Guthrie learned the song from Seeger and incorporated "Acres of Clams" into his shows with Shenandoah, helping to spread the song—and its antinuclear message—nationally. Guthrie was clearly inspired by the events at Seabrook. One month following the rally, Arlo told the *Milwaukee Sentinel*, "It was great, man. Hey, they closed the plant down." Guthrie also saw a parallel between the antiwar movements of the 1960s and the antinuke activists of the 1970s. "Today's youth movement's concerns are probably the same as everybody else's. . . . The Vietnam War was a concern for everybody, no matter what side of it you were on, and I think the same is probably true now with energy."[10]

In his stage shows and newspaper interviews from 1978 to 1980, Guthrie would discuss, at some length and with humor, the folly of nuclear power. He was optimistic that reason would eventually prevail. "I'm definitely opposed to nuclear power as an energy source," he told the *Christian Science Monitor* in March of 1978. "I think that once the weight of the scientific world gets over there, if the press covers it right, we won't have it." Two years later, with nuclear-energy plans continuing to press forward at home and around the world, Guthrie needed to amend his earlier statement. "We all know both sides of the nuclear issue, that low level radiation is dangerous," he told college-newspaper writer Bob Principe.

> The only disagreement in the health aspect of nuclear power is how dangerous are we willing to have it? From my point of view, I don't think it's moral to say we're only going to kill a certain amount of people for our toasters, air conditioners etc. In certain areas, like x-rays, it may be acceptable, but in trying to turn the whole world into a place where you have endless electricity at the risk of thousands of people's lives is absurd.

It was his view that, while costly, it would be best that existing nuclear power facilities were converted "into coal operating plants," though he added an important caveat that we would first have to "find out how to clean up the atmosphere as [we're] doing it." "There would be a lot of money involved," Guthrie admitted, "but I'd rather pay now than trying to fix all the leukemia patients and cancer victims that are going to happen as a result of nuclear energy."[11]

That August, following a brief tour of Western Europe, including a date at the New Morning Festival in Paris, Guthrie was back on the road with Shenandoah. The touring was relentless. His schedule had fallen into the pattern of five weeks on the road with twenty or so concerts scheduled on each run. Whenever feasible, Jackie and the kids would accompany him on the tour, but such arrangements were an exception. Some of his 1977 shows with Shenandoah had been recorded with the intent of releasing a live album. That mosaic album was now near completion.

With Guthrie in the midst of an East Coast tour, Warner Bros. released the "live-in-concert" *One Night* on September 15, 1978. The first half of the album was unreservedly great, perfectly capturing the musical brilliance and excitement of Guthrie and Shenandoah's current stage show. Three-quarters of the material comprising *One Night* was sourced from a Guthrie–Shenandoah gig in Raleigh, North Carolina. The rest came from shows in Cincinnati and Nashville. In late July Guthrie had been with engineers Donn Landee and Raffaello Mazza at Sunset Sound Recorders in Hollywood overseeing the album's final mix. In a telephone interview with journalist Bill Hammond of the *Milwaukee Sentinel*, Arlo offered that *One Night* would be mostly programmed with cover songs, since "I wanted to save some of my own stuff for the next album, which is going to be done in a studio, where we have a little more control over things." Guthrie's considerable skills as a guitarist, pianist, and banjoist were well represented and showcased on *One Night*: "I used to consider myself a guitar player because I couldn't sing, but now I'm more relaxed and into learning stuff. I'm actually playing more guitar on this album than I have on some of the other ones because it is live, and you can't get somebody to go into the studio and do it better." Though a concert album, there was, unusually, no "greatest hits" content, with all but one of the nine song/performances on wax for the first time. The Warner Bros. trade advertisement said it all:

What Sort of Contemporary Artist Could Get Away with Performing the Best Songs of Elvis Presley, the Beatles, Eddie Arnold, Eddie Fisher, the Weavers and Fats Domino—All on One Absurdly Brilliant New Album of His Own [12]

The first side was perfect. There was a dash of rock 'n' roll ("One Night"), a bluegrass rendering of the Lennon–McCartney classic "I've Just Seen a Face," three songs gleaned from Jack Elliott ("Anytime," "Buffalo Skinners," and "Tennessee Stud"), a delightful turn at a ragtime piano standard ("St. Louis Tickle"), and an exciting flat-picking tour de force via "Little Beggar Man." The single flaw of *One Night* was, arguably, the inclusion of Guthrie's opus "The Story of Reuben Clamzo and His Strange Daughter in the Key of A" that opens side B. Though the seventeen-minute, thirty-four-second monologue was not without its charms in live performance, the programming of the monologue on the LP was baffling, effectively ruining what had been a very fine musical collection. Prior to the album's release Guthrie defended his "Reuben Clamzo" monologue offering, "It's as much about the nuclear power issue as 'Alice' was about the war," but the satire of the former title was hardly as trenchant. Nearly every newspaper and magazine review was uniform in its praise of the album's rollicking and tuneful first side. The *Lakeland Ledger* suggested that *One Night* wasn't "half-bad. That is to say, that half of it is bad, and the other half isn't." "That ['Reuben Clamzo'] should take up an entire side of a record is remarkable," the review went on. "Regrettable too, because there's good material on the other side which could have been carried over to side two." The *Boston Globe* agreed that the first side was the better of the two. But although *One Night* was blessed as being musically "pleasant," the newspaper warned readers that "Reuben Clamzo" wasn't "strong enough throughout to merit taking up most of a single-record live LP." In the fair estimate of the music critic of the *Deseret News*, the monologue was "funny in person or the first two times you hear it on the record, but after thirty four minutes, you're really ready for something different." The critic ultimately dismissed the long-winded narrative, not unreasonably, as an "in-joke for Seabrookies and other clam lovers." The *Windsor Star* thought *One Night* a success as Guthrie "is a far more satisfactory performer when facing an audience than a studio control board," but he too agreed that while "Reuben Clamzo" was a "funny, friendly satire," it was nonetheless a miss as the saga ran so long nobody will "listen to it much." The crusty Robert Christgau of the *Village Voice* slagged "Reuben Clamzo" as "a tall tale that would have trouble making first string guard on a high school basketball team."[13]

The teaming of Pete Seeger with Guthrie and Shenandoah continued throughout 1978, and, assuming you were a fan of their type of folk music, the synergistic collaboration was entirely satisfying. In Vienna, Virginia, their filmed show at Wolf Trap Farm Park on August 22 was an outstanding success. That evening Pete sang "If I Had a Hammer," his robust performance igniting, according to a dispatch in the *Washington Post*, "a spontaneous standing ovation from a crowd grateful that Seeger has held on to his anger and his art." That concert was broadcast live in its entirety by a Washington, DC, PBS affiliate as part of that station's week-long *Live from Wolf Trap* program, a five-part series that also featured Sarah Vaughan's Gershwin tribute, a night of big-band music with Tex Beneke and His Orchestra, the trumpeter Chuck Mangione, and a sixtieth-birthday concert celebration for Leonard Bernstein. The Seeger and Guthrie installment was well received, and the program would be rebroadcast over the next several years, though often in truncated form, during the perennial PBS pledge drives.[14]

One week following their success at Wolf Trap, Guthrie and Seeger would play many of the same songs to a half-empty house at Boston's Hynes Veterans Auditorium. The *Boston Globe* groused that the show wasn't "particularly noteworthy. As a folk music program, it needn't have been exciting, but it shouldn't have been boring." Regardless of the naysayers, Seeger admitted to enjoying his sorties with Arlo and Shenandoah, though he conceded much of the music's intimacy was lost in the cavernous amphitheaters they would play each summer in front of thousands. "I'm very proud that [Arlo] likes to work with me," Pete told *Frets* magazine, "and I know that I love to perform with him . . . every summer we go out and do some concerts, usually in these great big open sheds, which frankly I think are too big. From the back, I don't know how they can see us without a telescope."[15]

That autumn Guthrie would enlist the assistance of Seeger for a small benefit event, a combination concert and picnic on the grounds of the Music Inn in Stockbridge. The event was to assist in raising $25,000 for the purchase of a new ambulance to serve the town of Washington and several neighboring communities. Though everyone in the area agreed that a new ambulance was essential, the town of Stockbridge nonetheless filed a preliminary injunction and restraining order against the benefit, arguing the law prohibited concerts on the grounds of the Music Inn following Labor Day. Though the Music Inn had previously signed off on that agreement, Guthrie argued that it was he and

Pete, not the Music Inn, who were renting the facility so the prohibition was nonstanding. The Guthrie–Seeger concert had been scheduled for September 16, and regardless of its selfless intent, the residents of Stockbridge, having just fended off the Berkshire Mountain summer vacationers, were fearful that the proposed concert would attract unruly crowds, litter, traffic, and noise. On Thursday, September 14, with the benefit only two days away and the promoters scrambling to find an alternate site, Guthrie and a lawyer from the Boston firm of Hale and Doar were in a Springfield courtroom where their case was heard by Hampden Superior Court judge John F. Moriarty. Guthrie's lawyer insisted that the event wasn't a concert at all but an "innocuous outing," to which the exasperated lawyer for Stockbridge countered, "There will be singing. . . . To call it anything else [but a concert] is a distinction without a difference." In the end, Moriarty ruled "that restrictions imposed on outdoor concerts at Music Inn in Stockbridge by a Berkshire Superior Court judge in 1977 were not binding" and that the concert could be staged as planned. Stepping out of the courtroom, Guthrie flashed a victory sign and announced to a small crowd of supporters and reporters, "OK, we go."[16]

That September it seemed as if Guthrie couldn't help but get embroiled in courtroom dramas. On September 21, he was in a U.S. district courtroom in Burlington, Vermont, set to defend himself against a promoter's charge of slander. The imbroglio dated back to Halloween evening 1976, when Guthrie was contracted to play at a small nightclub in Burlington. The singer had been guaranteed a payment of $2,500 cash for his show that night, to be delivered backstage at the intermission. The problem was that Guthrie was only paid $950 in cash, with the promoter, Clayton Fuller, guaranteeing the difference with a personal check. Guthrie and his road manager, Alan Clapper, were surprised since his contract stipulated that only a certified check was acceptable. When Guthrie returned to the stage following the intermission he surprised fans waiting for the second set, informing them that the show was over and "that everybody here is being ripped off." He also, reportedly, told everyone "never to patronize another concert promoted by Fuller." That was too much for the exasperated promoter, who believed that Guthrie breached the contract by not completing the show. Fuller sued Guthrie for slander, asking for "unspecified compensatory and punitive damages." In Burlington, Guthrie's lawyer, Spencer Knapp, told the seven-person jury that it was impossible for Guthrie to have damaged the promoter's reputation as "Fuller's reputation is beyond repair." Guthrie told the jury that he *did* recall telling everyone gathered that night they were being "ripped off" since "they had paid to see a show they were not going to see." As for the charge that he told concertgoers never to patronize another Fuller event, Guthrie coyly acknowledged, "I may have intoned that." On Tuesday, September 26, the verdict came in, and

Guthrie was cleared of the charge. He told reporters afterwards that he was feeling "pretty good" about the dismissal.[17]

In late autumn Arlo was back on the road for a series of shows on the West Coast and Canada. Guthrie was scheduled to perform with Shenandoah on October 24 at the Sports Arena in Anchorage, Alaska. The night prior to that concert, the local promoter had scheduled, much to Arlo's chagrin, a series of tight, fifteen-minute interview sessions with a number of local journalists. The best of these sit-downs was with writer Kathryn Phillips of the *Anchorage Daily News*, who found Arlo sitting in a corner of a local restaurant, grumbling his way through a number of topics. These ranged from nuclear power ("I'm totally opposed to nuclear power. . . . We all know it's dangerous. It's not a question of whether it's dangerous or not, it's really a question of how acceptable [the danger is]") to happiness ("I don't think the object of life is to be happy. I think if anybody is happy in this world, there is something wrong with them. . . . Anybody who's happy all of the time is not experiencing what there is to experience and therefore is not using all of the things that is within him to use"). The "falsely humble," in Guthrie's opinion, were as bad as those folks "who walk around all the time knowing everything." Arlo also corrected the misconception that he was a political folk singer, explaining again that his songs were moral fables, not tales of political realities. Though album sales had softened in recent years, he wasn't too concerned. As long as there were "people concerned with other people. . . . I'll always have an audience," he confidently told Phillips. The people who taught him the most, he explained, were Pete Seeger, his father, and his mother: all three had dedicated themselves to their crafts and the well-being of others.[18]

The songs comprising Guthrie's *Outlasting the Blues* (Warner Bros. BSK 3336) were mostly written and recorded during the first three months of winter 1979. The album, which was entirely recorded and mixed at Long View Farm Studios, North Brookfield, Massachusetts, was Guthrie's first non–Los Angeles studio album since 1967's *Alice's Restaurant*. Though old hand John Pilla remained at the control board as producer, a decision was made to forego the use of session men on the new recording project. Instead, Pilla chose to tap the considerable talents of Shenandoah. Other musical neighbors from the Berkshires, such as a local string orchestra, would be brought in to augment certain songs.[19]

It was important that the production of *Outlasting the Blues* was wrapped up by the end of winter as Guthrie and Shenandoah were set to embark in springtime for a number of concerts in Europe, with shows planned in Italy, Germany, Holland, Switzerland, and the United Kingdom. Just prior to heading off to Europe, Guthrie made last-minute plans to ride Amtrak's "endangered *Montrealer* train to Washington" on Tuesday afternoon, April 3. Nobody had asked for Guthrie's assistance in this case, but the folk singer had read in the newspapers that Amtrak was planning on shutting down train service on the line from Washington, DC, to Montreal. Guthrie thought the proposed suspension was "a real shame," the disappearing railroad one more symbol of lost Americana. Arlo proactively contacted a group called "Friends of the Railroad" who had been petitioning the Department of Transportation to continue the service. They suggested that Guthrie might use his celebrity status and ride the train with friends as that simple act alone "might attract some attention." "So some of us took our guitars and our horns," Guthrie recalled, "and we went down and took them all on the train." The idea was that the passengers, inspired by the bright music on the railroad cars, might write their senators and suggest that the train service not be suspended. The gentle protest was effective, and the *Montrealer* would get a temporary reprieve.[20]

At the conclusion of his first European tour of 1979, Arlo visited Elstree Studios, north of London, to tape an episode of Jim Henson's popular children's television program *The Muppet Show*. Guthrie was already something of a fan of the Emmy-winning program. His kids grew up watching it on TV, and Guthrie himself enjoyed it "because the show has consistently brought out something in the guests that you never see them reveal anywhere else. It's a childish quality, and it's nice to see people like that." In a sense, Guthrie was simply paraphrasing what his father had famously written some years earlier: "I don't wanna see kids act like grownups, I'd like to see the grownups act like kids." On the program Guthrie and a gaggle of Muppets performed "Grocery Blues" (from *Amigo*) on an upright piano, "Get Along Little Dogies" on guitar, and closed with Pete Seeger's "Sailing Down My Golden River" (recently recorded for *Outlasting the Blues*) with the augmentation of his bluesy mouth harp. He was also, much to the surprise of Kermit the Frog, memorably caught in a shocking romantic clutch with the show's fetching diva, Miss Piggy. The program was first broadcast in the United States on June 19, 1979.[21]

Copies of *Outlasting the Blues*, with its attendant wrestle of spiritual issues, hit the shelves of record stores in June 1979, a full ten weeks before Bob Dylan's first album of gospel rock, *Slow Train Coming*, was released that August. Critic Dave Marsh offered, "Guthrie finally resolves (successfully) the tensions between folk and rock, meaning mostly that he has put together some tough music . . . to complement some of his most unsettling songs ever. . . . 'Which Side' and 'Wedding Song' incorporate Biblical imagery as effortlessly and infectiously as I hope Bob Dylan does on his new record." The *New York Times* thought the album's "chilling" first line, "In the event of my demise," was not there by accident: as Guthrie "enters his 30's . . . he is likely to discover whether he has inherited Huntington's chorea," a possibility suggesting the album's spiritual ruminations. The *Christian Science Monitor* noted that the new album signaled that "Arlo Guthrie has outlasted the 60s as well as the blues." "In a world of cloned Top 40 hits," the review continued, "every song on this album has the unusual quality of sounding distinctive." Not every review was as glowing. The *Montreal Gazette* thought that *Outlasting the Blues* could not be rescued, despite the lovely resetting of Hoyt Axton's "Evangelina" that closed the album. The *Gazette* regretted that the contributions of Shenandoah could not "compensate for [Arlo's] wretched, grating wailing on most cuts." Ken Tucker in *Rolling Stone* thought Shenandoah's bar-band instrumental support "renders *Outlasting the Blues* a much duller and more ordinary LP than its informing intelligence should have allowed it to become." But he also believed that the album was a small masterwork of writing and programming, not only for its "meditation on mortality but [as] a chronicle of the cultural history that Arlo Guthrie has lived through." Acknowledging that while the pop arrangements and muscular electric guitar solos of *Outlasting the Blues* "[sounds] like the artist's first direct stab at commercial success in years," *Hi-Fidelity/Musical America* cautioned that "the conceptual underpinnings that emerge in the album's first side argue that [Guthrie's] determination to reach a broader audience is anything but mercenary."[22]

This time out, Warner Bros. seemed determined to aggressively market the LP, which was surely Guthrie's most rock 'n' roll–oriented album to date. Though his recent albums had been released with little fanfare or record company promotion, *Outlasting the Blues* would not suffer the same neglect. The afternoon of a concert at the Calderone Theater, West Hempstead, Long Island, Arlo was resting at a local Holiday Inn, having agreed to an interview with a reporter from Long Island's preeminent newspaper, *Newsday.* In that feature, later syndicated nationally, reporter Wayne Robins charged that Arthur Penn's *Alice's Restaurant* and Guthrie's media image as a hippie-everyman and songwriter of novelties "typecast him as a purveyor of a charming but lightweight musical style." "The comedy is not quite so dear" on *Outlasting the Blues*, Robins conceded, somberly noting the album's first side, with its treatises on morality and mortality, "is a bit depressing the first time you hear it." Guthrie countered that he hadn't entered the studio with the design of recording a "concept album" but wouldn't "deny the thematic unity of the first side." "Maybe it is a cycle," Guthrie conceded after reflection. "The songs just came together that way. . . . I confronted those thoughts in a direct way, and didn't pretend to be mystical."[23]

Though he was often prodded to, Guthrie rarely made public statements regarding Bob Dylan's controversial turn to Jesus Christ in 1979. Dylan would "be a great prophet. He's mysterious enough," Arlo told *Rolling Stone*, with a wry smile, but that's as little as he'd say on record. But two years following the release of Dylan's first all-gospel LP, Guthrie shared his conflicted feelings, conceding, "Truthfully, I like only two or three songs from *Slow Train Coming*," with two of those three apparently being the single "Gotta Serve Somebody" and the allegorical "Man Gave Names to All the Animals." By the autumn of 1980 Dylan had already returned to peppering his mostly gospel stage show with a small measure of classic songs. This was welcomed by Guthrie, as well as Dylan's fans, as he thought "Blowin' in the Wind" remained "a far better song than anything on *Slow Train* . . . and its application to spiritual life was far greater." Though Guthrie refused to second-guess or belittle Dylan's interest in religious matters, he wasn't all that enthused by the grim fundamentalism of Dylan's lyrics, which, as one critic noted, transformed rock's preeminent poet into little more than "a spiritual pamphleteer." But Guthrie was familiar enough with Dylan that he wasn't too concerned that the artist had staked a final claim. "Bob Dylan is not a person who has come to a place and stopped," Guthrie told writer Danny Smith. "Never was and he's not going to now. Remember that and give him room to move." This statement might have even been a reflection of some of Guthrie's own recent trials. Ever since his interest in Catholicism and Jesus Christ was widely reported in newspapers and magazines, his shows were beginning to attract an audience who were, as termed by the media, "born-again." Too often those who came to hear Guthrie deliver a sermon were unsettled by the fact that his concerts were anything but Christian revival meetings, and many were troubled by the perceived left-wing sentiments of "Victor Jara" and other songs. To Guthrie there was no contradiction. "People separate the religious and social aspects of life. I just can't make that distinction. The Jewish-Christian values expressed on *Outlasting the Blues* reaffirm who I am, my identity, my spiritual values."[24]

On July 21, Guthrie and Shenandoah played the Dr. Pepper Music Festival at Wollman Rink in Manhattan's Central Park. Guthrie was no stranger to the series at the venue, but this night's concert was more eventful as it was to be broadcast live on one of New York City's premier rock-music stations, WPLJ-FM. (The previous night's show in West Hempstead was also broadcast live in its entirety on station WLIR-FM.) The Dr. Pepper gig would allow Guthrie the opportunity to reaffirm his status as a mainstream rock 'n' roll act and would also serve as a platform to introduce songs from *Outlasting the Blues* to an audience of a million or more radio listeners. Not about to waste the promotional potentialities of a high-profile concert in the heart of the nation's media capital, the Warner Bros. publicity machine was in full press. They convinced Arlo to submit to a series of interviews prior to the show to help create buzz for *Outlasting the Blues*. That afternoon, Arlo and Jackie met with Mary Campbell of the Associated Press at a luncheon at their favorite Indian restaurant in Manhattan, the Shah Jahan. The Central Park show was sandwiched somewhere in the middle of a grueling thirty-one-city schedule. The current tour, which started on June 28 at the Casino Beach Club in Hampton Beach, New Hampshire, was to finish on September 9 with a cobill with Pete Seeger at the Pine Knob Music Theater, Clarkston, Michigan. Guthrie told Campbell that his style of songwriting hadn't changed all that much over the years, though he admitted that it probably "has freed up a bit. . . . It's a little more relaxed, probably because I'm not 18 any more." He acknowledged that he rarely wrote while on the road and working with the band. "I think I repress it when I'm touring, and let it seep out when I'm not. . . . If I think of something on the road, I just try and save it." But such work habits were problematic, as most years he was now on the road for some nine months, more or less, and when he returned to his home in Washington "my ears have had it. I don't want to hear anything but the birds and wind."[25]

Guthrie also confided to the AP that his "family" was to temporarily grow larger in the coming months. He and Jackie had been watching television and were very moved by two recent programs documenting the plight of the "boat people," refugees from communist-controlled Laos, Cambodia, and Vietnam fleeing political persecution. Their stories, in Guthrie's words, "broke my heart," so much so that he decided that he had to do something about it. He contacted his local congressman, who "put me in touch with the U.S. Catholic Conference, the closest agency for this to our house." Since there were two houses on his sprawling farm in Washington County, the Guthries were to soon welcome a Vietnamese father with seven sons and two grandsons. In the midst of everything else that was going on, the Guthries were hoping to find the refugees some construction work in the area. The idea of American citizens helping refugees from Southeast Asia return to their lives with a semblance of normality and dignity was an enterprise that appealed to Guthrie. "I see it as healing a lot of wounds," he explained. "I think if we open our hearts to these people, the Vietnam War could become a dead issue. . . . America has already taken in more of these people than any other country in the world, and I'm proud of that." The gesture was also a sign of his ever-deepening Christian faith. He was growing increasingly tired of "people who profess some sort of religious conviction" but rarely followed the example of Jesus, who tended to those who were neediest. He was later visited on his tour bus by Debra Rae Cohen, a correspondent from *Rolling Stone*, and the chat was anything but lighthearted. The two talked about *Outlasting the Blues*, Catholicism, death, God, and the possibility that Guthrie's recent interest in spiritual matters was the result of his living in the shadow of Huntington's disease. Guthrie somewhat nervously brushed off that suggestion, telling Cohen that, in the end, he was brought to the understanding there are "some things you can only do when you're alive." Though he always believed in God, he admitted, "I guess I didn't know as much about him when I was a kid as I probably do now." On *Outlasting the Blues*, Guthrie boldly proclaimed in "Which Side" that he was "satisfied to sing for God's own son." He told Cohen much the same, and that he "decided to pursue God in whatever way he would allow me to." "I guess a lot of things changed for me when I finally realized that I could see myself, all along, being utilized for things that I believed in."[26]

Though the majority of Guthrie's recent interviews were filled with discussions on matters of the spirit, neither he nor Warner Bros. were against selling some records as well. That night in Central Park the set list was slotted with five songs from the new LP as well as three unrecorded songs, "Waimanalo Blues," "No More Nukes," and Charlie King's rewrite of "Acres of Clams." With tongue firmly planted in cheek, Arlo also floated a creative new angle to increase album sales. Prior to launching into the two outright rockers from *Outlasting the Blues*, "Prologue" and "Which Side," Guthrie offered,

> We'd like to do a few songs here from a new album of ours. . . . We're trying to sell a lot of these albums, so we'll give a ride to anybody in the audience or anywhere on our bus. We've got a big bus out back there, and we'll take you anywhere you want to go. The first person that wants to buy *10,000 copies*, we'll drive you under the Hudson . . . or outer space. Don't matter to us.

Otherwise, the concert was business as usual, an engaging and rapturously received set of greatest hits ("City of New Orleans," "The Motorcycle Song," "Coming into Los Angeles"), as well as the songs of Dylan ("Percy's Song"), Seeger ("Sailing Down My Golden River") and his father ("This Land Is Your Land," "My Daddy [Flies a Ship in the Sky]," and "Deportee (Plane Wreck at Los Gatos)." He dedicated the last song ("Here's one written forty years ago, and it just as well could have been written yesterday") to those who "have not been eating Chiquita bananas lately," a reference to the ongoing United Farm Workers boycott of all products from the Sun Harvest and Chiquita Banana companies. The two antinuke songs ("Rosin the Beau/Acres of Clams" and "No More Nukes") were also rapturously received. The nuclear power issue was now on everyone's mind following the core meltdown of Unit 2 at the Three Mile Island facility near Harrisburg, Pennsylvania, on March 28. Arlo passed on a note to concertgoers to remind everyone that an antinuclear rally was to be staged at the Indian Point facility on August 5. It was an amazing concert from start to finish; one writer from *Variety* noted the excitement, offering that while Guthrie "neglected" to perform "Alice's Restaurant," "little else was denied shouting fans." The only dissenting opinion came from the *Village Voice*, which missed Arlo's comic monologues and found the "flat professionalism" of the concert similar to the songs on *Outlasting the Blues*; the songs were "grim [and] despairing" since "[Guthrie's] obviously not finding anything to laugh about these days."[27]

Arlo had a mere week's rest following the final show of his exhausting U.S. summer tour. He was due to again travel overseas. The summer of 1979 would mark the tenth anniversary of the Woodstock event, and a savvy European promoter managed to book original festival performers Joe Cocker, Country Joe McDonald, Richie Havens, and Arlo for a two-week-long "Woodstock in Europe" traveling show. There were nine shows traversing Germany, Italy, and Holland. The first was staged on September 16 at the Festplatz an der via Claudia, Augsburg-Gersthollen, Germany; the last was at Edenhal, Amsterdam, Holland, on September 27, with seven dates throughout Germany and Italy in the interim.

That November Guthrie was back in the United States and on the road for an East Coast swing. On Thanksgiving eve, November 21, Guthrie and Shenandoah appeared at the Van Wezel Performing Arts Hall in Sarasota, Florida. Following the show, Arlo agreed to chat with a feature writer from the Sarasota *Herald-Tribune*, telling the newspaperman that he had plans to spend Thanksgiving with friends. Afterwards, he and the band were scheduled to return to the road for a string of dates out west. Three weeks earlier Bob Dylan had inaugurated an unprecedented series of fourteen concerts at San Francisco's Fox-Warfield Theater on Mission Street, the heart of a crime- and drug-riddled neighborhood. The concerts made headlines as Dylan, who once famously cautioned, "don't follow leaders," was now telling everyone "there's only one authority / And that's the authority on High." Dylan's fans were, for the most part, blindsided and baffled by the bard's unexpected turn toward Jesus. The advertisements for the Warfield shows had offered no hint that Dylan would only be performing his gospel material from *Slow Train Coming* and songs from the as-yet-unreleased *Saved*. Dylan's Warfield concerts would soon be regarded as controversial and as challenging as his well-publicized defection to rock 'n' roll at Newport in 1965. Guthrie hadn't yet seen Dylan's gospel-revival show, but he thought that the hand-wringing, apoplectic, and hateful attacks on Dylan in the combined mainstream, music, and left-wing presses were, at the very least, *interesting*. "They didn't complain when he was singing about his Civil Rights ideals," Guthrie told writer Charlie Huisking. "When someone is strong and takes a stand about something, people are always going to be offended. There's no way around that."[28]

Dylan was not the only contemporary rock artist to infuse his music with musings on spiritual matters. Dave Marsh, writing in *Rolling Stone*, short-listed Robert Fripp, Van Morrison, Pete Townshend, Eric Clapton, Ronnie Lane, and Arlo as "rockers on the road to salvation." The difference between Bob Dylan and his contemporaries was the singer's unexpected heavy-handedness; Dylan's God was a vengeful one, and his brand of gospel music owed more to the bitter vitriol of his own "Positively Fourth Street" than, say, the uplifting sentiment of "'Tis So Sweet to Trust in Jesus." Marsh believed that Arlo's recent *Outlasting the Blues* was a winner and "among the finest records. . . . [Guthrie] has ever made . . . and far more prolific (and, for my money, effective) in its use of Biblical imagery than *Slow Train Coming*."[29]

Following his show in San Francisco, Arlo agreed to a backstage chat with Mary Neely for a segment to be broadcast on the syndicated *Rock and Religion* radio program. Based in nearby Sacramento, the program's producers had been issuing radio transcription discs of artists whose music reflected Christian themes. Host Tom McKenzie introduced Guthrie as an artist in the throes "of a deepening of his religious faith. Previously a 'humanitarian Jew,' as he called himself, Arlo now states that Christianity fulfills Judaism . . . and calls himself 'a Catholic Jew.'" Though he was also described by McKenzie as an "embodiment" of the "Woodstock generation," Arlo corrected that his songs were never of a "political dimension," as they were not "opposed to society per se." He wasn't willing to accept the media's tag that he was an antiauthority figure; he wasn't necessarily opposed to any specific authority as he recognized structure was necessary for people to get along in a "semi-civilized situation." His concern was with the moral character of that authority. Guthrie explained,

> I didn't turn to religion at all. I grew up in a house that was concerned about morality, and . . . concerned about it on a lot of different levels. It was concerned about it as the boss and the workingman, the poor and the rich, the corporate structure and the individual storeowner. All of these things . . . are all part of the social aspect of the gospel. . . . I grew up in that kind of atmosphere.

When questioned if the teachings of Jesus Christ were, in essence, "a format for social reform for nations and individuals," Arlo answered without hesitation, "Absolutely, absolutely." And when asked if he feared that his new-found spirituality might create backlash among his fans, Guthrie shrugged off the notion, telling Neely that while he couldn't speak for his audience he wasn't too concerned; after all, the civil rights and antiwar movements were won incrementally as more people began to understand the fundamental moral lessons playing out as history before them. The fire-and-brimstone Dylan gospel concerts at the Warfield that November were controversial, with critic Joel Selvin of the *San Francisco Chronicle* famously suggesting that "Dylan's conversion will serve as a concise metaphor for the vast emptiness of the era." Though Arlo was willing to discuss his own evolving spiritual views with those who asked or appeared interested, he chose not to use the concert stage as a platform for outright evangelism. When asked if he thought that lost souls might attend his concerts looking for answers, Arlo deferred, noting, "We're all looking for answers. No matter what names we give ourselves. We give ourselves names of religions . . . or ideals or things like that. But the nature of religion is mystery. The essence of it is mystery . . . so there is no answer. There [are] only steps closer to the mystery . . . only an acceptance of the mystery."[30]

One welcome aspect of his newfound spirituality was that it had strength-ened his recent songwriting. "I think that's part of what some of these new songs are about. It's real hard for me to get into the idea of writing songs about things I'm *pleased* with." If these were protest songs, Guthrie suggested they were protest songs of a different sort. "Coming out of the '60s," Arlo contin-ued, "the whole structure of what I wrote was, basically, concerned with what I was *displeased* with," but that, in a sense, was too simplistic an approach. One lesson that Guthrie learned through the years was "that not everybody who looks like you thinks like you. . . . There has to be something deeper than what somebody's job is, or what somebody's politics are. There has to be communication on levels that are not so 'issue' oriented."[31]

Though Guthrie and Shenandoah toured aggressively during the second half of 1979 to promote *Outlasting the Blues*, sales of the album never caught fire. The 1970s was the decade when the record business transformed into the record *industry*, and sales of rock 'n' roll albums, much less folk-rock albums with Christian underpinnings, were in decline. The phenomenon of disco mu-sic, which had germinated earlier in the decade, exploded onto the national stage in the last months of 1977, and disco was by 1978 easily the most popu-lar music form in the United States through the early 1980s. Though many rock 'n' roll fans and critics bemoaned the industry's turn from blues-based rock 'n' roll to the beat-driven dance rhythms of disco—a "Disco Demoli-tion" rally at Chicago's Comiskey Park in 1979 would turn into a small, and many believed racist-tinged, riot—Guthrie refused to align with the naysay-ers. He told the Sarasota *Herald-Tribune* that he didn't have any antipathy for disco, even though its emergence had certainly helped supplant him and many of his friends as record sellers. Disco was, in Arlo's view, essentially folk music, even in the absence of acoustic guitars or fiddles. He likened the contemporary disco dancing craze to the down-home square-dancing of 200 years earlier. Though he agreed that the lyrics of contemporary disco records tended to be "mindless," Guthrie reminded everyone that "nobody was look-ing for brilliant words in an old folk tune like 'Old Joe Clark' either. It was made for people to dance to."[32]

Nonetheless, the feeling that Guthrie, and similar artists, had been "pushed out" and off the record charts was prevalent. Guthrie conceded that was true "in terms of record labels and airplay. . . . Anybody up and coming would have a hard time presenting a kind of music that was different from the mainstream." But he was an established artist with his own loyal following, comfortable in the niche that he had carved for himself in the music business. Though he would have welcomed charting a hit record every now and again, he acknowledged, "I've never really been in the Top 40 anyway. I've never been part of the culture." This wasn't always the case, of course, but it was certainly true of 1973 through the present. In many ways, Guthrie's career began to resemble that of occasional tour mate Pete Seeger. Though Seeger could easily fill Carnegie Hall and attract reverent crowds wherever he strummed, he simply couldn't sell many records, regardless of how many foot-stomping standing ovations and multiple encores his concert performances inspired. Guthrie allowed himself the solace that it wasn't entirely his fault. Fate had, for whatever reason, decreed that he would never be a chart-topping artist. He sighed to writer Wayne Robins, "We did 'Alice,' and that was too long for most radio stations. ['Coming into Los Angeles'] came out at a time when drug songs were banned, and [the train that inspired] 'City of New Orleans,' crashed when we did it. After awhile, you begin to take the hint."[33]

As there was no new record in the works, Guthrie's media profile was diminished in 1980. He continued to tour relentlessly and began 1980 with the usual West Coast swing with Shenandoah. As he was on the opposite side of the country, Guthrie was unable to attend the world premiere of *Take It to the Limit*, set for March 5 at the Sunshine Mall Twin Cinema in South Daytona, Florida. Three years in the making, producer-director Peter Starr's homage to the motorcycle and the heroes of motorcycling was set to go into limited release on March 7. Starr had put together an impressive soundtrack for the film, weaving the music of Tangerine Dream, Foreigner, Jean-Luc Ponty, John McEuen, and Arlo Guthrie into his soon-to-be cult motorcycling movie. The local newspaper promised that at the premiere Starr would be putting "the theater's four channel Dolby stereo system to maximum use with the 'all around' sound of motorcycle and rock and roll." Guthrie was featured in the film, riding his motorcycle near his home in Washington and in an animated segment featuring, of all things, a talking pickle. The folk singer had recorded a new version of "The Motorcycle Song" specifically for the film. It was, perhaps, the only film premiere in history where tickets were available only at local Honda dealerships.[34]

Guthrie's touring would continue through the summer; there were the usual tandem dates with Pete Seeger as well as a series of cobills as support for singer-songwriter Harry Chapin. But there was a creeping consensus that the acoustic storytelling of the singer-songwriter movement was mere nostalgia. On Monday night, July 21, Guthrie was the underbill for Harry Chapin at the Greek Theater in Los Angeles. Though both artists were received rapturously by fans, a critic from *Variety* deemed their sets to be rehashes of some distant past. They complained that Guthrie's forty-five-minute segment suffered "from the same kind of terminal musical sameness as Chapin," and grumbled that "only his most ardent followers will last through his set without becoming bored." Thankfully, that sentiment was not shared by all. Steve Pond of the *Los Angeles Times* thought otherwise, suggesting "Arlo Guthrie, who deserves better, opened the show," though the singer's "short set barely scratched the surface of an extensive, eclectic repertoire."[35]

Guthrie's "extensive, eclectic repertoire" would be amply demonstrated on his follow-up to *Outlasting the Blues*. In April 1981, *Rolling Stone* reported that Arlo was in a Los Angeles studio and "recording his first new album in two years." The title, Guthrie revealed, was *Power of Love*, the name of a T-Bone Burnett song to be programmed as the album's opening salvo. The sessions that produced *Power of Love* were recorded at the Warner Bros. Recording Studio, North Hollywood, with producer John Pilla assembling the band from many of the same session musicians who had worked on *Amigo* five years earlier. Though sales of that LP had been disappointing, Guthrie told an Associated Press reporter that *Amigo* nonetheless remained his personal "favorite album. . . . I thought technically it was exquisite and emotionally very satisfying." Returning as the nucleus for *Power of Love* were Bob Glaub on bass, Russ Kunkel on drums and percussion, and Jai Winding on keyboards. Pilla would again produce and play a lush acoustic guitar on several songs. "It's a great band," Guthrie enthused to *Rolling Stone*. "They're pretty much the same guys I worked with on *Amigo*." But he also acknowledged, with some frustration, that "no one paid much attention" to that LP.[36]

That wasn't exactly true. Guthrie's song "Massachusetts" from *Amigo* would surprisingly resurface on radio playlists in a most unusual development. It all started in the late winter of 1980 when an elementary school teacher, Charlene Murphy, from the southwestern Massachusetts town of Chicopee, attended one of Guthrie's concerts and heard him sing the song. As she thought Arlo's paean to the state was absolutely "beautiful," Murphy bought a copy of *Amigo* and brought it to her classroom so she could play the song for her students. They too believed the song was something special, and, upon discovering that Massachusetts had no official state song, the students "thought it would be wonderful if Arlo's song could be made the official song." To that end the children wrote to state representative Kenneth Lemanski, who, according to *Rolling Stone*, "agreed to present a bill, sponsored by the children, to the state legislature." It might have remained a local, Don

Quixote–type story if a Boston DJ had not gotten wind of it. The DJ encouraged the campaign by putting the relatively obscure, and now four-year-old, song into rotation. It wasn't long before other schoolchildren from across the state began to lobby for the cause, writing to their own elected representatives and asking them to support the bill. On December 3, 1980, Representative Lemanski, as promised, presented the bill to the State Legislature of Massachusetts, where it was scheduled to go before a committee near February's end. The attention that the home-grown campaign was receiving in New England media outlets caused the usually sleepy publicity department of Warner Bros. to reissue "Massachusetts" as a two-sided single for FM/AM radio play. Guthrie was genuinely humbled by the campaign, telling the *Boston Globe*, "I feel really good about it because the move to do it came from a bunch of kids, not from a record company or anything like that. I thought it was great, although I never thought of the song—or any of my songs—as being akin to 'official-type' songs."[37]

With the recording of *Power of Love* wrapped, Guthrie traveled to Western Europe in early summer 1981, where he was to perform at several outdoor festivals. The biggest was held in St. Gallen, Switzerland, where the folk singer regaled a crowd estimated at 20,000 people. In Vienna, Austria, he performed a solo set before being joined on stage by his friend and old Woody Guthrie acolyte Donovan to sing duets on Dylan's "Blowin' in the Wind" and Donovan's own "Josie" to a crowd of swooning old folkies.

He returned to the United States for a series of summer concerts with Shenandoah, often sharing the bill with Pete Seeger, Jesse Winchester, and David Bromberg. Such outdoor package shows proved to be great attractions and tended to bring out the younger fans. Through his relentless touring, Guthrie had managed to attract a new generation of admirers, nearly all of whom had been born too late to have shared in the spirit of the original Woodstock experience. These fans, many of college age, gladly basked in that festival's many small re-creations. On July 11, 1981, Guthrie and Shenandoah were teamed with Bromberg, Winchester, and Kate and Anna McGarrigle at the Great Northeast Arts and Energy Festival, performing on a green hillside in the shadow of Ashby's Mt. Watatic ski slopes. Six thousand music fans came out for the concert, which at times resembled something of a mini-Woodstock, with scores of young people skinny-dipping in the waters nearby to escape the ninety-degree heat.[38]

Three days following a tandem concert with Seeger (July 19) at the Pine Knob Music Pavilion, Guthrie and Shenandoah were halfway through their concert at the University of British Columbia in Vancouver (July 22) when Arlo fell ill and had to leave the stage. He was admitted into the Health Sciences Center Hospital at the university, where the staff concluded the singer was suffering a kidney stone attack. Guthrie stayed overnight at the facility, was given fluids, and was released the following day, only to be readmitted a few hours later when test results determined that he was actually suffering from an inflamed pancreas. He was discharged on Sunday afternoon and returned to his hotel room, which is where he told an Associated Press reporter that while he was feeling OK, he was still a little weak. He returned home to Massachusetts, where it was expected he would recuperate for a week and a half before going on the road again. Two scheduled concerts with Seeger at the Greek Theater in Los Angeles and a concert with Shenandoah in Portland would be cancelled and rescheduled at a later time.[39]

*Power of Love* was released, with no promotional fanfare, in early summer 1981, though it wasn't until August that the first notices began to trickle in. Leslie Berman of the *Village Voice* wasn't unkind in his assessment, but he conceded that at this late date it was unlikely that fans would ever get a "perfect" Arlo Guthrie LP. Berman noted that Guthrie's talent had always been that of a stage artist, where his tools of "sophistication" and "wry wit" enabled him to transcend the "sentimentality" and "phoniness" of some of the time-worn material he chose to perform. He also alleged that Guthrie's charm, bountifully evident on the concert stage, simply wasn't "easily transferrable to vinyl," and that John Pilla's "swelling string arrangements" and the overall slick production of *Power of Love* was the "antithesis" of the very elements that made his stage shows so affecting. Mitchell Cohen of *High Fidelity* was in full agreement, arguing that *Power of Love* "nearly strips an engaging performer of his most distinctive qualities," but went further when he disparaged all but two of the album's ten songs as "musical driftwood" (only "Oklahoma Nights" and "If I Could Only Touch Your Life" were spared that unfortunate designation).[40]

Dave Marsh, a bona fide Guthrie fan writing in *Rolling Stone*, thought "Waimanalo Blues" and Richard Thompson's "When I Get to the Border" provided the album's only two "lovely moments." "Guthrie is probably the last great folk-rock singer we have left (well, maybe him and John Prine), but *Power of Love* doesn't do much to establish the fact," Marsh grumbled. The critic dismissed *Power of Love* as "one of Guthrie's least successful" albums, and Arlo's low-key duet with Rickie Lee Jones on "Jamaica Farewell" as "tedious and silly, ersatz folk from a performer whose glory has always been his intelligence and discrimination." Noel Coppage of *Stereo Review* was far more sympathetic, seeing the "elaborately produced" *Power of Love* as an obvious—though not necessarily a crass or misguided—attempt to enable Guthrie, whose album sales had flagged in recent years, to "attract a broader, more pop-conscious audience." Believing that, in artistic terms, *Outlasting the Blues* was Guthrie's most perfectly realized LP, Coppage wasn't entirely sure that the new, more pop-trending *Power of Love* hit its commercial target since "even in the thick of this expensive production, [Guthrie] doesn't come across as market-orientated." But the Coppage review does note, with acuity, that even when wrapped in extravagant sonic dross, the songs on *Power of Love* featured the artist's usual meditations on love and love lost, of the past and regret, of rootlessness and lost dreams. Though only two songs were penned by Guthrie, the material seemingly reflected all that "we have come to believe are Arlo's values or his vision." The success, or lack thereof, of *Power of Love* wasn't too surprising. Most American record buyers probably weren't even aware that a new Guthrie LP was available as Warner Bros. barely put up a penny in promotion. *Power of Love* didn't make much of a splash in England either. Though *Melody Maker* deemed the island rhythms of Guthrie's "Living Like a Legend" as "potentially interesting," the melancholic, piano-backed "Slow Boat," arguably one of the album's best songs, was deemed "undistinguished." In the end, though the music weekly allowed that the material for *Power of Love* had been carefully chosen by the artist, the resulting LP was merely one more "pleasant, if un-ambitious" effort.[41]

By August 5, Guthrie was recovered and back on the road, sharing a concert-in-the-round with Seeger at Long Island's Westbury Music Fair. He only performed a single song from *Power of Love*, David Mallet's "Garden Song," causing the *Village Voice* to note, "as with most folkies, his tours aren't intended to support his albums—they're an end in themselves." The politically minded *Voice* also noted that Guthrie's wandering monologues at Westbury "covered El Salvador, encroaching governments, and the environment." This was all true, but Guthrie was a raconteur and not a speechmaker, tending to address issues only in his personal fashion. That night at Westbury, Guthrie bridged his father's "Pretty Boy Floyd" with "Victor Jara," commenting,

> Some men are outlaws because of what they do and some are outlaws because of what they think, 'cause of what they say. This is a song about an outlaw, a folksinger-outlaw from the country of Chile. He used to go around singing folk songs down in South America, and his songs are sung all around there now. His name was Victor Jara. He wrote a lot of good songs. I started singing this song a few years ago when I was paying my taxes and I started thinking that the money was going to the government to help send men and money down to Chile to help knock off singers just like me.

Then, in a thinly disguised swipe at President Ronald Reagan's controversial decision to intervene in the civil war of El Salvador by sending economic and military aid to that country's right-wing rulers to combat leftist guerrillas, Guthrie offered this Vietnam war–era analogy: "You know, if you step on a dog turd and you can't help it, that's OK. But when you turn right around and step in it again, that's just *dumb*. . . . That's my thoughts on El Salvador."[42]

*Program booklet from a 1981 series of summer concerts featuring Pete Seeger, Arlo Guthrie, and Shenandoah. The summer tour shows were recorded by Warner Bros., and material from four separate concerts were seamlessly combined to produce the second Guthrie–Seeger collaboration LP,* Precious Friend *(BSK 3644). Author's collection.*

On August 15, Guthrie and Shenandoah performed at the Dr. Pepper Concert Series on Manhattan's Pier 84. Though *some* of the rain-soaked rock 'n' roll fans who sat on the windswept bleachers on the Hudson may have wanted to hear some material from the new album, one *Billboard* critic noted that Guthrie, once again, "virtually ignored lackluster new Warners [*sic*] album 'Power of Love.'" Instead, he chose to sing only his most popular songs (minus "Alice") and song-lead an unusually youthful crowd through Tom Paxton's trenchant parody "I'm Changing My Name to Chrysler."[43]

On August 26, Lee Hays, the ex-Weaver and Almanac singer, passed away a few short hours after his admittance into a Tarrytown hospital. He was sixty-seven years old and had been in ill health for some time. Four days later Guthrie, Seeger, and Shenandoah appeared at the Greek Theater in Los Angeles. That night both singers shared songs and reminiscences of their friend. Seeger closed the main set by performing a few fragments of Lee's best-known songs, followed by Arlo and the band joining him for the grand finale of "If I Had a Hammer" ("The Hammer Song"), a rousing protest number cowritten by Seeger and Hays in 1949 and first recorded by the Weavers on a rare 78 single. The press thought the evening's program unusually "subdued" but excused the somberness when Seeger closed with the news of the passing of Hays. Guthrie would subsequently finish all his summer concerts that year with "Amazing Grace," a song that Lee, in the guise of a revival-tent preacher, had sung in the *Alice's Restaurant* film. Halfway through one performance of the old spiritual, Guthrie offered Hays as "one of the few men I've known in this world who was not only an inspiration to me, but showed me that it's possible to do for yourself what you intend to do for the rest of the world."[44]

On November 28, Seeger, Guthrie, and Shenandoah ended their concert season with two performances at Carnegie Hall, a 2:30 afternoon program followed by a second full concert at 8:00 p.m. The notes of the Carnegie *Stagebill* program, written by Harold Leventhal and signed off by Seeger and Guthrie, began with the testimonial, "It is appropriate to dedicate today's concert to Lee Hays." The Thanksgiving weekend concerts at Carnegie Hall were something of a ritual among the New York City folk-song faithful, and many of those attending were also at the annual Seeger concert the previous year. It was, in fact, nearly a year to the day that the wheelchair-bound Hays, Fred Hellerman, and Ronnie Gilbert joined Seeger on the Carnegie stage for an emotional and highly publicized standing-room-only reunion of the original Weavers.[45]

On January 27, 1982, Warner Bros. issued their final Arlo Guthrie recording, *Pete Seeger & Arlo Guthrie: Precious Friend*. The two-record set, produced by John Pilla, was recorded live in concert during the summer tour of 1981. Twenty-six performances excerpted from their shows at the Poplar Creek Music Theater, Pine Knob Music Theater, Greek Theater, and Concord Pavilion were seamlessly blended into a single recording. *Stereo Review* found *Precious Friend* as "representative" of the most recent Seeger and Guthrie concert collaboration, a pleasing mix of original and traditional songs, ragtime numbers, and sing-alongs, with a dash of Woody Guthrie and Weavers classics tossed in for good measure. "The reason it works better than most live albums in one's home," critic Noel Coppage wrote, "is probably that the principals are such nice, decent, eternally optimistic people that they—and not just their product—would be *welcome* in one's home." Though the magazine had passed on reviewing *Power of Love* a year earlier, *Rolling Stone* offered that *Precious Friend* was something much "more than a collection of old folk memories. It is memory made alive."[46]

In a sense, that is what Arlo Guthrie's music has always been about. It has reflected his interest and, perhaps, his destiny, to connect the lessons and songs and stories of memory to the struggles and concerns of the present day. There was no question in Guthrie's mind that the 1960s generation—*his* generation—had changed the face of America for the better. It was *patriotic* to protest. "We no longer have one myopic view of what it is to be an American," Guthrie told *Boston Globe* staffer Jim McLaughlin in autumn 1982. "That's a change that traces back to the civil rights movement, and it's more significant than the Cultural Revolution in China. . . . Disagreeing on fundamental issues—abortion, prayer in schools, nuclear power—does not get you labeled un-American." A few years earlier, a reporter from the *Washington Post* pointed out to Guthrie that his concerts with Pete Seeger had an uncanny ability to attract the most diverse of audiences. The seats at their shows were populated not only by Seeger's fans, the old-lefties who "bring along their Brownies, their neckties and their memories," but with "kids who sit beside them [and] pass joints from hand to hand." Guthrie acknowledged, in effect, that not only was this true but it was almost the whole point of the collaboration, the generation-bridging blend of music and activism that manager Harold Leventhal termed the "Seeger-Guthrie Union." "If the '60s were a war," Guthrie told the *Post* with satisfaction, "there is no doubt who won." It would seem that everything, in the end, was solely dependent on how you chose to look at the world around you. Though homegrown radicals decried the international appeal of American music—popular, traditional, and otherwise—as one more example of U.S. "cultural imperialism," Guthrie mused on more than one occasion how proud he "was to come from a country where our songs are loved and known and sung all over the world by all kinds of people." In 1982, the little town of Pittsfield, Massachusetts, surprised Guthrie when it asked him to accept the honor of being the grand marshal of their annual July 4 parade. The town's officials told Arlo that he had been chosen for the honor as his songs were most representative of "Mom, apple pie, and America." "I liked that," Guthrie conceded with a grin.[47]

## NOTES

1. Paul Richard, "Arlo Guthrie at 30," *Washington Post*, July 29, 1977, B1; Joe Klein, "Notes on a Native Son," *Rolling Stone*, March 10, 1977, 52.

2. Robert Taylor, "Three Starry Spokesmen for Massachusetts," *Boston Globe*, June 28, 1977, 1, 27.

3. Georgia Pabst, "Summerfest Trims Free Passes," *Milwaukee Journal*, July 5, 1977, sec. 2, 9.

4. Paul Richard, "Arlo Guthrie at 30," B1, 16.

5. Janet Maslin, "Music: Witty, Winning Arlo Guthrie Rambles Round," *New York Times*, August 20, 1977, 12; Christgau *Village Voice* review. In Robert Christgau, *Rock Albums of the '70s: A Critical Guide* (New York: Da Capo Press, Inc., 1990), 164.

6. Joyce Wadler, "An Artist's Salute to Their Persecuted Peers," *Washington Post*, November 22, 1977, B1.

7. Jesse Lewis, "Arlo Guthrie: Last 'Brooklyn Cowboy' Comes South," *Ocala Star-Banner*, February 22, 1978, 2C; "Friends Gathre [*sic*] Tonight to Remember Will Geer," *New York Times*, May 12, 1978, C30; Eric Pace, "Will Geer Remembered at Tribute for Charm, Courage and Energy," *New York Times*, May 14, 1978, 49.

8. "Show Business," *Milwaukee Journal*, May 23, 1978, sec. "Accent," 2; "Trio Echoes Arms Theme," *Bangor Daily News*, May 23, 1978, 2; "Stars Support 'Survival Sunday,'" *Sarasota Herald-Tribune*, May 23, 1978, 10A.

9. Tom Smucker, "Recyclable Folk Music," *Village Voice*, July 3, 1978, 92; Carol Lawson, "An Old-Time Folk Festival on the Hudson," *New York Times*, June 16, 1978, C1; Joe Klein, "Notes on a Native Son," 56; Ward W. Smith, "Arlo: Too Busy for Stardom," *Christian Science Monitor*, March 30, 1978, 19.

10. E. J. Kahn, "Seabrook 2: Just When You Thought It Was Hopeless," *Village Voice*, July 3, 1978, 1, 19–21; Pete Seeger, notes *to Pete Seeger: Singalong—Demonstration Concert: Sanders Theatre, Harvard Campus, Cambridge, Mass.* (Folkways Records FXM 36055, 1980); Bill Hammond, "Arlo Guthrie: Hassles Are His Style," *Milwaukee Sentinel*, July 28, 1978, sec. "Let's Go," 4.

11. Ward W. Smith, "Arlo: Too Busy for Stardom," 19; Bob Principe, "Arlo Guthrie: Much More Than 'Perceptive Humorist.'" *Just in Time for the 80s, Imagine Presents the Return of the 60s* (September/October 1979), 17, 50.

12. Bill Hammond, "Arlo Guthrie: Hassles Are His Style," sec. "Let's Go," 4.

13. Linda Hamilton, "Let the Discs Fall Where They May," *Deseret News*, October 20, 1978, 6C; John Laycock, "All Grown Up," *Windsor Star*, January 13, 1979, 15; "Record Review," *Lakeland Ledger*, November 3, 1978, 3B; "Frank Dudgeon," "Records," *Boston Globe*, December 7, 1978, sec. Calendar, 6–7.

14. Steve Daley, "Performing Arts: Seeger and Guthrie," *Washington Post*, August 23, 1978, D3.

15. Ernie Santosuosso, "Guthrie and Seeger against Hynes Auditorium," *Boston Globe*, September 1, 1978, 24; Marty Gallanter, "Pete Seeger," *Frets* 1, no. 7 (September 1979), 28.

16. United Press International, "Arlo Even with Stockbridge," *Boston Globe*, September 16, 1978, 14; Rick Hampson, "The Guthrie Show Is On," *Nashua Telegraph*, September 15, 1978, 23.

17. "Promoter Sues Arlo Guthrie," *Sarasota Journal*, September 25, 1978, 8D; "People in the News: Found Innocent," *Reading Eagle*, September 27, 1978, 5; "Guthrie Case to Wind Up," *Lewiston Evening Journal*, September 26, 1978, 16.

18. Kathryn Phillips, "Arlo Guthrie: Sharing Music, Sharing Concerns," *Anchorage Daily News*, October 26, 1978, 17.

19. Judy Ball, "On the Road with Arlo Guthrie," *St. Anthony Messenger*, February 1980, 20.

20. "Singer to Attend Amtrak Rally," *New York Times*, April 1, 1979, 50; Marty Gallanter, "Arlo: Bound for His Own Glory," *Frets* 1, no. 5 (July 1979), 24.

21. Nancy Mills, "Arlo: Smiling the Odds Away," *Windsor-Star*, September 8, 1979, 17.

22. Ken Emerson, "Rousing Albums from Guthrie and Seeger," *New York Times*, December 16, 1979, D23; "P.G.," "Record Guide," *Christian Science Monitor*, August 30, 1979, 18; Hubert Bauch, "Spin Off," *Montreal Gazette*, July 21, 1979, 34; Ken Tucker, "The Last Folk Singer," *Rolling Stone*, November 1, 1979, 63; Sam Sutherland, "Backbeat," *Hi-Fidelity/Musical America*, September 1979, 144.

23. Wayne Robins, "Guthrie Succeeds at 'Outlasting the Blues,'" *Anchorage Daily News*, August 28, 1979, D8.

24. Debra Rae Cohen, "Arlo Guthrie's Faith Outlasts the Sixties," *Rolling Stone*, no. 299 (September 6, 1979), 22; Danny Smith, "A Pilgrim at Peace," *Melody Maker*, May 9, 1981, 36.

25. Mary Campbell, "Arlo Guthrie Asks Refugee Family In," *Harlan Daily Enterprise* (Harlan, KY), August 24, 1979, 6.

26. Mary Campbell, "Arlo Guthrie Asks Refugee Family In," 6; Debra Rae Cohen, "Arlo Guthrie's Faith Outlasts the Sixties," 22.

27. "Salt.," "Concert Reviews," *Variety*, August 1, 1979, 66; Jan Hoffman, "Arlo Guthrie Cuts the Comedy," *Village Voice*, July 30, 1979, 60.

28. Charlie Huisking, "Arlo Guthrie: The Troubadour of the 60s Hasn't Changed His Tune," *Herald Tribune* (Sarasota, FL), December 9, 1979, sec. *Florida West*, 16–17.

29. Dave Marsh, "American Grandstand: Rockers on the Road to Salvation," *Rolling Stone*, October 18, 1979, 43.

30. "Rock & Religion," "Arlo Guthrie Part I and II," RR-59/RR-60 (Original air date: March 9, 1980, and March 16, 1980); Joel Selvin, "Bob Dylan's God-Awful Gospel," *San Francisco Chronicle*, November 3, 1979.

31. "Rock & Religion," "Arlo Guthrie Part I and II," RR-59/RR-60 (Original air date: March 9, 1980, and March 16, 1980).

32. Charlie Huisking, "Arlo Guthrie: The Troubadour of the 60s Hasn't Changed His Tune," sec. *Florida West*, 16–17.

33. Bob Principe, "Arlo Guthrie: Much More Than 'Perceptive Humorist,'" 16; Wayne Robins, "Guthrie Succeeds at 'Outlasting the Blues,'" D8.

34. "World Premiere Tonight," *Daytona Beach Morning Journal*, March 5, 1980, 2B.

35. "Berg," "Concert Reviews," *Variety*, July 30, 1980, 77; Steve Pond, "Harry Chapin and Arlo Guthrie," *Los Angeles Times*, July 26, 1980, B6.

36. James Henke, "Arlo Guthrie a Home-State Hit," *Rolling Stone*, April 2, 1981, 56; Mary Campbell, "Arlo Guthrie Ready to Share His Life," *The Day* (New London, CT), August 23, 1979, 39.

37. James Henke, "Arlo Guthrie a Home-State Hit," 56. Steve Morse, "Like Old Times for Guthrie," *Boston Globe*, July 13, 1981, 31.

38. Steve Morse, "Like Old Times for Guthrie," 30–31.

39. "Arlo Guthrie Still Feels Weak after Treatment in Hospital," *Ocala Star-Banner*, July 27, 1981, 6A; "Notes on People: Arlo Guthrie on Mend," *New York Times*, July 28, 1981.

40. Leslie Berman, "Riffs: Arlo Guthrie Off the Record," *Village Voice*, August 12, 1981, 58; Mitchell Cohen, "Records: Arlo Guthrie: Power of Love," *High Fidelity/Musical America*, September 1981, 88.

41. Dave Marsh, "Record Reviews (*Rolling Stone*)," *Anchorage Daily News*, August 29, 1981, G5; Noel Coppage, "Recording: Arlo Guthrie: Power of Love," *Stereo Review*, October 1981, 90; Patrick Humphries, "Albums," *Melody Maker*, 5September 5, 1981, 19.

42. Leslie Berman, "Riffs: Arlo Guthrie Off the Record," 58.

43. Peter Krasilovsky, "Talent in Action," *Billboard*, September 5, 1981, 45.

44. Richard Cromelin, "Seeger, Guthrie, Team for Success," *Los Angeles Times*, September 2, 1981, G2.

45. Harold Leventhal, program notes of November 28 Carnegie Hall concert, *Stagebill*, 1981–1982 season, unpaginated.

46. Noel Coppage, "Guthrie/Seeger," *Stereo Review*, July 1982, 76; Allan Horning, "Records," *Rolling Stone*, May 27, 1982, 57.

47. Jeff McLaughlin, "Why Guthrie Gets Involved," *Boston Globe*, October 9, 1982, 8; Arlo Guthrie, spoken-word preface to "Can't Help Falling in Love," on *More Together Again* (Rising Son Records 0007, 1994); Paul Richard, "Arlo Guthrie at 30," B16.

*Chapter Seven*

# Epilogue

In 1965, seventeen-year-old Arlo Guthrie stepped onto the stage of New York's Town Hall to sing a song or two at a Woody Guthrie tribute concert. The year following he began his career in earnest, and by the autumn of 1967 he had scored an early commercial success with "Alice's Restaurant." The success of "Alice's Restaurant," first as an "underground" word-of-mouth phenomenon, second as a best-selling LP, and lastly as a critically acclaimed motion picture, cemented Guthrie's celebrity status as separate from that of his famous father. The success of "Alice's Restaurant" enabled him to blossom as a recording artist for Reprise/Warner Bros., but the singer's fifteen-year association with the label would come to an end following the release of *Precious Friend*. Though new recordings would be issued in subsequent years with no discernible drop-off in quality, it was rare to find these independent releases stocked in record shops, and most of Arlo's FM radio play was relegated to the odd spin of "City of New Orleans" on an oldies station. One misgiving about preparing a volume dedicated solely to Guthrie's fifteen-year association with Reprise/Warner Bros. is that such microscopy might suggest, however unintentionally, that only his albums recorded from 1967 to 1981 are worthy of interest. This is not the case, and though an oversimplification, Guthrie's recording career can be divided into two rough halves: the Reprise/Warner Bros. years (1967–1981), and what might be termed the "Rising Son" or, perhaps more accurately, the "independent label" years after 1984.

Though there had been a frustrating barren stretch of new material to reach public ears from the early winter of 1982 through the spring of 1986, the long gap between projects was understandable: Guthrie was in the midst of building his own record label so that he might market his own music. Though the fledgling record company president would endure a few business missteps along the way to solvency, it's near certain that had Guthrie remained an

*In concert at the Sharp Theater, Berrie Center, Ramapo College, Mahwah, New Jersey, March 7, 2010. Photo by Jim Phillips.*

artist-for-hire on the Warner Bros. label, many of the wonderful and worthwhile personal recording projects following his departure would likely have never come to pass.

In his essay "My Oughtabiography," Guthrie suggests that his eventual parting with Warner Bros. was due to simple arithmetic, that his "recording contract, which lasted 15 years . . . expired in 1983." Technically, Guthrie had signed three separate five-year contracts with Warner Bros., and that third contract expired after he delivered *Precious Friend*. In 1982, with the release of that austerely packaged Guthrie–Seeger double album, Arlo, John Pilla, and Shenandoah returned to Longview Farm Studios in North Brookfield, Massachusetts, to record *Someday*, a brilliant ten-song collection that featured mostly original material presented in a less folksy, more rock 'n' roll format. It was Guthrie's intent that *Someday* would be issued on the Warner Bros. label; the material on this new album was so strong that he was confident that he would be offered a fourth contract with the company. But once he brought the tapes of *Someday* to Warner Bros. in 1983, the company balked, and after some discussions Guthrie recalled "we mutually agreed [the company] didn't want [it]." The new team running the A&R arm of the Warner Communications Company was no longer interested in shepherding the careers of niche or cult artists. They were now primarily interested in selling units to a broad cross section of the pop-music market, preferably to an international market, and unless the team could move 200,000 copies—at a minimum and *right away*—a record was deemed unprofitable, no matter how artistically sketched and vital the vinyl document. In the 1980s there were virtually no folk singers or roots-music artists capable of moving their platters in those numbers, so they were simply—some might say cruelly—cut free and left to fend for themselves. This marketing strategy was not only unfortunate; it was shortsighted. The company was, in effect, choosing to concentrate on the teen demographic and all but ignore the musical interests and tastes of the adult baby boomers. This obvious slight was poor business as consumers born between 1947 and 1964 were not only the ad agencies' number one target demographic but also the very people who had supported the stable of artists on the label from the very beginning. In the words of fellow folk singer Tom Rush, a contemporary of Guthrie's who shared many folk-music package shows with him in the early 1980s, "the Baby-Boomers grew up, but the industry didn't." Guthrie told Jeff Tamarkin of the record-collecting magazine *discoveries* that the rupture with Warner Bros. was sad but inevitable. It was Arlo's opinion that "the people who knew how to make money moved in and the people who knew how to make records moved out." "There was a time when Warner Bros. Records was owned by people who knew how to make records," Guthrie mused. "Then that got bought, and merged, and sandwiched, and leveraged, and whatever else." Guthrie wasn't the only casualty of the infamous Warner Bros. "purge" of the early 1980s. By 1985 Van Morrison, Bonnie Raitt, Gordon Lightfoot, and some thirty other sincere artists from the Warner Bros. stable were unceremoniously shown the door due to flagging album sales.[1]

There was one element of being a free agent that was liberating. Though Guthrie had mostly enjoyed a relatively good working relationship with Warner Bros.—there had been few censorship issues—he was now free to pursue the more personal projects that his old employer would have likely dismissed as being too offbeat or uncommercial. On March 7, 1984, the New York City PBS station, WNET, hosted the premiere of the documentary film *Woody Guthrie: Hard Travelin'*. Produced by Jim Brown, Harold Leventhal, and Ginger Turek, the film was everything that Hal Ashby's Hollywood version of *Bound for Glory* was not, including historically accurate and entertaining. Jon Pareles, the television critic for the *New York Times*, described the film: "Part biography, part travelogue and part hootenanny, [*Hard Travelin'*] follows the singer's son, Arlo Guthrie, as he retraces his father's steps and collects reminiscences from his father's family, friends and musical partners." The film had been directed by Jim Brown, who had scored handsomely in 1981 with his award-winning documentary on the 1980 reunion at Carnegie Hall of the four original Weavers. Following Woody's life from the folk singer's beginnings in Okemah and on through his long stretch of hospitalization at the Brooklyn State and Greystone institutions, *Hard Travelin'* captures Arlo reminiscing and making music with many of the same people who had been touched by his father's life and art: Maxine "Lefty Lou" Crissman, Matt Jennings, Guthrie's first wife Mary Boyle, Rose Maddox, Sonny Terry, Herta Geer (for Will), Ronnie Gilbert, Holly Near, Pete Seeger, Ramblin' Jack Elliott, Bill Murlin (of the Bonneville Power Administration), Hoyt Axton, Judy Collins, and Joan Baez. The impromptu musical performances caught on film were so uniformly excellent that a decision was reached to issue an accompanying soundtrack album. Guthrie formed a one-off company, Arloco Records, to simultaneously issue *Woody Guthrie: Hard Travelin'—Soundtrack from the Film* (Arloco Records 284) that same winter. The soundtrack offered complete versions of many of the songs heard only in fragments in the film as well as several excellent performances that had been excised from the finished documentary. One such performance was Arlo's compelling "duet" with his father on "This Land Is Your Land." The morning of the first broadcast of *Hard Travelin'*, Guthrie recalled the circumstances of that "duet" with newsman Bryant Gumbel of the NBC *Today Show* program. "I was just sitting in the studio one night, nothing to do," Arlo remembered, "and I decided to just try that. So I went in the studio singing along with my dad, and it was very eerie and strange and very weird. It was almost like he was really there. . . . It was a very strange moment." One smiling face sadly absent from *Hard Travelin'* was that of Marjorie Guthrie. The former Mrs. Woody Guthrie, and mother of Arlo, Joady, and Nora, had passed away at age sixty-five on Sunday, March 13, 1983.[2]

On September 17 and 18, 1984, Guthrie shared the stage with Pete Seeger, Ronnie Gilbert, and Holly Near for two well-regarded concerts at the Universal Amphitheatre, Los Angeles. The concerts had been taped by the remote facilities of the Record Plant of Los Angeles, with Guthrie's tour manager, Bruce Clapper, providing the "sound supervision." The best performances were culled from the resulting tapes and issued as the single twelve-inch LP *HARP* (Redwood Records RR409, 1985), the album's title sourced from the upper-case letters of the principal's first names. The recording caught the four singers harmonizing and playing together throughout, with Guthrie's principal contributions being piano-backed versions of "City of New Orleans" and his new and as-yet-still-unreleased "All Over the World." He also contributed a verse or two to the album's opening and closing songs, "Oh, Mary, Don't You Weep" and the blues-songster classic "Pallet on the Floor." In 2001 Jim Musselman's Appleseed Recordings of West Chester, Pennsylvania, would issue an augmented two-CD set sourced from the *HARP* concerts that more completely captured the spirit of the event. The new issue featured the complete original recording as well as Guthrie's seminal performances of "Oh, Mom," "You and Me," and even a great cover of Dylan's "Mr. Tambourine Man."

On January 26, 1985, Steve Goodman's friends got together at Chicago's Arie Crown Theater for a proper send-off for their old pal, who passed away, at age thirty-six, following a losing battle with leukemia. On the bill that night were such friends as John Prine, David Bromberg, Bonnie Koloc, John Hartford, Richie Havens, the Nitty Gritty Dirt Band, and a host of others. Goodman's most recent label, the indie Red Pajamas Records, recorded the night's program and released a two-disc highlights set a year later as *A Tribute to Steve Goodman* (Red Pajama Records 004). Arlo sang "City of New Orleans," of course, Steve's wonderful paean to the disappearing railroad and a song that had proven durable and lucrative for both artists. Guthrie also played his own, and still unreleased, "All Over the World," a song written following the televised demonstrations of December 5, 1981, when hundreds of thousands of protestors marched throughout the streets of Europe and Japan calling for the nuclear disarmament of the world's superpowers. The song was later published in the pages of the struggling *Broadside* magazine, with new editor Jeff Ritter describing Arlo's hopeful anthem as "the work of an obviously mature songwriter."[3]

These recorded musical bits and pieces, no matter how well intentioned and executed, were hardly sufficient to sate the legion of Guthrie fans who wondered why all the wonderful new material performed on stage with Shenandoah was not yet available on LP (or rather on compact disc, a new but expensive format that had yet to supplant the beloved long-playing vinyl album). It was to that end that Guthrie founded Rising Son Records in 1986 so he might belatedly bring his *Someday* album to market. *Someday* would have the distinction of being the first release on the Rising Son label, but other titles would soon follow. In what proved to be a true masterstroke of business, Guthrie contacted old friends at Warner Bros. and asked for permission to license his back catalog and issue these (mostly moribund) titles as cassette tapes on his foundling label. As most of his Reprise and Warner Bros. albums had fallen out of print or were, for the most part, unavailable at retail outlets, Guthrie reasoned that should he be allowed to sell tapes through mail order and at his shows, Warner Bros. would get a cut of the proceeds. Amazingly, Warner Bros. agreed to the arrangement, though they initially resisted allowing Guthrie to market the three titles still making the corporation a little money: *Alice's Restaurant*, *Hobo's Lullaby*, and *The Best of Arlo Guthrie*. By the end of 1991 patience and common sense prevailed, and every one of Guthrie's Reprise and Warner Bros. albums (with the exception of *Alice's Restaurant*, his *Best of*, and the two concert albums with Pete Seeger) were made available through Rising Son.[4]

Properly marketing the albums was another issue. In the early and mid 1980s Guthrie was only occasionally featured in the pages of a mainstream rock 'n' roll magazine, so the folk singer–turned–record tycoon needed to find a cost-efficient vehicle in which to communicate with his loyal fan base. If he was to sell copies of the long-delayed *Someday*, he had to let his fans know that a new album was out and that out-of-print material was available once again. To that end Guthrie published the first issue of the infamous *Rolling Blunder Review* in the spring of 1986. The homegrown newsletter would serve as an important sales tool in those pre-Internet days, as it allowed Guthrie to stay in contact with his most dedicated fan base.

The newsletter began its humble life as a single-sheet, two-sided broadside whose primary function was to alert fans to his tour dates for May and June 1986. But the newsletter also introduced fans to the first releases of Rising Son Records. In his "Crop Report Spring 1986," Guthrie noted that the label's first three titles would include "bushels of our new record *Someday*. . . . Heaps of our re-released *Power of Love*. . . . Chunks of our re-released *Amigo*." Without enough working capital to press the new titles as twelve-inch vinyl LPs, and with the advent of the compact disc still two years away, the earliest titles were issued on high-grade Dolby-B chrome cassettes. A silver band on the earliest copies of *Someday* (RSR 0001) designated that title as a "25th Anniversary Edition," though it wasn't entirely clear what anniversary was being celebrated. Guthrie's first album had been issued only nineteen years earlier. Though *Someday* would eventually be released in the United Kingdom as an LP via C.M. Distribution of North Yorkshire, England, Guthrie informed U.S. readers of the *Rolling Blunder Review*, "These records are only available on cassette tapes, for now. At sometime in the future we may decide to grow them on regular record stuff. But being our own record company (these days), and not having as many options, we decided to grow some high quality, real-time recorded chrome type tapes, instead of the regular scratchy kind of records." Though *Someday* was a welcome addition to the canon, Guthrie had been playing several of the "new" songs from the album on stage with Shenandoah for more than four years. It wasn't too surprising that versions of "Oh, Mom," "You and Me," "All Over the World," and "Unemployment Line" were subsequently honed to near-perfection on stage, leaving many of the album's earlier "official" takes sounding somewhat austere and less vibrant.[5]

*Someday* was, sadly, the last Guthrie album to be produced by old friend John Pilla, who tragically passed away waiting on a heart transplant. John had first worked as a guitarist and "spiritual advisor" on 1969's *Running Down the Road* and went on to produce or coproduce every Guthrie album from *Washington County* (1970) through *Someday* (1986). The death of John Pilla was a heartbreaking double loss. Not only had Guthrie lost one of his best friends, but he had also lost his single most important musical collaborator. In the past, when Guthrie—or the record company—decided it was time to go into the studio and record, it was Pilla who arranged the studio time, assembled the session players, and hired the team of necessary engineers and technicians. These matters would now fall to Guthrie, and he himself suggested that he wasn't confident that he was up to the challenge of producing his own records. He told Jeff Tamarkin that he felt he was "working half-blind" following the passing of Pilla. "I was a little intimidated," Guthrie offered, "and it took me a long time to get my act together, to feel as though I could walk into a place, [and] know what was going on. . . . I needed to reassure myself that I could actually make records." Though he did not realize it at the time, Guthrie had an ace-in-the-hole in the guise of his laid-back, keyboard-playing son Abe. Having grown up in the age of computers and new technology, Abe was comfortable in a recording-studio setting, having already produced an album for his own band, Xavier.[6]

One of the singer's last collaborations with Pilla was the producer's overseeing of *The Arlo Guthrie Show*. Taped in Austin, Texas, following a nearly year-long 1986 tour with Shenandoah, the television program was a coproduction of the Southwestern Texas PBS Council and Rising Son International, Ltd. The program, produced by Terry Lickona and directed by Gary Menotti (both veterans of the long-running TV musical series *Austin City Limits*), featured Guthrie and the remnants of Shenandoah sharing a soundstage with guests Pete Seeger, Bonnie Raitt, David Bromberg, and Jerry Jeff Walker. Guthrie sang a cross section of songs from his career (including "Prologue," "Gates of Eden," "Coming into Los Angeles," and "Amazing Grace"), but the program was bittersweet as it captured on videotape the beginning of the end of his long association with his band. Arlo and Shenandoah would part ways following a final year of touring in 1987. Beginning in 1988 Guthrie would go it alone, touring regularly as a solo folk singer for the first time since 1975.

On January 20, 1988, at a $1,000-a-plate gala at the Waldorf-Astoria hotel in Manhattan, 1,200 "selected guests" planned to usher Bob Dylan, the Beatles, the Rolling Stones, the Beach Boys, and, more improbably, Woody Guthrie and Lead Belly into the Rock and Roll Hall of Fame. Guthrie and Lead Belly were to be feted as "early influences" on rock 'n' roll culture. The Guthrie family wasn't sure what to make of the honor, with Nora noting, "I didn't see my father's influence on rock and roll. We're here to see other people's perspective on it." In his accepting the award on his father's behalf, Arlo, in black tie and tails, offered, "You could figure a lot of things in this world, but this isn't one of them. I think if my dad were alive today, this is the one place he *wouldn't* be. I understand that. . . . [But] his spirit is still around, still writing, still singing. And I think this is why I had to come anyhow, to say thank you." Getting into the spirit of the commemoration, on August 24, 1988, Columbia Records issued *Folkways: A Vision Shared—A Tribute to Woody Guthrie & Leadbelly* (Columbia OC 44034), a soundtrack album designed to accompany Jim Brown's HBO television special of the same name. The producers of the soundtrack asked Arlo to contribute a song to the album, with the caveat that he choose a more obscure title of his father's and allow the project's "superstars" (Bob Dylan, Bruce Springsteen, Willie Nelson, Brian Wilson, Emmylou Harris, and John Mellencamp) to have first crack at Woody's better-known titles. Guthrie obliged, delivering what is arguably the most authentic performance on the album, a solo guitar version of Woody's obscure ballad "East Texas Red." Guthrie would also feature prominently in the HBO television special, singing his father's "Grand Coulee Dam" with guitar and harmonica as well as performing duets with Pete Seeger on Lead Belly's "Alabama Bound" and with Emmylou Harris on "Deportee (Plane Wreck at Los Gatos")." The intent of the accompanying Columbia soundtrack album was to raise funds for the Smithsonian Institution to acquire the thousands of recordings and manuscripts Moses Asch had left behind following his passing, at age eighty-one, on October 19, 1986. Perhaps recognizing that the end was near, the previous Thanksgiving weekend at Carnegie Hall, Pete Seeger and Guthrie dedicated their annual holiday program to Asch, who watched, with his wife Frances, from his plush orchestra seat.[7]

In some respects, the transition of the Folkways collection to the Smithsonian was something of a karmic event. That spring, at a solo concert in Minneapolis on April 21, 1989, Guthrie shared,

> When [Moses Asch] passed on about two years ago, people began to wonder what was going to happen to Folkways Records. . . . And they decided to send it down to the Smithsonian Institute [*sic*] in Washington, D.C. So along with the Folkways record collection, a bunch of stuff of my dad's also went down to the Smithsonian at the same time: all his writings, and notes, and lyric sheets, and manuscripts, and books, and paintings—all kinds of stuff that we had hanging around our house that we didn't want people coming over to *our* house to look at. It was also sort of, at least, *cosmically* interesting, to see the U.S. government, in the end, [be responsible for] preserving and taking care of all that stuff.[8]

With the last of the of the baby-boom generation passing into the parenting phase of their lives, it was inevitable that they would resurrect their own heroes as musical and storytelling babysitters for their children. In October 1990, the Lightyear Records Company issued *Baby's Storytime*, an unusual cassette tape that captured Guthrie's nasal recitations of such well-worn children's tales as "The Gingerbread Man" and "The Three Little Pigs." In another strange turn of events, that same year Guthrie agreed to a temporary return to the acting profession when he accepted a small role in the motorcycle film *Roadside Prophets*. Guthrie admitted that he only consented to take on the role of Harvey, a philosophical and slightly stoned graying biker/gas station attendant, when he was assured that the part was so small that he "could actually memorize all of his lines on the way to the set from the motel." The trippy feature, which was heralded as a '90s companion to the legendary *Easy Rider* (1969), costarred the musician John Doe (of the Los Angeles punk band X) and the Beastie Boys' Adam Horovitz. The film also teased off-the-wall cameos from the likes of David Carradine, Timothy Leary, and a young John Cusack. In March 1992 *Roadside Prophets* was released, to mixed reviews, on a limited basis in U.S. markets but was soon rushed—some might say banished—to home-video oblivion.[9]

In the weeks leading up to Christmas 1991, the mainstream newspapers caught wind of a story that had been familiar to Guthrie's fans for some time. The current artist-owners of the deconsecrated Episcopal Church in Great Barrington, formerly Alice and Ray's church, were planning on putting the building up for sale, and there were rumors that Guthrie was interested in taking ownership. It was true that Guthrie had met with the owners in the summer of 1990 when he first learned of its availability, but as the original asking price for the property was $350,000, Guthrie was flummoxed on where he was to come up with that sort of cash in the time frame demanded. The owners were not necessarily unsympathetic to Guthrie's design for their transient home and eventually lowered their asking price to $320,000. By December 1991, with the sale in a prolonged inert state, Guthrie was given until March of 1992 to come up with the cash. That winter, Guthrie began to ask fans attending his concerts—and subscribers to his newsletter—to contribute a few dollars to the campaign so that the church might, in a sense, be returned to "the family of the 1960s." "I can't wait to get back in there," Guthrie told the *New York Times*, suggesting that at least twenty of his earliest songs were written at the church, and "I think there are a couple more in there." Guthrie's Rising Son Record Company had already moved belongings and inventory into the building, having agreed to lease office space on the property until monies could be raised. In the autumn of 1991, Guthrie announced that he was in the process of buying the church and had filed for tax-exempt status with the Internal Revenue Service and the Commonwealth of Massachusetts. Thus began the founding of the Guthrie Center, an interfaith community space named in honor of his parents.[10]

It seemed that everything in the universe was cyclical. Sometimes you just had to hang on long enough to see things turn your way. In 1991 Guthrie met with Warner Bros. president Lenny Waronker. Waronker had, of course, coproduced or served as executive producer on most of Guthrie's albums for Reprise/Warner Bros. dating back to *Running Down the Road* in 1969. Though Guthrie was hoping that Waronker might be interested in a "regular record," the Warner Bros. president was primarily concerned about getting Guthrie on board for a children's album in the planning stage. The genesis of what would become *Woody's 20 Grow Big Songs* (Warner Bros. 9 45020-2, 1992) was almost as interesting as the resulting CD. It seems that sometime in 1948, a year or two following the first issue of Woody's children's album on the Asch label, Woody and Marjorie decided to collaborate on a song folio that would feature many of the compositions. Woody illustrated the proposed book with his colorful caricatures, and Marjorie, sitting at the piano each night, would studiously write out a simple musical notation. In his introduction to the volume, written circa August and September 1948, Woody dedicated the collection to the memory of Cathy Ann, to his three children from his previous marriage to Mary Jennings, and "to Arlo Davy, just climbing up into your fourteenth month." It was a wonderful idea, but the project got sidetracked for one reason or another, and the manuscript was misplaced and summarily forgotten. That was until 1990 when the original manuscript was found in the holdings of the library at Sarah Lawrence University, Bronxville, New York. Marjorie Guthrie had earlier taught dance at the college, and she had either absentmindedly, or purposefully, left the manuscript behind. Following their contacting Harold Leventhal, the librarians at Sarah Lawrence generously returned the manuscript to Woody Guthrie Publications. Mindful of the significance of this lost treasure, Arlo's sister, Nora Guthrie-Rotante, was put in charge of readying the book for publication by HarperCollins Children's Books of New York. It was Leventhal who suggested to Nora's older brother that he might consider re-recording the songs for an accompanying CD release, but it was Arlo's belief that the project should include the contributions of the entire Guthrie family. To that end he brought his sister Nora and brother Joady, as well as all of their children, into the recording studio. The sessions were held from August through December 1991 at Derek Studios, in Dalton, Massachusetts, the heart of the Berkshires. Though the plan was for the recording sessions to be fun and lighthearted, Arlo recalled that he and his siblings went directly into a "pressure-cooker environment that boils off all diplomacy. We were all flashing back to when we were little kids. It makes you remember why families go in different directions." Nora remembered going into the studio completely relaxed on a "wonderfully goofy morning, filled with high expectations." Things changed immediately when they began to play back the original tapes of Woody singing. The enthusiasm of everyone gathered in the studio dipped in an instant. Nora remembered listening to the songs: "Half were out of tune, the rest were just . . . 'out.' We heard Woody put extra beats where no man had gone before. We heard keys hovering strangely between those we had learned from our music teacher. We heard words combining dialects from Oklahoma, Texas, and Coney Island." As Arlo would recall, "It was hard enough to sing along with Woody Guthrie when he was alive, let alone on a fixed recording. . . . The guy had very little sense of time and meter." Once they made a decision to tackle the recording process "genetically," things fell into place, and *Woody's 20 Grow Big Songs* was honored with a Grammy nomination in 1993 in the category of "Best Album for Children."[11]

If Guthrie had experienced extra stress during the recording of *Woody's 20 Grow Big Songs*, it was understandable. The children's album was being concurrently recorded at Derek Studios along with Guthrie's third release on the Rising Son label, *Son of the Wind* (Rising Son 0003). (Rising Son 0002 was a compilation of previously recorded songs titled *All Over the World*). *Son of the Wind* was precisely the sort of project that Guthrie would have found difficult selling to the accountants at Warner Bros., as most of the twelve tracks featured fresh recordings of traditional songs ("Red River Valley," "Shenandoah," "The Gal I Left Behind") and cowboy ballads ("Streets of Laredo," "Utah Carroll," "I Ride an Old Paint"), with two of his father's, "Dead or Alive" and "Woody's Rag/Hard Work," thrown in for good measure. These were the dusty, and sometimes grim, songs that Arlo had learned from the recordings of his father, Cisco Houston ("Utah Carroll"), Jimmie Rodgers via Woody's cousin Jack Guthrie ("When the Cactus Is in Bloom"), Gene Autry ("Riding Down the Canyon"), and Ramblin' Jack Elliott ("South Coast"). "I grew up listening to these guys sing these songs," Arlo wrote in his liner notes, "and the older I get, the more I realize how important it is for us to hand down these stories and songs to future generations." Guthrie was proud of the new CD as it was Rising Son's first original project. While *Someday* was Rising Son's first new-to-issue recording, that album had been originally made for Warner Bros. Records in 1983. *Son of the Wind*, on the other hand, was "really the first project conceived and delivered on the RSR label." "These songs are at the root of who we are as a people and a nation," Guthrie would inform readers of his newsletter. He also promised that he was willing to record a second batch of more traditional songs "if this record meets with an appreciative audience."[12]

Two rarer Guthrie releases of 1992 were a "Special Limited Edition," two-song cassette (Rising Son 0006) which featured Guthrie performing the Joe Manning and Steve Vozzolo song "Norman Always Knew." It was a syrupy but sincere tribute to the illustrator Norman Rockwell, the Berkshire's most famous past resident. Rockwell was, of course, the artist who gained fame and acclaim for his idyllic portraits of Americana that graced the covers of the *Saturday Evening Post* and other magazines (Stockbridge police chief William B. "Officer Obie" Obanhein was previously immortalized in one of the artist's advertising sketches for an insurance company). The B-side of the cassette featured a re-recording, on solo piano, of Guthrie's own "Massachusetts." The tape was sold exclusively through Rising Son and in the gift shop of the Norman Rockwell Museum in Stockbridge, Massachusetts. It was also in 1992 that the Audio Literature Company, a books-on-tape publishing outfit, issued a two-cassette abridged version of Woody Guthrie's *Bound for Glory*, read by Arlo.

Guthrie continued to tour as a solo artist throughout most of the period from 1988 through 1991. Starting in 1992, however, Guthrie began to go out on occasional sorties with Xavier, a rock 'n' roll band cofounded in 1984 by Guthrie's son Abe, Randy Cormier, and Tim Sears. The Xavier dates were a refreshing change from the lone guitar-and-harmonica shows, and Guthrie may have continued to tour more extensively with the band had he not made another surprising return to acting near the end of 1993. His return to Hollywood began when Guthrie agreed to appear on a cable television program hosted by friend Bill Rosenthal. Following the fun but otherwise uneventful taping, Rosenthal joked to Arlo that he would soon be fielding casting calls as the "cable show goes to Hollywood, where a lot of producers are." Amazingly, and almost as if on script, a few weeks later Guthrie was contacted by a producer working for television bigwig Steven Bochco. The producer wanted to know if Arlo would read for a role on the new ABC television drama *The Byrds of Paradise*. Guthrie wasn't all that interested in returning to acting until he learned that the program was to be shot in Hawaii. It was too good an offer to pass on. Unfortunately for his tan, *The Byrds of Paradise* would only last a single season. Arlo was cast as Alan Moon, described by *People* magazine as "a semi-regenerate hippie who enrolls in prep school at 45." Though Alan Moon wouldn't prove to be a major character—Guthrie would appear in brief but memorable walk-ons—he was one of the series's best-loved characters, trailing in popularity only to teenage heartthrob Jennifer Love Hewitt. The pilot episode debuted on March 3, 1994, but the series was cancelled after only thirteen episodes. Guthrie told *People* magazine that he was disappointed for his newfound actor friends that the show had been cancelled so soon, but in his own case he was sure to survive as "It's too late to ruin my career." He would return to music, which is exactly what he did, without missing a beat. In this spirit *People* noted the upcoming autumnal release of *More Together Again* (Rising Son Records 0007/0008). The two-CD set featured an enchanting live recording of Pete Seeger, Arlo Guthrie, and Xavier from their concert at the Wolf Trap Farm Performing Arts Center, Vienna, Virginia, on August 8, 1993. That same year Guthrie also sang Townes Van Zandt's "Tecumseh Valley" with Nanci Griffith as a guest artist on the angelic Texan's collaborative LP *Other Voices, Other Rooms* (Elektra 61464-2).[13]

Anyone attending Guthrie's concerts throughout the late 1980s and early 1990s knew that the folk singer was still writing songs. He would lightly sprinkle some of them into his set lists comprised mostly of old folk revival–era favorites and songs recorded during his Reprise/Warner Bros. tenure. Though fans had enjoyed *Son of the Wind*, Guthrie had not released an album of original material since *Someday* was belatedly issued in 1986. The long drought would come to an end in 1996 with *Mystic Journey* (Rising Son Records 0009). Guthrie's self-description as a "Catholic Jew" had meshed with an interest in interfaith dialogue and interspirituality, and *Mystic Journey* (the title track was, ironically, the only song on the album *not* written or cowritten by Guthrie) was dedicated to Guthrie's guru, Ma Jaya Sati Bhagavati. "Ma," as she was commonly known, was a fellow child of Brooklyn who now served as the spiritual director of the interfaith Kashi Ashram Foundation in Florida. Some of the songs on *Mystic Journey* clearly reflect some of Ma's teachings and spiritual concerns, particularly "Doors of Heaven," "Wake Up Dead," and "Under Cover of Night." "Moon Song," which opens

up *Mystic Journey*, was written during Guthrie's time in Hawaii while filming *The Byrds of Paradise*; "You Are the Song" was adapted from a poem
that silent film star Charlie Chaplin had written for his wife Oona. Chaplin's
iconic "Little Tramp" character was a favorite of both of Guthrie's parents,
and Guthrie had earlier decided to put a melody to the silent actor's little-
known poem. He had sung the song, very occasionally, on past concert tours.
"Stairs" was also an "old" song, perhaps an outtake originally intended for
inclusion on *Someday*, as Arlo had been singing the song on his concert tours
with Shenandoah since the mid-1980s. One of his greatest new songs in the
protest realm was "When a Soldier Makes It Home." A concert favorite for
some time, Guthrie wrote it shortly after the Soviet Union began to extract
its bloodied troops from neighboring Afghanistan in 1989. The closing two
songs, "All This Stuff Takes Time" and "I'll Be with You Tonight," ended
the album on a light tone, both new to practically everyone outside of Guthrie's inner circle.

Released simultaneously with *Mystic Journey* was an odd re-recording
of Guthrie's album *Alice's Restaurant* (Rising Son Records 0010). The B-
side tracks of the "new" *Alice's Restaurant* CD were recorded, once again,
at Derek Studios and featured contributions from Shenandoah alumni Steve
Ide, David Grover (guitars), and Terry a la Berry (drums), with augmentation courtesy of Xavier's Sean Hurley (bass) and Abe Guthrie (keyboards).
Though the re-recording would serve as an excuse to capture for posterity
his updated "Watergate Tapes" version of his most famous talking blues,
there was another factor in the peculiar decision to re-record his first album.
Though Warner Bros. had agreed to lease nearly all of Guthrie's back catalog to Rising Son, the company barred the folk singer, with some frustration, from getting control of the golden goose that was the original *Alice's
Restaurant*. This was an issue well into the 1990s, as concertgoers visiting
the sales table at Guthrie's concerts would inevitably request CD copies of
the *Alice's Restaurant* album. Guthrie admitted to *Guitar World Acoustic*
magazine that his decision to go into the studio and re-record his first LP
was "because it was the one album I couldn't get back from Warner Bros."
After warning his old company, "We have ways of dealing with that," Guthrie chose to re-record the talking blues at the church that had been his initial
inspiration. Though his plan was to market the new *Alice's Restaurant* as a
"30th Anniversary" retrospective, Guthrie took great care that it sounded as
identical as possible to the earlier release so as to not betray memories. This
was a somewhat ironic turn of events as Guthrie had long claimed that he had
never been happy with the production of *Alice's Restaurant* since the original
producers "really didn't have the sensitivity to what the songs could have
been." Guthrie considered issuing the two new recordings on vinyl, and test

pressings were produced for both the remade *Alice's Restaurant* and *Mystic Journey*, but they never appeared.[14]

In September 1996, the Rock and Roll Hall of Fame in Cleveland hosted "Hard Travelin': The Life and Legacy of Woody Guthrie," a week-long series of programs and conferences culminating in an "all-star" tribute concert at Severance Hall on the 29th. Though Guthrie was pressed to serve as an entertaining last-minute replacement for an ailing Studs Terkel (who had been scheduled to deliver the conference's keynote address), he more naturally teamed with such Woody fans and disciples as Ani DiFranco, Ramblin' Jack Elliott, Fred Hellerman, the Indigo Girls, Country Joe McDonald, and Bruce Springsteen for the Severance Hall concert. That evening Guthrie recited some of his father's prose and sang a solo on "Dust Storm Disaster." He also contributed guitar and vocals to the ensemble performances of "Hard Travelin'" and "This Land Is Your Land." The latter song would be the featured title the following year on the Rounder Records release of *This Land Is Your Land: An All-American Children's Folk Classic* (Rounder Kids CD 8050, 1997). The Rounder album, which featured Woody and Arlo Guthrie performing a selection of Woody's classic songs, was designed to serve as the soundtrack to an animated VHS release of the same name. In the summer of 1997, Guthrie's rock 'n' roll credentials would be reestablished when he was invited to perform—and serve as master of ceremonies—at the 1997 edition of the Further Festival, a traveling caravan of such "hippie" jam bands as Rat-Dog (featuring Grateful Dead alumni Bob Weir and Mickey Hart), the Black Crowes, moe, pianist Bruce Hornsby, and an assortment of similar tie-dyed recording and touring acts.

Though Guthrie could rock with the best of them, he was best served as an artist of more intimate, graceful music. In 2002 Rising Son Records acted as the American distributor of *Banjoman: A Tribute to Derroll Adams* (Rising Son Records, RSR-2012-2, 2002). Beautifully recorded and packaged with a colorful sixty-page booklet, *Banjoman* was a true musical labor of love for the principals involved. Virtually unknown in the United States, Derroll Adams (1925–2000), was an Oregon-born folk-singing banjo player with a sepulchral bass voice and a penchant for melancholy songs. A U.S. expatriate, Adams was better known among traditional music fans of Western Europe, having lived most of his adult life in Brussels, Belgium. An early singing partner of Ramblin' Jack Elliott (the singer first brought Derroll to England in February of 1957), Adams settled in Belgium the following year and soon attracted a devoted circle of musician friends and fans. Just prior to Derroll's passing at age seventy-five, many of his friends, particularly the Dutch blues guitarist Hans Theessink and Arlo Guthrie, decided to celebrate his life with an album of his songs performed by his friends and disciples. Though Adams wouldn't live long enough to hear the results of the sessions, the producers got commitments from Ramblin' Jack Elliott, Donovan, Dolly Parton, Allan Taylor, Billy Connolly, Tucker Zimmerman, Youra Marcus, Wizz Jones, and Happy Traum. Guthrie, who would coproduce the album with Theessink, contributes guitar, lead, and background vocals on several tracks, including "Columbus Stockade Blues," "Portland Town," "The Cuckoo," "Freight Train Blues," "The Valley," "Dixie Darling," "Muleskinner Blues," and "24 Hours a Day."

Such niche recordings were artistically and personally satisfying, but it was touring that paid most of the bills. From June 4 through June 19, 2004, Guthrie, alongside tour mates Gordon Titcomb (mandolin, pedal-steel guitar, five-string banjo) and son Abe (keyboards), was in Australia for ten concerts. Just prior to setting off for Australia, Guthrie had been contacted by the Academy Award–winning cinematographer and film director Haskell Wexler, who had photographed *Bound for Glory* in 1975. Wexler, whose politics had always been proudly left of center, asked if the singer would be willing to contribute a few songs to the soundtrack of his proposed film *From Wharf Rats to the Lord of the Docks*, a stage drama documenting the life and times of the Australian-born union leader Harry Bridges. Woody, Pete, and the Almanac Singers had written a couple of songs praising the outspoken Bridges, a radical fighting deportation by U.S. officials, for his leading the International Longshore and Warehouse Workers Union through a series of militant strikes. Wexler asked Guthrie if he would consider recording one of the mostly forgotten "Songs for Bridges" for his film, and Arlo readily agreed. With Abe assisting on keyboard and Gordon on mandolin, the trio retired to a small recording studio where they were filmed singing "The Ballad of Harry Bridges" and "Waltzing Matilda." Sarah Lee Guthrie, the youngest of Arlo's three daughters and a musician herself, also contributed a song to the project, performing her grandfather's previously unrecorded "Harry Bridges." While in Australia, Wexler and his crew also recorded and filmed Guthrie's concert at Sydney's Seymour Centre on June 12. It was from that line recording that Guthrie decided to issue the double CD *Live in Sydney* (Rising Son Records, RSR 1124, 2005). Capturing a vivid snapshot of Guthrie's stage show at the time, the recording was welcomed by longtime fans for including such songs as Guthrie's own haunting "Haleiwa Blues" and "My Old Friend" and such traditional tunes as "Green Green Rocky Road" and "St. James Infirmary." These four songs were made available on an official Arlo Guthrie CD for the first time.

Thirty years following his passing, "new" Woody Guthrie songs continued to surface. Primarily through the efforts of Nora Guthrie, many of Woody's unseen or forgotten "notebook" songs were being farmed out and recorded by select contemporary bands and artists. Though he had recorded any number of his father's songs through the years, the closest to an "all Woody Guthrie" project Arlo allowed himself was his contribution to the soundtrack recording of the *Hard Travelin'* documentary. But the idea of a "songs of Woody Guthrie" album had long simmered, and as early as December 1976 Arlo suggested to *Rolling Stone* that "he was thinking about doing an album of songs by Woody that no one had ever heard," with most dating from the 1950s. As most of his father's most famous songs were written during the 1930s and 1940s, Woody's writings from the 1950s had been mostly untouched and unheralded. Nevertheless, Arlo, who enjoyed unfettered access to his father's rare materials and notebooks, believed that the songs dating from the 1950s were Woody's most "amazing."[15]

In the spring of 1981, during an otherwise routine interview with *Melody Maker*, Guthrie would tell music writer Danny Smith the same. Smith informed readers that one of the singer's "long-term projects is to record some of Woody's material; songs that have never been recorded, some that have never been put to song." In 1998, some seventeen years following that interview, Guthrie would finally get around to his oft-delayed Woody Guthrie recording project. The impetus for the recording was the announcement that the U.S. Postal Service was planning to honor his father by putting his image on a postage stamp. In June 1998 the post office issued four new postage stamps in their "American Music Series—Folk Singers," the others feted being Lead Belly, Sonny Terry, and Josh White. In much the same manner that the U.S. Department of the Interior's "conservation" award had surprised the Guthrie family thirty-odd years earlier, the fact that the U.S. government was planning on honoring Woody by putting his image on a stamp was, well, mind-boggling. In the preface to his singing of his father's "The Sinking of the Reuben James" at his annual Thanksgiving weekend concert at Carnegie Hall, Arlo admitted to the standing-room-only crowd that such commemoration came with a cost beyond that of the stamp itself: "For a man like my father who fought his entire life against being respectable, this really comes as a final, stunning defeat." Following a ceremony with the U.S. postmaster general, Guthrie chose to celebrate the honor by gathering his bluegrass-playing friends the Dillards for a relaxed recording session in a Branson, Missouri, studio.

Unfortunately, Arlo's long-simmering idea of recording an album of Woody's less well-known songs was sadly abandoned, for the time being at least. In some ways, this was acceptable as the responsibility no longer fell to Arlo to rescue his father's songs from unpublished oblivion. Newly minted recordings of rare materials sourced from original Woody Guthrie typescripts were already circulating and achieving surprising successes. This was primarily due to the vision of his sister Nora, now president of the Woody Guthrie

Archives, who was determined to see that some of the thousands of extant lyrics left behind by her father were put to music by contemporary artists. The most well known and successful of these experiments was when the popular Americana band Wilco and the British singer-songwriter Billy Bragg collaborated on some forty or so previously unpublished lyrics and put them to music. Thirty of these collaborative songs were collected together for two widely heralded albums, *Mermaid Avenue* (Warner/Elektra 62204-2, 1998) and *Mermaid Avenue Vol. II* (Warner/Elektra 62522-2, 2000). Choosing a different tack, Arlo decided to go "old school" with his own recording/tribute project by bringing in the Dillards. In a press release Guthrie enthused that it was his desire that the new album might replicate "the authentic sound and feel of Woody's music." The title of the recording was to be *Thirty-Two Cents*, which was the cost of the new Woody Guthrie postage stamp circa 1998. He explained his decision to bring the Dillards onboard (with whom he had recorded Woody's version of "Going Down the Road" on the *We Ain't Down Yet* LP of 1976) as "I thought it [would] be the closest thing to the kind of music people actually play from that part of the world—Oklahoma is close enough to the Ozarks." Guthrie and the band ran through a selection of Woody's best-known songs ("This Land Is Your Land," "So Long, It's Been Good to Know Yuh," "The Sinking of the Reuben James"), though there was a dash of songs less well known among enthusiasts ("Sally, Don't You Grieve," "Ludlow Massacre," and "East Texas Red"). The songs for the proposed album were recorded quickly, in a loose and informal manner, with bluegrass tempos. But after listening to the playbacks Guthrie discovered to his horror that the resulting tapes were bedeviled by a number of technical problems. The recordings were shelved, with no little frustration, for a period of almost ten years until new technologies allowed the original tapes to be painstakingly mended digitally. The album was finally released in 2008 under the self-deprecating and amended title *Thirty-Two Cents: Postage Due* (Rising Son Records, RSR 1127).[16]

Having successfully and blessedly dodged the onset of Huntington's disease (as had brother Joady and sister Nora), Arlo hit the half-century mark in 1997. Upon the occasion of his fifty-fifth birthday in 2002, Guthrie had outlived his famous father, and his uncontested status as the preeminent torchbearer of the Woody Guthrie, Cisco Houston, and Pete Seeger legacies was becoming ever more obvious. Starting in 2000, Guthrie became a much-sought-after "talking head" in such award-winning documentary films as Aiyana Elliott's *The Ballad of Ramblin' Jack* (2000), Jim Brown's *Isn't This a Time* and *Pete Seeger: The Power of Song*, and Stephen Gammond's *Woody Guthrie: This Machine Kills Fascists* (2005). Acknowledging the contributions that those of a radical stripe had in the shaping of American history, Guthrie's music appeared in the aforementioned staging of Harry Bridges' life as well as in Peter Miller's documentary recalling the tragedy of the Sacco and Vanzetti case. In the rolling end credits of the latter film, Guthrie sang Woody's relatively obscure song "Red Wine," one of a cycle of Sacco and Vanzetti ballads that Woody had written on commission from Moses Asch in 1947. Guthrie was also featured on a number of retro tribute CDs, including *What's That I Hear: The Songs of Phil Ochs* (Sliced Bread Records), *If I Had a Song: The Songs of Pete Seeger Vol. 2* (Appleseed 1055, 2001), and *Spain in My Heart: Songs of the Spanish Civil War* (Appleseed 1074, 2003). Occasionally Guthrie would sign onto projects under the radar of most folk-music devotees. One such contribution was the CD *Sharin' in the Groove: Celebrating the Music of Phish* (Mockingbird Foundation). Guthrie also contributed to the country and western novelty album *All Gone Fishin'* (Bandit Records). The latter featured an impressive star-spangled roster of mainstream country-music artists performing songs on the single subject of fishing. Guthrie's contribution was a perfect, and previously unissued, solo turn on his father's "Talking Fishing Blues."

Arlo's own catalog of solo recordings continued to grow. His most ambitious recording project, *In Times Like These* (Rising Son 1126, 2007) will be long remembered as one of the artist's most magnificent. The album was recorded, after nearly a decade of rehearsal, in a program with the University of Kentucky Symphony Orchestra. That concert, which featured Guthrie on guitar and piano with John Nardolillo conducting, was staged at the Singletary Center for the Arts, Lexington, Kentucky, on March 10, 2006. Nardolillo, a Peabody Conservatory–trained violinist and conductor, was an Arlo fan from way back who happened to cross paths with the folk singer at an outdoor show at Lincoln Center in Manhattan. Nardolillo suggested to Guthrie that he might consider rescoring some of his own music for a symphonic folk-music opus in the style of Aaron Copland's "Appalachian Spring" or Leonard Bernstein's series of folk music–themed "Young People's Concerts." Guthrie was intrigued, but as he was a folk singer and not a Julliard-trained musician with proper training, he hired an arranger to work on the charts for a number of songs. The earliest charts were undistinguished at best, and the collaboration floundered until pianist James Burton, a friend of Nardolillo's, was brought aboard and successfully worked out a set of new charts with contributions from Guthrie and several principal players of the orchestra. Beginning in 1998, Guthrie would perform in a symphonic setting on a select number of dates each year, most famously in 2001 with the Boston Pops during their nationally televised July 4 concert. In 2007, Arlo finally made the commitment to rise to the challenge of the "logistical nightmare" of professionally recording one of his symphonic concerts, and the result was *In Times Like*

*These*. On this sparkling recording, Guthrie chose not only to revisit a cross section of original songs from his own career (1970 through the present) but to introduce songs of Lead Belly, Charlie Chaplin, and Elvis Presley to moving symphonic resettings.[17]

On the other end of the spectrum was Guthrie's *Tales of '69* (Rising Son Records RSR 1128, 2009), a seminal, if likely misattributed, recording of a stage show circa 1968, and *Every Hundred Years* (matrosenblau/12, 2009), a live album recorded September 19, 2006, at Wartburg Castle in Eisenach, Germany. The latter was in collaboration with the German cabaret artist Hans Eckardt Wenzel, who, in 2003, recorded two albums of unreleased Woody Guthrie songs (one in English, one with German translations) titled *Ticky-Tock* (Contraer Musik). The latter is also of note as the disc features Guthrie's first official recording of "My Peace," an endearing poem of goodwill composed by his father while in the gloomy isolation of "Wardy Forty" in Greystone Hospital.

In the year preceding the twentieth anniversary of the original Woodstock Music and Arts Festival, Guthrie quietly began to incorporate a new song, "Keep the Dream Alive," into his set lists. That song, still unreleased at the time of this writing, is a poignant and personal recounting of an era when both internal and external possibilities seemed unlimited. Guthrie's piano-backed song, written and performed in the intimate and reflective manner of his best songwriting efforts, gently calls on everyone touched by the dreams of the Woodstock era to recommit to the idealism once shared. In one verse, Guthrie sings that he has "shared the journey of a father and a son / And though at times they're different / They're still one." This is the song's most beautiful couplet, an affirmation that the struggle for peace, for freedom, for goodwill, for the dignity of the individual is never-ending, and that this struggle connects generations and transcends transient political agendas and movements.

This commitment to coexistence and matters of social welfare was as much Marjorie Guthrie's as Woody's, and it is a vision that resonates in nearly every verse and note of Arlo Guthrie's music. It's a struggle without end, and, when the time comes, the singer has expressed confidence that others younger and stronger will be there to pick up the baton. As Arlo moved gray-haired but graceful into his sixth decade, he rolled out what was termed the Guthrie Family Legacy Tour, inviting siblings, children, and grandchildren to join him on stage and share in the communal music making. In doing so, Arlo was able to realize his father's long-standing dream of fielding a Guthrie family musical troupe, one that would sing some old songs for new times.

There will hopefully be new Arlo Guthrie songs and albums and stories in future years. But as has been the case with his friend and folk-singing mentor, Pete Seeger, it's possible that Guthrie will be best remembered not

*In concert at the Sharp Theater, Berrie Center, Ramapo College, Mahwah, New Jersey, March 7, 2010. Photo by Jim Phillips.*

for his impressive recorded legacy but for his engaging stage presence, his considerable musical skills, and his abilities as a raconteur in the manner of Will Rogers and Woody Guthrie. Perhaps Arlo's most important contribution has been his capacity to encourage concertgoers around the world to "keep the dream alive" by existing and acting, in his father's terminology, as "Hoping Machines."

## NOTES

1. Arlo Guthrie. "My Oughtabiography," *Rolling Blunder Review*, November 1989 (special edition), 2; Mick McCuistion, "Arlo Guthrie," *On the Tracks* 3, no. 2, 1995, 30; William Knoedelseder Jr., "Small Labels Big for Baby-Boomers," *San Francisco Chronicle*, January 20, 1985; Jeff Tamarkin, "Arlo Guthrie at 50: In the House of the Rising Son," *Discoveries*, no. 111 (August 1997), 46.

2. Jon Pareles, "TV Reviews—Woody Guthrie: Hard Travelin'," *New York Times*, March 7, 1984, C22; Arlo Guthrie interview, *Today Show*, NBC-Television, taped March 7, 1984.

3. Jeff Ritter, ed., *Broadside* no. 166 (September 1985), 2, 12.

4. Arlo Guthrie, undated *Rising Son Records* mailing, circa spring 1986.

5. Arlo Guthrie, undated *Rising Son Records* mailing, circa spring 1986.

6. Jeff Tamarkin, "Arlo Guthrie at 50: In the House of the Rising Son," 46.

7. Jon Bream, "Rock Hall of Fame Induction, Program Provided Contrast in Good, Bad Vibes," *Star-Tribune* (Twin Cities), January 21, 1988, sec. Variety, 16E; "Rock Hall of Fame Ceremonies Fail to Unite Beatles," *Star-Tribune* (Twin Cities), January 21, 1988, sec. News, 07A; "Rock and Roll Hall of Fame," *Rolling Stone* no. 521 (March 10, 1988), 8–17, 97.

8. Arlo Guthrie, Minneapolis, MN, April 21, 1989. That the U.S government was to custodian the holdings of the Woody collection isn't entirely true. Though the Smithsonian retains all of the Asch masters, the bulk of Woody's writings and personal papers are under the curatorship of the Woody Guthrie Foundation and Archives, 125–131 East Main Street, Suite 201, Mt. Kisco, NY, 10549.

9. "Guthrie Says 'OK' to Movie," *Rolling Blunder Review* no. 17 (Winter 1990), 7.

10. "Church for Sale," *Rolling Blunder Review*, no. 17 (Winter 1990), 3–4; "Great Barrington Journal: Folk Singer Hopes Fans Can Save 'Alice's Church,'" *New York Times*, December 6, 1991; "There & Back Again," *Rolling Blunder Review*, no. 20 (Fall 1991), 2.

11. "What's Happening," *Rolling Blunder Review*, no. 18 (Spring 1991), 5; "In Record Time," *Arlo Guthrie's Rolling Blunder Review & Get Stuff*, November 1991, 1; Arlo Guthrie, "In Record Time," *Rolling Blunder Review*, no. 20 (Fall 1991), 5; Janet Schnol, "A Collection of Folk Songs for a New Generation," *Publisher's Weekly*, October 5, 1992, 33; Nora Guthrie, "Notes from Woody Guthrie's Daughter," *Woody's 20 Grow Big Songs* (Warner Bros. 9 45020-2, 1992).

12. Arlo Guthrie, notes to *Son of the Wind* (Rising Son Records 0003, 1991); Arlo Guthrie, "In Record Time," *Rolling Blunder Review*, no. 20 (Fall 1991), 5.

13. Mark Goodman with Tom Cunneff, "Aloha, Arlo!" *People*, June 13, 1994, 67–68; Ben DiPietro, "Arlo's a Free Bird in 'Paradise,'" *New York Post*, March 8, 1994, 75.

14. Isaiah Trost, "Coney Island Okie," *Guitar World Acoustic*, no. 24 (1997), 92; Jeff Tamarkin, "Arlo Guthrie at 50: In the House of the Rising Son," 45.

15. Joe Klein, "Notes on a Native Son," *Rolling Stone*, March 10, 1977, 56.

16. Danny Smith, "A Pilgrim at Peace," *Melody Maker*, May 9, 1981, 36; Arlo Guthrie, Carnegie Hall, New York City, NY, November 27, 1998.

17. Arlo Guthrie, notes to *In Times Like These* (Rising Son Records, RSR 1126, 2007).

# Basic U.S. Discography (1967–2011)

The following discography documents the officially released recordings (in the author's collection or familiar to the author) that feature Arlo Guthrie on LP, CD, cassette, reel-to-reel, and 45-rpm formats. The discography is separated into six categories: Guthrie's solo recordings (which, in exception, will include the artist's three collaborative albums with Pete Seeger); songs of Guthrie's that appear on the legendary Reprise/Warner "Loss Leader" Series; anthologies, soundtracks, and festival recordings; Guthrie's appearances on the albums of other artists; a singles listing; and a miscellaneous section that includes, among other titles, foreign-release long-playing albums that feature unique compilations of previously issued materials, and other unusual recorded documents of interest to collectors. Though Guthrie's best-selling recording of Steve Goodman's "City of New Orleans" has been featured on a number of compilations with such titles as *Super Hits of the '70s: Have a Nice Day* and *Baby Boomer Classics: Mellow Seventies*, I've chosen to forego a list of these collections due to page constraints.

## SOLO ALBUMS

### *Alice's Restaurant* (1967)

LP: Reprise RS 6267 (Stereo)
Eight-track: RM-6267 and M8 6267
Cassette: M5 6267
Reel-to-reel: RST-6267-C
CD: WEA 6267

Produced by Fred Hellerman for Loom Productions, Inc. (with an assist by Al Brown).

Side A:

Alice's Restaurant Massacree (Arlo Guthrie)

Side B:

Chilling of the Evening (Arlo Guthrie)
Ring-around-a-Rosy Rag (Arlo Guthrie)
Now and Then (Arlo Guthrie)
I'm Going Home (Arlo Guthrie)
The Motorcycle Song (Arlo Guthrie)
Highway in the Wind (Arlo Guthrie)

### *Arlo* (1968)

LP: Reprise RS 6299 (Stereo)
Eight-track: M8 6299
Cassette: M5 6299
Reel-to-reel: RST-6299-C
CD: Koch/Rising Son Records KOC-CD-7948
Produced by Fred Hellerman for Loom Productions, Inc. Recording engineer Tony Brainard, mixing engineer Bill Scymzyk. Recorded live at the Bitter End Café, New York City, December 1968.
Musicians: Arlo Guthrie (guitar), Bob Arkin (bass), Stan Free (piano and harpsichord), and Ed Shaughnessy (tabla and drums).

Side A:

The Motorcycle Song (Arlo Guthrie)
Wouldn't You Believe It (Arlo Guthrie)
Try Me One More Time (Ernest Tubb)
John Looked Down (Arlo Guthrie)

Side Two:

Meditation (Wave upon Wave) (Arlo Guthrie)
Standing at the Threshold (Arlo Guthrie)
The Pause of Mr. Claus (Arlo Guthrie)

### *Running Down the Road* (1969)

LP: Reprise RS 6346 (Stereo)
Eight-track: M8 6346
Cassette: M5 6346
Reel-to-reel: RST-6346-B
CD: Koch/Rising Son Records KOC-CD-7949.

Coproduced by Lenny Waronker and Van Dyke Parks. Head engineer Doug Botnick, additional engineering Donn Landee, spiritual advisor (union scale) John Pilla.

Musicians: Arlo Guthrie (guitar, piano), John Pilla (guitar), Clarence White (guitar), James Burton (guitar), James Gordon (drums), Gene Parsons (drums, harmonica), Ry Cooder (bass, mandolin), Jerry Scheff (bass), Chris Ethridge (bass), Milt Holland (percussion).

Side A:

Oklahoma Hills (Woody Guthrie)

Every Hand in the Land (Arlo Guthrie)

Creole Belle (John Hurt)

Wheel of Fortune (Arlo Guthrie)

Oh, in the Morning (Arlo Guthrie)

Side B:

Coming into Los Angeles (Arlo Guthrie)

Stealin' (Gus Cannon/arranged and adapted by Arlo Guthrie)

My Front Pages (Arlo Guthrie)

Living in the Country (Pete Seeger)

Running Down the Road (Arlo Guthrie)

### *Washington County* (1970)

LP: Reprise RS 6411

Eight-track: M8 6411

Cassette: M5 6411

Reel-to-reel: RST-6411-B

CD: Koch/Rising Son Records KOC-CD-7950 (1997)

Coproduced by Lenny Waronker and John Pilla, "Valley to Pray" coproduced by Van Dyke Parks. Engineer Donn Landee, "Gabriel's Mother's Hiway Ballad #16 Blues" arranged by Fred Myrow.

Musicians: Arlo Guthrie (guitar, piano, five-string banjo, autoharp), John Pilla (guitar, autoharp), Chris Ethridge (bass), Richie Hayward (drums), Ry Cooder (bottleneck guitar), Clarence White (electric guitar), Doug Dillard (five-string banjo), Gary Walters (bass), Hoyt Axton (bass, vocals).

Side A:

Introduction (Arlo Guthrie)

Fence Post Blues (Arlo Guthrie)

Gabriel's Mother's Hiway Ballad #16 Blues (Arlo Guthrie)

Washington County (Arlo Guthrie)

Valley to Pray (Coutson-Pilla-Guthrie)

Lay Down Little Dogies (Woody Guthrie)

Side B:
  I Could Be Singing (Arlo Guthrie)
  If You Would Just Drop By (Arlo Guthrie)
  Percy's Song (Bob Dylan)
  I Want to Be Around (Arlo Guthrie)

### *Hobo's Lullaby/Hobo's Lullabye* (1972)

LP: Reprise MS 2060
Eight-track: M8 2060
Cassette: M5 2060
Reel-to-reel: RST-2060-B
CD: Koch/Rising Son Records KOC-CD-7951 (1997)
Coproduced by Lenny Waronker and John Pilla. Engineer Donn Landee.
Musicians ("people who contributed to this album"): Arlo Guthrie, Hoyt Axton, Max Bennett, Byron Berline, Roger Bush, William Cole, Ry Cooder, John Craviotto, Nick De Caro, Jim Dickinson, Doug Dillard, Chris Ethridge, Vanetta Fields, Wilton Felder, Ann Goodman, Gib Guilbeau, Richie Hayward, Jim Keltner, Clydie King, Daniel Labbatte, William Lee, Judy Maizel, Thad Maxwell, Gene Merlino, Arnie Moore, Larry Nicholson, Spooner Oldham, Thurl Ravenscroft, Fritz Richmond, Linda Ronstadt, Jessica Smith, Clarence White.
Side A:
  Anytime (H. Lawson)
  The City of New Orleans (Steve Goodman)
  Lightning Bar Blues (Hoyt Axton)
  Shackles and Chains (Jimmie Davis)
  1913 Massacre (Woody Guthrie)
  Somebody Turned On the Light (Hoyt Axton)
Side B:
  Ukulele Lady (Richard Whiting and Gus Kahn)
  When the Ship Comes In (Bob Dylan)
  Mapleview (20%) Rag (Arlo Guthrie)
  Days Are Short (Arlo Guthrie)
  Hobo's Lullaby (Goebel Reeves)

### *Last of the Brooklyn Cowboys* (1973)

LP: Reprise MS 2142
Eight-track: M8 2142
Quad eight-track: L9M-2142
Cassette: M5 2142

Reel-to-reel: RST-2142-A

Quad reel-to-reel: RSTQ-2142-QF

CD: Koch/Rising Son Records KOC-CD-7952 (1997)

Coproduced by John Pilla and Lenny Waronker. Engineers Lee Hershberg, Donn Landee, Bobby Hata, and Terry Geiser. Recorded, mixed, and mastered at Amigo, Warner Bros. Recording Studios, North Hollywood, and Buck Owens Studios, Bakersfield, CA.

Musicians: Arlo Guthrie (guitar, piano, harmonica), Kevin Burke (fiddle), Jim Keltner (drums), Bob Glaub (bass), Jesse Ed Davis (electric guitar), Jim Gordon (piano), Nick De Caro (accordion), Jerry Wiggins (drums), Doyle Singer (bass), Don Rich (electric guitar, fiddle, dobro), Buddy Alan (rhythm guitar), Bob Morris (rhythm guitar), Jim Shaw (piano, organ), Jerry Brightman (steel guitar), Don Crislieb (bassoon), Buddy Collette (clarinet), William Greene (oboe), Ernie Watts (flute), Lee Sklar (bass), Ry Cooder (bottleneck guitar, guitar), John Pilla (rhythm guitar, bass), Gene Parsons (drums), Thad Maxwell (bass), Doug Dillard (five-string banjo), Gib Gilbeau (fiddle), Clarence White (electric guitar), Grady Martin (guitar), Richie Hayward (drums), Chuck Rainey (bass), Mike Utley (organ), George Bohanon, Dick Hyde, Gene Coe (horns), Jesse Smith, Clydie King, Vanetta Fields, Gene Merlino, Thurle Ravenscroft, Robert Tebow, Bill Cole (background vocals).

Side A:

Farrell O'Gara (traditional, arranged and adapted by Kevin Burke)

Gypsy Davy (Woody Guthrie)

This Troubled Mind of Mine (Johnny Tyler and Billy Hughes)

Week on the Rag (Arlo Guthrie)

Miss the Mississippi and You (Bill Halley)

Lovesick Blues (Irving Mills and Cliff Friend)

Uncle Jeff (Arlo Guthrie)

Side B:

Gates of Eden (Bob Dylan)

Last Train (Arlo Guthrie)

Cowboy Song (Arlo Guthrie)

Sailor's Bonnett (traditional, arranged and adapted by Kevin Burke)

Cooper's Lament (Arlo Guthrie)

Ramblin' Round (Woody Guthrie)

### *Arlo Guthrie* (1974)

LP: Reprise MS 2183

Eight-track: M8 2183

Cassette: M5 2183

CD: Koch/Rising Son Records KOC-CD-7953

Coproduced by John Pilla and Lenny Waronker. Engineers Lee Herschberg and Donn Landee, "Me and My Goose" arranged by George Bohanon, "Go Down Moses" by Southern California Community Choir under the direction of Rev. James Cleveland, orchestration by Nick De Caro. Recorded, mixed, and mastered at Warner Bros. Studios, North Hollywood, CA.

Musicians ("thanks to everyone"): Arlo Guthrie, Byron Berline, Roger Bush, Ry Cooder, Jesse "Ed" Davis, Nick De Caro, Doug Dillard, Buddy Emmons, Chris Ethridge, Wilton Felder, Jim Gordon, Darryl Hardy, Milt Holland, Jim Keltner, Clydie King, Marty McCall, Kenny Moore, Spooner Oldham, John Pilla, Greg Prestopino, Jessie Smith.

Side A:

Won't Be Long (Arlo Guthrie)

Presidential Rag (Arlo Guthrie)

Deportee (Plane Wreck at Los Gatos) (Woody Guthrie/Martin Hoffman)

Children of Abraham (Arlo Guthrie)

Nostalgia Rag (Arlo Guthrie)

Side B:

When the Cactus Is in Bloom (Jimmie Rodgers)

Me and My Goose (Arlo Guthrie)

Bling Blang (Woody Guthrie)

Go Down Moses (traditional, arranged and adapted by Arlo Guthrie)

Hard Times (Arlo Guthrie)

Last to Leave (Arlo Guthrie)

## Pete Seeger & Arlo Guthrie: Together in Concert (1975)

LP: Reprise 2R 2214

Cassette: Reprise 2R5 2214

Eight-track: Reprise 2R8 2214

CD: Rising Son Records RSR 00011

Produced by John Pilla, associate producer Russ Titelman. Remix engineer Bobby Hata. Assembled at Shaggy Dog Studios, Stockbridge, MA. Mixed and mastered at Warner Bros. Recording Studios, North Hollywood, CA. Recorded live in concert at Carnegie Hall, New York City, March 8, 1974; Opera House, Chicago, March 9, 1974; Place des Arts, Montreal, March 17, 1974; and the Music Hall, Boston, March 30, 1974.

Musicians: Arlo Guthrie (guitar, piano, vocals), Pete Seeger (twelve-string guitar, five-string banjo, vocals).

Side A:

Way Out There (Bob Nolan)
Yodeling (traditional)
Roving Gambler (Cisco Houston)
Don't Think Twice, It's All Right (Bob Dylan)
Declaration of Independence (W. Gibbs/C. Dougherty)
Get Up and Go (Pete Seeger)
City of New Orleans (Steve Goodman)
Side B:
Estadio Chile (Victor Jara)
Guantanamera (H. Angulo/J. Marti/P. Seeger)
On a Monday (Huddie Ledbetter)
Presidential Rag (Arlo Guthrie)
Walkin' Down the Line (Bob Dylan)
Side C:
Well May the World Go (Pete Seeger)
Henry My Son (traditional)
Mother, the Queen of My Heart (Hoyt Bryant/Jimmie Rodgers)
Deportee (Plane Wreck at Los Gatos) (Woody Guthrie/Martin Hoffman)
Joe Hill (Earl Robinson/Alfred Hayes)
May There Always Be Sunshine (Oshanin/Ostrovsky/Botting)
Three Rules of Discipline and the Eight Rules of Attention
Side D:
Stealin' (Gus Cannon)
Golden Vanity (traditional)
Lonesome Valley (traditional)
Quite Early Morning (Pete Seeger)
Sweet Rosyanne (Bright Light Quartette/A. Lomax)


*Amigo* **(1976)**

LP: Reprise MS 2239
Eight-track: Reprise M8 2239
Cassette: Reprise M5 2239
CD: Koch/Rising Son Records KOC-CD-7954
Produced by John Pilla. Executive producer Lenny Waronker. Engineers Donn Landee and Lloyd Clift. Recorded at Amigo, Warner Bros. Recording Studios, North Hollywood, CA. Strings arranged by Nick De Caro.
Musicians: Arlo Guthrie (guitar, piano), Russ Kunkel (drums, percussion), Bob Blaub (bass), Jai Winding (keyboards), Waddy Watchell (guitar), Gayle Levant (harmonica on "Ocean Crossing" and "Manzanillo Bay"),

Milt Holland (percussion on "Guabi, Guabi"), Rick Jaeger (drums on "Grocery Blues"), Leah Kunkel (electric piano, background vocals), Billy Green (guitar on "Walking Song"), Linda Ronstadt (vocals on "Connection"), Nick De Caro (accordion on "Manzanillo Bay").

Side A:

Guabi, Guabi (adapted by Arlo Guthrie)
Darkest Hour (Arlo Guthrie)
Massachusetts (Arlo Guthrie)
Victor Jara (Adrian Mitchell/Arlo Guthrie)
Patriot's Dream (Arlo Guthrie)

Side B:

Grocery Blues (Arlo Guthrie)
Walking Blues (Leah Kunkel)
My Love (Arlo Guthrie)
Manzanillo Bay (Robb "Rabbitt" Mackay)
Ocean Crossing (Arlo Guthrie)
Connection (Jagger-Richards)

### *The Best of Arlo Guthrie* (1977)

LP: Warner Bros. BSK 3117
Cassette: WB M5 3117
Eight-track: WB M8 3117

Side A:

Alice's Restaurant Massacree
Gabriel's Mother's Hiway Ballad #16 Blues
Cooper's Lament

Side B:

Motorcycle (Significance of the Pickle) Song (previously unreleased)
Coming into Los Angeles
Last Train
City of New Orleans
Darkest Hour
Last to Leave

### *Arlo Guthrie with Shenandoah—One Night* (1978)

LP: Warner Bros. BSK 3232
Eight-track: WB M8 3232
Cassette: WB M5 3232

Produced by John Pilla. Recorded and engineered by Peter V. Giansante. Remixed by Raffaello Mazza and Donn Landee at Sunset Sound Recorders, Hollywood, CA. Recorded live in Raleigh, NC; Cincinnati, OH; and Nashville, TN.

Musicians: Arlo Guthrie (piano, guitar, five-string banjo, vocals), David Grover (guitar, five-string banjo, vocals), Carol Ide (guitar, percussion, vocals), Steve Ide (guitar, trombone, vocals), Dan Velika (bass, vocals), Terry a la Berry (drums, vocals).

Side A:

One Night (Bartholomew/Steiman/King)

I've Just Seen a Face (Lennon-McCartney)

Tennessee Stud (Jimmy Driftwood)

Anytime (H. Lawson)

Little Beggar Man (traditional, arranged by Arlo Guthrie)

Buffalo Skinners (traditional, arranged by Arlo Guthrie)

St. Louis Tickle (traditional, arranged by Arlo Guthrie)

Side B:

The Story of Reuben Clamzo & His Strange Daughter in the Key of A (Arlo Guthrie)

Last Night I Had the Strangest Dream (Ed McCurdy)

## *Outlasting the Blues* (1979)

LP: Warner Bros. BSK 3336

Cassette: WB M5 3336

CD: Koch/Rising Son Records KOC-CD-7956 (2000) (paired with *Power of Love*)

Produced by John Pilla. Engineer Les Kahn, assistant engineer Jesse Henderson.

Musicians: Arlo Guthrie (guitar, piano, vocals), David Grover (guitars, vocals), Dan Velika (bass, guitar, vocals), Steve Ide (guitars, vocals), Carol Ide (percussion, vocals, "scarf"), Terry a la Berry (drums, marimba, vocals), Peter Sacco, Ann Saughnessy, Davis Brooks, Michael Gillette (violin), Paul Yarbrough, Helen Huybrechts (viola), David Darling, Thomas Austin (cello), Gordon Johnson (bass), Peter Adams (steel guitar), John Pilla (guitar, vocals, finger cymbals), John Sauer (piano on "Carry Me Over" and organ on "Wedding Song"), John Culpo (accordion), Ron Sloan (harmonica on "World Away from Me"). Recorded and mixed at Longview Farm Studios, North Brookfield, MA. Mastered at Warner Bros. Recording Studios, North Hollywood, CA.

Side A:
  Prologue (Arlo Guthrie)
  Which Side (Arlo Guthrie)
  Wedding Song (Arlo Guthrie)
  World Away from Me (Arlo Guthrie)
  Epilogue (Arlo Guthrie)
Side B:
  Telephone (Arlo Guthrie)
  Sailing Down This Golden River (Pete Seeger)
  Carry Me Over (Arlo Guthrie)
  Underground (Arlo Guthrie)
  Drowning Man (Arlo Guthrie)
  Evangelina (Hoyt Axton/K. Higginbothan)

## *Power of Love* (1981)

LP: Warner Bros. BSK 3558
Cassette: Warner Bros. M5 3558
CD: Koch/Rising Son Records KOC-CD-7956 (2000) (paired with *Outlasting the Blues*)
Produced by John Pilla for Route 183 Productions, executive producer Lenny Waronker. Engineered by Mark Linett, assistant engineers Stuart Gitlin, Ken Deane, Rudy Hill, and Bobby Hata. Recorded, mixed, and mastered at Amigo, Warner Bros. Recording Studio, North Hollywood, CA.
Musicians: Arlo Guthrie (acoustic guitars, piano), Russ Kunkel (drums, percussion), Bob Glaub (bass), Hadley Hockensmith (guitars), Jai Winding (keyboards), John Pilla (acoustic guitars), Robben Ford (electric guitar on "Oklahoma Nights"), Fred Tackett (acoustic guitar on "When I Get to the Border"), Dean Parks (electric guitar on "Power of Love" and "Give It All You Got"), Hank De Vito (steel guitar on "Jamaica Farewell"), Jim Horn (recorders on "Power of Love"), Jay Dee Maness (steel guitar on "Slow Boat"), Rickie Lee Jones (vocals on "Jamaica Farewell"), Leah Kunkel (vocals on "If I Could Only Touch Your Life" and "Waimanalo Blues"), Penny Nichols (vocals on "Waimanalo Blues" and "When I Get to the Border"), Abraham Guthrie (vocals on "Garden Song"), Cathy Guthrie (vocals on "Garden Song"), Annie Guthrie (vocals on "Garden Song"), Sarah Lee Guthrie (vocals on "Garden Song"), Joey Waronker (vocals on "Garden Song"), Anna Waronker (vocals on "Garden Song"), Amos Newman (vocals on "Garden Song"), Tracy Brown (vocals on "Garden Song"), Tom Kelly (vocals on "Oklahoma Nights"), Bill Champlin (vocals on "Oklahoma Nights"), Clydie King (vocals on "Living Like a Legend"

and "Give It All You Got"), Sherlie Matthews King (vocals on "Living Like a Legend" and "Give It All You Got"), Gwen Dickey King (vocals on "Living Like a Legend" and "Give It All You Got"), Phil Everly (vocals on "Power of Love").

Side A:

Power of Love (T-Bone Burnett)

Oklahoma Nights (Jimmy Webb)

If I Could Only Touch Your Life (Aaron Schroeder/David Grover)

Waimanalo Blues (Thor Wold/Liko Martin)

Living Like a Legend (Arlo Guthrie)

Side B:

Give It All You Got (Steve Ide/Carol Ide)

When I Get to the Border (Richard Thompson)

Jamaica Farewell (Erving Burgess)

Slow Boat (Arlo Guthrie)

Garden Song (David Mallet)


## Pete Seeger & Arlo Guthrie: Precious Friend (1982)

LP: Warner Bros. 2BSK 3644

Cassette: Warner Bros. 2K5 3644

Produced by John Pilla. Recorded and mixed by Mark Linett. Assistant engineers Jack Crymes, Jimmy Sandweiss, David Bianco, Jim Scott, Bill Hutchinson, and Jesse Henderson. Mobile recording by the Record Plant, Los Angeles, CA. Mastered at Amigo, Warner Bros. Recording Studios, North Hollywood, CA.

Musicians: Arlo Guthrie (guitar, harmonica, piano), Pete Seeger (twelve-string guitar, five-string banjo, recorder), Steve Ide (lead guitar, trombone, vocals), Terry a la Berry (drums, percussion), Bob Putnam (guitar, piano on "Sailin' Up, Sailin' Down," organ on "Amazing Grace," vocals), Dan Velika (bass, vocals), Carol Ide (percussion, vocals, organ on "Ocean Crossing").

Side A:

Wabash Cannonball (public domain)

Circles (Harry Chapin)

Hills of Glenshee (public domain)

Ocean Crossing (Arlo Guthrie)

Celery-Time (Arlo Guthrie)

Run, Come See Jerusalem (Blind Blake)

Sailin' Up, Sailin' Down (Based on Jimmy Reed's "Baby, What Do You Want Me to Do?")

Side B:

How Can I Keep from Singing? (Doris Penn)

Old Time Religion (public domain)

Pretty Boy Floyd (Woody Guthrie)

Ladies Auxiliary (Woody Guthrie)

Please Don't Talk about Me When I'm Gone (Sidney Clare/Sam Stept/ Bee Palmer)

Precious Friend (Pete Seeger)

Side C:

Do-Re-Mi (Woody Guthrie)

Tarantella (public domain)

The Neutron Bomb (Arlo Guthrie)

I'm Changing My Name to Chrysler (Tom Paxton)

St. Louis Tickle (traditional, arranged by Arlo Guthrie)

Wimoweh (Mbube) (Solomon Linda/Paul Campbell)

Will the Circle Be Unbroken? (public domain, arranged and adapted by Arlo Guthrie)

Side D:

Garden Song (David Mallett)

Kisses Sweeter Than Wine (Paul Campbell/Joel Newman)

Raggedy Raggedy (Lee Hays)

In Dead Earnest (Lee Hays)

If I Had a Hammer (The Hammer Song) (Lee Hays/Pete Seeger)

Amazing Grace (John Newton, arranged and adapted by Arlo Guthrie)

### *Someday* (1986)

LP: Rising Son Records RSR 0001 (United Kingdom only)

Cassette: Rising Son Records RSR 0001

CD: Rising Son Records CD 0001

Produced by John Pilla. Engineer Jesse Henderson, assistant engineers Bill Robinson and Mike Mullaney, technical assistance Bill Ryan. Recorded, mixed, and mastered at Longview Farm, North Brookfield, MA.

Musicians: Arlo Guthrie (vocals, guitar, piano, synthesizers), Terry a la Berry (drums, percussion), Steve Ide (guitars, background vocals), Dan Velika (bass, guitar, background vocals), David Grover (guitar, background vocals), Chuck Hammer (synthesizer guitars), "Diamond" Jim Baker (saxophone), John Pilla (guitars), Penny Nichols, Carol Ide, Leah Kunkel, Judy Lunseth (background vocals).

Side A:

All Over the World (Arlo Guthrie)

Russian Girls (Arlo Guthrie)

Here We Are/Way Out in the Country (Arlo Guthrie)
Someday (Arlo Guthrie)
Satellite (Arlo Guthrie)
Side B:
Oh, Mom (Arlo Guthrie/Terry Hall)
Unemployment Line (Robb E. MacKay)
Eli (Arlo Guthrie)
Major Blues (Arlo Guthrie)
You and Me (Arlo Guthrie)

## *All Over the World* (1991)

CD: Rising Son Records CD 0002
This CD is "a new collection of previously recorded songs":
All Over the World
Oklahoma Nights
Massachusetts
Ukulele Lady
Manzanillo Bay
Miss the Mississippi
When I Get to the Border
City of New Orleans
Russian Girls
Gaubi, Guabi
Waimanalo Blues
Evangelina
Last Night I Had the Strangest Dream

## *Son of the Wind* (1991)

CD: Rising Son Records RSR CD 0003
Coproduced by Arlo Guthrie and David Grover. Engineered and mixed by
    Greg Steele. Recorded at Derek Studios, Dalton, MA.
Musicians: Arlo Guthrie (vocals, guitar), David Grover (guitar), Ed Gerhard
    (guitar), Dan Velika (bass), Terry a la Berry Hall (drums), Rick Tivens
    (fiddles and mandolin), Paul Kleinwald (banjo), Tim Gray (hammered
    dulcimer), John Culpo (accordion), Zip Zantay (clarinet), Mike Joyce, Jim
    Labbee, Bow Bowes, Dick Delmolino (background vocals).
Songs:
Buffalo Girls (arranged and adapted by Arlo Guthrie)
Dead or Alive (Woody Guthrie)
Streets of Laredo (arranged and adapted by Arlo Guthrie)

Ridin' Down the Canyon (Gene Autry and Smiley Burnett)
South Coast (Lillian Bos Ross, Sam Eskin, Richard Dehr, and Frank Miller)
Shenandoah (arranged and adapted by Arlo Guthrie)
The Girl I Left Behind (arranged and adapted by Arlo Guthrie)
When the Cactus Is in Bloom (Jimmie Rodgers)
Woody's Rag/Hard Work (Woody Guthrie)
I Ride an Old Paint (arranged and adapted by Arlo Guthrie)
Utah Carroll (arranged and adapted by Arlo Guthrie)
Red River Valley (arranged and adapted by Arlo Guthrie)

## *Arlo Guthrie and Pete Seeger: More Together Again—In Concert* (1994)

CD: Rising Son Records RSR 0007 (Volume One)
CD: Rising Son Records RSR 0008 (Volume Two)
Produced by Arlo Guthrie. Recorded by Ed Eastridge, Big Moe Recording Studios, Kensington, MD. Engineered and mixed by Greg Steele, Derek Studios, Dalton, MA. Digitally mastered by Toby Mountain, Northeastern Digital Recording, Inc., Southborough, MA. Recorded live at Wolf Trap Farm Park for the Performing Arts, Vienna, VA, August 8, 1993.
Musicians: Arlo Guthrie (vocals, guitar, keyboard, harmonica), Pete Seeger (vocals, guitar, five-string banjo, recorder), Tao Rodriguez-Seeger (vocals, guitar, maracas), Abe Guthrie (vocals, keyboard), Tim Sears (electric guitar, vocals), Jason Webster (acoustic and electric guitar, vocals), Kali Baba McConnell (drums, tabla, vocals), Sean Hurley (bass, vocals), Cathy Guthrie, Annie Guthrie, Sarah Lee Guthrie (vocals).
Volume One:
Midnight Special (H. Ledbetter, collected and arranged by John A. Lomax and Alan Lomax)
Abiyoyo (Pete Seeger, traditional music arranged by Rev. H. C. N. Williams and J. N. Maselwa)
Where Have All the Flowers Gone? (Pete Seeger)
Mooses Come Walking (Arlo Guthrie)
When the Ship Comes In (Bob Dylan)
Guantanamera (Marti/Dias/Orbon/Angulo/Seeger)
The Ross Perot Guide to Answering Embarrassing Questions (Calvin Trillin/Pete Seeger)
Sailing Down My Golden River (Pete Seeger)
If I Had a Hammer (Lee Hays/Pete Seeger)
When a Soldier Makes It Home (Arlo Guthrie)
Can't Help Falling in Love (Luigi Creatore/Hugo Peretti/George Weiss)

Volume Two:
De Colores (traditional)
Solo le pido a Dios (Leon Geico)
Wake Up Dead (Arlo Guthrie)
Gabriel's Mother's Hiway Ballad #16 Blues (Arlo Guthrie)
Hills of Glenshee (traditional)
A Little of This and That (Pete Seeger)
City of New Orleans (Steve Goodman)
Jacob's Ladder (traditional, additional lyrics by Pete Seeger)
Wimoweh (Mbube) (Solomon Linda/Paul Campbell)
Amazing Grace (John Newton)
This Land Is Your Land (Woody Guthrie)

## *Mystic Journey* (1996)

CD: Rising Son Records 0009
Produced by Arlo Guthrie and Abe Guthrie. Engineered by Greg Steele. Recorded at Derek Studios, Dalton, MA.
Musicians: Arlo Guthrie (vocals, six- and twelve-string guitars, piano, harmonica), Cyril Pahinui, Ed Gerhard (guitar), Abraham Guthrie (keyboards, Hammond B-3 organ), Darren Todd (bass), Terry a la Berry (drums), Greg Steele (percussion), Tim Sears (guitar), Steve Ide (guitar, trombone), Sean Hurley (bass), Kali Baba McConnell (drums), Jason Webster (guitar), John Culpo (accordion), David Grover (guitar), Jeff Stevens (trumpet), Charlie Tokarz (saxophone).
Songs:
Moon Song (Arlo Guthrie)
Face of Time (Arlo Guthrie)
The Mystic Journey (James Rider)
Under Cover of Night (Arlo Guthrie)
You Are the Song (Glen Anthony/Charlie Chaplin)
Doors of Heaven (Arlo Guthrie)
Wake Up Dead (Arlo Guthrie)
When a Soldier Makes It Home (Arlo Guthrie)
Stairs (Arlo Guthrie)
All This Stuff Takes Time (Arlo Guthrie)
I'll Be with You Tonight (Arlo Guthrie)

## *Alice's Restaurant* (1996)

CD: Rising Son Records 0010
Produced by Arlo Guthrie and Abe Guthrie. Engineered by Greg Steele. Recorded at Derek Studios, Dalton, MA.

Musicians: Arlo Guthrie (vocals, guitar, harmonica, piano), Steve Ide (guitar), Sean Hurley (bass), David Grover (guitar), Abraham Guthrie (keyboards), Terry a la Berry (drums).

Songs:

Alice's Restaurant (The Massacre Revisited) (Arlo Guthrie)
Chilling of the Evening (Arlo Guthrie)
Ring-around-a-Rosy Rag (Arlo Guthrie)
Now and Then (Arlo Guthrie)
I'm Going Home (Arlo Guthrie)
The Motorcycle Song (Arlo Guthrie)
Highway in the Wind (Arlo Guthrie)

### *In Times Like These* (2007)

CD: Rising Son Records RSR 1126

LP: Rising Son Records 1126

Produced by Arlo Guthrie, George Massenburg, and John Nardolillo, with the University of Kentucky Symphony Orchestra, music director and conductor John Nardolillo, assistant conductor Eric Paetkau, assistant conductor Robert Seebacher. Recorded March 10, 2006, at the Singletary Center for the Arts, Lexington, KY.

Musicians: Arlo Guthrie (vocals, guitar, twelve-string guitar, piano, harmonica).

Songs:

Darkest Hour (Arlo Guthrie)
Last Train (Arlo Guthrie)
St. James Infirmary (traditional, arranged and adapted by Arlo Guthrie)
If You Would Just Drop By (Arlo Guthrie)
Last to Leave (Arlo Guthrie)
Epilogue (Arlo Guthrie)
In Times Like These (Arlo Guthrie)
Patriot's Dream (Arlo Guthrie)
City of New Orleans (Steve Goodman)
You Are the Song (Glen Anthony/Charles Chaplin)
Goodnight, Irene (Huddie Ledbetter)
Can't Help Falling in Love (Luigi Creatore/Hugo Peretti/George Weiss)

### *Arlo Guthrie with the Dillards—Thirty-Two Cents: Postage Due* (2008)

CD: Rising Son Records 1127

Produced by Arlo Guthrie and Rodney Dillard. Engineered by Barry Taylor. Mixed by Abraham Guthrie.

Recorded at Caravell Studios, Branson, MO.

Musicians: Arlo Guthrie (vocals, guitar), Doug Dillard (five-string banjo), Rodney Dillard, Dean Webb, Mitch James, Abe Guthrie, Cathy Guthrie, Annie Guthrie, Sarah Lee Guthrie (background vocals on "Ship in the Sky [My Daddy]").

Songs:

Grand Coulee Dam (Woody Guthrie)

Hard Travelin' (Woody Guthrie)

East Texas Red (Woody Guthrie)

Pastures of Plenty (Woody Guthrie)

Ludlow Massacre (Woody Guthrie)

The Sinking of the Reuben James (Woody Guthrie)

Sally Don't You Grieve (Woody Guthrie)

Tom Joad (Woody Guthrie)

Ship in the Sky (My Daddy) (Woody Guthrie)

The Ranger's Command (Woody Guthrie)

Do Re Mi (Woody Guthrie)

So Long, It's Been Good to Know Yuh (Woody Guthrie)

This Land Is Your Land (Instrumental)

## *Tales of '69* (2009)

CD: Rising Son Records RSR 1128

Produced by Arlo Guthrie. Mastered by Toby Mountain at Northeastern Digital Recording.

Musicians: Arlo Guthrie (vocals, guitar), Bob Atkins (double bass).

Songs:

The Unbelievable Motorcycle Tale (Arlo Guthrie)

What a Gas

Coming into Los Angeles (Arlo Guthrie)

If You Would Just Drop By (Arlo Guthrie)

If Ever I Should See the Mountain (Arlo Guthrie)

Finger Pickin' Good (Simply Tuning)

Alice—Before Time Began (Arlo Guthrie)

Road to Everywhere (Arlo Guthrie)

Hurry to Me (Arlo Guthrie)

## *Arlo Guthrie & Wenzel—Every 100 Years* (2010)

CD: matrosenblau /12 (Germany)

Recorded live at Wartburg Castle, Eisenach, Germany, September 19, 2006. Recording by MDR Figaro and Siegbert Schneider. Live sound, mix, mastering, new recording, and sound restoration by Thommy Kiawallo at Domino-Studio, Berlin.

Musicians: Arlo Guthrie (vocals, guitar, harmonica), Hans Eckardt Wenzel (vocals, piano, accordion), Gordon Titcomb (vocals, mandolin, pedal steel), Abe Guthrie (keyboards), Hannes Scheffler (guitar), Karla Wenzel (vocals, percussion, organ), Cornelius Ochs (bass), Nora Guthrie (vocals), Georg Schwark (tuba), and Stefan Meinking (drums).

Songs:

Green Green Rocky Road (traditional, arranged and adapted by Arlo Guthrie)

In Times Like These (Arlo Guthrie)

Nächtliche Überfahrt (Wenzel)

Ridin' Down the Canyon (Gene Autry/Smiley Burnett)

Ninety Mile Wind (words by Woody Guthrie; music by Wenzel)

The Red Haired Boy (traditional)

Every 100 Years (words by Woody Guthrie; music by Wenzel)

St. Louis Tickle (Theron Catlan Bennett)

Herbstlied (Wenzel)

St. James Infirmary (traditional, arranged and adapted by Arlo Guthrie)

In meiner schwarzen Stunde (Arlo Guthrie; German translation by Wenzel)

Darkest Hour (Arlo Guthrie)

My Peace/Mein Frieden (Woody Guthrie)

Goodnight, Irene (Huddie Ledbetter)


## REPRISE/WARNER BROS. "LOSS LEADER" SERIES

### *Some of Our Best Friends Are* (1968)

(PRO 290)
The Motorcycle Song


### *The 1969 Warner/Reprise Songbook* (1969)

(PRO 331)
The Pause of Mr. Claus (from *Arlo*)


### *The 1969 Warner/Reprise Record Show* (1969)

(PRO 336)
Every Hand in the Land (from *Running Down the Road*)

### The Big Ball (1970)

(PRO 358)
Coming into Los Angeles (from *Running Down the Road*)

### Schlagers! (1970)

(PRO 359)
Stealin' (from *Running Down the Road*)

### Looney Tunes & Merrie Melodies (1970)

(PRO 423)
Valley to Pray (from *Washington County*)

### The Whole Burbank Catalog (1972)

(PRO 512)
Ukulele Lady (from *Hobo's Lullaby*)

### Display Case 6 (1972)

(PRO 527)
Ukulele Lady (from *Hobo's Lullaby*)

### Burbank (1972)

(PRO 529)
Voter Registration Rag (previously unreleased)

### The Days of Wine and Vinyl (1972)

(PRO 549)
The Ballad of Tricky Fred (from Reprise single 0994)

### Appetizers (1973)

(PRO 569)
Lovesick Blues (from *Last of the Brooklyn Cowboys*)

***Deep Ear* (1974)**

(PRO 591)
Me and My Goose (from *Arlo Guthrie*)

***I Didn't Know They Still Made Records Like This* (1975)**

(PRO 608)
City of New Orleans (from *Hobo's Lullaby*)

***The People's Record* (1976)**

(PRO 645)
Patriot's Dream (from *Amigo*)

***Pumping Vinyl* (1979)**

(PRO A-773)
(Last Night) I Had the Strangest Dream (from *One Night*)


## ANTHOLOGIES, SOUNDTRACKS, AND FESTIVAL RECORDS

***Something to Sing About!* (1968)**

LP: MOS 1
Produced by Milton Okun. Three-LP set to supplement the *Something to Sing About!* songbook (New York: Macmillan, 1968).
The Motorcycle Song

**Alice's Restaurant—*Original Motion Picture Score* (1970)**

LP: United Artists UAS 5195
Side A:
    Traveling Music (Arlo Guthrie)
    Alice's Restaurant Massacree, Part I (Arlo Guthrie)
    The Let Down (Garry Sherman)
    Songs to Aging Children (Joni Mitchell; vocal: Tigger Outlaw)
    Amazing Grace (Guthrie/Sherman)
Side B:
    Trip to the City (Arlo Guthrie)
    Alice's Restaurant Massacree, Part II (Arlo Guthrie)

Crash Pad Improvs (Arlo Guthrie)
You're a Fink (Guthrie/Sherman; vocal: Al Schackman)
Harps and Marriage (Gary Sherman)

## Woodstock—Music from the Original Soundtrack and More (1970)

LP: Cotillion Records SD 3-500
Eight-track: Cotillion TP-500
Cassette: Cotillion CS-500
Reel: Cotillion T-500
Coming into Los Angeles

## A Tribute to Woody Guthrie, Part One (1972)

LP: Columbia Records KC 31171
Recorded at Carnegie Hall, January 20, 1968, and the Hollywood Bowl, September 12, 1970.
Songs:
This Train Is Bound for Glory
Oklahoma Hills
Do Re Mi

## A Tribute to Woody Guthrie, Part Two (1972)

LP: Warner Bros. Records BS 2586
Recorded at Carnegie Hall, January 20, 1968, and the Hollywood Bowl, September 12, 1970.
Jesus Christ

## Superstars of the '70s (1973)

LP: Warner Special Products SP 4000
Four-LP set
City of New Orleans

## The Bitter End Years (1974)

LP: Roxbury Records RLX 300
The Motorcycle Song

### Philadelphia Folk Festival '74 (1974)

LP: WMMR/Promo 1
This single promo LP features musical highlights of the WHYY-TV (Wilmington/Philadelphia) PBS station recording of the Philadelphia Folk Festival, Upper Salford, PA, August 23 through 25, 1974. Other artists featured on the LP include David Bromberg, John Hartford, Leon Redbone, and Tom Rush.

### A Tribute to Woody Guthrie (1976)

Two LPs: Warner Bros. Records 2W 3007
CD: WB 26036-2
Recorded at Carnegie Hall, January 20, 1968, and the Hollywood Bowl, September 12, 1970.
Songs:
  This Train Is Bound for Glory
  Oklahoma Hills
  Do Re Mi
  Jesus Christ
  This Land Is Your Land (with Odetta and cast)

### Woody Guthrie's "We Ain't Down Yet" (1976)

LP: Cream Records CR-1002
CD: Diablo Records DIAB 812
Goin' Down the Road (with Doug and Rodney Dillard)

### A Tribute to Leadbelly (1977)

Two LPs: Tomato Records TOM-2-7003
CD: Tomato 2696192
Recorded at Hunter College–CUNY, March 15, 1975, with Pete Seeger, the Lunenberg Travelers, Sonny Terry, and Brownie McGhee. Released on CD in 1989 as Tomato 2696192.
Songs:
  The Bourgeois Blues (with Pete Seeger)
  Redbird
  Pigmeat
  Lord Lord Lord
  On a Monday
  Midnight Special (with cast)

Meeting at the Building (with cast)
Goodnight, Irene (with cast)

## Arthur B. Morrison Presents President Jimmy Carter in Project Tooth Decay, Dateline Washington (1977)

LP: Cornucopia Records (Beverly Hills, CA), no catalog no.
Produced and directed by Arthur B. Morrison.
The U.S. government–sponsored "juvenile sound recording" promotes dental
  hygiene and features contributions of such celebrity guests as Muhammad
  Ali, Pat Boone, President Jimmy Carter, Howard Cosell, Ossie Davis, Arlo
  Guthrie, Richie Havens, Billie Jean King, Lily Tomlin, and Frank Sinatra.

## Bread & Roses: Festival of Acoustic Music (1978)

Two LPs: Fantasy F-79009, recorded at the Greek Theater, UC-Berkeley
CD: FAN 79009
Me and My Goose (as "Al the Goose")

## Soundtrack from the Film Woody Guthrie: Hard Travelin' (1984)

LP: Arloco Records ARL-284
CD: Rising Son Records RSR 0013
Side A:
  Oklahoma Hills (with the Oklahoma Swing Band)
  Philadelphia Lawyer (with Rose Maddox and the Oklahoma Swing Band)
  Hard Travelin' (with Ramblin' Jack Elliott and Sonny Terry)
  Deportee (Plane Wreck at Los Gatos) (with Hoyt Axton)
  Roll Columbia Roll (with Bill Murlin)
  Union Maid (with Pete Seeger)
  New York Town (with Ramblin' Jack Elliott and Sonny Terry)
Side B:
  The Sinking of the Reuben James (with Pete Seeger)
  Riding in My Car (with Judy Collins)
  Hobo's Lullaby (with Pete Seeger)
  This Land Is Your Land (with Woody Guthrie)

## Tribute to Steve Goodman (1985)

Two LPs: Red Pajamas Records RPJ 004.
Songs:
  All Over the World
  City of New Orleans

## *HARP* (1985)

LP: Redwood Records RR 409
Musicians: Arlo Guthrie, Pete Seeger, Holly Near, Ronnie Gilbert, and Jeff
  Langley
Songs:
  Oh, Mary, Don't You Weep
  City of New Orleans
  All Over the World
  Pallet on the Floor

## *Folkways: A Vision Shared—A Tribute to Woody Guthrie and Lead Belly* (1988)

LP: Columbia 44034
East Texas Red

## *Audio Literature Presents* Bound for Glory (1992)

Audio Literature, Berkeley, CA, no catalog no.
This two-cassette book-on-tape set features Arlo reading an abridged version
  of his father's novel *Bound for Glory*.

## *Rainbow Sign* (1992)

CD: Rounder CD 8025
Oh, Mary, Don't You Weep (from *HARP*, Redwood Records RR 409)

## *Woody's 20 Grow Big Songs* (1992)

CD: Warner Bros. 9 45020-2
Executive producers Arlo Guthrie and Nora Guthrie; coproduced by Arlo
  Guthrie, Nora Guthrie, and Frank Fuchs. Recorded by Greg Steele at Derek
  Studios, Dalton, MA, August through December 1991.
Musicians: Woody Guthrie (vocals, guitar, harmonica), Arlo Guthrie (vocals,
  guitar, keyboards), Joady Guthrie (vocals, guitar), David Grover (guitar),
  Dan Velika (bass), Terry Hall (drums), Rick Tiven (fiddle, mandolin), John
  Culpo (accordion), Nora Guthrie-Rotante, Abraham Guthrie, Cathyaliza
  Guthrie, Annie Guthrie, Anna Rotante, Sarah Lee Guthrie, Damon Guthrie
  (vocals).
Songs:
  Wake Up
  Clean-O

All Work Together
Dance Around
Pretty and Shiny-O
Don't You Push Me Down
Little Seed
Needle Sing
Merry-Go-Round
Howdy-Doo
Mailman
Riding in My Car
Bling Blang
Pick It Up
My Dolly
Put Your Finger in the Air
Race You down the Mountain
Jig Along Home
Little Bird
Sleep Eye

### *Further More* (1997)

CD: Hybrid HY-20003
Highway in the Wind (from *Alice's Restaurant*)

### *This Land Is Your Land—An All-American Children's Folk Classic* (1997)

CD: Rounder Kids CD 8050
Produced and arranged by Frankie Fuchs. Engineered by Bob Kearney and Eric Fischer. Mixed by Bob Kearney, Frankie Fuchs, and Marc Desisto. Recorded at Music Grinders Studio and Track Record Studio.
Musicians: Woody Guthrie (vocals, guitar), Arlo Guthrie (vocals, guitar, piano, harmonica), James "Hutch" Hutchinson (bass), Russ Kunkel (drums), Bob Jones (steel guitar), Emil Richards (Native American percussion), Sid Page (violin), Steve Conn (accordion), Danny Wilson (mandolin), Frank Fuchs (guitar), Tom Burton (vocals, spoons), Sam Riney (clarinet, saxophone), Eric Weissberg (banjo, jaw harp, mandolin), Doug Norwine (soprano sax), and Vincent Tividad (flute).
Songs:
Howdi Do
Riding in My Car
Along Home

Mail Myself to You
This Land Is Your Land
Bling Blang
All Work Together
Grassy Grass Grass
So Long, It's Been Good to Know Yuh
This Land Is Your Land (instrumental)
All Work Together (instrumental)

### *What's That I Hear? The Songs of Phil Ochs—Various Artists* (1998)

CD: Sliced Bread Records SLBR 71176
I Ain't Marchin' Anymore (Phil Ochs)

### *Lost Hits of the '60s: 40 Solid Gold AM Radio Classics* (1999)

CD: Warner Special Products/Echo 4573
Alice's Rock & Roll Restaurant (Arlo Guthrie) (from Reprise single 0877)

### *Sing Out for Seva—Various Artists* (1999)

CD: Arista/Grateful Dead Records GDCD 4067
Guthrie's contribution recorded live at the Nob Hill Masonic Center, February 13, 1994.
Can't Help Falling in Love (Luigi Creatore/Hugo Peretti/George Weiss)

### *'Til We Outnumber 'Em . . . : The Songs of Woody Guthrie* (2000)

CD: Righteous Babe Records RBR019-D
Produced and mixed by Ani DiFranco. Recorded live on September 29, 1997, at Severance Hall, Cleveland, OH.
Musical and spoken-word guests include Billy Bragg, Ani DiFranco, Ramblin' Jack Elliott, Arlo Guthrie, Peter Glazer, Fred Hellerman, Indigo Girls, Country Joe McDonald, David Pirner, Tim Robbins, Bruce Springsteen, and Craig Werner.
Songs:
Hard Travelin' Hootenanny (with cast)
Regular Fires
Free in Every Moment
Dust Storm Disaster
Change the Moment
'Til We Outnumber 'Em (This Land Is Your Land) (with cast)

**The Best of Broadside 1962–1988: Anthems of the America Underground from the Pages of Broadside Magazine (2000)**

CD: Smithsonian Folkways SFW 40130
Reissue produced by Jeff Place and Ronald D. Cohen.
Victor Jara

**Bright Spaces: Children's Music to Benefit the Homeless—Various Artists (2000)**

CD: Rounder Kids 11661-8061-2
Songs:
Bling Blang
This Land Is Your Land (with Woody Guthrie)

**Washington Square Memoirs: The Great Urban Folk Boom 1950–1970 (2001)**

CD: Rhino Records
The Motorcycle Song (Arlo Guthrie)

**Philadelphia Folk Festival 40th Anniversary (2001)**

CD: Sliced Bread Records SLBR 74440
Ring-around-a-Rosy Rag (Arlo Guthrie)

**If I Had a Song: The Songs of Pete Seeger, Vol. 2 (2001)**

CD: Appleseed Recordings APR CD 1055
Executive producer Jim Musselman. The Arlo Guthrie–Pete Seeger duets were recorded at 1-800-PRIMECD Studio, New York City, NY, 1989.
Songs:
66 Highway Blues (Woody Guthrie/Pete Seeger; Arlo Guthrie: vocals, guitar; Pete Seeger: vocals, five-string banjo)
This Old Car (Pete Seeger: vocals, guitar; Arlo Guthrie: vocals, guitar; Mark Dann: bass)

**Sharin' in the Groove: Celebrating the Music of Phish—Various Artists (2001)**

CD: Mockingbird Foundation
Bouncing around the Room (Arlo Guthrie and Xavier)

### *Banjoman—A Tribute to Derroll Adams* (2002)

CD: Rising Son Records RSR-2102-2 (U.S.); Blue Groove CD BG-1420
Produced by Hans Theessink and Arlo Guthrie. Mastered by Toby Mountain at Northeastern Digital Recording, Inc., Southboro, MA.
Songs:
Columbus Stockade Blues (traditional; Arlo Guthrie: vocal, guitar; Donovan: guitar, vocals; Hans Theesink: vocals, guitar, mandolin; David Ferguson: guitar)
Portland Town (Derroll Adams; Arlo Guthrie: vocal, guitar; Hans Theessink: guitar)
The Cuckoo (traditional; Ramblin' Jack Elliott: vocal, guitar; Arlo Guthrie: guitar)
Freight Train Blues (traditional; Hans Theessink: vocals, guitar; Arlo Guthrie: guitar, accompanying vocals; Donovan: harmonica)
The Valley (Derroll Adams; Hans Theessink: vocals, guitar, mandola; Arlo Guthrie: guitar; Donovan: vocal)
Dixie Darling (A. P. Carter; Dolly Parton: vocal; Arlo Guthrie: vocal; Hans Theessink: guitar, accompanying vocal; Barney McKenna: banjo, accompanying vocal; John Shehan: fiddle, accompanying vocal; Jack Clement: ukulele; David Ferguson: upright bass).
Muleskinner Blues (Rodgers/Vaughn; Ramblin' Jack Elliott: vocals, guitar; Arlo Guthrie: vocals, guitar)
24 Hours a Day (Derroll Adams; Hans Theessink: vocal, guitar; Arlo Guthrie: guitar, foot tap)

### *Celebration: 45th Philadelphia Folk Festival* (2002)

CD: Sliced Bread Records SLBR 74445
Recorded live at the Philadelphia Folk Festival, August 24 through 26, 2001.
When the Ship Comes In (Bob Dylan)

### *Seeds: The Songs of Pete Seeger, Volume 3* (2003)

CD: Appleseed Recordings APR CD 1072
Produced by Jim Musselman and David Seitz. Recorded in New York City circa 1989.
Song: Trouble at the Bottom (Pete Seeger; Pete Seeger: vocal, guitar; Tao Rodriguez-Seeger: vocal, guitar; Arlo Guthrie: vocal; Mark Dann: bass)

### *Spain in My Heart: Songs of the Spanish Civil War* (2003)

CD: Appleseed Recordings APR CD 1074
Executive producer Heather Rose Bridger; produced by Joe Weed and Heather Rose Bridger.

Song: Jarama Valley (Lee Hays/Woody Guthrie/Pete Seeger)
Musicians: Pete Seeger (vocals, five-string banjo), Arlo Guthrie (vocals), Marty Atkinson (rhythm guitar), Joe Weed (lead guitar), Derek Jones (bass), Norton Buffalo (harmonica)

### *Wildflower Festival—Judy Collins* (2003)

CD: Wildflower WLFL 13002
Judy Collins and friends (Tom Rush, Arlo Guthrie, and Eric Andersen) recorded live at Humphrey's Concerts by the Bay, San Diego, CA, June 30, 2002.
Songs:
St. James Infirmary
Mooses Come Walking
City of New Orleans (with cast)
Thirsty Boots (with cast)
Will the Circle Be Unbroken (with cast)

### *Sing Along with Putumayo* (2004)

CD: Putumayo World Music 222-2
Bling Blang (Woody Guthrie)

### *America—The Boston Pops Orchestra* (2005)

CD: Artemis Classics ARCL 5
Songs:
City of New Orleans (Steve Goodman)
This Land Is Your Land (Woody Guthrie)

### *All Gone Fishin'—Various Artists* (2006)

CD: Bandit Records BAN 79818
Talking Fishing Blues (Woody Guthrie)

### *Sowing the Seeds—The 10th Anniversary* (2007)

CD: Appleseed Recordings APR CD 1102
Selection track sourced from *HARP—A Time to Sing!* (Appleseed Recording APR CD 1054).
Somos el barco (We Are the Boat) (Pete Seeger with Arlo Guthrie, Holly Near, and Ronnie Gilbert)

*Step by Step: Music from the Film* **From Wharf Rats to Lords of the Docks (2008)**

The Ballad of Harry Bridges (with Gordon Titcomb, mandolin; Abraham Guthrie, keyboards)
Waltzing Matilda (with Gordon Titcomb, mandolin; Abraham Guthrie, keyboards)

*Go Waggaloo—Sarah Lee Guthrie & Family* **(2009)**

CD: Smithsonian Folkways Recordings SFW CD 45069
Produced by Johnny Irion with Rte 8 Records and John Smith of Smithsonian Folkways.
Songs:
   Big Square Walkin' (Sarah Lee Guthrie; Sarah Lee Guthrie: guitar, vocals; Arlo Guthrie: autoharp; Johnny Irion, Olivia Irion, Jacklyn Guthrie: backup vocals)
   Brush Your Teeth Blues #57 (Johnny Irion; Sarah Lee Guthrie: lead vocals, melodica; Arlo Guthrie: ukulele; Johnny Irion: acoustic guitar; Amanda Kowalski: upright bass)

## ON OTHER ARTISTS' RECORDS

*I Saw the Light: With Some Help from My Friends—Earl Scruggs* **(1972)**

LP: Columbia KC 31354
Picture from Life's Other Side (as "Arloff Boguslavski")

*Sonny & Brownie—Sonny Terry and Brownie McGhee* **(1973)**

LP: A&M Records SP 4379
CD: Mobile Fidelity Sound Lab UDCD 641
Songs:
   People Get Ready (on acoustic guitar)
   Sail Away (on vocals and acoustic guitar)
   God and Man (on piano)

*What Were Once Vices Are Now Habits—Doobie Brothers* **(1974)**

LP: Warner Bros. W 2750
Guthrie is credited as contributing autoharp to this LP.

## *Southbound—Hoyt Axton* (1975)

LP: A&M SP4510
Roll Your Own

## *Cobble Mountain Band—Cobble Mountain Band* (1979)

LP: Singlebrook CMB-1579
Produced by John Pilla for Rt. 183 Productions. Recording engineers Les Kahn and Jesse Henderson. This LP from the Massachusetts-based western-swing-honky-tonk band includes musical contributions from Arlo Guthrie and former Weaver Fred Hellerman.

## *Christmas—Ed Gerhard* (1991)

CD: Virtue VRD 1920
Produced by Ed Gerhard
Silver Bells (with Arlo Guthrie, twelve-string guitar)

## *Counting the Ways—Ed Gerhard* (1996)

CD: Virtue VIU 1922
My Creole Belle (Mississippi John Hurt) (with Arlo Guthrie: vocals, guitar)

## *Friends of Mine—Ramblin' Jack Elliott* (1998)

CD: Hightone HCD 8089
Produced by Roy Rogers. Recorded February 2, 1996, at Prairie Sun Recording, Cotati, CA.
Musicians: Ramblin' Jack Elliott (vocals, guitar), Arlo Guthrie (vocals, guitar), Ruth Davies (bass), Tom Rigney (violin), Jimmy Sanchez (snare drum).
Ridin' Down the Canyon (Gene Autry/Smiley Burnett)

## *Sarah Lee Guthrie—Sarah Lee Guthrie* (2001)

CD: Rising Son B0002M730Q

## *The Girls Won't Leave the Boys Alone—Cherish the Ladies* (2001)

CD: Windham Hill 01934-11583-2/Sony Music SBMK 748779

## The Well—Jennifer Warnes (2001)

CD: SDR Limited SD8960
Produced by Martin Davich and Jennifer Warnes. Mixed by George Massenburg and mastered by Bernie Grundman. "Patriot's Dream" also released as a CD single (SD 1233-2).
Patriot's Dream (Arlo Guthrie) (with Jennifer Warnes)

## Top of the World—Jimmy Sturr (2002)

CD: Rounder 6104
City of New Orleans
This Land Is Your Land

## Entirely Live—Sarah Lee Guthrie & Johnny Irion (2005)

CD: Rt. 8 Music B00075U0AI
Songs:
    In a Young Girl's Mind
    DC Niner
    There'll Be No Church Tonight

## Woodyboye: Songs of Woody Guthrie (and Tales Worth Telling), Volume II—Joel Rafael Band (2005)

CD: Appleseed Records APLE 1086
Stepstone

## The Last Train—Gordon Titcomb (2005)

CD: Rising Son B000A8QSVC
Musicians include Mike Auldridge, Mark Schatz, Bill Keith, and Arlo Guthrie.

## Great American Song Series, Vol. 2—Eric Andersen (2005)

CD: Appleseed Recording APLE 1092

### U.S. SINGLES (1967–1982)

1967—Reprise 0644 (White Label promo)—"The Motorcycle Song" (Arlo Guthrie) / "Now and Then" (Arlo Guthrie). Produced by Fred Hellerman for Loom Productions, Inc. From *Alice's Restaurant*.

1968—Reprise PRO 304 (White Label promo)—"The Motorcycle Song" (Arlo Guthrie) / "The Pause of Mister Claus" (Arlo Guthrie). Produced by Fred Hellerman for Loom Productions, Inc. Recorded "live" at the Bitter End Café, New York City, December 1967. From *Arlo*.

1968—Reprise 0793 (White Label promo)—"The Motorcycle Song (Part I)" (Arlo Guthrie) / "The Motorcycle Song (Part II)" (Arlo Guthrie). Produced by Fred Hellerman for Loom Productions, Inc. From *Arlo*.

1969—Reprise 0877 (stock copy)—"Alice's Rock & Roll Restaurant" (Arlo Guthrie) / "Coming into Los Angeles" (Arlo Guthrie). Produced by Lenny Waronker and John Pilla. "Alice's Rock & Roll Restaurant" features Doug Kershaw on violin. Side A previously unreleased. Side B from *Running Down the Road*.

1970—Reprise 0951 (White Label promo)—"Valley to Pray" (D. Coutson/J. Pilla/Arlo Guthrie) / "Gabriel's Mother's Hiway Ballad #16 Blues" (Arlo Guthrie). Side A produced by Lenny Waronker and John Pilla. Musical directors: Kirby Johnson and Van Dyke Parks. Side B produced by Lenny Waronker and John Pilla. Both songs from *Washington County*.

1970—Reprise 0951 (stock copy)—"Valley to Pray" (D. Coutson/J. Pilla/ Arlo Guthrie) / "Gabriel's Mother's Hiway Ballad #16 Blues" (Arlo Guthrie). Side A produced by Lenny Waronker and John Pilla. Musical directors: Kirby Johnson and Van Dyke Parks. Side B produced by Lenny Waronker and John Pilla. Both songs from *Washington County*.

1970—Reprise 0994 (White Label promo)—"Ballad of Tricky Fred" (Arlo Guthrie) (stereo) / "Ballad of Tricky Fred" (Arlo Guthrie) (mono). Produced by Lenny Waronker and John Pilla. Previously unreleased but later featured on the Warner Bros. promotional LP *The Days of Wine and Vinyl* (PRO 540, 1972).

1972—Reprise REP 1103 (stock copy)—"The City of New Orleans" (Steve Goodman) / "Days Are Short" (Arlo Guthrie). Produced by Lenny Waronker and John Pilla. From *Hobo's Lullaby*.

1972—Reprise REP 1137 (White Label promo)—"Cooper's Lament" (Arlo Guthrie) / "Ukulele Lady" (Richard Whiting/Gus Kahn). Produced by Lenny Waronker and John Pilla. Side A previously unreleased but later included on *Last of the Brooklyn Cowboys*. Side B from *Hobo's Lullaby*.

1972—Reprise REP 1137 (stock copy)—"Cooper's Lament" (Arlo Guthrie) / "Ukulele Lady" (Richard Whiting/Gus Kahn). Produced by Lenny Waronker and John Pilla. Side A previously unreleased but later included on *Last of the Brooklyn Cowboys*. Side B from *Hobo's Lullaby*.

1973—Reprise REP 1158—(White Label promo)—"Gypsy Davy" (Woody Guthrie) / "Week on the Rag" (Arlo Guthrie). Side A produced by Lenny Waronker and John Pilla. Side B produced by Lenny Waronker and John Pilla. Woodwinds arranged by George Bohanon. From *Last of the Brooklyn Cowboys*.

1974—Reprise REP 1211 (promo)—"Presidential Rag" (Arlo Guthrie) / "Nostalgia Rag" (Arlo Guthrie). Produced by Lenny Waronker and John Pilla. From *Arlo Guthrie*.

1976—Reprise RPS 1363 (promo)—"Ocean Crossing" (Arlo Guthrie) / "Patriot's Dream" (Arlo Guthrie). Produced by John Pilla. Engineered by Donn Landee. From *Amigo*.

1976—Reprise RPS 1363 (stock copy)—"Ocean Crossing" (Arlo Guthrie) / "Patriot's Dream" (Arlo Guthrie). Produced by John Pilla. Engineered by Donn Landee. From *Amigo*.

1976—Reprise RPS 1376 (promo)—"Guabi, Guabi" (Arlo Guthrie) (stereo) / "Guabi, Guabi" (Arlo Guthrie) (mono). Produced by John Pilla. Engineered by Donn Landee. From *Amigo*.

1976—Reprise RPS 1388 (promo)—"Massachusetts" (Arlo Guthrie) (stereo) / "Massachusetts" (Arlo Guthrie) (mono). Produced by John Pilla. Engineered by Donn Landee. From *Amigo*.

1979—Warner Bros. PRO-S-813—"Prologue" (Arlo Guthrie) / "Which Side" (Arlo Guthrie). This disc is Record 4, Side 1 and 2, of the *Warner Bros. Preview Pack June 1979*, a six-disc boxed release featuring new music by label mates Guthrie, Devo, Junior Walker, Gruppo Sportivo, Jakob Magnusson, and Adam Mitchell. Technically, these are not 45 rpm singles, as the seven-inch discs play at 33 1/3 rpm. The Guthrie sides were produced by John Pilla and are sourced from the then-forthcoming *Outlasting the Blues*.

1979—Warner Bros. WBS 49037 (promo)—"Prologue" (Arlo Guthrie) (stereo) / "Prologue" (Arlo Guthrie) (mono). Produced by John Pilla. From *Outlasting the Blues*.

1981—Warner Bros. WBS49796 (promo)—"If I Could Only Touch Your Life" (Aaron Schroeder/David Grover) (stereo) / "If I Could Only Touch Your Life" (Aaron Schroeder/David Grover) (mono). Produced by John Pilla for Rt. 183 Productions, Inc. Engineered by Mark Linett. From the album *Power of Love*.

1981—Warner Bros. WBS49889 (promo)—"Oklahoma Nights" (Jimmy Webb) (stereo) / "Oklahoma Nights" (Jimmy Webb) (mono). Produced by John Pilla for Rt. 183 Productions, Inc. Engineered by Mark Linett. From *Power of Love*.

1988—Rising Son Records RSRS 0001—"Russian Girls" (Arlo Guthrie) / "All Over the World" (Arlo Guthrie). From *Someday* (RSR 0001). (UK release only).

1992—Rising Son Records 0006—"Special Limited Edition—2 Songs" cassette single. "Norman Always Knew" (Joe Manning and Steve Vozzolo) / "Massachusetts" (Arlo Guthrie). Both song versions previously unreleased.

## ODDS AND ENDS

### *Arlo* (1969)

LP: Armed Forces Radio and Television Service, Los Angeles (P-11134/ RL-31-9)
Transcription disc featuring three tracks from *Arlo* (Reprise RS 6299). The alternate side of the disc features five tracks from *Donovan in Concert*.
Songs:
  The Motorcycle Song
  John Looked Down
  Meditation (Wave upon Wave)

### United Artists Alice's Restaurant *Spots for Radio Play* (1969)

LP: United Artists ULP 82669
This promotional transcription disc features four different radio spots advertising the *Alice's Restaurant* film.

### *Seventy-Two Vote* (1992)

This rare Warner Bos. promo-single features several of the label's artists (America, Beach Boys, Beaver and Krause, Arlo Guthrie, the Phlorescent Leech & Eddie, and Todd Rundgren), encouraging teen radio listeners to register and vote in the 1972 presidential election. Arlo's contribution was his "Voter Registration Rag."

### *Quadradisc Sampler* (1973)

LP: Warner Bros./Elektra 7/Atlantic PR 186
Gypsy Davy

### *Radio Spots from Warner/Reprise* (1973)

Reel-to-reel: R-555-A, 60 seconds, 7.5 st.
Radio spot for *Six Pack* promotion featuring Guthrie and Foghat.

### *Radio Spots from Warner/Reprise* (1974)

Reel-to-reel: R-601, 30 seconds, 7.5 st.
Radio spot for *Arlo Guthrie* LP (MS-2183).

### *Arlo Guthrie on Guthrie Thomas* **(1975)**

45 rpm single: Capitol SPRO-8216 (promotional record)
"Includes phone interview with Arlo Guthrie and excerpts of songs by
  Guthrie Thomas from his new Capitol Album *GUTHRIE THOMAS* (ST-
  11435)."

### *Rock & Religion* **(1980)**

LP: Rock & Religion RR59/RR60
This transcription disc features Mary Neely's interview with Arlo Guthrie regarding the artist's interest in "moral and spiritual issues in America." The
program was broadcast in two parts on March 9, 1980, and March 16, 1980.

### *Rock Age* **(aka *Rock Age Campaign*)**

Japan
Two LPs: Warner Bros./Pioneer Records PS-9/10
Valley to Pray (from *Washington County*)

### *The Very Best of Arlo Guthrie* **(1971)**

Australia
LP: REPRISE RS-5258
Side A:
  Washington County
  Percy's Song
  Highway in the Wind
  Oklahoma Hills
  Alice's Restaurant
Side B:
  Valley to Pray
  Ballad of Tricky Fred
  The Motorcycle Song
  Living in the Country
  Shackles & Chains
  Running Down the Road

### *Star Collection: Arlo Guthrie* **(1972)**

Germany
LP: MIDI-MID 24 003 ("A Product of WEA Musik")
Side A:
  Now and Then

Meditation (Wave upon Wave)
Fence Post Blues
Highway in the Wind
Oklahoma Hills
Side B:
The Motorcycle Song
Wouldn't You Believe It
Standing at the Threshold
Try Me One More Time
John Looked Down

## *Arlo Guthrie* (1972)

Italy
LP: Charter Line CTR 24003
Side A:
Now and Then
Meditation (Wave upon Wave)
Fence Post Blues
Highway in the Wind
Oklahoma Hills
Side B:
The Motorcycle Song
Wouldn't You Believe It
Standing at the Threshold
Try Me One More Time
John Looked Down

## *Arlo Guthrie—Live at APA: My Peace* (2005)

This unusual CD is a privately circulated, nonmastered pressing of a line
recording taken from Guthrie's members-only concert of August 18, 2005,
at the 113th annual convention of the American Psychological Association
in Washington, DC.
Songs:
Ridin' Down the Canyon
Gypsy Davy
City of New Orleans
This Land Is Your Land
Alice's Restaurant
My Peace

# Bibliography

Aarons, Leroy. "Award for Woody Guthrie: Songwriter Honored at Last." *Boston Globe*, April 8, 1966, 21.

Abramson, Rudy. "Pageantry and Tumult: Ford, Concord Join in a Historic Salute." *Los Angeles Times*, April 20, 1975, 1.

Adams, Marjory. "'Alice's Restaurant' Caters to Hippies." *Boston Evening Globe*, August 20, 1969, 29.

Andrews, Harvey. "Record Reviews" (review of *Last of the Brooklyn Cowboys*). *Folk Review* 2, no. 11 (September 1973), 27, 29.

———. "Record Reviews" (review of *Arlo Guthrie*). *Folk Review* 4, no. 1 (November 1974), 19–20.

Arnold, Gary. "Film: Alice in Guthrieland." *Washington Post*, September 18, 1969, G1, 13.

Aronowitz, Alfred G. "Arlo Guthrie, 20, Takes Own Road—Woody's Son, at Carnegie, Sings of Urban Dust Bowl." *New York Times*, November 12, 1967, 85.

Atkinson, Bob. "Book Reviews." *Sing Out!* 19, no. 6 (June/July 1970), 41.

Atkinson, Terry. "Brief Reviews of Pop Albums" (*Amigo*). *Los Angeles Times*, October 17, 1976, sec. "Calendar," 77.

Baggelaar, Kristin, and Donald Milton. *Folk Music—More Than a Song*. New York: Thomas Y. Crowell, 1976.

Baker, Robb. "Concert: A Spell-Binding Albatross." *Chicago Tribune*, July 21, 1968, A6.

Ball, Judy. "On the Road with Arlo Guthrie." *St. Anthony Messenger* 87, no. 9 (February 1980), 16–21.

Bauman, Irma, and Mordecai Bauman. *From Our Angle of Repose: A Memoir*. New York: Author, 2006.

"Bent." "Hipsters Get a New Hero in Arlo Guthrie Who Pulls SRO $7,800 in N.Y. Debut." *Variety*, November 15, 1967, 61.

———. "Bitter End, N.Y." *Variety*, December 27, 1967, 45.

———. "Concert Review: Judy Collins/Arlo Guthrie." *Variety*, July 3, 1968, 48.

——. "Concert Reviews: Arlo Guthrie (Carnegie Hall, N.Y.)." *Variety*, December 18, 1968, 49.

"Berg." "Concert Reviews: Harry Chapin/Arlo Guthrie (Greek Theatre, L.A.)." *Variety*, July 30, 1980, 77.

Berman, Leslie. "Riffs: Arlo Guthrie Off the Record." *Village Voice*, August 12, 1981, 58.

Bernstein, Carl. "Sings of Real Events: Arlo Guthrie Shines at Lisner." *Washington Post*, January 15, 1968, D7.

——. *Loyalties: A Son's Memoir*. New York: Simon and Schuster, 1989.

Blando, Bill. "Arlo Hoes His Own Row." *Knickerbocker News*, November 11, 1967, B11.

Bosworth, Patricia. "Mrs. Guthrie: 'Kids Know Arlo's Still Searching.'" *New York Times*, September 28, 1969, D15.

Brack, Ray. "New Acts: Arlo Guthrie." *Variety*, February 23, 1966, 61.

——. "Chicago." *Billboard*, April 16, 1966, 34.

Braudy, Susan. "As Arlo Guthrie Sees It . . . Kids Are Groovy, Adults Aren't." *Sunday New York Times Magazine*, April 27, 1969, 56–57ff.

Braun, Saul. "Alice & Ray & Yesterday's Flowers." *Playboy* 16, no. 10 (October 1969), 120–22, 142, 192, 194, 196–98.

Bream, Jon. "Rock Hall of Fame Induction, Program Provided Contrast in Good, Bad Vibes." *Star-Tribune* (Twin Cities), January 21, 1988, sec. Variety, 16E.

Brewster, Susan. "The Coop Interview: Arlo Guthrie." *Coop/Fast Folk Musical Magazine* 1, nos. 8, 9 (September and October 1982).

Brock, Alice May. *My Life as a Restaurant*. Woodstock, NY: Overlook Press, 1975.

Brooks, Michael. "Woody & Arlo." *Guitar Player* 5, no. 5 (August 1971), 26–29, 34–35.

Brown, James. "Hoyt Axton Hosts Variety Special." *Los Angeles Times*, May 20, 1975, E18.

Bryant, Nelson. "Wood, Field and Stream." *New York Times*, July 14, 1968, S24.

Burton, Chas. "Records" (review of *Running Down the Road*). *Rolling Stone*, December 27, 1969, 58, 60.

Butler, Janet. "Arlo Guthrie: Mystic Journey." *American Songwriter* (November 1995).

Campbell, Mary. "Arlo Guthrie Blends Humor with Protest." *Los Angeles Times*, November 25, 1968, C23.

——. "Arlo Guthrie Ready to Share His Life." *The Day* (New London, CT), August 23, 1979, 39.

——. "Arlo Guthrie Asks Refugee Family In." *Harlan Daily Enterprise*, August 24, 1979, 6.

Canby, Vincent. "Our Time: Arlo and Chicago." *New York Times*, August 31, 1969, D1.

Champlin, Charles. "'Restaurant' Based on Guthrie Song." *Los Angeles Times*, August 26, 1969, C1.

Christgau, Robert. "The Christgau Consumer Guide" (review of *Hobo's Lullabye*). *Creem* 4, no. 6 (November 1972), 15.

———. "The Christgau Consumer Guide" (review of *Arlo Guthrie*). *Creem* 6, no. 3 (August 1974), 13.

———. "Christgau's Consumer Guide" (review of *Amigo*). *Village Voice* 21, no. 44 (November 1, 1976), 79.

Clark, David. "Rock" (review of *Last of the Brooklyn Cowboys*). *Records and Recording*, July 1973, 80.

Clark, Matt, with Marianna Gosnell. "Medicine: The Cruelest Killer." *Newsweek*, September 27, 1976, 67–68.

Clines, Francis X. "L.I. Narcotics Raid Nets 33 on Campus." *New York Times*, January 18, 1968, 1.

———. "Students Decry Stony Brook Raid." *New York Times*, January 19, 1968, 22.

Coates, James. "Ford Camp Errs; Reagan's Not Broke." *Chicago Tribune*, March 20, 1976, sec. 1, 6.

Cobb, Bertha B., and Ernest Cobb. *Arlo*. Boston/Newton Upper Falls, MA: Arlo Publishing Company, 1915.

Cobb, Nathan. "Arlo at South Shore Makes You Smile." *Boston Globe*, July 14, 1969, 15.

Coburn, Randy Sue. "On the Trail of Ramblin' Jack Elliott." *Esquire*, April 1984, 80–82, 84–85.

Cohen, Debra Rae. "Arlo Guthrie's Faith Outlasts the Sixties." *Rolling Stone*, no. 299, September 6, 1979, 22.

Cohen, Mitchell. "Backbeat" (review of *Power of Love*). *High Fidelity/Musical America*, September 1981, 88.

Cohen, Ronald. D. *Rainbow Quest—The Folk Music Revival & American Society 1940–1970*. Amherst and Boston: University of Massachusetts Press, 2002.

———. *A History of Folk Music Festivals in the United States*. Lanham, MD: Scarecrow Press, 2008.

Colander, Pat. "Soundstage: Where It's Happening in Chicago." *Chicago Tribune*, November 10, 1974, O3.

Cooney, Michael. "Record Reviews: The Woody Guthrie Tribute: Another View." *Sing Out!* 22, no. 2 (March/April 1973), 43.

Cooper, Richard T. "Even Judge Amused: Guthrie and 'Alice' Liven Chicago Trial." *Los Angeles Times*, January 16, 1970, 4.

Coppage, Noel. "Recordings of Special Merit" (review of *Last of the Brooklyn Cowboys*). *Stereo Review*, September 1973, 90, 94.

———. "Recordings of Special Merit" (review of *Arlo Guthrie*). *Stereo Review*, September 1974, 93.

———. "Recordings of Special Merit" (review of *Together in Concert*). *Stereo Review*, September 1975, 97.

———. "Arlo Guthrie" (review of *Power of Love*). *Stereo Review*, October 1981, 90.

———. "Guthrie/Seeger" (review of *Precious Friend*). *Stereo Review*, July 1982, 76.

Cramer, Carol. "VD Blues: Taking the Worry Out of Being Close." *Chicago Tribune*, October 8, 1972, sec. 10, 2.

Cray, Ed. *Ramblin' Man—The Life and Times of Woody Guthrie*. New York: W.W. Norton, 2004.

Cromelin, Richard. "Music Review: Seeger and Guthrie Share Bowl Stage." *Los Angeles Times*, August 21, 1972, sec. IV, 17.

———. "Arlo Guthrie at S.M. Civic." *Los Angeles Times*, November 19, 1973, sec. IV, 14.

———. "Arlo Guthrie—Nice and Normal." *Los Angeles Times*, April 14, 1977, F14.

———. "Seeger, Guthrie Team for Success." *Los Angeles Times*, September 2, 1981, G2.

Crowe, Cameron. "Pop Album Briefs" (review of *Arlo Guthrie*). *Los Angeles Times*, July 21, 1974, sec. Calendar, 60.

Cunningham, Sis, and Gordon Freisen. "Ed. Note." *Broadside* 80 (April/May 1967), 17–18.

———. "Ed. Note." *Broadside* 81 (June 1967), 2–3.

Dallas, Karl. "One of America's Most Interesting Young Folk Singers for Some Time." *Melody Maker*, December 10, 1966, 14.

———. "Caught in the Act: Arlo Guthrie." *Melody Maker*, December 17, 1966, 20.

———. "Focus on Folk: Arlo Doesn't Need the Famous Dad Bit." *Melody Maker*, December 16, 1967, 11.

———. "The Tragedy of Alice's Restaurant." *Melody Maker*, November 15, 1969, 7.

———. "Arlo—Trying to Escape from Alice's Restaurant." *Melody Maker*, February 21, 1970, 9.

———. "Arlo Looks Back." *Melody Maker*, August 12, 1972, 45.

———. "Guthrie's Survival Course." *Melody Maker*, July 27, 1974, 24.

Daley, Steve. "Performing Arts: Seeger and Guthrie." *Washington Post*, August 23, 1978, D3.

Davidson, Sara. "Arlo Guthrie." *Boston Globe Sunday Magazine*, June 9, 1968, 18–22, 26–27.

Dellar, Fred. "Current Pop" (review of *Hobo's Lullaby*). *Hi-Fi News & Record Review*, September 1972, 1683.

DiPietro, Ben. "Arlo's a Free Bird in 'Paradise.'" *New York Post*, March 8, 1994, 75.

Dove, Ian. "Seeger and Guthrie Salute Leadbelly." *New York Times*, March 17, 1975, 38.

Dreazen, Phyllis. "Folk: Arlo Guthrie's Concert Talk-Fest." *Chicago Tribune*, April 21, 1968, sec. 1A, 6.

Druse, Bobbi. "Rapping with Arlo Guthrie." *Broadside of Boston* circa November 1967, reprinted in *Broadside* (New York), no. 166 (September 1985), 12.

Dudgeon, Frank. "Records" (review of *One Night*). *Boston Globe*, December 7, 1978, sec. Calendar, 6–7.

Dunaway, David King. *How Can I Keep from Singing: Pete Seeger*. New York: McGraw-Hill, 1981.

Edwards, Henry. "The Lighter Side: In Brief" (review of *Hobo's Lullaby*). *High Fidelity* 22, no. 9 (September 1972), 108.

Eliot, Marc. *Death of a Rebel: Starring Phil Ochs and a Small Circle of Friends*. Garden City, NY: Doubleday, 1979.

Emerson, Ken. "Rousing Albums from Guthrie and Seeger." *New York Times*, December 16, 1979, D23.

Erlich, Nancy. "Arlo Guthrie, Carnegie Hall, New York." *Billboard*, April 10, 1971, 20.

Farren, Mick. "Platters" (review of *Together in Concert*). *NME*, June 28, 1975, 18.

Feron, James. "Concert by Arlo Guthrie Aids Harris's Campaign." *New York Times*, March 21, 1976, 42.

Ferretti, Fred. "Troubadour, L.A." *Variety*, January 31, 1968, 69.

———. "New Acts: Arlo Guthrie, Songs, Instrumentals, 55 Mins. Troubadour, L.A." *Variety*, July 2, 1969, 60.

———. "Arlo Guthrie Weds in Berkshire Meadow." *New York Times*, October 10, 1969, 34.

———. "Concert Reviews: Arlo Guthrie, Santa Monica Civic Aud." *Variety*, April 20, 1977, 108.

Fishel, Jim. "Talent in Action: Arlo Guthrie, Carnegie Hall, New York." *Billboard*, June 7, 1975, 39.

Fong-Torres, Ben. "Radio: One Toke behind the Line." *Rolling Stone*, April 15, 1971.

Fox, Hank. "Woodie Guthrie's Son Is Making It on His Own Talent." *Billboard*, November 25, 1967, 33.

Fricker, Richard. "Talent in Action: Arlo Guthrie, Cain's Ballroom, Tulsa." *Billboard*, May 29, 1976, 36.

Friedman, Mickey. "Record Reviews," *Sing Out!* 19, no. 5 (March/April 1970), 47.

Fripp, Bill. "Berkshires: A Massachusetts Uninfluenced by Bostonians." *Boston Globe*, June 16, 1974, sec. Living, A9, 14.

Gahr, David, and Robert Shelton. *The Face of Folk Music*. New York: Citadel Press, 1968.

Gallanter, Marty. "Arlo—Bound for His Own Glory." *Frets* 1, no. 5 (July 1979), 24–26, 28–29.

Geisel, Ellen. "Arlo Guthrie (The Story of Reuben Clamzo . . .)." *Dirty Linen*, no. 39 (April/May 1992), 20–21, 23, 54.

Gent, George. "2 Concerts to Sing Folk Festival Blues." *New York Times*, July 6, 1972, 42.

Gilbert, Jeremy. "Caught in the Act: Arlo Guthrie." *Melody Maker*, February 14, 1970, 14.

Goldman, Stuart. "At Royce Hall: Guthrie Touches All the Bases." *Los Angeles Times*, December 13, 1979, F37.

Goldsmith, Peter. *Making People's Music: Moses Asch and Folkways Records*. Washington, DC: Smithsonian Institution Press, 1998.

Goldstein, Richard. "Pop: Arlo Takes a Giant Step." *New York Times*, November 5, 1967, D22.

Goodman, Mark, and Tom Cunneff. "Aloha, Arlo!" *People*, June 13, 1994, 67–68.

Graham, Donald, and Carl Bernstein. "335 War Protestors Arrested." *Boston Globe*, May 1, 1971, 1.

Grail, Celia. "Talent in Action: Arlo Guthrie, Royce Hall, UCLA." *Billboard*, January 5, 1980, 29.

Grant, Derek. "Popular Records" (review of *Arlo Guthrie*). *Gramophone*, November 1974, 978.

———. "Popular Records" (review of *Together in Concert*). *Gramophone*, August 1975, 371.

Grant, Lee. "Guthrie: Word Volcano Will Erupt as a Film." *Los Angeles Times*, October 19, 1975, sec. Calendar, 1, 49, 51–52.

Grier, Peter. "Record Guide" (review of *Outlasting the Blues*). *Christian Science Monitor*, August 30, 1979, 18.

Gross, Mike. "From the Music Capitols of the World: New York." *Billboard*, May 28, 1966, 36.

Gussow, Mel. "Arlo: 'Kids Want to Be Free.'" *New York Times*, January 11, 1970, 81.

Gustafson, Robert. "Coffee House Circuit: The Tempo Is Up." *Boston Globe*, September 11, 1966, A43.

———. "Coffee House Circuit: Similarities . . . Yes, but No Imitation." *Boston Globe*, October 16, 1966, 18A.

Guthrie, Arlo. *This Is the Arlo Guthrie Book*. Edited by Happy Traum. New York: Amsco Music Publishing Company, 1969.

———. Notes to *Swampwater* (RCA Records 4572).

———. "House of the Rising Son." *Esquire*, September 1984, 80–82.

———. "Despite the Shadow of His Father's (and Possibly His Own) Deadly Disease, a Folk Hero Celebrates Life." *People* 28, no. 10 (September 7, 1987).

———. "My Oughtabiography." *Rolling Blunder Review* (special edition), November 1989, 2.

———. "Church for Sale." *Rolling Blunder Review*, no. 17 (Winter 1990), 3–4.

———. "Guthrie Says 'OK' to Movie." *Rolling Blunder Review*, no. 17 (Winter 1990), 7.

———. "Car Talk Junkie Speaks." *Rolling Blunder Review*, no. 18 (Spring 1991), 3.

———. "What's Happening." *Rolling Blunder Review*, no. 18 (Spring 1991), 5.

———. "There & Back Again." *Rolling Blunder Review*, no. 20 (Fall 1991), 2.

———. "In Record Time." *Rolling Blunder Review*, no. 20 (Fall 1991), 5.

———. Notes to *Son of the Wind* (Rising Son Records, RSR 003), 1991.

———. "Notes on the Program." *Carnegie Hall Stagebill*, November 30, 1996, 18.

———. "Foreword" in *Early Dylan*. Boston/New York/London: Little, Brown and Company, 1999.

Guthrie, Nora. "Notes from Woody Guthrie's Daughter." *Woody's 20 Grow Big Songs* (Warner Bros. 9 45020-2), 1992.

Guthrie, Woody. "Woody Guthrie Says . . . New People's Songster on Way." *People's World*, June 3, 1947, 5.

———. "Correspondence." *People's Songs* 3, nos. 1 and 2 (February/March 1948), 23.

———. "Woody." *Sing Out!* 17, no. 6 (December 1967/January 1968), 10.

———. *Pastures of Plenty: A Self Portrait*. New York: HarperCollins, 1990.

Haber, Joyce. "No More Alice." *Los Angeles Times*, March 22, 1968, C17.

Haberman, Paula. "Toronto News." *Hoot* 2, no. 5 (September 1966), 3.

Halvorsen, Jon. "Seeger, Guthrie in Benefit." *Evening News*, June 30, 1975, 7B.

Hammond, Bill. "Arlo Guthrie: Hassles Are His Style." *Milwaukee Sentinel*, July 28, 1978, sec. "Let's Go," 4.

Hampson, Rick. "Most of All They Remember Mama." *Lewiston Evening Journal*, October 17, 1978, 29.

Heckman, Don. "Nyro, Donovan, Zappa and More." *New York Times*, November 9, 1969, D36.

———. "Taylor Leads Good Vibes at Folk Festival Benefit." *New York Times*, July 8, 1972, 16.

Hedgepeth, W. "The Successful Anarchist." *Look* 33 (February 4, 1969), 60–62, 64.

Heller, Jean. "Guthrie's Songs Catch On—But It's Too Late." *Los Angeles Times*, March 4, 1966, 20.

———. "Woody Guthrie Wins Hearts of Hundreds." *Free-Lance Star* (Fredericksburg, VA), April 25, 1966, 2.

Henke, James. "Arlo Guthrie's a Home-State Hit." *Rolling Stone*, April 2, 1981, 56.

Hentoff, Nat. "Woody Guthrie Still Prowls Our Memories." *New York Times*, April 16, 1972, D28.

Hilburn, Robert. "Music Review: Collins, Guthrie at Bowl." *Los Angeles Times*, August 3, 1970, sec. IV, 1, 18.

———. "Tribute to Woody Guthrie." *Los Angeles Times*, September 14, 1970, E1.

———. "Pop Album Briefs" (review of *Last of the Brooklyn Cowboys*). *Los Angeles Times*, August 12, 1973, sec. Calendar, 41.

———. "Woody Guthrie Born Again in LP Reissues." *Los Angeles Times*, December 14, 1976, G1.

Hillier, Tony. "Arlo and a Song Like Alice." *Rhythms*, May 2008, 44–45.

Himes, Geoffrey. "Guthrie and Seeger at Wolf Trap." *Washington Post*, August 14, 1980, F13.

Hoffman, Frank, and George Albert. *The Cash Box Album Charts, 1955–1974*. Metuchen, NJ, and London: Scarecrow Press, 1988.

Hoffman, Jan. "Arlo Guthrie Cuts the Comedy." *Village Voice*, July 30, 1979, 60.

Hoffman, Louise. "Joady Guthrie." *Broadside*, no. 174, 10.

Holden, Stephen. "Cabaret: Vintage Arlo Guthrie at Bottom Line." *New York Times*, January 29, 1982, C23.

Horing, Allan. "Records" (review of *Precious Friend*). *Rolling Stone*, May 27, 1982, 57.

Howard, William. "Guthrie, Seeger at Music Hall." *Boston Globe*, April 2, 1974, 40.

Hughes, Allen. "WNYC Folk Concert Sung in 6 Segments." *New York Times*, February 19, 1967, 71.

Huisking, Charlie. "Arlo Guthrie: The Troubadour of the 60s Hasn't Changed His Tune." *Herald Tribune* (Sarasota, FL), December 9, 1979, sec. Florida West, 16–17.

Humphries, Patrick. "Albums—Arlo Guthrie: Power of Love." *Melody Maker*, September 5, 1981, 19.

Hunter, Marjorie. "Prominent Foes of War Arrested." *New York Times*, May 25, 1972, 20.

Iwata, Edward. "Joady Guthrie: Arlo's Brother Tries to Make It on His Own." *San Francisco Chronicle*, January 5, 1986, sec. Sunday Datebook, 37.

Jahn, Mike. "Pop Music: Arlo and Alice." *Escapade* 13, no. 3 (April 1968), 10, 69.
————. "Love Tales Sung by Arlo Guthrie—Talking Blues-Style Marks Concert at Carnegie Hall." *New York Times*, December 27, 1969, C14.
————. "Arlo Guthrie Gives a Concert Marked by Country Songs." *New York Times*, April 2, 1971, 32.
————. "The Lighter Side" (review of *Together in Concert*). *High Fidelity/Musical America* 25, no. 8 (August 1975), 111.
————. "The Lighter Side" (review of *Amigo*). *High Fidelity/Musical America* 27, no. 1 (January 1977), 143.
Jasper, Tony. "Folk" (review of *Together in Concert*). *Hi-Fi News & Record Review*, September 1975, 117.
"Jeff." "Concert Reviews: Arlo Guthrie (Carnegie Hall, N.Y.)." *Variety*, December 31, 1969, 34.
————. "Concert Reviews: Arlo Guthrie/Swampwater (Carnegie Hall, N.Y.)." *Variety*, April 7, 1971, 54.
Johnson, Pete. "Popular Records." *Los Angeles Times*, October 22, 1967, S37.
Joyce, Mike. "Arlo Guthrie." *Washington Post*, August 17, 1981, B13.
Kahn, E. J. "Seabrook 2: Just When You Thought It Was Hopeless." *Village Voice*, July 3, 1978, 1, 19–21.
Kauffman, Bruce. "Easy at the Bushnell . . . Arlo." *Hartford Courant*, April 4, 1971, 6B.
King, Nick. "People's Bicentennial Gambles on Angry Patriots." *Boston Globe*, April 14, 1975, 3.
"Kirb." "Concert Reviews: Arlo Guthrie/Harry Chapin (Wollman Rink, N.Y.)." *Variety*, August 2, 1972, 43.
————. "Concert Reviews: Pete Seeger/Arlo Guthrie (Carnegie Hall, N.Y.)." *Variety*, March 13, 1974, 62.
————. "Concert Reviews: Arlo Guthrie, Carnegie Hall, N.Y." *Variety*, May 7, 1975, 336.
————. "Concert Reviews: Arlo Guthrie (Wollman Rink, N.Y.)." *Variety*, August 25, 1976, 54.
————. "Concert Reviews: Arlo Guthrie/Shenandoah (Wollman Rink, N.Y.)." *Variety*, July 26, 1978, 66.
Kirby, Fred. "Arlo Guthrie Folk Singer with Rapport." *Billboard*, December 21, 1968, 14.
————. "From the Music Capitals of the World: New York." *Billboard*, September 6, 1969, 34.
Klein, Joe. "Notes on a Native Son." *Rolling Stone*, no. 234 (March 10, 1977), 50–57.
————. *Woody Guthrie: A Life*. New York: Alfred A. Knopf, 1980.
Klemesrud, Judy. "A Cookbook by That Restaurant's Alice." *New York Times*, July 30, 1969, 44.
Kneeland, Douglas E. "Pace of New Hampshire Campaigning Slows before the Primary Tomorrow." *New York Times*, February 23, 1976, 29.
Knoedelseder, William, Jr. "Small Labels Big for the Baby Boomers: Independents Find Market for Their Work." *San Francisco Chronicle*, January 20, 1985.

Kramer, Carol. "VD Blues: Taking the Worry Out of Being Close." *Chicago Tribune*, October 8, 1972, sec. 10, 2.

Krasilovsky, Peter. "Talent in Action: Arlo Guthrie, Pier 84, New York." *Billboard*, September 5, 1981, 45.

Krogsgaard, Michael. *Positively Bob Dylan*. Ann Arbor: Popular Culture Ink, 1991.

Lambert, Gary. "Capsule Reviews" (review of *Amigo*). *Crawdaddy*, November 1976, 80.

Lang, Michael, and Holly George Warren. *The Road to Woodstock: From the Man behind the Legendary Festival*. New York: Ecco/HarperCollins, 2009.

Lawson, Carol. "An Old-Time Folk Festival on the Hudson." *New York Times*, June 16, 1978, C1.

Lawson, Dorie McCullough. *Posterity: Letters of Great Americans to Their Children*. New York: Doubleday, 2004.

Lee, Laura. *Arlo, Alice & Anglicans: The Lives of a New England Church*. Lee, MA: Berkshire House, 2000.

Legro, Ron. "Relaxed Arlo Guthrie Sings a Good Show." *Milwaukee Sentinel*, July 23, 1975, 10.

Lehman, June. "Guthrie to Grace UWM Stage." *Milwaukee Sentinel*, April 1989, 13.

Leonard, John. "TV Review: Dime-Store Display of Imagination." *LIFE*, February 19, 1971, 16.

Leventhal, Harold. Notes to *Alice's Restaurant* (Reprise RS 6267), 1967.

———. Notes to *Pete Seeger & Arlo Guthrie: Together in Concert* (Reprise Records 2R 2214), 1975.

———. Program notes of November 28 Carnegie Hall concert. *Stagebill*, 1981–1982 season, unpaginated.

Lewis, Jesse. "Arlo Guthrie: Last 'Brooklyn Cowboy' Comes South." *Ocala Star-Banner*, February 22, 1978, 2C.

Lifeset, Roger. "Music on Campus." *Billboard*, October 15, 1966, 60.

Lowe, Steven. "The Lighter Side." *High Fidelity*, January 1968, 100.

Lukas, J. Anthony. "Song by Guthrie Barred at Trial." *New York Times*, January 16, 1970, 10.

Lurtsema, Bob. "I Want to Know." *Sing Out!* 17, no. 3 (June/July 1967), 50.

Maas, Jan A. "Troubadour for Our Times." *New York Sunday News*, November 16, 1969, 12–13.

Maddocks, Melvin. "Two Nations Indivisible." *Christian Science Monitor*, April 21, 1975, 1, 11.

Marsh, Dave. "American Grandstand: Rockers on the Road to Salvation." *Rolling Stone*, October 18, 1979, 43.

Maslin, Janet. "Records" (review of *Hobo's Lullabye*). *Rolling Stone*, July 20, 1972, 50.

———. "Records" (review of *Last of the Brooklyn Cowboys*). *Rolling Stone*, June 21, 1973, 64.

———. "Arlo Guthrie Lives Up to His Name." *Village Voice* 21, no. 46 (November 15, 1976), 97.

———. "Music: Witty, Winning Arlo Guthrie Rambles Round." *New York Times*, August 20, 1977, 12.

Mathews, Linda. "Arlo Guthrie on Troubadour Stage." *Los Angeles Times*, January 25, 1968, A10.

Mayer, Ira. "Riffs: The Time of Year." *Village Voice* 16, no. 16 (April 22, 1971), 43.

———. "Pop: Arlo Guthrie: Hobo's Lullaby." *New York Times*, August 27, 1972, D19.

———. "Generations without a Gap." *Village Voice* 19, no. 11 (March 14, 1974), 56–57.

McCuistion, Mick. "Arlo Guthrie." *On the Tracks* 3, no. 2 (1995), 30–34.

McCullaugh, Jim. "Talent in Action: Arlo Guthrie, Civic Auditorium, Santa Monica, Calif." *Billboard*, April 30, 1977, 36.

McDonald, Gregory. "Rap-Up." *Boston Globe*, November 19, 1969, 49.

———. "Rap-Up: Arlo Always Liked Playing Solo." *Boston Globe*, March 18, 1970, 14.

McDonough, Jack. "Talent in Action: Arlo Guthrie, Boarding House, San Francisco." *Billboard*, March 27, 1976, 46.

McLaughlin, Jeff. "Why Guthrie Gets Involved." *Boston Globe*, October 9, 1982, 8.

McLellan, Joseph. "Funny—Even Profound." *Washington Post*, August 31, 1974, C5.

McMillan, Gary. "'Peoples' Rally Jams Concord." *Boston Globe*, April 19, 1975, 1, 5.

McMillan, Gary, and Nick King. "Peoples Bicentennial: Rally More Like a Party with Raspberry for Ford." *Boston Globe*, April 20, 1975, 49, 61.

Miller, Edwin. "Spotlight! The Hollywood Scene." *Seventeen*, February 1974, 42, 54, 56.

Millet, Michael. "Guthrie: Traveling Light & Versatile." Source unknown.

Mills, Nancy. "Arlo: Smiling the Odds Away." *Windsor-Star*, September 8, 1979, 17.

Mitchel, Jeff. "Arlo." *News Record* (University of Cincinnati), February 28, 1969, 8.

———. "Arlo Guthrie's 'Alice's Restaurant,' 'Running Down the Road,' Too Commercial." *News Record* (University of Cincinnati), October 7, 1969, 18.

———. "Arlo, Santana at X." *News Record* (University of Cincinnati), October 7, 1969, 18.

Mohr, Charles. "Harris's Fate Is Linked to Defeating Bayh." *New York Times*, February 29, 1976, 42.

Moore, Steve. "Performance: The Son Becomes a Star." *Rolling Stone*, December 20, 1973, 88.

Morse, Steve. "Arlo Guthrie Has His Day." *Boston Globe*, November 8, 1976, 16.

———. "Like Old Times for Guthrie." *Boston Globe*, July 13, 1981, 30, 31.

Naha, Ed. "Record Lovers Guide" (review of *Arlo Guthrie*). *Circus* 8, no. 12 (September 1974), 60.

Nelson, Paul. "Record Reviews" (review of *A Tribute to Woody Guthrie, Part One and Two*). *Rolling Stone*, July 20, 1972, 50.

———. "Records" (review of *Together in Concert*). *Rolling Stone*, August 28, 1975, 74.

Nic Schenk, Mary. "Music Review: Sound New, Message Isn't." *St. Petersburg Times*, November 15, 1971, 3D.

Norman, Bob. "Record Reviews." *Sing Out!* 21, no. 5 (September/October 1972), 38.

Nyren, Neil. "Review of American Festival of Music." *Broadside* (Cambridge) 2, no. 6 (May 10, 1967), 23.

Pace, Eric. "Will Geer Remembered at Tribute for Charm, Courage and Energy." *New York Times*, May 14, 1978, 49.

Pareles, Jon. "TV Reviews—Woody Guthrie: Hard Travelin'." *New York Times*, March 7, 1984, C22.

Parmentier, Ernest, ed. "Alice's Restaurant." *Filmfacts: A Publication of the American Film Institute* 12, no. 13 (1969), 289–93.

Paseman, Lloyd. "Folksinger Demonstrates He Takes Work Seriously: Arlo Guthrie Performs for UO Audience." *Eugene Register-Guard*, December 7, 1971, 1.

Perault, Peter Z. "*Alice's Restaurant* World Premiere Attracts 1500." *Boston Evening Globe*, August 20, 1969, 29.

Pettifer, Alan. "On Record" (review of *Arlo Guthrie*). *Country Music Review* 3, no. 5 (September 1974), 34.

Phillips, B. J. "Arlo Solo—Without His Bride." *Washington Post*, October 11, 1969, E1.

Phillips, Kathryn. "Arlo Guthrie: Sharing Music, Sharing Concerns." *Anchorage Daily News*, October 26, 1978, 17.

Pond, Steve. "Harry Chapin and Arlo Guthrie." *Los Angeles Times*, July 26, 1980, B6.

Principe, Bob. "Arlo Guthrie: Much More Than 'Perceptive Humorist.'" *Imagine Presents the Return of the 60s* (September/October 1979), 16–17, 50.

Quinn, Sally. "Indian Benefit: A Vanishing Breed?" *Los Angeles Times*, December 5, 1974, 122.

Rachlis, Kit. "Records" (review of *Amigo*). *Rolling Stone*, January 27, 1977, 65.

Radcliffe, Joe. "Talent in Action: Arlo Guthrie, Bottom Line, N.Y." *Billboard*, February 20, 1982, 56.

Reilly, Peter. "The Deadly Satiric Aim of Arlo Guthrie." *Hi-Fi Review*, February 1968, 81.

Reuss, Richard A. *Woody Guthrie Bilbliography*. New York: Guthrie Children's Trust Fund, 1968.

Richard, Paul. "Arlo Guthrie at 30." *Washington Post*, July 29, 1977, B1, 16.

———. "Arlo Guthrie: Hearing the Infinite." *Los Angeles Times*, September 7, 1977, 110.

Robbin, Ed. *Woody Guthrie and Me*. Berkeley, CA: Lancaster-Miller, 1979.

Robertson, Nan. "Woody Guthrie's Widow: Carrying On the Fight the Folk Singer Lost." *New York Times*, January 27, 1977, 40.

Robins, Wayne. "Guthrie Succeeds at 'Outlasting the Blues.'" *Anchorage Daily News*, August 28, 1979, D8.

Robinson, Barry. "Despite Her Protestations—Film Makes Folk Hero of Alice." *Chicago Tribune*, November 16, 1969, sec. 5, 2.

Rockwell, John. "The Lighter Side" (review of *Arlo Guthrie*). *High Fidelity/Musical America* 24, no. 10 (October 1974).

———. "Arlo Guthrie's Band Politically Active." *New York Times*, August 19, 1976, 48.

"Ron." "New Acts: Arlo Guthrie." *Variety*, February 23, 1966, 61.

Rose, Frank. "I Don't See Any Stars. Do You See Any Stars?" *Village Voice*, May 16, 1974, 74.

———. "Talking Chile Blues." *Zoo World*, no. 61 (June 20, 1974), 14–15.

———. "At Home with Arlo: Conversation in the Berkshires." *Zoo World*, no. 62 (July 4, 1974), 22–23.

Ross, Joe. "Ramblin with Jack." *Folk Roots*, January/February 1993, 40–41, 43.

Roxon, Lillian. "The Guthrie Concert." *Sydney Morning Herald*, quoted in *Bob Dylan: A Retrospective*, edited by Craig McGregor. New York: William Morrow, 1972.

Russcol, Herbert. "I Gave My Love a Cherry, Tell It Like It Is, Baby!" *High Fidelity* 18 (December 1968), 54–58.

Russell, Tony. "Folk Song" (review of *A Tribute to Woody Guthrie* and *Hobo's Lullabye*). *Gramophone*, November 1972, 989.

Sagar-Fenton, Mike. "Reviews: Records" (review of *Together in Concert*). *Folk Review* 4, no. 11 (September 1975), 30.

Sakol, Jeanne. "The Hit Generation: Sweet Satire Seen for the Future." *Milwaukee Journal*, April 17, 1968, 2.

"Salt." "Concert Reviews: Arlo Guthrie/Side of the Road Gang (Wollman Rink, N.Y.)." *Variety*, August 1, 1979, 66.

Santelli, Robert, and Emily Davidson, eds. *Hard Travelin'—The Life and Legacy of Woody Guthrie*. Hanover, NH, and London: Wesleyan University Press, 1999.

Santosuosso, Ernie. "Arlo Guthrie on Stage at Symphony Hall." *Boston Globe*, April 3, 1971, 17.

———. "Arlo Guthrie to Top Bill." *Boston Globe*, October 3, 1975, 20.

———. "Guthrie and Seeger against Hynes Auditorium." *Boston Globe*, September 1, 1978, 24.

Seawell, Mary Ann. "Generation of Arlo Guthrie." *Los Angeles Times*, September 17, 1967, C14.

———. "Gentle Arlo's World for People, Not Machines." *Washington Post*, August 9, 1968, C4.

Seeger, Pete. *The Incompleat Folksinger*. New York: Simon and Schuster, 1972.

Semple, Robert B., Jr. "U.S. Award Given to Woody Guthrie." *New York Times*, April 7, 1966, 45.

Scheimann, Eugene. "Fight Waged by Family." *Montreal Gazette*, August 25, 1971, 41.

Schmidt, Arthur. "Record Reviews" (review of *Arlo*). *Rolling Stone*, October 26, 1968, 28.

Schnol, Janet. "A Collection of Folk Songs for a New Generation." *Publisher's Weekly*, October 5, 1992, 33.

Scoppa, Bud. "Records" (review of *Arlo Guthrie*). *Rolling Stone*, July 18, 1974, 64.

Shelton, Robert. "Guthrie Honored by Folk Concert." *New York Times*, April 19, 1965, 38.

———. "Tribute to the Life and Legend of Woody Guthrie." *New York Times*, January 22, 1968, 31.

———. "Folk Folk Meet at Newport Fest." *New York Times*, July 28, 1968, 64.

———. "Folk Music Trends Emerge at Newport Festival." *New York Times*, July 30, 1968, 32.

Shephard, Sam. *Rolling Thunder Logbook.* New York: Penguin Books, 1978.

Silber, Irwin. "What's Happening . . ." *Sing Out!* 17, no. 5 (October/November 1967), 1.

———. "Fan the Flames." *Sing Out!* 17, no. 6 (December/January 1968), 55.

"S.L." "Arlo's Fresh Chapter" (review of *Arlo Guthrie*). *Melody Maker*, August 17, 1974, 47.

Sloman, Larry. *On the Road with Bob Dylan.* New York: Bantam Books, 1978.

Smith, Danny. "A Pilgrim at Peace: Danny Smith Rolls the Tape and Replays the Past with Arlo Guthrie." *Melody Maker*, May 9, 1981, 30, 36.

Smith, Ward W. "Arlo: Too Busy for Stardom." *Christian Science Monitor*, March 30, 1978, 19.

Smucker, Tom. "Pete and Arlo: All in the Family." *Village Voice* 20, no. 31 (August 4, 1975), 89.

———. "If Every Concert Were a Benefit, Pete Seeger Would Be Frank Sinatra." *Village Voice*, October 18, 1976, 76, 78.

———. "Arlo Guthrie and the Communist Mystical Tradition (a Tall Tale)." *Village Voice* 22, no. 35 (August 29, 1977), 38–39.

———. "Recyclable Folk Music." *Village Voice*, July 3, 1978, 37, 92.

Steele, Richard. "Woody's Boy." *Newsweek* 67 (May 23, 1966), 112–13.

Stern, Micahel. "87,000 March in War Protests Here." *New York Times*, April 28, 1968, 1, 72.

Sterritt, David. "The Pop Scene: They Dress in Hippie Disguises." *Christian Science Monitor*, January 3, 1968, 15.

———. "Everyone 'Together' in a Free-Form Festival." *Christian Science Monitor*, August 3, 1968, 6.

———. "New Guthrie—'Less Contented.'" *Christian Science Monitor*, November 2, 1968, 21.

———. "Arlo's 'Alice' in a Film by Penn." *Christian Science Monitor*, September 8, 1969, 6.

Stickney, John. "Alice's Family of Folk Song Fame Becomes a Movie." *LIFE* 66, no. 12 (March 28, 1969), 43–45, 48, 50.

Stinson, Craig. "Newport's Folk Festival Scores with Varied Acts." *Billboard*, August 9, 1969, 32.

Stokes, Geoffrey. "Art & Politics: A Certain Tension." *Village Voice*, June 6, 1974, 62–63.

Sullivan, Jim. "A Multifaceted Arlo Guthrie." *Boston Globe*, August 13, 1979, 24.

Sutherland, Sam. "Talent in Action: Pete Seeger/Arlo Guthrie, Carnegie Hall, New York." *Billboard*, March 23, 1974, 20.

———. "Backbeat" (review of *Outlasting the Blues*). *Hi Fidelity/Musical America*, September 1979, 144.

Sweeny, Louise. "Arthur Penn: 'No Preconceptions.'" *Christian Science Monitor*, August 8, 1969, 4.

Sylvester, Bruce. "Guthrie and Watson Bring 'Country Folk' to Boston." *Boston Globe*, June 29, 1972, 25.

——. "Tall Tales and Country Rock by Arlo Guthrie." *Boston Globe*, April 13, 1973, 29.

Tamarkin, Jeff. "In the House of the Rising Son—Arlo Guthrie at 50." *Discoveries*, no. 111 (August 1997), 40–49.

Taylor, David. "3000 Fans 'Bubble' over Arlo." *Boston Globe*, September 29, 1969, 15.

Taylor, Robert. "Three Starry Spokesman for Massachusetts." *Boston Globe*, June 28, 1977, 1, 27.

Tharp, Thelma. "Arlo Guthrie's Gamble." *Sarasota Herald-Tribune/Family Weekly*, April 12, 1970, 28–29.

Thomas, Bob. "Putting the Woody Guthrie Story on Film." *Boston Globe*, December 24, 1975, 17.

Tiegel, Eliot. "Guthrie Drawing 'Em In." *Billboard*, February 10, 1968, 14.

——. "W-7 Creates 'Now' Power." *Billboard*, July 20, 1968, 8.

Tolces, Todd. "Caught in the Act: Seeger and Guthrie." *Melody Maker*, March 22, 1975, 47.

Trammell, Robby. "Okemah Shows Collective Pride for Native Sons." *Sunday Oklahoman*, April 30, 1989, 1A, 4A.

Traum, Happy. "The Eighth Annual Cambridge Folk Festival." *Sing Out!* 21, no. 5 (September/October 1972), 13.

Trost, Isiah. "Coney Island Okie." *Guitar World Acoustic*, no. 24 (1997), 25–26, 91–92.

"Trot." "Concert Reviews: Pete Seeger/Arlo Guthrie (Civic Ctr., Madison, Wis.)." *Variety*, December 15, 1982, 74.

Tucker, Ken. "Singing People." *People's Songs* 2, no. 6 and 7 (July/August 1947), 13.

——. "Folk Singer Opposed—Cashmore Lauds Veterans' Protest on Seeger." *New York Times*, April 13, 1956, 51.

——. "Puerto Ricans Brief Traveling Students on the Homeland." *New York Times*, March 21, 1964, 14.

——. "Guthrie Jnr: Living in the Shadow of a Legend." *Melody Maker*, July 10, 1965, 7.

——. "Tops in Pop to Appear at Boston Music Fest." *Billboard*, April 8, 1967, 26.

——. "From the Music Capitals of the World." *Billboard*, May 6, 1967, 50.

——. "Boston Music Festival Ends with C&W Acts." *Billboard*, May 13, 1967, 28.

——. "Folk Fest & Workshops to Adorn Philly Countryside." *Billboard*, August 19, 1967, 23, 53.

——. "Talent Signings." *Billboard*, September 9, 1967, 30.

——. "Arlo Guthrie Makes Own Mark on Contemporary Folk Scene." *Hartford Courant*, October 14, 1967, 36A.

——. "Arlo Guthrie Caffee [*sic*] Lena Star Tonight." *Knickerbocker News*, November 3, 1967, 12A.

——. "The Talk of the Town: Arlo Guthrie." *New Yorker*, January 6, 1968, 18–21.

——. "WB's Lee in Talent Hunt." *Billboard*, January 6, 1968, 1, 6.

——. "Recordings: Woody's Boy" (review of *Alice's Restaurant* LP). *Time* 91 (January 12, 1968), 50.

———. "WB-7 Sales Up %15; 7.5 Mil. in Quarter." *Billboard*, April 6, 1968, 3.

———. "Blind Date: Arlo Guthrie Singles Out the New Singles." *Melody Maker*, April 20, 1968, 14.

———. "Festival, Folk Upswing Seen as Newport Lures Whopping 70,000." *Billboard*, August 10, 1968, 10.

———. "And Here's Arlo." *Sunday New York News Coloroto Magazine*, November 10, 1968, 6.

———. "Random Notes." *Rolling Stone*, May 3, 1969, 4.

———. "Random Notes." *Rolling Stone*, August 23, 1969, 4.

———. "Alice, Officer Obie Get Along Fine Now." *Hartford Courant*, September 22, 1969, 15.

———. "Arlo Guthrie to Be Married." *Hartford Courant*, September 26, 1969, 17.

———. "Arlo's Mother Pleads for Disease Cure." *Los Angeles Times*, September 26, 1969, G21.

———. "A Joyful Happening." *Time* 94 (October 17, 1969), 66.

———. "Newsmakers." *Los Angeles Times*, January 4, 1970, A.

———. "Arlo Guthrie's Tune Livens Chicago Trial (AP)." *Sarasota Journal*, January 16, 1970, 2.

———. "Chicago Court Entertained by Guthrie (UPI)." *Times-News* (Hendersonville, NC), January 16, 1970, 3.

———. "Guthrie Analyses Country Music." *Variety*, January 21, 1970, 53.

———. "Newsmakers." *Los Angeles Times*, April 8, 1970, sec. 1, 2.

———. "Singer Arlo, Lullabyist." *Washington Post*, April 10, 1970, C4.

———. "Tribute to Guthrie Will Be Benefit." *Los Angeles Times*, August 30, 1970, D13.

———. "Arlo Guthrie's Mother Urges Disease Crusade." *Hartford Courant*, January 24, 1971, 13A.

———. "Philly DJ Out—Lyrics Cited," *Billboard*, March 27, 1971, 4.

———. "Guthrie Recognized by His Hometown." *Los Angeles Times*, July 15, 1971, sec. 1, 25.

———. "The Evolution of Arlo." *Warner Bros./Reprise Circular* 4, no. 19 (May 15, 1972), not paginated.

———. "Fast Spins: The City of New Orleans." *Warner Bros./Reprise Circular* 4, no. 24 (June 18, 1972), not paginated.

———. "Dots and Dashes." *Warner Bros./Reprise Circular* 4, no. 28 (July 17, 1972), not paginated.

———. "Dots and Dashes." *Warner Bros./Reprise Circular* 4, no. 38 (September 25, 1972), not paginated.

———. "Fast Spins: Cooper's Lament/Ukulele Lady." *Warner Bros./Reprise Circular* 4, no. 48 (December 11, 1972), 9.

———. "Items." *Warner Bros./Reprise Circular* 4, no. 48 (December 11, 1972), not paginated.

———. "Random Notes." *Rolling Stone*, December 21, 1972, 7.

———. "Studio Watch: Recording in Hollywood, North and Otherwise." *Warner Bros./Reprise Circular* 5, no. 5 (February 5, 1973), not paginated.

——. "Watergate Tentacles Tighten, Stock Market Plummets." *Warner Bros./Reprise Circular* 5, no. 21 (May 28, 1973), not paginated.

——. "On Record" (review of *Last of the Brooklyn Cowboys*). *Country Music Review* 2, no. 8 (October 1973), 29.

——. "A Little Booze, Song and Dance, and One Loud Anthem for Chile." *Rolling Stone*, June 20, 1974, 32.

——. "The Southland." *Los Angeles Times*, October 21, 1974, sec. 1, 2.

——. "Random Notes." *Rolling Stone*, February 27, 1975, 22.

——. "Campaign '76: 4 Democratic Candidates Discuss Economic Issues in Boston." *Boston Globe*, February 23, 1976, 7.

——. "Pulling Out All the Stops to Win the First Primary." *Chicago Tribune*, February 24, 1976, not paginated.

——. "Longplayers" (review of *Amigo*). *Circus*, no. 145 (December 14, 1976), 16.

——. "Bob Fass Building Vocal 'Community' over WBAI-FM, N.Y." *Billboard*, January 22, 1977, 1.

——. "Alice Cooks." *Newsweek*, October 30, 1978, 20.

——. "The Last Folk Singer." *Rolling Stone*, November 1, 1979, 63–64.

——. "Rock and Roll Hall of Fame." *Rolling Stone*, no. 521 (March 10, 1988), 8–17, 97.

——. "Great Barrington Journal: Folk Singer Hopes Fans Can Save 'Alice's Church.'" *New York Times*, December 6, 1991.

——. "Seeking Sanctuary: Forget Alice's Restaurant; It's Alice's Old Church That Arlo Guthrie Wants to Buy." *People*, February 10, 1992, 89.

UPI. "Guthries Respond to Okemah." *Washington Post*, July 15, 1971, C4.

——. "Arlo Even with Stockbridge." *Boston Globe*, September 16, 1978, 14.

——. "Singer to Attend Amtrak Rally." *New York Times*, April 1, 1979, 50.

Van Huesen, Philip. "Music: Arlo Doesn't Forget, but He's Memorable." *Chicago Tribune*, September 6, 1974, sec. 2, 5.

Van Matre, Lynn. "Arlo Lets 'Em Down." *Chicago Tribune*, November 23, 1969, sec. 1A, 6.

——. "Sound" (review of *Washington County*). *Chicago Tribune*, October 18, 1970, sec. 5, 4.

——. "Sound: It's a Feast of Folk in Memory of Woody." *Chicago Tribune*, April 23, 1972, sec. Arts & Fun, 9.

——. "Concert Ends Abruptly: Ravinia's Rain Clouds Arlo's Joy." *Chicago Tribune*, July 13, 1972, sec. 2, 6.

——. "Pete Seeger: Plucking a Banjo of Brotherhood." *Chicago Tribune*, March 3, 1974, E8.

——. "Pete and Arlo: A Pleasant Bit of Art with Politics." *Chicago Tribune*, March 11, 1974, sec. 2, 17.

——. "Nothing's Changed about Arlo Guthrie." *Chicago Tribune*, November 21, 1975, sec. 3, 7.

Van Osdol, Ken. "Arlo Guthrie: Music . . . Tunes a Soul." *Eugene Register-Guard*, February 1, 1976, 4C.

Vassal, Jacques. *Electric Children*. New York: Taplinger Publishing Company, 1976.

Wadler, Joyce. "An Artists' Salute to Their Persecuted Peers." *Washington Post,* November 22, 1977, B1.

Ward, Alex. "Seeger, Guthrie: Soft Politics." *Washington Post,* March 26, 1975, B16.

Ward, Ed. "Records" (review of *Washington County*). *Rolling Stone,* November 26, 1970, 38.

———. "Records" (review of *Last of the Brooklyn Cowboys*). *Creem* 5, no. 3 (August 1973), 66.

Watts, Michael. "Caught in the Act: Arlo Guthrie." *Melody Maker,* August 5, 1972, 29.

Wenner, Jann. "Records" (review of *Alice's Restaurant*). *Rolling Stone,* November 9, 1967, 20.

Whitman, Arthur. "The Apotheosis of Woody's Kid." *Chicago Tribune Magazine,* November 10, 1968, 16, 20, 22.

Willens, Doris. *Lonesome Traveler: The Life of Lee Hays.* New York and London: W.W. Norton & Company, 1988.

Willis, Thomas. "Mississippi River Festival Opens Friday at Edwardsville." *Chicago Tribune,* June 15, 1969, sec. 5, 9–10.

Wilson, John S. "Newport Is His Just for a Song—Arlo Guthrie Festival Hero with Alice's Restaurant." *New York Times,* July 18, 1967, 30.

———. "Folk Fete Shines without Superstars." *New York Times,* July 22, 1969, 32.

———. "Can Rock and Pop Be Folk Music?" *New York Times,* August 29, 1974, 24.

Wilson, Tony. "Dylan's Dilemma—Arlo Guthrie Confirms the Wall of Silence That Surrounds Bob Dylan Now." *Melody Maker,* April 13, 1968, 14.

Wold, William. "Arlo's 'Alice' from Song to Screen." *Los Angeles Times,* July 13, 1969, M20.

Young, Israel G., and Paul Nelson. "Good News from a Far Country." *Sing Out!* 17, no. 6 (December 1967/January 1968), 42.

Yurchenco, Henrietta. *A Mighty Hard Road: The Woody Guthrie Story.* New York: McGraw-Hill, 1970.

Zimmerman, Paul D. "Alice's Restaurant's Children." *Newsweek,* September 29, 1969, 101–4, 106.

Zito, Tom. "Guthrie, Collins in Superb Concert." *Washington Post,* August 21, 1970, B1.

# Index

# About the Author

**Hank Reineke** has written about folk, blues, and country music for such publications as the *Aquarian Arts Weekly*, *Soho Arts Weekly*, *Downtown*, *East Coast Rocker*, *Blues Revue*, *On the Tracks*, *ISIS*, and *The Bridge*. His first book, *Ramblin' Jack Elliott: The Never-Ending Highway* (Scarecrow Press) was awarded a Certificate of Merit for Best Research in Folk, Ethnic, or World Music by the Association for Recorded Sound Collections. He also served as a research consultant on Aiyana Elliott's award-winning documentary film *The Ballad of Ramblin' Jack*. Hank resides in New Jersey with his wife, Christa, and their two daughters, Emily and Sara.

CPSIA information can be obtained at www.ICGtesting.com
Printed in the USA
BVOW070210180512

290493BV00002B/7/P